AWESOME SEGA™ GENESIS™ SECRETS 5

J. Douglas Arnold & Zach Meston

SANDWICH ISLANDS PUBLISHING CO., LTD.
POST OFFICE BOX 10669 • LAHAINA, MAUI, HI 96761

Library of Congress Cataloging-in-Publication Data

Arnold, J. Douglas, 1966-
    Awesome Sega Genesis secrets 5 / J. Douglas Arnold, Zach Meston
    p. cm. – (Gaming mastery series) ; 5)
    ISBN 1-884364-05-5

    1. Sega Genesis video games. I. Meston, Zach, 1972-. II. Title. III. Titles: Awesome Sega Genesis secrets five. IV. Series

GV 1469.25.S43A75 1995   794.8'15365
                                                   QBI95-523

94 95 96 — 10 9 8 7 6 5 4 3 2 1

HOW TO ORDER:

Quantity discounts are available from the publisher, Sandwich Islands Publishing, P.O. Box 10669, Lahaina, HI 96761; telephone (808) 661-5844. On your letterhead, include information concerning the intended use of the books and the number of books you wish to purchase.

U.S. Bookstores and Libraries: Please submit all orders to Sandwich Islands Publishing.

Printed in the United States of America.

ACKNOWLEDGEMENTS

From Both Authors:

Thanks to Brian Goss, Patrick Wilson, Kraig Kujawa, and Ethan Bott for helping us with Super Street Fighter II, Earthworm Jim, and Madden '95. If not for them, this book would have been out another month late! Thanks a ton, guys!

Thanks to our excellent team of game players for helping us master the games and find the secrets that fill the pages of this book: Brett LaBore, Mark Elies, Ari Stines, Paz Derham, Corey LaBore, and Nick & Willie.

From Zach Meston:

Instead of thanking a bunch of people I've already thanked before and who are so jaded by seeing their name in print that they will shrug their shoulders and say "Ehhh" when I show them this book, I've decided to thank the people who've really pissed me off over the past few months. These folks inspired me to work really hard to keep myself from thinking about the various ways I wanted to kill them.

Thanks to Mike Davila for printing one of my private e-mail messages to him in the pages of *Computer Player* magazine, making me look like a complete idiot. (I had to laugh when he misspelled my hometown of Lahaina as "Kalani," though.)

Thanks to a certain "friend" on Oahu for totally flaking out on us during deadline and leaving us with a huge workload. By the way, Danny, you *still* haven't sent back those cartridges. You're only an inter-island flight away, pal, remember that.

Thanks to Jer Horwitz for badmouthing me at an Internet IRC conference at which I was the guest. You might want to have your ego deflated, O Self-Important One.

Okay, now that I've gotten that out of my system, I'd like to thank a few people who I've never thanked before and therefore won't be jaded: Garth Bradley, Claudette Castillo, April Garofalo, Tara Herman, Don Hicks, Amy Johns, and Jeff Kitts.

Special thanks to my sweet princess, for whom I am completely mental.

From J. Douglas Arnold:

Special thanks to my mother, Joan, for being the best.

Thanks to Joe Harabin for his essential help.

Thanks to our new secretary (and my sister-in-law) Jamie Arnold for helping us keep things in control.

Thanks to Gavin Campbell for making the most difficult time in my life a little easier. You'll always be the best friend I ever had.

Greetings to Larry Antonio, Adam Dotson, Mike Oue, Steve "Smike" Henke, Scott Wery, Ruth Ko, Barbara & Stan, Angelo, Nicholas Wakida, Gregg Abbott, Tom Fernandez, Josh Arlidge, Adam Tornatore, Ed Duncan, Chris & Jamie & Matthew Arnold; Jack, Val, Tera & Kyle Kidd; Dan Schaut, Damon & Yvonne, Clint Crabtree, Gary Clisby, Fran & Don Mitsumura, Helen & Rob Reed, Dan & Naomi Malone, Linda & Bill Pierce, all my chat buddies on CompuServe, and anyone else I've ever met! Thanks for everything!

A special "howdy" to the folks in Missouri: Granny, Grandpa, and the Henke Family.

CONTENTS

Complete Strategies for...

ANIMANIACS

CATEGORY: Action/Puzzle   DEVELOPER: Konami
PLAYERS: 1   PUBLISHER: Konami

Introduction

Konami is easily one of the most consistent companies in the video game market. Their games are known for excellent graphics and sounds, as well as some of the most entertaining and innovative gameplay. Programmers at Konami avoid the generic and come up with new ways to play old games. Therefore, *Animaniacs* is a little hard to categorize. It's a platform game, but also has many puzzles to solve along the way (much more than most platform games). By using the skills of Yakko, Wakko and Dot you must overcome obstacles and traps in an attempt to collect various items from the Warner Bros. Studio so they can open their own "hip pop culture" shop. One player uses all three characters, switching between them during the game.

Forget all those mindless platform games. In *Animaniacs* you have to use your brain to defeat Pinky and Brain.

Basic Strategies

✦ **Controls:** In the default setup (the settings when you turn on the game) the A button is for action, B is to jump, and C switches between the three characters. Yakko can paddleball attack with A, and push objects (mostly crates) by walking into them (or pull them by holding A while walking away from them). Wakko can pound with a hammer by pressing A (this will light fuses, destroy blocks, hit switches, etc.). Dot can flirt with another character by pressing A to blow a kiss.

✦ Collect 100 **stars** for a **1-Up** and collect **food** to restore your energy.

✦ The Animaniac you control is the only one that can get hurt by enemies and obstacles. If the Animaniac you control gets hit, all three will feel the pain.

✦ There are many **crates** throughout the game that must be stacked to form stairs. If you push or pull a crate too far and cause the crates to fall, walk to the left or right until the crates are off the screen, then go back and they'll be restacked.

Jump while launching from a seesaw to reach higher platforms and items.

- If you jump as you're being launched from a **seesaw** you can reach higher platforms.
- Whenever you see the **nurse** switch to Dot to avoid having your selected character lose control by falling in love.
- Whenever you see a **1-Up** near the beginning of a room you can always gain extra lives by collecting nearby stars, grabbing the **1-Up**, losing a life, then repeating until you collect enough stars (100) to gain a life. It's a long and tedious process, but it's the only way to build up extra lives.

Practice Scene

- At the beginning of the practice area you'll jump out of the water tower. Hold left to land on the pigeons ("The Goodbrothers") below the water tower, then go left and right to bounce on all of the pigeons. If you knock all of the pigeons off you'll reveal three hidden stars.
- The rest of this area is just for practice. Push the block, hit the fuse with the hammer and throw a kiss to the dog.

Scene 1: Bungle in the Jungle

- Push the block and climb on, then throw a kiss to the bird and jump to the swinging platform. Drop off the second swinging platform to grab stars. Go right and jump over the **cannon** to collect stars, then light the cannon by hitting the fuse with the hammer and jump into the cannon. Throw a kiss to the guy with headphones and jump on his head to reach the ledge to the right. Jump on the **robotic walker** and switch to Wakko (red hat). Use the hammer to hit the red button on the walker's head and he'll duck down, then hit it again to go back up.
- Jump in the **speedboat** and ride to the studio lights, then jump across the lights to collect the stars and avoid the alligator. Jump on the elephant and hit him in the head with the hammer, then jump back into the boat. Select Yakko and rapidly use his paddleboard attack to hit the guard.
- Ride the **logs** down to collect a **clock** and hit a switch at the bottom-right of the waterfall, then jump back up the logs and collect any remaining stars as you go to the door on the upper-right.
- While riding on the **railcart** use Wakko's hammer to guide the cart up or down the various rails. At the second junction go down for fruit if you need the energy boost. Go up at the third and fourth junctions. The stars are a bit tricky to jump for, so only go for them if you feel daring. As you head down the next hill stand on the right edge of the cart and you'll collect lots of stars on the way down. At the top of the next hill is a **1-Up**, but you have to jump for it and land back in the cart or you'll lose a life in the process. When you see the X ahead jump up to the small platforms and leap across them to the exit.
- Hit the **seesaw** with your hammer, then jump on for a boost up as the ball lands back on the seesaw. You can reach the stars above the seesaw by holding left and hitting your head on the inside of the cave as you're launched. After launching from the seesaw you'll need to jump

You have to be ready to jump early for the 1-Up at the top of the hill in the railcart.

onto a **large boulder** and ride it down. This jump is *very* tricky, but try to time your jump from near the hole to the seesaw and land on the boulder right as the boulder is landing. Also try to avoid landing on the security guard that appears between boulders.

✦ Launch from the next seesaw and go left, then pull the bottom of the **three stacked crates** until it is almost out from below the top two crates (don't pull it too far or the top crates will fall and you'll have to scroll the crates off the screen to restack them). When the bottom crate is almost completely pulled out from under the other two crates, jump on it and pull the second crate to the right so all three crates form stairs to the platforms above. If you want to grab the four stars to the left of the three stacked crates hold left on your way down, then climb back up the hill and ride another boulder down.

Timing the jump onto the boulder is very tricky. Try to land on the rock as it lands on the ground.

✦ In the next area jump onto the **disappearing blocks** as they appear, and try to pay attention to what blocks are about to disappear. Hit the crate to the right for a star, then leap for the **food** above to discover hidden blocks. Leap across the hidden blocks by remembering where they are when they flash. Pull the wood crate to the left, then hit the grey rocks with your hammer.

✦ In the **water fountain** hold Down to launch yourself up. In the next area go to the bottom and pull the wooden crate from the wall, then push it to the right into the passage for **food** and a **clock**. If you walk into the passage without the crate you'll enter a hidden warp that takes you back to the beginning of this area. Pull the crate back out of the passage and use it as a step. When you reach the two red buttons hit the one of the right to open the exit door to the boss.

✦ **RALPH, THE SECURITY GUARD:** Use Wakko's hammer to hit the seesaws. Stay on the right seesaw. If the mice run by, quickly rush to the far right to avoid Ralph, then go back to the seesaw. If a bomb drops nearby, move away until it explodes, then return back to the seesaw. Hit the seesaw with the hammer as Ralph walks overhead, then run to the right quickly to avoid the falling debris. After a few hits Ralph will go ballistic and drop a lot of bombs, and hiding out on the right side is the best way to wait out his temper. It takes seven hits to defeat Ralph.

Hammer the seesaw when Ralph is overhead, then rush to the right to avoid the debris.

Scene 2: Space Trucking

✵ Hit the button with the hammer to turn the rocket's hydraulic lift on, then jump on the rocket. Jump off the rocket after it passes through the wall to collect the stars below. Go right and hit the camera with the hammer.

✵ There are **two crates** that can be used to reach the ledges above. Pull the bottom crate left to form a very small step. Jump up on the bottom crate and push the top crate to the right edge of the bottom crate. Don't push it too far or you'll have to reset them by scrolling the screen to the left until the crates disappear. Push the bottom crate to the right until there's only a small step again, then repeat as before by pushing the top crate to the right until it's on the edge of the bottom crate. The crates should be at the center of the floor so you can reach the area above with the blue steps. Move the crate below the stars to collect them, then push it all the way left. Stand on the crate and smash the grey rock under the higher crate. Throw a kiss at the dog to put him asleep. There are **three boxes** ahead. Hit the first box (far right) to collect an **extra life.** Go back to the right and back down to the original two crates of this stage. Grab the lower crate and pull it to the right, then push it so it hangs over the edge of the pit.

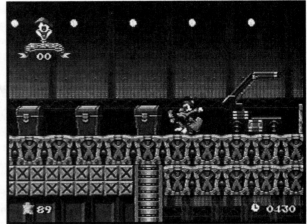

Hit the far right of the three boxes in this area to collect an extra life.

✵ Go right until you see a **hen carrying a rocket.** Throw a kiss at the hen, then jump on the rocket. Jump on the yellow and black striped elevator. As you ride up the elevator, stand on the left side of the elevator to avoid all of the laser cannons and collect the stars.

✵ Jump to the top platform with the word "GAS" written on it and push the crate over the right side to land on the button below. Quickly go through the lower passage and collect the stars. If the doors shut before you escape out the right side, jump up through the ceiling and push the crate back onto the button. On the next floor down go to the far left and drag the crate up against the left wall, then stand on it and hit the wall with the hammer to collect the **apple.** Jump to the **conveyor belt** at the upper right and go right. Jump over the gap to land on the lower-right conveyor belt.

✵ As you enter the next room walk three or four steps onto the blocks and ride up, then continue walking to the right. Pull the crate to the left to climb to the ledge above, then go left and hit the four buttons to make a star pop out of the **volcano.** You might be able to make other items pop out of the volcano with the right combination, but we didn't have seven years to test out every possible combination. Go back to the right and push the crate to the right. Then leap over to the right and hit the button.

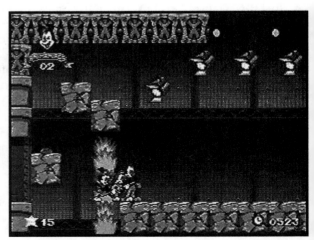

Walk three or four steps onto the rocks and wait to ride up, then continue walking across to the right.

- **Ralph the security guard** makes another appearance. If you stay on the ground he'll attack you, so jump onto the rockets and leap from rocket to rocket. If you land on one of the treasure chests on the top row you can safely walk off to the right and land on something every time. When the rockets stop you'll have to fight Ralph by using Yakko's paddleball attack.

- Climb up the left side on the blue platforms to reach a **clock**, then collect the stars to the right. In the next area fall down to the bottom floor to collect stars and a **clock**, then use the seesaw to get back up. Go right until you reach **three crates and four breakable stones.** You need to jump up and hit the top breakable stone (it has a **1-Up** in it), then climb to the top right. If you break the bottom stone you'll have to drop down below and relaunch off the seesaw to reset the crates.

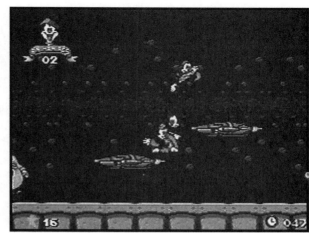

Stay on the rockets to avoid being attacked by Ralph.
Use your paddleboard if he does attack you.

- In the next room is **Ralph the security guard,** again! This time you have to race up a series of ladders while avoiding him. Use Yakko the entire time so you can attack with the paddleboard and push the crates around. Collect the stars and **food** while using the paddleboard to distract Ralph, then climb up a ladder immediately after knocking him down until you reach the top. Go right and Ralph won't be able to follow you.

- Push the crate under the **steel gate** to keep it from smashing you, but don't push it all the way. Jump over the crate as the gate rises, hit the button, then jump back over the crate. Go left and fall down the elevator shaft to the bottom floor, then select Dot and follow the **nurse** to the left for an **apple.** Go right, ride the elevator up one floor, and jump to the left. Push the crate onto the **triangle button,** then go left into the wall and drag the crate out to place it on the **circle button.** Go across to the right and stand on the button until the gate below is completely open, then quickly drop down and run through the door before it closes.

- In the next room, ride the **rotating elevators** up to the top and go right. Drag the right of the two crates up against the breakable stone, then push the other crate on top of the first crate. Drag both crates to the right to form steps. Go to the far right wall. To get the **clock** and the **1-Up**, stand on the right edge of the elevator below, then leap up to the items as the elevator is rising. Go left and back up the rotating elevators, then drop down to the two crates again. This time hit the breakable stone on the left and hit the button to activate the elevator, then drop down to it and jump into the exit.

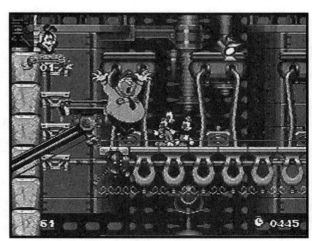

Avoid the sparks and green clouds while attacking
Ralph with the paddleboard and running up a ladder.

- Hit the fuse on the **cannon** and jump in for a launch to the **walking robot.**

- **Ralph the security guard** is the boss again. This time you need to climb to the top of the room while avoiding Ralph, green clouds of toxic dust, sparks, and a few falling spotlights. Take your time, since there's plenty of time available. Wait for the sparks to go by before jumping to those platforms, and try to knock Ralph off before climbing up a floor so you won't have to fight him on your way up.

Scene 3: Remember the a la Mode

⚡ Jump on the cactus and wait for Ralph to stop bombing, then jump over the horse as it charges you. Continue jumping over cactuses and horses as you run to the right. Use Yakko's paddleboard attack to hit Ralph when he attacks. Scare Mindy (the little girl) with the paddleboard, then grab the **apple** after the dog chases the girl. In the next room grab the stars and push at least one crate onto the spikes to get across the gap.

⚡ In the next room jump to the **bridge** with the camera and knock the **skull and crossbones block** down, then hit it to lower the bridge and break the camera. Use Yakko's paddleboard to knock Ralph into a silly rage, then run past him into the next room.

⚡ In the **hotel** climb up the steps and jump across the **hippos,** then climb up while avoiding the barrels until you see a button. The **barrels** come in groups of four, so wait until four pass before making a run to the next safe area. Hit the button with the hammer, then continue to the right avoiding more barrels until you find the culprits responsible for launching them.

The barrels come in groups of four. Wait for the gap between groups, then make a run for a safe spot.

⚡ In the **Indian village** there are **three crates** that must be stacked in the right area. Push the bottom crate to the far right against the rock next to the pit of flames, then pull it back one small step. Go to the second crate (not the top one) and pull it to the right as far as you can, then leap over the crate to land on the left side and push the crate until it's halfway off the platform. Push the top crate completely off the right side so it lands in the pit below, then go back to the second crate and push it off the right side so it lands on the first crate. Stand on the first crate and pull the second crate to the right, then pull the bottom crate to the far right, then pull the second crate right again until it falls off. Place the second crate on top of the third crate (which is in the pit of fire). Push the second crate off the right side so it lands next to the third crate in the pit, then run across them and leap to the right bank of the pit. For the next **two crates,** push the top crate to

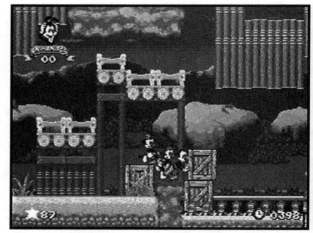

The method to using the three crates to get across the flaming pit is very tricky.

the right so you can see it in the window, then break the stone below and grab the star and **clock** in the passage below, then return to the top crate and push it into the pit of flames to cross safely.

✴ **Near the exit** there are lots of stars above a see-saw and disappearing platforms. By now you should have the necessary skills to collect them with a little patience. You should still have plenty of time left on the **clock** by the time you grab all the stars. Jump across the disappearing platforms to the right to reach the exit.

✴ In the next room you'll have to jump across collapsing platforms. There's a **1-Up** dangerously placed above the flaming pit below. You can't get it without losing a life, but if your energy is low you can grab the life and restart with full energy. If you do fall to the pit below later, be sure to jump for the **1-Up** before you lose all your energy.

✴ In the bottom-left wall of this area is a **hidden bonus game** where you can spin a wheel and win extra stars (or more likely, lose stars!). Place your bet of which character you think you'll land on, then spin the wheel and try to stop it on the character you bet on. The characters at the bottom are on the wheel less often than those at the top, so the odds of landing on them is much lower. Either way, odds are you'll lose more than you'll win.

✴ When you see **Mindy and her dog Buttons** switch to Dot because the **nurse** is in the stagecoach below and Dot is the only one who can resist her temptation. Grab the **clock** in the stagecoach, then fall off the cliff to collect lots of goodies below. Go into the cliff on the left and drag the crate to the right into the pit of flames to leap across. Hit the **stilt legs of Brain** (mouse) with the paddleboard to knock him down. Go right and use the **seesaw** to launch up

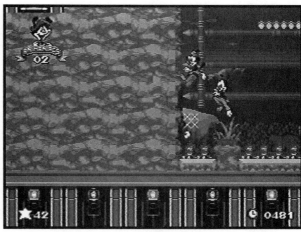

Jump into the left wall of the Indian village area with the collapsing platforms...

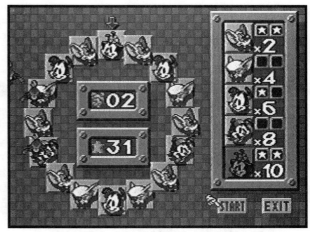

...and you'll find this hidden bonus game where you'll have the opportunity to lose all your stars!

to the top floor on the left, then collect the **hidden stars** behind the fort wall. Go left to the yellow and black striped platform, then hit it with the hammer to make it fall. As it's falling jump right to the second floor and go right. Hit the detonator to open the exit door.

✴ **In the train** move the bottom-left crate two steps to the left, then climb up the steps on the far left of the screen and push the top crate on top of the bottom-left crate. Drag the top crate to the right on to the other crate, then leap up to the **clock** and stars.

✴ **Outside the train,** switch to Wakko and use his hammer to launch pies at **Ralph** while dodging pies he throws at you. After you hit him five times you'll continue back inside the train.

✴ **Back inside the train** go to the crate on the bottom floor. There's a group of three crates in the background — pull the crate so it's in front of the bottom left of those three crates in the background. Climb to the top floor along the left wall and push both crates to the right so they drop below. Stack all three crates up and pull them slowly to the right until they form steps to the ice cream cone above.

✴ **As you exit the train** quickly *push* the crate to the right and jump onto the camera before the rest of

| Use the paddleboard to knock Ralph silly... | ...then use the hammer to knock coal into the train. |

the train separates. Jump into the front train. Use Yakko to knock **Ralph** back with the paddleboard, then quickly switch to Wakko to hit coal into the train as the lid opens. Switch back to Yakko when you see Ralph catching up to hit him again, then repeat this pattern until you reach the right side of the screen and collect the next valuable item for your museum.

Scene 4: To Scream or Not to Scream

✦ Jump up with Dot and kiss the Grim Reaper to stun him. Fall into the hole and push the tombstone to the left to grab the star, then drag it to the far right. Push the top tombstone to the right, then hit the breakable block and push the lower tombstone to the right. Push the top tombstone against the haystack to jump over it. If you land on the haystack you'll hit a hidden spring that sends you back to the beginning of the stage. Go through the log ahead to collect an extra star. Drag the stone block onto the button to raise the door protecting one star. Drag the crate on the right to the right, then hit the breakable block with your hammer. Push the left crate onto the button to open the door to the haunted house.

✦ **Inside the haunted house** avoid the books while grabbing the stars on the pegs above.

✦ In the second room of the haunted house beware of **falling chandeliers.** Check the last mirror for a cool effect — he's the boss in the next room.

✦ **Vampire:** Walk quickly to the crate and pull it to the left until it's at the center of the screen. Switch to Dot and stay on the left side of the crate. When the vampire lands to the right of the crate, jump and throw a kiss at him to make him disappear.

✦ Go right and grab the star, then climb up and go right. Jump on the chandelier for another star, then drop down to the left. Push the crate to the right against the statue and hit the statue with

Quickly pull the crate left to the center of the screen, then hide behind it and blow Drac a kiss.

your hammer. Push the crate to the far right and climb up the steps. Fall to the area below and stay in front of the table. Jump to avoid the **dishes** while running to the right to avoid the pull of the trumpet. Go to the left and smash the breakable blocks, then drag the crate to the right past the table.

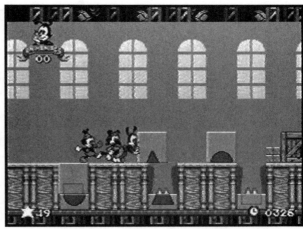

🗲 Go right and push each one of the blocks into the holes nearest them (to the right). The shapes won't match up, but that's not important yet. Go right and collect the stars and **clock**, then smash the breakable block. Go back to the left and push the red triangle block into its matching hole, then drag the blue circle block to the left into its hole and the yellow square block to the right into its hole. Push the crate to the right into the pit, then pull and push it against the right side of the pit. Push the next crate forward and leap over to the exit.

The first time you see these blocks just push them into their nearest holes.

🗲 As you drop into the next room go straight down for a **clock**. Go back up and drag the crate to the left next to the water. Push the crate onto the log the moment it stops and walk onto the log while avoiding the water that falls from above. You'll have to push the crate a little more than half way off the log. When you reach the other side of the water quickly push off the crate and place it over the blue pipe. Go to the left until you see a **1-Up**. If you're low on energy you can grab the **1-Up** now and

when you start at the beginning of this room you'll have full energy (you can get the **1-Up** without dying in a minute, but if you're low on energy you might as well grab it now and take the fall). Go left and jump down the platforms to the bottom, then push the crate left to drain the water. Climb back up and drop down to grab the **1-Up**. Go right and smash the treasure chest for an **apple**, then climb up and go into the left passage to drag a crate out to the far right ledge. The block should be almost off the ledge, then climb on it and jump across to the right for a treasure chest with an **apple**. Push the crate over the ledge and drop down, then drag the crate to the right to reach the exit.

Throw a kiss at the vampire, then hit the button to drop him off the platform he's standing on.

🗲 **Vampire Boss — Second Encounter**: Use Dot and throw a kiss at the vampire as soon as possible. The arrows next to the buttons point to the platform across the room that will collapse when that button is hit with the hammer. After kissing the vampire while he's on a platform quickly hit the button that will collapse the platform he's standing on. Jump to the center platform and prepare to throw another kiss, then repeat the pattern.

Scene 5: Once There Was a Man Named Oscar

✸ The first room is a breeze. In the second room go to the second seesaw and *jump* as the ball lands on the seesaw to reach the floor above. When you reach the **elevator** don't ride it up! Go left into the wall and drag the block in the next wall to the right. Climb up and hit the machine above the yellow gas ball, then go back down and push the other half of the wall through to the left. Climb up and hit the machine to the right, then grab the stars on your way back down. Go to the elevator and ride it up. Go left and hit the plunger when the **mice** step on the plunger to the left. They'll leap up and eventually destroy the machine above. Go back to the elevator and ride it up to the next stop. Jump down between the **two crates** and grab the star. Jump back up on the left side of the left crate and push it to the right to the edge of the ledge without letting it drop into the pit. Jump up and to the right to grab the third crate and drag it to the left so it lands on the other two crates. Drag the top crate as far left as possible on top of the bottom left crate (it should line up directly above the pit below). Drag the bottom left crate to the left so the top crate falls into the pit, then push the crate to the right so it falls into the pit. Drag the top crate to the left so you can get into the passage it blocks. Drop down and hit the treasure chest for a star. Go left and drop down the row of stars, then go right.

✸ **Outside of the factory** fall down the stream of stars, then jump to the bird's nest on the left and leap up and right to grab the **1-Up**. If you want you can plummet to your death and repeat this area over and over until you collect 100 stars for an extra life. You must jump across the **yellow and black platforms** without getting hit by the falling debris. Jump across the bottom three, then time the jump from the third platform to the center platform. Jump to the top left platform, then leap across to the right onto the top of the sign. Drop down to the platform on the right side of the sign, then time your leaps to the two platforms on the right. Leap to the **hot dog sign,** then quickly leap to the exit.

✸ **Back inside the factory** switch to Yakko and drop down to the bottom of the room to collect stars while hitting **Ralph** the security guard with your paddleboard attack. Go up and right. Hit the breakable block under the **swinging steel ball,** then drag the crate to the right to climb up. Go down the steps in the next area and hit the fuse, then quickly climb up out of the hole before the bomb explodes. Climb up to the exit.

✸ In the next area you must quickly hit all **three buttons** to move the walls out of the way while you run to the right. Don't stop for any stars. When you see the crates stay on the bottom floor and push the bottom crate to the edge of the

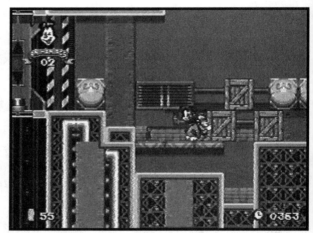

After riding the elevator to the top, place the third crate on top of the first, then pull the first to the left.

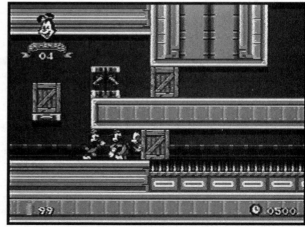

Push this bottom crate to the right slightly for a 1-Up, then pull it left and climb quickly.

ledge next to the spikes to collect a hidden **1-Up**, then pull the crate to the left until there's enough of the top of the crate exposed to jump up onto. Jump to the upper-left crate, then quickly to the upper-right. Quickly push the next crate until you can jump over it, then select Wakko to hit another **two red buttons** with the hammer. Keep Wakko in charge and jump across the collapsing platform until you see a **red button.** Hit it with a hammer, then drag the crate a little to the right and use it to jump up and right to the exit ahead.

Dodge the embers and hammer the hydrant
to put out the fire.

- In the next room you'll see a **helicopter** outside. Push the crate to the right quickly to jump over the wall. Grab the next crate and drag it to the left to reach the button above. Go to the exit for the final area.

- It's Backdraft II as you run through a **city of flames.** Dodge the falling embers and hit the **fire hydrant** with the hammer. Go to the right and jump across the collapsing platforms. Drop down in the next area and drag the crate to the left until you're against the wall, then leap up and go right to hit the next fire hydrant. Push the crate to the right to climb up, then leap from the next crate to get **food**. Go right and hit another hydrant. Go down the slope and hit the next hydrant, then drop down on the left and grab the stars below. To the left is **Mindy** and a star. Jump up to grab the star, then push the left crate to the left until it drops. Pull the crate on the right to the left, then drop down and jump up on the right side of the crate. Push the crate to the left until it drops, then push it to the right into the hole. Once the crates fill both holes Mindy will run to the right and Buttons will follow. You could have easily jumped over Buttons and saved yourself some trouble without rescuing Mindy, but don't you feel better knowing she's safe?

- In the next area just jump onto the **car** and enjoy the ride.

- **THE FINAL BOSS:** Use Dot to throw a kiss at Pinky so he'll forget to light the bomb before he drops it. Use Yakko to push the bomb to the feet of the robot, then use Wakko to ignite the bomb. Get away from the bomb, then after it explodes move back towards the robot's feet to avoid the next lit bomb

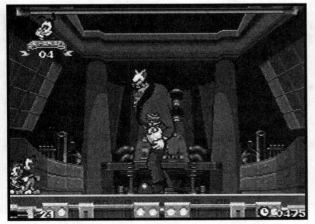

Throw a kiss at Pinky so he'll drop an unlit bomb,
then push it into the foot and hammer it.

Avoid the legs while using Dot's powerful kiss to get
more unlit bombs, then push it into Pinky and hammer it.

thrown at you. Repeat the pattern until you hit him with six bombs, then he'll split and you'll have to fight only the legs.

✦ For the second phase, switch to Dot and run under the legs when they jump, then throw a kiss at Pinky in the robot's pocket. Push the bomb up to Pinky and hit it with the hammer, then move back. Avoid the legs and lit bombs until it's safe to move in and throw another kiss. Repeat the pattern, taking your time, until you hit him with six more bombs. You'll be treated to a long ending sequence showing all of the characters.

Awesome Secrets!

PASSWORD: Practice Cleared.

PASSWORD: Scene 1 Cleared.

PASSWORD:
Scene 1+2 Cleared.

PASSWORD:
Scene 1+2+3 Cleared.

PASSWORD: Scene 4 Cleared.

BALLZ

CATEGORY: Fighting	DEVELOPER: P.F. Magic
PLAYERS: 1 or 2 (Simultaneous)	PUBLISHER: Accolade

Introduction

In the overcrowded market of clone-like fighting games, P.F. Magic and Accolade decided to make their fighting game a little different. By creating the characters from a bunch of spheres, or balls, they were able to make the characters move quickly and fluidly while also being allowed to change the point of view constantly. Since the animation of the characters in most games takes up a lot of memory, the programmers are limited by the number of actual moves a character can perform. Since animating a bunch of balls doesn't take up nearly as much memory, the average character in Ballz has 29-35 moves.

It ain't Virtua Fighters, but Ballz offers one of the most extensive moves list of any fighting game.

Basic and Advanced Moves

✦ All of these moves assume you haven't changed the default settings):

Punch: A	**Kick:** B	**Jump:** C

(The longer you hold the jump, the higher or longer you'll jump. Lighter fighters can jump higher.)

Low Punch: A + down	**Low Kick:** B + down
Lunging Punch: Toward + A	**Lunging Kick:** Toward + B
Short Punch: Away + A	**Short Kick:** Away + B

✦ **BLOCKING:**

Retreating block: Away	**High block:** Away + up
Crouching block: Away + down	**Roll away when down:** A + Up or Down

✦ **BEGGING FOR MERCY:** Press down rapidly when fatigued to grovel and regain your health.

✦ **TAUNT:** Press Punch + Kick + Jump all at the same time (A + B + C) to taunt the other player. Taunting increases the damage delivered on the next attack by either player.

✦ **GRAPPLE:** Press A repeatedly to grapple. Rapidly press punch (A) to fight while grappling. Whichever player presses A the fastest will perform a special move against the other fighter.

✦ **AIR KICK/PUNCH:** Press C then B to perform an Air Kick, or C then A to perform an Air Punch.

✦ **LATERAL MOVES:** Left + B + C for a Lateral Move Left, or Right + B + C for a Lateral Move Right.

Morphing

You can morph into any of the other characters at any time by performing these combinations.

MORPH TO	BY PRESSING
Boomer	Right, Left, A + C
Bruiser	Down, Left, , A + C
Crusher	Down, Right, A + C
Divine	Up, Left, , A + C
Kronk	Left, Left, , A + C
Tsunami	Left, Right, A + C
Turbo	Right, Right, A + C
Yoko	Up, Right, A + C

Other Stuff To Know

AFTER SHATTER STOMP: If you perform a finishing move on your opponent, you can stomp the remains of your opponent by pressing A four times. Each character has a different way of paying their last respects to their opponent.

FINISHING MOVES: The finishing move for every character is the same — Up three times. The finishing move performed by each character is totally different. The Finishing move can only be performed when your opponent has 2.5 energy ballz or less.

SPECIAL MOVES: We have provided the special moves for each character. When a move is listed as letters with commas, do each move one after another. If the move is listed with a plus sign (+), then press the buttons at the same time or move the control pad as you press the button(s) at the same time.

If you perform a finishing move on your opponent, you can do an After Shatter Stomp on their remains.

Boomer

RATINGS:

Speed 3	Throw Damage 4	Explosion/Cyclone Damage . 5
Punch Damage 3	Grapple Damage 4	Other Special Moves 1
Kick Damage 3	Charge Attacks 1	Defense 2
Missile Attacks 5	Aerial Attack Damage . . 1	Aerial Defense 3

SPECIAL MOVES:

Bowl Head . . . . Away, Toward, B
Dive . . . . Down, Up + C
Jack-In-The-Box Head . . . . Up + A
Sideshow Left (Handstand Kick) . . . . . Left, Left, B
Colossal Kick (Power Kick) . . . . Toward, Toward, B (near opponent)
Sideshow Right (Handstand Kick) . . . . Right, Right, B
Rude Gesture . . . . Away, Toward, Up + A   or   A + B + C
M-80 (Self Destruct) . . . . Right, Down, Left, Up, A
Slinky Punch (Telescoping Arms) . . . . Down + A + B
Throw (Suspended Spin) . . . . B when close to opponent
Throw Head . . . . Away, Toward, A

Boomer juggles while riding on the back
of his opponent for his fatality.

Press Away, Toward, A to throw your head
at your unsuspecting opponent.

Bruiser

RATINGS:

Speed 3	Throw Damage 2	Explosion/Cyclone Damage . 4
Punch Damage 4	Grapple Damage 2	Other Special Moves 3
Kick Damage 2	Charge Attacks 2	Defense 3
Missile Attacks 3	Aerial Attack Damage . . 3	Aerial Defense 5

SPECIAL MOVES:

Buckle Heave	Down, Up, A
Buckle Kick	Away, Toward, B
Buckle Toss	Away, Toward, A
Cannonball	C, Down + A or C, Down, Down
Cartwheel Left	Left, Left, B
Cartwheel Right	Right, Right, B
Charge	Toward, Toward, Toward
Torqueno (Cyclone)	Right, Down, Left, Up, A
Ducking Uppercut	B + C (while ducking)
Jump Kick Two Feet	C, A + B
Jumping Jacks	Up, Down, Up, Down
Leg Grab from Duck	A + B (while ducking)
Leg Sweep	Down, A + B
Italian Salute (Rude Gesture)	A + B + C
Slide Tackle	Down, Down, B
Throw (Spinning Bodyslam)	B when close
Tornado	Toward, Away, Toward

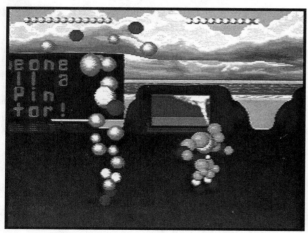

You can suck your opponent in with the cyclone and rearrange his ballz.

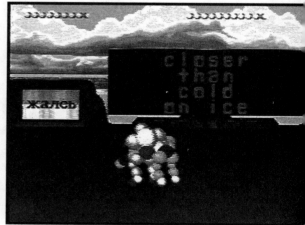

Move close to your opponent and grapple to grab him in a head lock and pummel his head.

Crusher

RATINGS:

Speed	1	Throw Damage	4	Explosion/Cyclone Damage	4
Punch Damage	5	Grapple Damage	3	Other Special Moves	3
Kick Damage	5	Charge Attacks	5	Defense	5
Missile Attacks	2	Aerial Attack Damage	4	Aerial Defense	2

SPECIAL MOVES:

Arrow Spear	A + B (while in air)
Charge Attack	Toward, Toward, Toward
Jumping Head Butt	Left, Down, A or Right, Down, A
Lunge with Horn	Toward, Toward, A
Pile Driver (Over the Top Body Slam)	Up, Down, A
Rude Gesture	Away, Toward, Up + A, or A + B + C
Rumble Charge	Up, Down, Up
Stomp on Foot	Up, Toward, B
Throw (Spear on horn)	B when close
Horn Heave (high)	Away, Up, A
Horn Heave (low)	Away, Toward, A
Wind Up Kick	Away, Away, B
Wind Up Punch	Away, Away, A

Crusher jumps onto the back of his opponent to destroy him with a fatality.

Hold your opponent by his legs and bounce his head against your knee.

Divine

RATINGS:

Speed 5	Throw Damage 3	Explosion/Cyclone Damage . 3
Punch Damage 2	Grapple Damage 4	Other Special Moves 2
Kick Damage. 5	Charge Attacks 1	Defense 3
Missile Attacks 1	Aerial Attack Damage . . 5	Aerial Defense 3

SPECIAL MOVES:

Bump & Grind	Toward, Away, Toward, Away
Ducking Uppercut.	Down, Toward, A
Fake Dizzy.	Down, Down, Away
Flip & Throw	A + B when close
Jump Left, Kick Right	Left, Left, B
Jump Right, Kick Left	Right, Right, B
The Knee (Knee to Groin).	Down, Down, Toward
Low Lunge Kick	Down, B + C
Jette (Lunge Kick).	Up, Up, B
Opera Assault.	Down, Down, Up
Reverse Cartwheel Head Scissors	Toward, Toward, Toward
Ride on Back & Bite	C then land on opponent
Rude Gesture	Away, Toward, Up + A or A + B + C
Tornado Punch (Spin)	Away, Up, Toward
Throw (Nut Grab).	B when close

The ever painful knee to groin.
They don't call it *Ballz* for nothing!

Jump on the back of your opponent with
a grappling move, then bite the back of his head.

Kronk

RATINGS:

Speed 4	Throw Damage 4	Explosion/Cyclone Damage . 1
Punch Damage 3	Grapple Damage 4	Other Special Moves 2
Kick Damage 2	Charge Attacks 3	Defense 3
Missile Attacks 2	Aerial Attack Damage . . 2	Aerial Defense 5

SPECIAL MOVES:

Bone Sweep	Down + A + B
Club Uppercut	Up, Down, Up
Duck, Dive & Roll	Toward, Toward, Toward
Fencing Lunge	Toward, Toward, A
Flying Down Spear	C, Down, Down
Flying Phlegm	Away, Toward, A
Lobber Loogie	Away, Up, A
The Klub	Down, Down, A
Overhead Club	Up, A
Kranium Krunch	C then land on opponent
Rude Gesture	Away, Down, A or A + B + C
Throw (Tee Off)	B when close
Wind Up Club	Toward, Away, A

Hock a loogie at your opponent
for a minimal amount of damage.

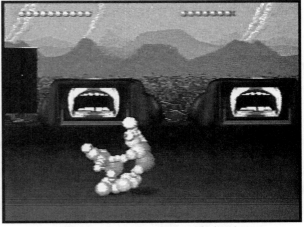

Hold your opponent from behind,
then join a club and beat him over the head with it.

Tsunami

RATINGS:

Speed 2	Throw Damage 5	Explosion/Cyclone Damage . 2
Punch Damage 5	Grapple Damage 3	Other Special Moves 4
Kick Damage 3	Charge Attacks 5	Defense 4
Missile Attacks 1	Aerial Attack Damage . . 4	Aerial Defense 3

SPECIAL MOVES:

Dynamite Roll (Belly Charge)	Toward, Toward, Toward
Wasabit Slam (Flying Somersault)	Away, Away, C
Sumo Sidekick Left (Jump Kick)	Left, Left, B
Sumo Sidekick Right (Jump Kick)	Right, Right, B
Karate Chop	Up, Toward, A
Meditate	Up, Up, C
Rude Gesture	Away, Toward, Up + A or A + B + C
Sumo Splash	C, A + B
Throw (Pound on Ground)	B when close
Wind Up Kick	Toward, Away, B
Wind Up Punch	Toward, Away, A

Hold your opponent against the ground,
then pound his head into that very same ground.

Use the meditate move
to float away or toward your opponent.

Turbo

RATINGS:

Speed 4	Throw Damage 4	Explosion/Cyclone Damage . 1
Punch Damage 3	Grapple Damage 4	Other Special Moves 4
Kick Damage 3	Charge Attacks 3	Defense 3
Missile Attacks 2	Aerial Attack Damage . . 4	Aerial Defense 3

SPECIAL MOVES:

Charging Flip Kick	Toward, Toward, Toward
Javelin Kick (Flying Dart)	C, Down, Down
Head Pound	Up, Toward, A
Turbo Thruster (Hovering)	C, B + C
Turbine Punch (Rising Punch)	Down + A + B
Rude Gesture	Away, Toward, Up + A or A + B + C
Spinning Pile Driver	C, A + B when close in midair
Super Blow	Toward, Toward + A
Throw (Toss & Punch)	B when close
Wind Up Punch	Away, Toward, A

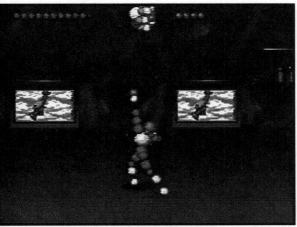

Toss your opponent into the air,
then punch him as he falls.

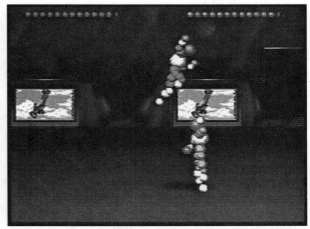

Use the Turbo Thruster move
to float above your opponent.

Yoko

RATINGS:

Speed	3	Throw Damage	5	Explosion/Cyclone Damage	1
Punch Damage	2	Grapple Damage	2	Other Special Moves	5
Kick Damage	2	Charge Attacks	2	Defense	3
Missile Attacks	1	Aerial Attack Damage	4	Aerial Defense	4

SPECIAL MOVES:

Backflip	Up, B
Forward Roll	Toward, Toward, Toward
Gamera Spin Attack	Toward, Up, Up
Pole Swing	Right, Right, Up, or Left, Left, Up
Pull Off Leg & Swing	Down, B
Congo Cranium (ride back)	C then land on opponent
Rude Gesture	Down, Toward, B or A + B + C
Sphincter Blast (Stun Fart)	Away, Away, Away
Swinging (Start Swinging)	C, Up, Up
Swing Around Hit	Left, Left, B or Right, Right, B
Swing Punch	A (while swinging)
Swing Kick	B (while swinging)
Throw (Gorilla Spin)	B when close
Uppercut	Up, A

Move in close to your opponent, jump and land
on him to ride on his back, then punch away.

Yoko can maneuver quickly around the screen
by swinging from vines only he can see.

BATTLETECH

CATEGORY: Action	DEVELOPER: Malibu Interactive
PLAYERS: 1-2 (Simultaneous)	PUBLISHER: Extreme Entertainment

Introduction

Extreme really should be paying royalties to Electronic Arts, because *Battletech* is one of the most blatant "tributes" to *Desert Strike* and *Jungle Strike* we've ever seen. Which is not a bad thing, mind you, since *Desert Strike* and *Jungle Strike* were both rather butt-kickin' games. *Battletech* isn't quite as good as either—there are only five levels, the missions in each level aren't as involving as they could be, and the ending sequence blows meaty chunks—but the difficulty level is definitely challenging (to the point of frustration) and the graphics are gorgeous. This chapter is filled with maps, pictures, and strategies to make your journey through the game much easier than ours!

Battletech looks and plays very much like the *Strike* series of helicopter games from Electronic Arts.

Basic Strategies

✦ When an enemy Mech attacks you, attack it immediately with your most powerful weapons and take it out ASAP. 'Mechs are simply too dangerous to mess around with for longer than absolutely necessary.

✦ Position yourself behind enemy targets and let the enemy destroy them for you. You save plenty of ammo this way. This technique works particularly well with enemy 'Mechs, which you can often destroy by goading the other enemies into shooting at you and hitting the enemy 'Mech.

✦ Blow up all the buildings you come across to find ammo. Our maps label the locations of ammo and Coolant containers on each level (except for the ammo and Coolant carried by enemy 'Mechs).

✦ Each player has his own idea of the best weapon selection. Our personal faves were the Gauss Rifle (more ammo and damage than the other Heavy Ordnance weapons), Auto Cannon (a good combination of ammo and power), and the Long Range Missile (much more useful in combat than either the Inferno or the Thunder Mines). Experiment on your own to find out what you like the most.

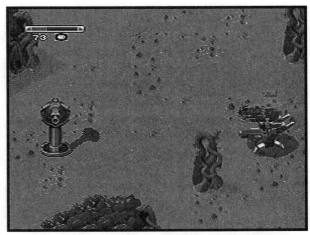

Against the cannons that move up and down, shoot them from the side so that they can't shoot back at you.

✦ With most of the enemies in *Battletech,* your strategy is simply to run and shoot, but there's a hand technique you can use against the cannons that move up and down; shoot them from the side, fa enough away so that they can't return fire.

Level 1: Alshain

MISSION 1

✦ **Briefing:** The **radar site** is located in the **south east** sectors. This installation feeds your coordinates to all ground based guns. **Take it out.**

✦ You start the mission at the south end of the map, just to the east of a supply cache with one of each ammo type (and a Coolant container). Return here if you're running low on ammo and have already raided nearby buildings for the hidden ammo inside.

✦ The radar site is covered with mines that explode when the Madcat stomps on them. You can use the Main Gun to strafe the field and blow up

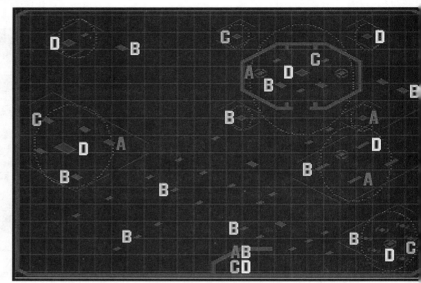

LEVEL 1 MAP (ALSHAIN)

A: Heavy Ordnance (Button A)   C: Tactical Weapon (Button C)
B: Main Gun (Button B)   D: Coolant

the mines before stepping on them, although you certainly won't hit them all. Attack the cannons on the perimeter of the site before you charge through the fence to blow up the radar dishes. There'

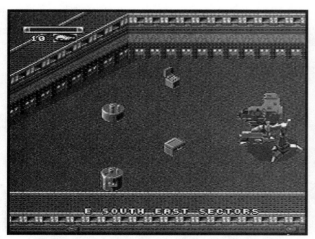

There's a supply cache of goodies kindly placed very close to your starting location in the mission.

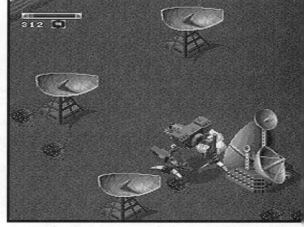

Use the Main Gun to strafe the minefield and blow the mines up–much better than stepping on them.

Coolant underneath one of the dishes, to make up for the damage you take from the mines. You're also attacked by an enemy Mech carrying a second Coolant container. Use your Main Gun and Tactical Weapon to very quickly destroy the Mech.

MISSION 2

✦ **Briefing: Aerotech** attacks are frequent and deadly. Take out the **Aeroport** in the **eastern** sectors to rid yourself of this vicious nuisance.

✦ Aerotechs are the aircraft flying so high in the sky that you can only see their shadows as they make strafing runs on your Madcat. These runs can be avoided if you notice them early enough. Use your Heavy Ordnance to destroy each of the four Aerotech hangars.

MISSION 3

✦ **Briefing:** DMCS Mech and tank bays in the western sectors manufacture 'Mechs and tanks. Eliminate this zone quickly or they will amass an overwhelming force against you.

✦ There's a 'Mech-producing building in the middle that you should take out immediately. To give you even more incentive, there's a Coolant container inside it. Once the 'Mechs stop attacking, the rest of the zone is easy by comparison. Use your heavy weaponry to take out the buildings; there's simply too much firepower here to mess around with.

MISSION 4

✦ **Briefing:** We have just discovered our captured **Star Captain** is being held in the **north west** sectors. He will deactivate the **DMCS Compound's** bay doors for you.

✦ The only defense in this area is ground cannons, which are easy to destroy. Stay out of their attack range and pick them off one at a time. There's no time limit, so don't rush. There's one tank-producing building that should be destroyed as soon as possible. Destroy the two buildings and the captured Star Captain runs to your 'Mech for pickup. (You can also position yourself behind the buildings and let the cannons destroy them for you.)

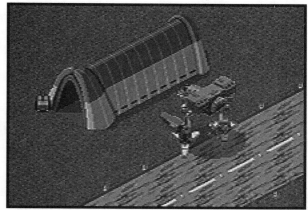

Use your more powerful weapons to destroy the four Aerotech hangars quickly.

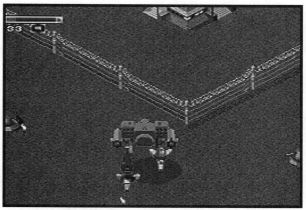

The only defense in the northwest corner of the map are ground cannons that are easy to blow up.

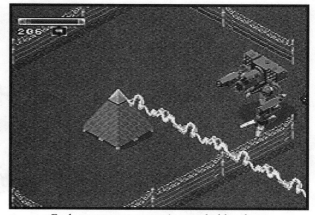

Each power generator is guarded by three cannons and has a power-up item underneath it.

MISSION 5

- ✦ **Briefing:** The **DMCS Compound** has a very effective internal defense system. Destroy the **power generators** at the four corners of the compound to disable this system.
- ✦ Each power generator is guarded by three cannons. As you did in the previous mission, shoot the cannons from long range, and destroy the generator when the coast is clear. There's one of each ammo type, and a Coolant, under the generators.

MISSION 6

- ✦ **Briefing:** Take out the **main DMCS compound** itself. **Level the place.**
- ✦ Blow the main gate and immediately run around the perimeter of the compound, using everything you have to destroy the enemy buildings and

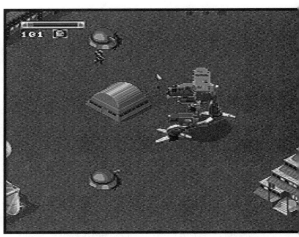
Run around the perimeter of the main compound and cut loose with everything you've got.

vehicles. This is the final mission, so you might as well let loose! The building in the center of the compound has a Coolant inside, so destroy it if you're running high on damage. Blow up all the buildings to complete the level.

Level 2: Satalice

MISSION 1

- ✦ **Briefing: Rasalhague** will send a shipment of **parts** off the planet in a **few minutes.** Unfortunately, we do not know which of the **two launch sites** they plan to ship the parts out from. Locate and **destroy both** sites before the shipment can leave the planet.
- ✦ The first launch site is in the south section of the level, and the second launch site is in the northeast corner. From your starting location, walk southeast through the mountains to the first site, destroy it, and then go northeast to the second site. (Refer to the

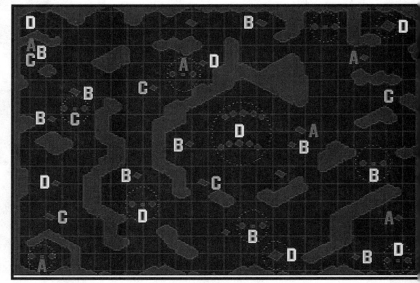

LEVEL 2 MAP (SATALICE)

A: Heavy Ordnance (Button A)   C: Tactical Weapon (Button C)
B: Main Gun (Button B)   D: Coolant

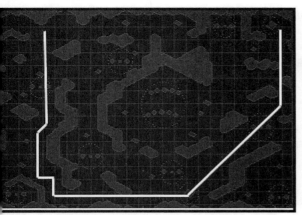

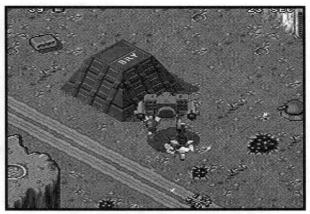

Follow this path to quickly strike both of the missile launch sites while avoiding the enemy forces.

This is a missile launch site. Any questions?

map with delineated path.) Don't waste any time fighting enemies unless it's absolutely necessary to take them out. Trying to hit the sites the other way around is all but impossible because of the huge number of enemies you encounter (including an enemy 'Mech) while cutting across the north section of the level. Each launch site has a Coolant under it, so you simply need to survive until you reach each site. If you make it to the first site with 80 seconds to spare, you're making very good time.

MISSION 2

✵ **Briefing:** Take out the **eight material gathering stations.** You must destroy them all or the **main assembly plant** will be too volatile to attack. If the **smoke stacks** on the main plant are still smoking, you have **not** taken out all the gathering sites.

✵ With the launch sites destroyed, you can now take your time exploring the rest of the level. Go to each station, destroying any guards and weapons around it, then the station itself. The enemies are much more aggro in this level, so you must have your aiming/shooting skills down pat to survive. Especially make sure you blow up the doors in the canyon walls that release enemy tanks and soldiers—the fewer enemies you have to face, the better.

Don't just scurry past the doors in the canyon walls–destroy them to stop the flow of enemy vehicles.

Watch out for this enemy 'Mech. It's fast and deadly!

- The station near the southwest corner of the map is in the middle of a large field of lava. Approach it from the north path, which is much easier to negotiate than the deadly lava fields to the south.
- You can completely avoid confronting the enemy 'Mech at the north end of the map, but if you want to fight him, approach from the west side. The east side has an erupting crater that combines with the enemy 'Mech's shots to overheat you in seconds.
- The station in the southeast corner of the map has two tanks guarding its north side. Lure the tanks into following you, then walk north and let the lava from the erupting crater hit and destroy the tanks.

MISSION 3

- **Briefing:** Destroy the **main assembly plant.** It is heavily guarded so be prepared for a wild fire fight. Good luck.
- Attack the plant from the southwest corner to deal with the enemy 'Mech right away. (Notice that it stays within the plant area and doesn't come out to follow you.) If your damage is running high, go for the coolant from the nearby station you blew to hell earlier. Once the 'Mech is gone, you can venture into the plant and start blasting away.
- The mines make their first appearance on the north side of the plant, popping out of the ground when your 'Mech gets close and explod-

Keep an eye out for the mines that appear at the north end of the main assembly plant.

ing a few moments later. These mines are stationary, so you can easily shoot them or simply run away before they blow. There are homing mines in later levels that move towards your 'Mech, and are much harder to avoid or shoot.

Level 3: Ridderkerk

MISSION 1

- **Briefing:** Your radar is being completely jammed. **Fed-Com** has **five radar jamming sites** in the area. Locate and destroy all of these sites.
- You start in the southwest corner of the level, which is filled with homing mines, so walk slowly north and be ready to run south if a mine pops out of the snow. Remember, a mine only appears once, so after it has been triggered, it won't appear again.

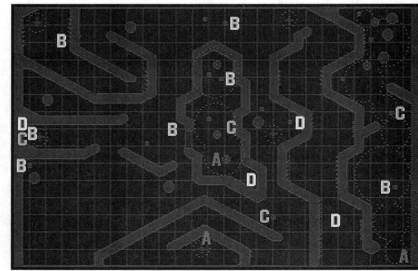

LEVEL 3 MAP (RIDDERKERK)

A: Heavy Ordnance (Button A)   C: Tactical Weapon (Button C)
B: Main Gun (Button B)   D: Coolant

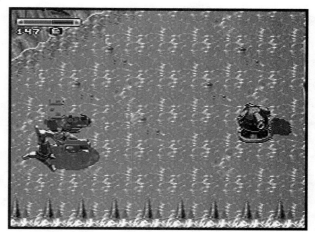

The mines in this level slide at you before exploding. Run away or shoot them in the snow.

Your 'Mech slips and slides on the ice like a liquored-up figure skater and is almost as amusing to watch.

✵ Three of the five radar dishes are located on ice. Ice slows down your 'Mech and makes it slip around instead of turning immediately. On the ice, firing a weapon pushes your 'Mech backwards. For example, if the 'Mech is facing west and you shoot, the 'Mech slides rapidly to the east. Make sure not to slide into the walls by firing uncontrollably or unnecessarily. Try to stand on solid ground (there are a few snow patches on the ice) if possible before shooting.

✵ Use the shoot-recoil trick to quickly get you out of trouble—for example, if a homing mine appears and you have to quickly back away from it. If you try to turn around, the mine hits your 'Mech, but if you fire a weapon or two, your 'Mech slides back out of range.

MISSION 2

✵ **Briefing:** You should be able to locate the **research center** on your radar screen as well as the **weak area** in the **center's** defensive perimeter. Break through it and take out everything in the **center.**

✵ Once you're through the weak spot, clear out the enemies in the south side of the center, then hit the north side. (The enemies in the south side are easier to take out, and there's a much-needed Coolant container to be had.)

MISSION 3

✵ **Briefing:** Now, take out the **main base** where all the research information is stored. The only way to reach this area is by traversing down the frozen river. The river is heavily guarded by the **First Lyran Regulars,** so watch out.

There's a much-needed Coolant container at the south end of the research center.

✵ There are two approaches to the frozen river: simply run like hell through it, or take your time and pick off each enemy vehicle or cannon as you come to it. If you (wisely) choose the run-like-hell approach, there are still a few points where you *have* to shoot to clear a path for your 'Mech. Use your Heavy Ordnance to get rid of the obstacle as quickly as possible.

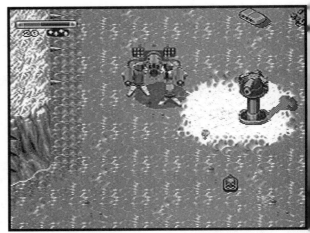

* One of the first enemies at the main base is a 'Mech; fortunately, it has a Coolant inside, so you can attack it aggressively. Once it's destroyed, slowly make your way to the north and take out each group of targets as you come to them. The north side of the base is teeming with homing mines, so watch out for them.

Don't try to destroy every enemy on the
frozen river. Just through it as quickly as you can.

Level 4: Avon

MISSION 1

* **Briefing:** Locate the **four installations** that hold the device pieces. Each installation is protected by an **enclosed wall.** Break through these walls and pick up each piece to the **fuel air demolition device.** Make sure to choose the Large Laser as your Main Gun weapon, because this level is loaded with Main Gun ammo (and precious little of anything else).

* You might be tempted to immediately break into the installation next to your starting point in the southeast corner, but don't do it! You need to save this installation for last, and here's why: the moment you grab the fourth piece of the demolition device, it becomes active and starts counting down. The southeast installation is the only one close enough to the wall that you can run to it and plant the device before it goes off. Comprende?

* This level is filled with caves spilling forth tanks and soldiers. You shouldn't waste too much time or ammunition destroying all the caves, but you should definitely take out some of them.

* Go after the northeast installation first; the enemy 'Mech there is surprisingly weak. There are mines near the ammo in this area, so tread carefully.

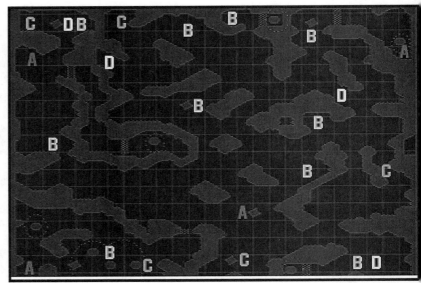

LEVEL 4 MAP (AVON)

A: Heavy Ordnance (Button A)   C: Tactical Weapon (Button C)
B: Main Gun (Button B)   D: Coolant

"All in all, you're just a...'nother brick in the wall."

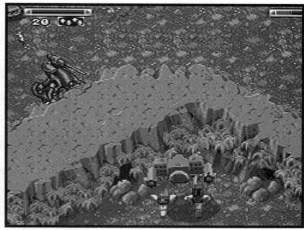

Trick the enemy guns into destroying this 'Mech for you.

- The second installation you hit should be the north one. There are more mines along the route, along with plenty of cannons.
- The extremely well-guarded installation is your third target. Before going inside, you can stand outside the installation and position yourself so that the cannons inside destroy the enemy 'Mech. Don't get too close or you might get whacked by a Gauss Rifle shot.
- Use your Heavy Ordnance (preferably the Gauss Rifle) to clear a path straight through the minefield on the west side of the map.

Use the Gauss Rifle to blast through the minefield on the west side of the campaign map.

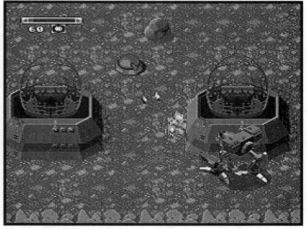

Destroy these plant buildings and you complete the level.

MISSION 2

- **Briefing:** The defensive wall has been destroyed. Move in and take out the drop ship manufacturing plant. Good luck.
- Mow down the group of soldiers just behind the wall (easy) and then take on the 'Mech halfway through the plant (not easy). Destroy all the plant buildings to complete the level.

Level 5: Swamp

MISSION 1

✸ **Briefing:** Eliminate the **two radar jamming sites** that are interfering with your radar.

✸ This level is extremely cruel, with massive numbers of gunboats and helicopters, precious few ammo refills or Coolants, and swampy areas that slow your 'Mech down and make you an easy target for the enemy hordes. Don't slog through the swampy areas unless absolutely necessary (which it is at several points) and use our map to find your way around.

✸ Use the Machine Gun as your Main Gun weapon on this level, because you run out of ammo too quickly with the others.

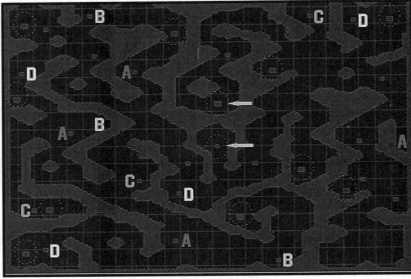

LEVEL 5 MAP (SWAMP)

A: Heavy Ordnance (Button A)   C: Tactical Weapon (Button C)
B: Main Gun (Button B)   D: Coolant

MISSION 2

✸ **Briefing:** Retrieve the **genetic material** located in the **gene storage centers.**

✸ With the radar jammers destroyed, you can see just how brutally tilted the odds are against you! You already had to take out most of the forces on the east side of map to reach the jammers, but now you have to hit the west. Go for the storage centers with the Coolants at first, so that you can return to them later when you need them (and you *will* need them). Try to leave one or two ammo refills untouched so that you can fill up before fighting the Thunderbolt 'Mech.

The swampy areas slow down your 'Mech and make you an easy target. Avoid them unless absolutely necessary.

The Thunderbolt 'Mech is the game's "final boss." Destroy it to win the game and earn the really lame ending.

MISSION 3

✵ **Briefing:** Destroy the **Thunderbolt Mech.**

✵ Search along the south side of the map to find the Thunderbolt, which is the fastest and most intelligent 'Mech in the game—no big surprise since it's the final boss! There's no real secret to success: just lay into the T-Bolt with everything you've got and kill him before he kills you. When the T-Bolt goes up in smoke, you earn the privilege of watching the extremely disappointing ending sequence. You played this level thirty million times for *this*?!

Awesome Secrets

✵ **Passwords:** Level 2: STJNNN; Level 3: GRBCHV; Level 4: BBYLND; Level 5: BMBRMN.

"Merging Through" by J. Douglas Arnold

This stereogram is actually two stereograms merged electronically. Once you focus on the image, study the two different patterns, then notice how they cross paths to form a sphere at the center. See page 325 for more 3D information.

BEAVIS AND BUTT-HEAD

CATEGORY: Action   DEVELOPER: Viacom New Media
PLAYERS: 1 or 2 (Simultaneous)   PUBLISHER: Viacom New Media

Introduction

If you enjoy the bizarre humor of Beavis and Butt-head on MTV, then you're very likely going to love this game. We did! Viacom has done an excellent job of capturing the jokes and animation that made them famous, and best of all two players can join forces to help them in their quest. What is their heroic quest, you ask? To find the scattered pieces of their Gwar concert tickets, of course. What could be more heroic? In most cases you'll need a combination of items to get a ticket piece, and it helps to have a twisted mind when trying to figure out what item is used where. A password system keeps the game from becoming too difficult, but getting started is still a challenge. If you like Beavis and Butt-head, then this game rocks!

Fans of Beavis and Butt-head rejoice! This game doesn't suck. If you don't get them, then you probably shouldn't get this game.

Basic Strategies

✴ Controls: In the one-player game you can switch between Beavis and Butt-head by pressing Start to see your stuff, then press B to switch characters. Hold the A button to run. Press B to jump. You can long jump by running and then jumping. Press C to pick up an object when standing near it, or to attack an enemy.

✴ Your basic **weapons** to begin with are Butt-head's natural gas (fart) and Beavis' burp. Both are lousy for defeating enemies, so your first stop should be Burger World to get a **straw** for shooting spitwads. There's another straw at the Yoghourt shop in the mall which you can pick up later. The straws are the best weapon because they give you rapid fire, but they aren't so rapid that they knock characters off the screen (like the toy gun does). If an enemy doesn't move when shot (like the chef in the hospital), then the toy gun is a good weapon.

✴ Don't grab **food items** unless you need them. Most of them will stick around so you can grab

Fighting with only your "natural abilities" can be frustrating, so head for Burger World and get a straw.

them later when you do need them.

💢 When playing a **one-player game,** only the lead character can get hit.

💢 When walking around, always shoot spitwads ahead of you to hit any enemies that appear before they can hit you.

💢 After getting a **ticket piece,** always return to the Gwar poster in your room and always **write down your password!**

💢 Don't buy anything from the toy shop until you've entered the drive-in.

💢 If you ever run out of **money,** go to the street scene and pass through the sewers to find a duck that reappears after each time you pawn it.

💢 Never use the **Sucks** option. It causes you to lose anything you've gained, so you might as well enter your last password and start from there.

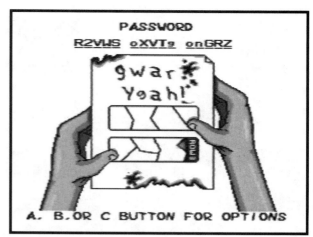

After getting a ticket piece, return to the Gwar poster
in your room and write down your password.

Walkthrough

💢 There are many different paths to take, but we tried to take the most logical for this walkthrough with the least amount of back-tracking necessary.

HOME

💢 You don't need the pants and camera in the bedroom yet, and you might need the room in your pockets, so leave those items and grab the **remote** next to the couch. Select Burger World on the TV.

BURGER WORLD

💢 We begin in Burger World because that's where the **straw** is located, and it makes the enemies everywhere else easier to deal with. Run to the right to go behind Burger World. Go to the right of the **dumpster** to grab the **straw** on the ground. Jump back down and run around to the left to lure the rats that direction, then jump over them and make a run for the **dead rat** hanging out of the dumpster. Jump back over the rats again and go left to the door of Burger World (don't grab the rotten hamburger yet). The trick to getting into the **back door of Burger World** is guessing what the code is for the lock. Considering the manager probably realized what an idiot Butt-head is, he must have come up with something Butt-head could remember. Numbers would be too difficult, especially eight digits! So

Let's see here... there's eight digits in the code
for the back door of Burger World. Hmmm...

Put the fries and the dead rat into the fryer,
then serve the results to the angry customer...

After the customer hurls, go around to the front
entrance of Burger World and grab the ticket piece.

look at the letters on the keypad. If you hit the numbers that correspond with the letters in Butt-head, then you're in (28884323). Put the **fries** and the dead rat into the deep frier. When the fries appear, go right to give the fries to the angry customer. In his vomit is a **concert ticket piece.** Go out the back door and in through the front door to collect the ticket piece, then return home by going to the exit sign and using the remote control. There's a piece of hidden food around the left corner of Burger World, just above the exit sign. When you get back home, go to your bedroom and put the ticket piece on the Gwar poster, then write down your password. Go back to the couch and select Turbo Mall 2000.

TURBO MALL 2000: Go left to enter the mall. Use your straw to fight off the security guards and other enemies in the mall. Go to "We 'B' Cars" to get a **free oil sample.** The character in this shop is very easy to knock out, so anytime you need food return here to fight him again. Go into the pet shop and buy the **snake** with the money you made at Burger World, then the moment the guy ducks under the counter to pack up the snake, grab the **key** off the register. If you miss it, hand the package back to the clerk and he'll re-pack it for you. When you get the key, go to the right and let the bird out, then grab the **concert ticket piece** out of the bottom of the cage. When the bird drops eggs, go down to

Buy the snake in the pet shop and grab the key on the
register when the clerk ducks down to wrap the snake...

Use the key to let the parrot out of its cage,
then grab the ticket in the bottom of the cage.

Go to the pawn shop in the mall and sell the headset
to make some money.

Go into the Army Recruiting Center and drop the snake,
then grab the book on the desk to find a ticket piece.

avoid them and run left. Grab your snake package if you don't already have it, then leave the store. Go right to the Yoghourt shop and run past the counter under the cones. Grab the **straw** from the table (whichever character doesn't currently have a straw must grab it). Go into the bathroom and grab the **soap** from the far left sink. Go left to the elevator and take it to the second floor. You can avoid the **girls** by staying in front of them or behind them, then running past them at the moment they bend their arm. Go right to the **pawn shop** and sell your headset. Go left to the Army Recruiting Center and grab a **cherry bomb,** then drop the snake. When the wussy takes cover, grab the book on his desk to reveal a **ticket piece.** (If you grab the book on his desk before dropping the snake you'll be seriously killed.) You can grab the snake if you want, but there's no use for it. Go into the **laundromat** once you have the pants and the soap. If you wake up **granny** you're gonna be sorry, so open the dryer to her right for **food** (if you need it), then go to the dryer on the far left of her and use the oil on the door to prevent it from squeaking. Open the dryer and get the **ticket piece.** Go back home to drop off your ticket pieces and write down the password. (If you're in desperate need for energy you can go into the Yoghourt shop and use the cherry bomb in the toilet to get **food**.)

Put some oil on the door of the dryer
in the laundromat before opening...

...then grab the concert ticket piece inside
and run before granny wakes up!

Take your time in the sewers,
and use long jumps to clear wide areas.

You have to go all the way to the right past the sewers
to collect this bone for Mr. Anderson's mutt.

THE STREET

Always keep shooting your straw while walking. Go into the **sewer** to the right. The green stuff is very toxic, and the rats on the floor will bite. Use a running jump to make it over wide gaps. Take your time — this is about the toughest area of the entire game. When you reach the other side, climb up the ladder and grab the **food** and **white bird** next to the road block, then go up to find an area with a free **toy gun.** Jump over the toxic puddle, then continue going to the right jumping over the wrecked cars and tires while avoiding the rats and swooping birds. Watch for the **boot** along the way. Grab the **bone** at the far right, then go all the way back through the sewers. If you're low on energy at this point, you should go back to the Gwar poster in your room to get a password. Otherwise, go to the **house with the open gate** on the Street level and use the gun to fire rapidly at **Mr. Anderson** on his riding lawn mower. Go to the right and select the bone, then press C to throw it. After the **dog** chases the bone, go to the door of the shed and open it. Get the **fishing pole** (bottom-left) and the **chainsaw** (upper-right). Exit the toolshed and use the chainsaw on the tree to collect a **ticket piece.** Go back home and write down your password.

Get the fishing pole and the chainsaw from
inside the toolshed at Mr. Anderson's house...

...then use the chainsaw on the tree outside
to collect another concert ticket piece.

Collect the two chemicals from room 102 by gagging the teacher with burps...

...then drop the chemicals in front of Principal McVicar to knock him out and collect a ticket piece.

HIGHLAND HIGH SCHOOL

✻ You can only enter the classrooms that have posters on them. The guys in the hall will keep coming, and each time you knock them out you'll get **food.** This is a great way to recover any lost energy. Enter **room 102.** Make sure you have two spaces open in your pockets so you can grab the potions when it's safe. Burp at the teacher about a dozen times to gag him. It's very difficult to avoid the fireballs, so just go for it and use the guys in the hall to regain your energy. Once the teacher's gagged he'll take his finger off the switch for a brief moment and you can safely grab one of the **chemicals** before he hits the switch again. Go out in the hall for more energy if you need it, then go back and gag the teacher again (this time it only takes 9 hits). Grab the remaining chemicals, then go out and right to **room 108.** Grab the **gum** under the right leg of the teacher's desk, then talk to him for advice. He changes his advice every once in a while. Go out and right to the **principal's office.** If you need energy you can enter the **bathroom** and drop a **cherry bomb** in the toilet for food. There's also a **hot dog** just beyond the door of the principal's office. In the principal's office you'll see McVicar with the ticket on his head. Drop the A+B potion on his desk to make him faint, then grab the **ticket piece.** Go back home and write down the next password. If you want, you can skip to the **couch fishing** section now and play around with it.

DRIVE-IN

✻ It cost $3 to enter the drive-in. If you don't have enough money, go to the pawn shop at the mall with the bird and any other items you have that can be sold. You'll also need a cherry bomb and the camera at the drive-in. Enter the **snack bar** and use the **cherry bomb** to blow up the soda machine. Go outside and to the right to see the cars. Go to the far right while dodging the rats. Collect the **binoculars** and **food** (is that a burrito or what?!). Go left to the **van that's rocking** and use the camera to take a picture. A crazed woman will chase after you. Run to the left while

Blow up the grape soda machine in the snack bar with a cherry bomb...

avoiding the rats and the puddles that slow you down. Rush back into the snack bar and the woman will slip on the grape soda and drop a **ticket piece.** Grab it and go back to your Gwar poster.

HOSPITAL

First go to Burger World and eat the **rotten hamburger,** then go back home and select the Hospital. Be ready to shoot security guards while jumping over the bowling balls. If you let a skateboard hit your foot it will stop and no more will appear while you're standing next to it. Go inside the hospital and enter the **sick room.** The nurse will cure you. Jump on the table and grab the **scissors.** Exit the room and go right. Shoot the chef with your toy gun, then jump on the **scooter.** The handsome guy on the treadmill will chase after you. If you hit three medical kits in a row you'll slow down too much and get crushed by the jogger. The more time between hitting medical kits, the less likely you are to get crushed by the jogger. If there's a lot of time between hits, you can take as many as six hits before getting crushed. If you make it to the exit you'll fall down the stairs and get the **ticket piece.** Go back home and write down the next password. The game is not over! Go up to the Gwar poster and **grab the tickets** (this

Take a picture of the van that's rocking with your camera, then run for the snack bar.

Avoid hitting the medical kits while being chased by the crazed jogger...

...then grab the ticket piece after you tumble down the hospital stairs.

can be tricky, because you have to be standing in the correct spot, just to the right of the poster). Even with tickets you're going to have to fight to get backstage and rock with the band. If both of your characters don't have toy guns, go back to the pawn shop and sell anything you can, then buy another toy gun at the toy store in the mall.

At the Gwar concert you can enter the first doors you see for the lame ending...

or venture backstage to battle an army of guards with the reward of going onstage with Gwar!

GWAR CONCERT

- Give your ticket to the guard and go past the barrier. If you enter the **doors to the concert** you'll get to see the ending that "sucks", so go past the entrance to the show. When you see the first lightpost, get the **cat** selected in your inventory, then rapidly press the C button as you walk forward so the cat will run the moment it sees the dog and the dog will run right past you. Keep shooting with the toy gun and moving forward slowly until you reach the backstage doors. You'll have to get past a *lot* of guards before reaching backstage. As you shoot them with the gun they'll be pushed backward — don't let them go off the screen. Take a step or two forward, then start shooting again. When you get backstage, use the **scissors** to cut the rope on the bag over the head of the guy throwing banana peels. Go to the right and look for **costumes** on the ground to grab, then select them and press up to enter the stage. You can control their unsuccessful attempts at stage diving.

COUCH FISHING

- Once you've collected the fishing pole, you can sit on the couch and use various items as bait. Reeling in is very difficult. You have to press the C button rapidly, but a turbo controller can make it much more enjoyable.

- **Army Documents:** Catches [Daria]. He gives you information.
- **Boot:** Catches Earl (bald guy with gun). He'll kill you with one shot, so be ready to run to your room the moment he appears. Use the baseball bat to hit him when you return to the living room. You're best off avoiding him altogether. He gives you food if you defeat him. After you kill him, he'll reappear each time you come out of your room, so be careful.
- **Donut:** Catches the security guard from the mall. Have a weapon ready. He'll give you food if you defeat him.
- **Gum:** Used to get a piece of the concert ticket.

Using different bait while couch fishing will catch you different items or, more likely, people.

- 💲 **Pizza:** Used to get the cat, which is used to distract the dog at the Gwar concert.
- 💲 **Walkman** (Yellow): Catches [Stuart]. She gives you information.

Items List

- 💲 **A&B Chemicals:** Found at the Highland High School in the first classroom you can enter. Used to knock out principal McVicar.
- 💲 **Army Documents:** Found in the Army Recruiting Station in the mall. Bait used for couch fishing.
- 💲 **Baseball Bat with Glove:** Found in the toy store of the mall. Used as a weapon. Hit shopping carts to stop them and get food.
- 💲 **Binoculars:** Found at the end of the drive-in. Used to pawn at the mall for money (most items are worth 50¢, but this is worth $1.90).
- 💲 **Bird:** Found on the street after going through the sewer. Used to pawn at the mall for money (50¢). Boot: Found on the Street level in the junkyard.
- 💲 **Bone:** Found on the far right of the junkyard on the Street level. Used to distract the dog at Mr. Anderson's house.
- 💲 **Camera:** Found in the dresser in bedroom of home. Used to take a picture of the bouncing car in the drive-in.
- 💲 **Cat:** Found while couch fishing. Used to distract Mr. Anderson's dog at the Gwar concert.
- 💲 **Chainsaw:** Found in Mr. Anderson's toolshed (Street level). Used for cutting down the tree next to the toolshed (no other use).
- 💲 **Cherry Bomb:** Found in the Army Recruiting Station. Used to blow up toilets or at the snack bar to blow up grape soda machine. You can go

The binoculars is the most valuable items that can be traded in at the pawn shop.

If you need to make money you can keep going back for the white bird after pawning it off.

Couch fish for the cat, then use it to get backstage at the Gwar concert.

back and get another each time you use one.

- **Dead Rat:** Found in the dumpster behind Burger World. Used to get money from customer when fried up with french fries.
- **Donut:** Found in couch of home. Bait used for couch fishing.
- **French Fries:** Found next to deep frier in Burger World. Used to get money from customer when fried up with dead rat.
- **Funky Costumes:** Found backstage at the Gwar concert. Used to blend in with the band on stage (yeah, right!).
- **Gum:** Found under the desk of the second classroom you can enter at Highland High School. Used as bait for couch fishing.
- **Headset for Drive-Thru:** Found near the deep frier in Burger World. Used to pawn at the mall for money.
- **Oil Sample:** Found in the mall at "We 'B' Cars". Used to grease up the door at the laundromat before you open it.
- **Pants:** Found under the bed in the bedroom of the house. Used to get into the laundromat (also need the soap).
- **Pizza Slice:** Found in couch of home. Bait used for couch fishing.
- **Remote Control:** Found next to couch. Used to search for different channels/stages.
- **Rotten Hamburger:** Found next to the dumpster at Burger World. Eat it, then make a run for the hospital so you can enter the sick room.
- **Scissors:** Found in the sick room of the hospital. Used to cut a rope at the Gwar concert.
- **Snake:** Found at the pet shop (cost 50¢). Used to scare the army recruiter in the mall.
- **Soap:** Found in far left bathroom sink of the Yoghourt shop. Used to get into the laundromat (also need the pants).
- **Toy Gun:** Found in the toy store of the mall. Used as a weapon.
- **Walkman (Yellow):** Found in couch of home. Bait used for couch fishing.

You'll need the pants and the soap to get past the guard in front of the laundromat.

Eat the rotten hamburger, then make a run for the hospital to enter the sick room.

Awesome Secrets!

- **Passwords:** The passwords on the next page follow the flow of this chapter. Check the screen shot for the number of ticket pieces and the exact lettering in the password.

R2VWS oXVT9 onGRZ

SsD7S 96cD- 4+jKb

oLnQs PGJEC +p7Cd

rØRR1 6cJMA -puYN

dGSrC DN9T9 MTIHn

8Pkhk BFit+ F5bN-

8Pkhk BFit+ F5bN-

c8Oyo Qaxhj jdd6d

CONTRA: HARDCORPS

CATEGORY: Platform   DEVELOPER: Konami
PLAYERS: 1 or 2 (Simultaneous)   PUBLISHER: Konami

Introduction

There are several ugly trends occurring in the video game market — at least their ugly trends if you have our job of playing through dozens of games for one single book. The ugly trend here is the level of difficulty in some of the latest games. Contra: Hard Corps is one of the toughest games we've ever played. And to add fuel to the fire, there are SIX different endings to this game! And each path is as challenging as the average single game. Of course, all of this is great news to you, the game player, who's looking for a game that will keep them entertained for longer than the 1-2 day average. This latest in the Contra series will keep you busy for weeks, at the very least! There are four characters to choose from, tons of weapons, and awesome bosses everywhere!

Huge bosses, tons of enemies, and six different paths with different endings are bound to challenge you!

Basic Strategies

✸ **CONTROLS:** Use A to select weapon (can also do when game is paused), use B to shoot selected weapon, use C to jump. Hold B and press A to toggle between shot types. Shot I allows you to move while firing, while Shot II will keep your character still while aiming with the control pad. Press C plus down/right or down/left diagonally to slide. Press Down + C to jump down through floors.

✸ **CHARACTERS:** There are four characters to choose from, each with various weapons. Our favorite is Browny, since his height allows him to avoid most bullets without ducking. He can't jump as high as the other characters, but he can perform a double jump to reach higher ledges. Each character can collect up to four different special weapons, placed in the holes marked as A, B, C and D along the top of the screen. We always like to assume you don't have any special weapons when writing these guides, since if you lose that weapon, and you're reading our book, you're going to need more help. If you *are* car-

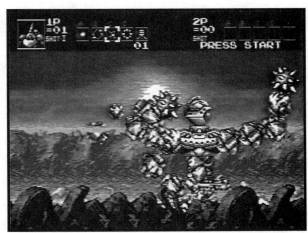
The slide attack is the most useful move in the game. As you slide you can't be hit by enemies.

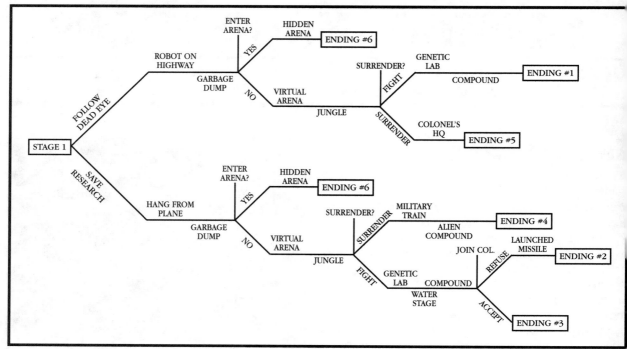

There are six different paths to take through Contra, each with a totally different ending.
Some paths have areas in common, but each has totally unique areas.

rying one of the special weapons, feel free to use it. It will only make your job easier, and the strategies we discuss will still apply.

🔅 **The slide attack** is the most important move to master, since it will allow you to pass through bosses and enemies without getting hit.

🔅 With the **two-player option** you'll be able to defeat enemies and bosses more easily, thanks to doubled fire power, but you'll also have to fight over the special weapons that become available, and keeping track of your character on the screen can be difficult as the other player jumps around near you. You're best off practicing by yourself to get the hang of the game, then join with an experienced player to gang up on the enemies.

🔅 **PATHS:** There are several paths that can be taken during the course of the game. A total of six different endings can be reached, depending on the course you take. Check the flowchart we've provided above for a complete diagram of each path (it wasn't easy!). Konami claims that ending #2 is the best, but they all have nearly equal quality as far as ending sequences go. Ending #2 doesn't have any more detailed animation than the others, but it probably is the toughest to reach.

Stage 1

🔅 From the start, head to the right and blast everyone in sight. The first mini-boss is a spider that only requires a few hits in the head to destroy. The rotating robot is next. Stand on the far right and fire at the robot until it catches on fire. When the robot speeds in your direction, jump over or slide through him, then run to the opposite side of the screen and continue firing. The next boss will appear walk-

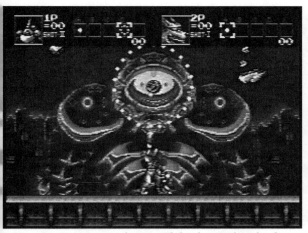

Line up your aim on the eye of this boss when he first appears, then stand still and fire straight up.

Start in the left corner and shoot to the right, then slide through the boss before he corners you.

ing in the background, then he lands behind the building you're on and rises up to fight. He's huge! Stand at the center of the screen and fire straight up. Your weapon should shoot straight through his eye as he rises if you're lined up correctly. As long as you're standing in this position you can't get hurt until he throws a car at you. When you see the car in his hand, jump or slide to the side to avoid it.

⚡ **The main boss** is a manned robot that jumps down from the top of a building. Stand on the far left and shoot to the right while ducking. If you're using Browny, you won't have to duck. As the boss hops toward you, move left or right to avoid him, but stay in the left area. Once he falls to the ground, he'll hop back up and the top half of his body will spin off and hover in the air.. His head will fly by twice, then it will return to his body and he'll charge at you twice. Use the slide attack to slide through him as he charges. Shoot him the rest of the time.

⚡ After finishing the main boss of the first stage you'll be given a choice to go after Deadeye Joe or rescue the Research Center. The path you follow will depend on your choice.

Follow Dead Eye Joe

⚡ **HIGHWAY:** You'll begin on motor bikes. Jump and shoot the enemies as they swoop down. If they get too close, they'll shoot down at an angle and hit you. When the ship in the background crashes into the building, rush to the right side and shoot to the left to hit a maniac with a missile. The next enemy is a blue crab. He'll start on the ceiling, then he rotates down to the floor. Stay on the right side and keep jumping and shooting to avoid his bullets. He'll move to the right side eventually, so be ready to jump over him. While he's on the right side, he'll drop bouncing white balls that you must maneuver in between (or double jump over with Browny). When he returns to the roof he'll drop his arm to the floor. Stay to the left and continue jumping and shooting until he's destroyed.

⚡ In the next area you'll be on a robotic ostrich running with a large ship above. Stay to the left side. The ship will begin by dropping three groups of white balls. Make the first jump early so you can jump again before the second and third group shoot by. Move to the right, then prepare to jump a longer stream of white balls. Move back to the left and dodge the bouncing stream of balls that appears next. Shoot the red orb each time it appears to defeat the ship.

⚡ **RUNNING ROBOT:** The boss will run behind you in the distance. His arms reach up toward you, so keep moving from side to side to avoid it. After reaching up a few times, he'll leap forward and try to land on you. He usually lands in the opposite lane than the lane he was running in while in the background. The boss will shoot spiked balls, which you can slide through, and then he'll run next to you. Jump and shoot from beside him, or select Shot II and aim diagonally at him while standing nearby. He'll explode and only his chestplate will remain. It bounces forward and backward — just keep away from it and shoot.

When the boss leaps from the background, he'll usually land on the opposite side of the road.

⚡ **GARBAGE DUMP:** Shoot the bikers as they come over the hill. When they stop coming, go to the right and keep moving quickly while shooting to hit each biker and avoid damage. The boss is a trash heap with spiked balls on his hands. Stand to the far right when he appears and shoot while jumping. When he leaps toward you, stand directly next to him and slide through him, then run to the opposite side of the screen. After beating the boss you'll head underground. Keep walking quickly to stay ahead of the turrets on the walls and avoid their bullets. Before you enter the door at the bottom of the hill, you can climb the wall above the door and talk to a man. He offers you money to enter the hidden Battle Arena. If you answer yes, you'll enter the arena and battle a few monsters, then you'll see an ending sequence (#6). If you answer no, you'll return back down to the door you climbed above and head into the Virtual Arena.

⚡ **HIDDEN BATTLE ARENA (ENDING #6):** The first enemy is a man with a *big* head. He walks back and forth, throwing a fish at you if you stand in front of him. Climb to the ceiling quickly, then fire down diagonally at him. If you stay above him, he'll jump up and hit you with his extending arm, so always move away as he walks below you. After his head explodes you'll still have to fight his body, so don't let go of the controller! The next boss is a mutant with a baby carriage, and his baby ain't very cute either. Jump onto the left wall and hang in the location shown in the picture. You want your feet to be above the grey connector in the background. If you're even a hair too low, you'll get smashed. While hanging in the correct position you can fire down diagonally at the carriage and hit the mutants and everything they shoot at you. The third and final boss is a floating red blob. Stand to the far left and

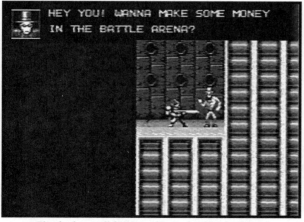

Climb the wall here and accept the challenge of the stranger on the ledge above...

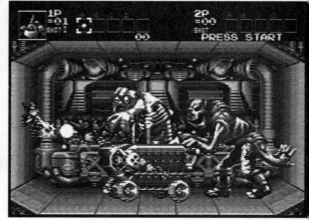

...and you'll enter the Hidden Battle Arena, where you'll fight mutants like this happy little family.

jump and shoot rapidly toward the boss. The only threat in this position is the steel balls that fall to the floor. When you see them coming, quickly jump and grab the left wall, then drop back to the floor. You need to keep jumping so you can hit all of the rockets that fire during each round of the pattern, otherwise you could hang from the wall. Defeat this boss and you'll get a weird little ending sequence.

* **VIRTUAL ARENA:** If you chose not to fight in the Battle Arena, or you didn't even climb the wall to talk to the mysterious man, you'll head for the Virtual Arena next. The first boss is **Taurus.** Shoot him until he starts wiggling his legs, then slide or jump to avoid him as he swoops down with a charge attack. Next is **Sagittarius.** The most important objective is to shoot the arrows he fires so they won't hit you. While hitting the arrows you'll hit the boss plenty of times. The third boss is **Gemini.** These twins shoot out a spray of white bullets in an arc. Keep as far away as possible at all times. When they come toward you in between attacks, jump over them or slide through them. The next bosses are formed from a **group of blocks.** Shoot the red block at the center to cause damage. If you're using Browny, you'll have to jump while shooting to hit the red block, or use one of your special weapons. Blocks in the form of the letter "T" will attack from the group of blocks. Avoid them as they bounce near you while continuing your assault on the red block. The second formation of blocks is a **tank.** Duck or jump to avoid the bullets, then shoot (or jump and shoot with Browny) to hit the red block. The third and final formation is a **helicopter.** Try not to stand directly below the helicopter, because it drops blocks. The tail rudder will swoop down toward you, so always be prepared to slide away or through it.

* **JUNGLE:** You'll be greeted by huge tribes of enemies. Spray bullets as you walk to the right. The head of a statue drops from above (you'll see the feet of the statue first). Various insects fly out of the ears of the head. There's no strategy other than the usual — dodge and shoot, using your slide often.

* Next is a **bridge.** Walk to the right until the screen stops scrolling, then go back to the left

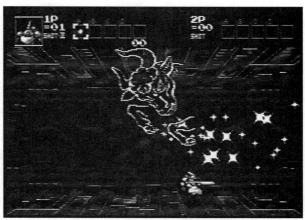
Shoot Taurus until his legs move, then slide or jump to avoid his charge attack.

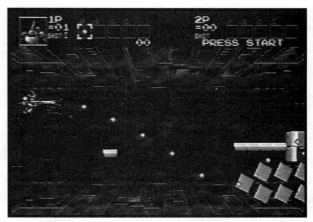
Stay to the far left and jump or duck to avoid the bullets, then shoot the tank between bullets.

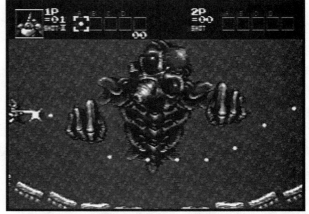
When on the bridge, stay on the far left block and fire away. The boss won't hurt you on this block.

and stand on the block that is barely visible on the left edge. Select Shot II and fire away while staying on the far left block. When the bridge blows up you'll land on a dinosaur neck. Keep jumping and firing in all directions to destroy the rolling bugs that appear. As you jump off the head of the dinosaur, don't shoot his head or he'll blow smoke at you.

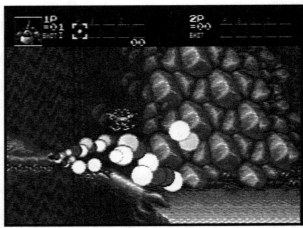

If you shoot the head of the dinosaur, you'll trigger steam and take damage.

✷ To the right is a **ball with legs.** His pattern is widely varied and is different each time you meet him. The best advice we can offer is stick to the corners until he jumps towards you, and use the slide attack to get through him when you're cornered. When the ball forms a beak, it will spit flames onto the ground in three groups — jump over them, or slide through them. When the boss falls on its back, it will throw its legs like a boomerang. Once the ball shoots flames, it will be joined by a second ball. Stay in either corner and slide or jump as they approach. When the boss flies into the air, shoot diagonally (using Shot II). After you defeat this boss, you'll head to a tunnel to the right.

✷ The next boss will attack you as you run and climb through this twisting **tunnel.** It will begin by sucking in energy. As you shoot the head, it will rotate. After sucking in energy, the head will shoot beams, and if you shoot the head at this time it will spin around and shoot you, so wait until it shoots all of the beams, then shoot it again while it's sucking in energy. Run to the right as it crawls toward you, then climb the wall when you reach it and climb up out of the screen to stay away from the propeller of the boss. The boss will attach to the ceiling and swing back and forth while rolling up the tunnel. If you stay on the ceiling and run ahead of him or stay behind him, you'll avoid his head as it swings. If you are behind him, you'll automatically be pulled forward as the screen scrolls. The head will fall to the floor and spin from side to side. Use the slide attack to go through the boss as he rolls towards you. He'll start dragging himself up the next slope and then attach to the wall and ceiling to reach the top passage. Stay behind him and keep your guard up. When you reach the top passage he'll fall to the floor and shoot a few missiles. Shoot them before they hit you. Then the boss will attach to the ceiling and

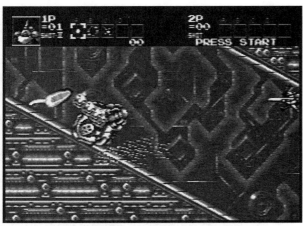

It's easiest to stay behind the boss and let the scrolling screen drag you with the boss.

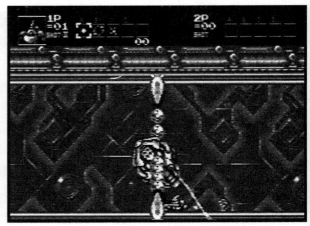

At the end of this battle, use the slide attack to get through the beams as they circle the screen.

floor like he did the first time, only this time he'll shoot three rays while spinning his head. You have to stay near the bottom of the boss, then slide under him as the rays approach, then back under him and through the rays to let them pass you by.

Follow Dead Eye Joe... Fight

✦ **GENETIC LAB:** If you chose to fight, you'll find yourself in the Genetic Lab. The crazed doctor sits in his chair above you. He'll choose two creatures to place in the chambers, then he genetically combines them into the center chamber, and you get to destroy whatever comes out. **The first creature** is like a flying centipede. It moves slow, and the head seems to be the place to hit. The tail will sting, so move cautiously. **The second creature** is a flying ghoul. He has two attacks, but regardless of what he's going to do you should concentrate on avoiding the space directly below him. If you're under him, he'll drop straight down and stomp you. For his other attack, he shoots two fireballs straight down that quickly curve and slide along the floor toward you. Jump over them or use your slide attack through them. **The third creature** is a flying flower. It moves fairly slowly, and drops yellow pollen as it moves from side to side. Stay against either wall (left is usually better), then jump and shoot. If the flower drops pollen over you, move until it sinks

The fourth creature will drop weapons.
If you shoot it too often you'll destroy it.

off the screen, then continue hanging out in the corner. Use the slide attack to get through any pollen that traps you in the corner. **The fourth creature** is on your side. Don't shoot him! He drops weapon items, which will make the rest of this battle much easier. If you're using Browny (you should be), try to save the C weapon for the final creature. **The fifth creature** is a ghoul that walks on a long tail. The tail will whip left and right, so keep clear. Since you should have just collected several weapons, this creature shouldn't last long. Aim for his head and slide under him if you become cornered. **The sixth creature** is a ghoul that walks on his arms and has a long tail with a flower on the end, swinging up in the air. This creature will shoot fireballs into the air that sink at a fairly slow rate. Again, use the slide to avoid being cornered. After this creature is defeated the machine will overload, and the doctor will get what's coming to him, but you'll still have to fight the creature that appears. If you're using Browny and you have the C weapon, you can stand on the far side of the screen and use the tracking abilities of the C weapon to home in on the red ball between the creature's legs (hey, we don't design these games — we just write strategies for them!). The creature will usually leap from side to side, so when he's in the air, make a run for the opposite cor-

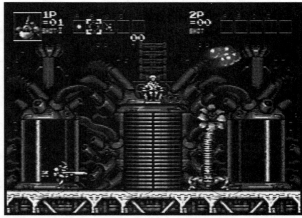
The fireballs shot into the air by the sixth creature will sink very slowly. Use the slide to avoid being cornered.

ner. If you don't have the C weapon, you're best bet is to chance getting under the creature so you can cause major damage to the red ball. If you're using a character other than Browny, you'll have to do a lot more sliding and maneuvering to avoid getting hit while aiming for the red ball.

✦ **COMPOUND (ENDING #1):** Here's the final stage to reach the first ending. You can choose to make a run for the first boss to the right and hope the ostrich creatures don't demolish you, or you can take your time and try to destroy each ostrich creature one-by-one as you slowly advance forward. The first sub-boss has a deadly stream of bullets, which it will fire diagonally when it nears the center of the screen. Stay very close to the body, which moves slowly, and shoot up at the head. You'll have to get through another pack of ostrich creatures before meeting the second sub-boss. When you see the explosion of the boss coming through the ceiling, run to the far left, then use jumps while firing to destroy the larvae shooting from the boss. When the boss reaches out its arm, slide to the right to avoid it, then quickly return to the left corner. Move forward slowly after destroying the boss, shooting each group of yellow eyes as you come to them. It's easier to jump over and run away from the second group of eyes.

✦ **The next sub-boss burrows out of the ground,** so jump to the ceiling and grab on. Move to the center of the ceiling and shoot diagonally down at the creature as he moves around. When the creature stops moving and raises the front of its body up, drop from the ceiling and run to the far corner to avoid the fireballs that rain down. A second creature will appear from the ceiling, directly above the first creature. The key to survival is knowing that you can walk on the back of the bottom creature. The tough part is timing the moment to drop to his back and run past before the two creatures smash together. When the second creature disappears, drop down and prepare to dodge another rainstorm of fireballs. The creature will repeat these patterns for another round or two before beginning the final part of the pattern. The second creature will appear, then it will drop onto the first creature and form a ball. The ball will roll around all four walls of

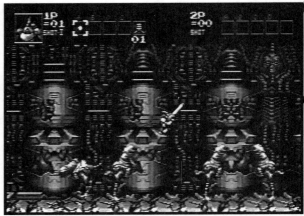

The ostrich creatures attack in huge numbers. Move slowly and kill them one-by-one to play it safe.

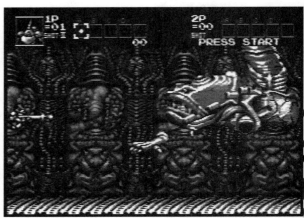

Stay in the left corner and jump while shooting to destroy the larvae, then slide right to avoid the arms.

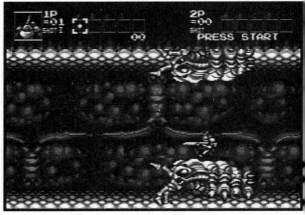

When the creature's twin appears, you must move between them in between bounces.

the room in a clockwise direction. Move to the lower-right corner and shoot the creature as he moves around the screen, then as he rolls down the wall toward you, slide toward the corner to pass through the creature unharmed. Move back to the left about one-third of the way, then repeat the pattern. The ball will roll faster and faster until you destroy it. Be ready to grab two weapons after you beat this boss.

* After defeating the rolling ball, go right and climb upward. Jump to the far right wall and shoot as you climb to destroy the scorpions. The head at the center of the room will reach to the side walls, so try to destroy it before you climb that high. When you reach the top, prepare to fight the final boss.

* **Final Boss:** The alien begins in female form. She shoots blue drones your direction. Move to the bottom-left corner and face right, then select Shot II so you won't move while shooting. Your first priority is to shoot the blue drones, because they're your only threat at the beginning. Use Browny's yo-yo weapon (C) to make this battle a breeze. Once you defeat this part of the boss, you'll enter the final battle with the alien heart. While fighting the heart, you must also deal with a pair of eyes that take on three formations. They begin on separate sides of the screen, then they rotate around the screen in a clockwise direction. Stand at the center, below the alien heart, and shoot it while jumping to avoid the eyes. The second set of eyes are attached at the center. They will bounce around the screen, pulling each other by the chord that connect them. The

Move to the lower-left corner, select Shot II, and concentrate on shooting the blue drones.

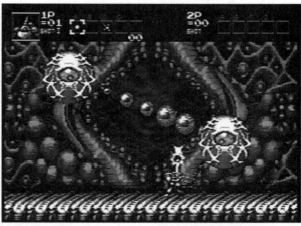

Avoid the eyeballs while shooting the alien heart. You can jump through the chord in the second formation.

chord won't hurt you, so if the eyes are far enough apart you can jump between them. The corners are safe most of the time, but be ready to jump or slide if an eyeball comes your way. The third formation has the eyes on the ground, with enough space between them for another eyeball. The balls will rotate around each other, one at a time, walking along the outside walls of the room in a counter-clockwise direction. Stand at the center of the screen, then as they eyes come around, use the slide to pass through one of them safely. The pattern will repeat with the first set of eyes. If you shoot the heart as often as possible, you should destroy it before the eyes can begin the three-part pattern for a third time. You'll be treated to a short animation and long credits.

Follow Dead Eye... Surrender

* **COLONEL'S HQ (ENDING #5):** If you chose to surrender and fight later when challenged by the colonel, you'll enter the Colonel's Headquarters. The Colonel will zap his soldiers, making them become

green frog mutants. You'll be chased by a wall of fire from the left, so quickly run to the right, blasting all of the frog mutants along the way. Having a second player in this part will make the battle against the frog mutants much easier. When you enter the elevator you'll meet an ED-209-type robot. He'll jump to the center of the walls and ceiling a few times, so stick to the floor or corners of the ceiling and fire away. When he stops, his mouth will open and he'll attack with one of three randomly-chosen attacks. Always move to the opposite side of the room. If you see robots marching out, climb the wall fast to avoid them. They'll explode the moment they touch anything, but they won't climb the walls. If you see small red "flashlights" come out of its mouth, watch them closely and be ready to slide or jump to avoid being in the path of the beams they fire

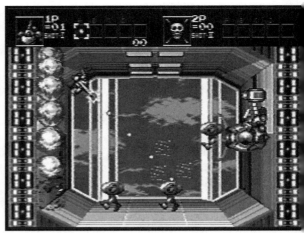

If you see the marching robots escaping from the mouth of the boss, quickly climb the wall.

when they stop moving. The final attack has six small silver drones fly out, which turn into propellers when they stop, then begin floating around again. They'll repeat this a few times before going away. After about five or six of these random attacks, the boss will begin walking around all four walls of the room in a clockwise direction. With each lap of the room he makes, his legs will grow a bit longer, making him tougher to avoid. Stand at the bottom of the screen and shoot the head, then each time he walks toward you, slide through his legs. After defeating this boss you'll shoot up to the top floor, then you'll find the final boss to the right.

* **Big Magnum:** The final boss will be on the right side of the screen. Climb up the left wall and climb to the top of the wall, then shoot to the right as the metal arm of the boss rises up to meet you. When the cannon at the tip of the arm retracts inside, then reappears, watch the energy burst at the tip of the cannon for a clue of what's coming, then react accordingly. If you see **small blue spots** in the energy burst, the cannon will shoot four fireballs that stretch across the screen, stop, then drop straight down. Immediately drop to the ground. Each set of four fireballs has a gap, which you must stand under as

the fireballs drop. If the energy burst has **large blue spots,** the cannon will fire one fireball that will float up near the cannon, then it will explode into streams that curve down and shoot at you (jump or slide to avoid taking a hit). If you see **large yellow spots** in the energy burst, move away to avoid a stream of bullets that shoot directly where you're standing. If the energy burst has **small yellow spots,** the cannon will fire a swirl of balls that will shoot directly at the spot you're on, so move quickly. Once the cannon explodes (it will be after about a dozen of the above four patterns), you'll get a weapon power-up. The arm will retract, then the face will appear on the tip of the arm as it stretches back out. Stand at the bottom-right corner and shoot up at the face while avoiding the large yellow

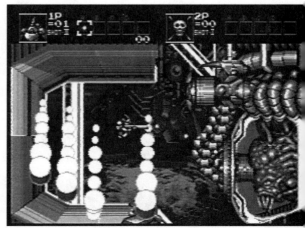

When small blue spots appear in the energy burst, drop to the floor and stand in between the gap in the fireballs.

stream of bullets that floats around. Use jumps to avoid the bullets, or slide to the left, quickly returning to shoot the face. After many hits, the face will explode and another weapon will appear. This time the arm will rise back up to the top, with a claw-like weapon. A ball appears at the center of the area you can move around in, then three beams shoot out from the ball and rotate in a clockwise direction. It's possible to crawl the walls to stay ahead of the beams, dropping to the floor when you reach the top-right side of the ceiling. The tough part is timing the drop from the ceiling to the floor without hitting the beam. The safer maneuver is to stay on the floor and use the slide attack to get through the beams. You can't fall off the right side of the floor, so slide away! When you see flames fill the screen, the battle is over and you'll see ending #5.

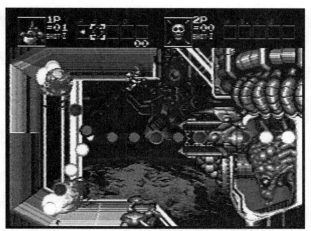

Climb around the room to keep up with the beams, or drop to the floor and slide through each beam.

Save the Research Center

✤ **HANGING FROM PLANE:** Face to the right as the **missile launcher** approaches from behind. Jump to avoid each missile (if you're using Browny, use double jumps). As you land from the jump, face left and shoot the soldier that appears from the exploded missile. The falling soldiers will hit the missile launcher, eventually destroying it. As you're lifted into the clouds, continue hanging from the bottom of the plane and shoot the man that attaches and swings from the bottom of the plane. Once he's defeated, jump to the top wing of the plane and face to the right. Shoot the rocket man, and continue shooting him while staying prepared to jump if the rocket man shoots a beam your direction. A plane will appear above you next. The middle cannon shoots flames straight down, while the wings each shoot a triple-shot spread of fireballs. The plane will take a hit and land. Be prepared to shoot the weapons that appear when you land, then go to the right and blast through the door. Go to the right and climb the wall to the top floor, and be prepared to grab two more weapons as you head to the right. You'll enter the battle room for the fight against a big alien.

✤ **ALIEN CELL BOSS:** The boss hangs from the ceiling and drops blue and white blocks, then he stacks them in various formations and they fly around the room. Jump to either wall and climb halfway up to the line in the wall separating the two colors. Constantly shoot the boss while he's stacking the blocks, then give the blocks all of your attention. If you don't destroy them quickly, they'll fly in a formation that varies each time, and is very tough to avoid. The first stack is a straight up stack that will tip over to the side, but

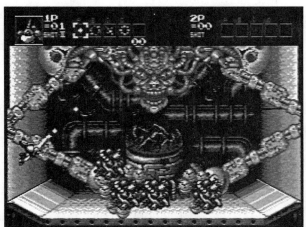

The boss will drop blue and white blocks, stack them, then they'll fly around the room in patterns.

if you shoot it from the time the boss finishes stacking it, you'll destroy the blocks before they hit the ground. The second formation of blocks will be two sets of two blocks that frog leap over each other as they move from wall to wall. They'll hit the lower part of the wall, so keep enough height up on the wall to avoid them. The next four blocks will be in a square formation. They'll bounce across the screen, getting higher as they go. When they come your direction, quickly run and jump to the other wall, then continue your assault on them. The final formation will be in the shape of the letter "T". The bottom side of the "T" will point toward you as it chases you around the room. Keep moving and sliding to avoid getting hit while shooting it. The boss will repeat the formation from this point until

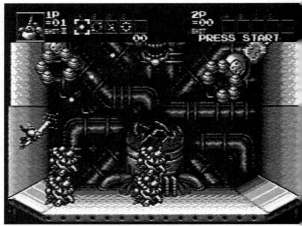

The frog-leaping blocks will not climb the walls so climb to avoid them before they corner you.

you destroy him, which shouldn't be long after the first pattern in the formation (the straight up stack)

- **GARBAGE DUMP:** From this point until you are given the option of surrendering, see the section on Follow Dead Eye Joe (for Garbage Dump, Arenas, Jungle).

Save Research Center... Surrender

- **MILITARY TRAIN:** Be prepared to shoot two weapons that appear at the very beginning of this stage. There are dozens of foot soldiers attacking from both sides. Blast through them and get outside to meet the first sub-boss. It's a pair of cool-looking robots — one hanging from each side of the screen. They move up and down while taking turns shooting at you with their cannons. Concentrate on avoiding their cannons while shooting the entire time. One robot will blow up and the other will fall to the ground. It will crawl from side to side while screaming, but it won't hurt you if you stay on the platform above the ground. Keep firing until he's defeated. As you jump to hang from the red train car, be

prepared to shoot the weapons that appear. The next sub-boss is a spike on an arm that sticks out of the top of one of the train cars. It has a countdown timer on it that will tell you when it's going to shoot (nice feature!). When an exclamation mark (!) appears, it will slam into the surface of the train with the spike tip. Your measly weapons aren't enough to hurt the base of the boss, but his weapon is plenty strong. Move left and right across the base to make the boss shoot itself. The final boss is a very cool blue running robot. He's cool looking, but he ain't friendly! After he runs to the front of the train he'll stop it by grabbing the front of the train and digging his feet into the ground. He'll start by shooting an arcing fireball that will bounce along the surface of the train. Move between the bounces. He'll

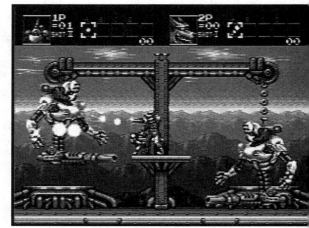

The first bosses on the train will take turns shooting at you while moving up and down.

shake the train, then he'll shoot blue and red bombs that land on the front of the train and slide down to the left. Jump over them. He'll then climb onto the train and shoot a few missiles that can be shot, then he'll move to the left side, so slide across. For the rest of the battle he'll move left and right across the top of the train, stopping on the right side to kneel and shoot flames across the train. You'll have to do a lot of quick sliding each time he cross the train, then jump over the flames. If you stay in the corner he'll kick you, so keep moving.

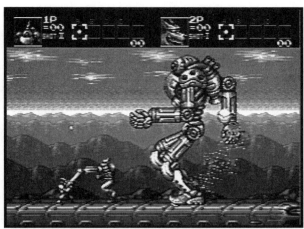

The final boss on the train is extremely fast and difficult. Sliding is the key to survival. Dodge and shoot.

ALIEN COMPOUND (ENDING #4): About one screen into this stage be prepared to shoot the weapons that fly by. Shoot the aliens that escape from their cases. When you reach the first room you'll have to fight Dead-Eye Joe in his red battle pod. It will move to the center of the room, then it will sprout four arms. The arms will detach and move about 45°, then reattach to the wall, one at a time in a clockwise direction. Stand near an arm and move left or right to avoid the arms as they move. They retract into the body each time, so you won't have to avoid them swinging from spot to spot. They will speed up their relocating, then slow back down. Next the pod will slam into the walls with its arms extended. Move to the top corner and shoot, then quickly drop and slide to avoid it when it nears your corner. After you shoot the arms off, the pod will split into two blinking pieces, then pick a spot to come back together (usually directly above you). When the two pieces rejoin, they'll rapidly slam into the floor and ceiling in a straight vertical line. Slide away and shoot. When the battle is over you'll have to climb to the top and fight the mutated doctor.

DOCTOR: The colonel zaps the **doctor** and he transforms into an alien spider. The spider will shoot a beam that riccochets off the walls to form a web-like path, then it will crawl along the path. The web beam won't hurt you, but the creature and his blue beam will. The flashing blue beams are in a four-part pattern. First the spider shoots one straight at you that will stop and turn toward you as you run away. Use the slide at the last moment to get past it. Next, the spider will shoot a beam that explodes

The two pieces will split apart and flash, then rejoin directly above you. Move before it drops to the floor.

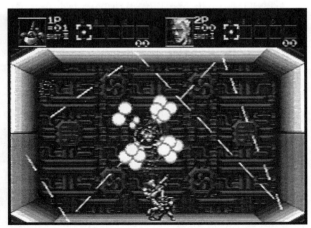

This boss will shoot a web around the screen, then it will crawl along the web. The web won't hurt you.

into every direction. Be sliding as the beams cross your path. A simple single beam is next, which is usually shot into the corner of the ceiling, then a diagonal four-way beam is shot, which can be avoided as long as you straight to the sides or directly above or below the spider. The patterns of the beams change as the battle progresses. After about five webs the spider will be smashed and you'll be off to face the Colonel in the final battle.

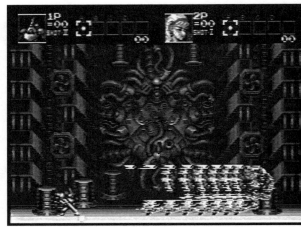

The colonel will count down before he attacks.
Slide through him the moment he makes his move.

🔸 **COLONEL:** The colonel mutates into a monster. The countdown above his head will warn you when he's going to charge to the opposite side of the screen (jump or slide through him). When the boss jumps to the top corner of the screen, he'll shoot a diagonal spray of fireballs to the opposite bottom corner of the screen. When he holds a fireball to his hip, it will suck in energy and then he'll throw it straight across the screen. You can't jump over it, so slide. As if that weren't enough, after a few minutes of this he'll mutate into a big creature with heads on each end. It will move to one side of the screen, then it will stretch its neck out and slam its head into the ground rapidly, causing red and blue bombs to drop from the ceiling. Stay to the far left and you should avoid most of the bombs and his head easily. When he hops to the center of the screen, be ready to slide past him when he hops to the left side of the screen. Move directly under the next of the boss to avoid his head as it stretches and creates a circle. This pattern repeats until the creature explodes and all that's left is the heart of the alien surrounded by heads. Shoot the heart while avoiding the pulsing ball of heads that protect it. Move under the mass of heads when they're near the top of the screen, or between pulses. This is the last pattern for the last boss. Destroy the heart and you'll view one of the many endings.

Save Research Center... Fight

🔸 **GENETIC LAB:** See the section in Follow Dead Eye Joe for tips in the Genetic Lab.

🔸 **WATER STAGE:** You'll begin this stage on the front deck of a ship about twice as tall as you (geez, that's pretty small!). A plane attacks first. It will aim it's guns, stop moving and lock aim, then shoot. As long as you move or slide when it locks aim, you can avoid the bullets. For its second attack it will fly near the top of the screen while dropping blue and red mines. If the mines come into contact with you they will explode — stand between them or slide to avoid them. A creature will attack from below the ship next. The creature will reach its arm up to hit you. Sliding is the only sure way to avoid the arm, since it will move from side to side if you try to

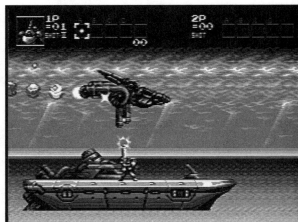

The plane above will lock it's crosshairs on you. The moment the crosshairs stop, move to avoid being shot.

walk away. After destroying the underwater creature, the ship will take damage and you'll have to jump onto a jet ski. A jumping fish attacks next. He makes small jumps from left to right that can easily be jumped over, then when he reaches the right side he'll make a larger jump to the left side, which you must move under. Stick near the center and fire away while dodging the robotic fish. When you reach land, be ready to shoot the two weapons that fly by.

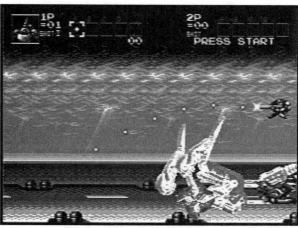

* When you get back on land after the water stage you'll have to fight an incredibly tough robot that transforms, and he's more than meets the eye! You can shoot the robots missiles. He'll run, hop, flip, and walk on his hands while moving back and forth across the screen. Slide attacks are once again the key to survival, and you'll need to

After the robot runs along the left side and disappears, be ready to dodge him as he dives along the ground.

do a lot of them. Keep an eye out for when he runs along the left side and disappears, because he usually follows with a dive across the bottom of the screen. Once you shoot the boss often enough he will break apart into his three different parts, then transform into a bird. It will begin with a swooping attack from the skies. The spot where it hits the ground will vary, so be ready with a slide attack each time he disappears off the screen. After it tires of swooping ti will jog behind you and attack with its beak. You can stay near its body and shoot up diagonally, or stay ahead of its reach and shoot back at it. Next the bird will stick near the left side and hover in the air. This is a great opportunity to move in close and blast him with your best weapon. It will start spitting a rapid stream of seeds while moving its head up and down, but if you stay under its neck you won't get hit. When it stops spitting it will move to the right side of the screen and drop eggs. Stay to the far left and jump over them while shooting. Be ready for the bird to repeat any of its previous patterns, but soon it should split apart and transform into the next creature — a robotic tank. This final formation, like the previous, will sometimes vary its attack pattern. When you see a large spear appear in the arm of the boss, move to the right side of the screen (slightly to the left of the edge) to avoid being hit by the spear as it crashes down into the ground. The boss will drag the spear across the ground while moving left and right, so keep

up with him or you'll get crushed. When the body of the robot lifts off the tank base, quickly move to the opposite side of the screen and jump each time the tank base bashes into the side of the screen. When the boss shoots a ton of fireballs into the screen, watch for the target that appears and quickly move onto it (very cruel, guys! Very cruel!). The target is the only spot on the screen where the bullets *don't* hit. If you shoot him as often as possible the boss should have enough time to perform about five or six of these patterns.

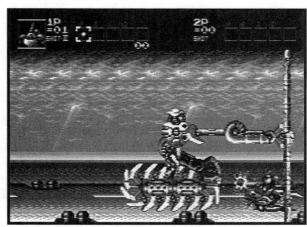

When the boss raises his spear, move to this position to avoid being destroyed as he slams it down.

* **COMPOUND:** You'll be attacked by foot soldiers from all sides. Keep shooting while moving forward to reach the battle room. The boss is various formations of foot soldiers. The first forma-

tion is a giant circle that rolls towards you. They don't require too many hits, so stand to the far left and fire away to destroy them. In the second formation the soldiers will stack straight up, then they'll bend to form an arc and the bottom soldiers will become the top soldiers, upside down. They'll "walk" across the screen this way. Stand under the arc as it forms and shoot. The third formation is a pyramid. Try to get to the far right side before they finish building their formation. The soldier at the top is blue, while the rest are red. Shoot the blue guy, because he's the only one that can be damaged. As the soldiers move toward you, slide through them and continue shooting them from the other side. It's easiest to slide through them while their halfway through their twist (and very thin). Once you defeat this last formation you'll meet up with the colonel again, and you'll have to choose which path you want to take to the end.

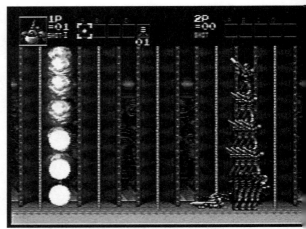

The final formation of the soldiers is a pyramid. Only the top soldier can be hurt, so attack him!

- ✿ **JOIN COLONEL?:** If you answer yes, you'll get Ending #3, which ain't that great. If you refuse to join the colonel, you'll have to fight him.

- ✿ **REFUSE TO JOIN — FIGHT THE COLONEL (ENDING #2):** If you decided to refuse the colonel's offer to join forces (as well you should — I think he's the bad guy!), you'll have to fight him. Like most of the other bosses, his pattern is varied, only he moves even faster than most of the previous bosses. The only way to survive is to do a lot more sliding than firing. The colonel will grab a claw from his ultra-secret storage bin at the top of the screen, then he'll slide at you with the claw ahead of him. He'll hop around for a while, then he'll jump in the air and spin like a saw blade down to the center, then up to the opposite side of the screen. He'll hop around some more, then he'll grab a piece of scrap metal from the top of the screen and throw it at you. Slide, slide, then slide some more and you might survive. This battle lasts a long time, and if you do conquer him you'll still have one more major battle before reaching Ending #2.

- ✿ **LAUNCHED MISSILE:** Move to the far left missile and shoot Dead-Eye Joe each time he appears. As

long as you shoot him quickly when he moves to the left side, he'll drop below and move to the right side. Once Joe is defeated, the missiles on the right will drop out of sight, and you'll reach the main missile above. Jump to the missile and shoot straight up to hit the two weapon power-ups that appear. Select Shot II, then shoot everything in sight before moving up the missile. A large worm will reach out of the left side of the missile as you near the top. If you move up the missile without destroying each enemy you see first, you'll be attacked by all of the enemies at once, creating an impossible battle. When you reach the top of the missile you'll have to battle the alien. At the beginning of the battle, move to the opposite side of the missile and avoid the

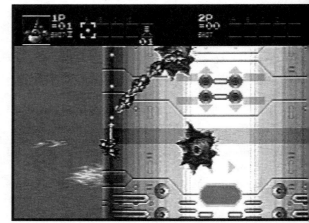

As you climb up the side of the missile, select Shot II and shoot everything in sight, then move up slowly.

flames shot by the alien worm. If the flames move too close, slide through them and run to the opposite side. Shoot the head of the alien worm to cause damage. The alien worm will occasionally ram its head into the ground. When the worm is defeated, the heart of the alien (hey, that's a different game!) will rise from the missile, sprout arms, and attack. If you shoot the entire arm it will disappear and another will form, so you're better off shooting the lower part of the arm and leaving the small bone from the shoulder that won't be able to reach you. The alien will eventually sprout a head with a long neck that spits larvae. Shoot the larvae to easily destroy it, then shoot the head when the red membrane appears. You must shoot the larvae, then shoot up diagonally at the head, then slide

Try to shoot only part of the arm.
If you shoot it all the way off it will reform.

to the other side as the head swings down and moves to the other side. After a few hundred hits the alien will be destroyed and you'll get to see one of the many endings.

"Where There's Smoke" by J. Douglas Arnold
This stereogram is a tricky two-level stereogram. The darker part of the pattern floats above the lighter, creating a smoke effect. See page 325 for more 3D information.

DYNAMITE HEADDY

CATEGORY: Platform   DEVELOPER: Treasure
PLAYERS: 1   PUBLISHER: Sega of America

Introduction

If you were lucky enough to discover Gunstar Heroes, or daring enough to discover McDonald's Treasure Island, then you've already experienced the talent of one of the best programming teams for the Genesis — Treasure. They are pioneers in graphics and gameplay, and Dynamite Headdy is their latest masterpiece. Tons of levels, tons of bosses, and totally awesome gameplay make this game a must buy. As Dynamite Headdy you must survive 9 scenes with 3 or more stages each, and a boss on nearly every stage (not scene — stage!). There's an excellent practice area on the first scene, and "next level" graphics that include 3-D objects that rotate, and bright, Super Nintendo-quality graphics.

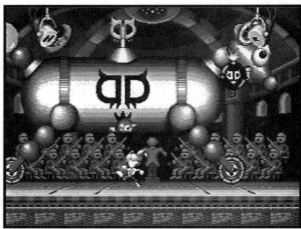

The masters of programming at Treasure are ready to take you to yet another "next level" with Dynamite Headdy.

Basic Strategies

- ✹ **CONTROLS:** You can change the controls in the Options menu. The defaults are A to cancel a head, B to attack, C the jump.
- ✹ There are various heads that Headdy can collect, and it's important to learn what each head can do so you can put them to work. Headdy can attack with his normal head, and he can climb to higher areas if there's a **HangMan** above (a yellow creature about the size of a lemon, assuming Headdy is about five feet tall). The best way to learn how the various heads and creatures help Headdy is to play the first stage and enter each of the three **practice rooms.** You'll also receive a **Secret Bonus Point** for each practice room you complete (see the end of this chapter for a complete list of Secret Bonus Points).
- ✹ Your **energy** is displayed in the top-left corner in the form of a spotlight. When the light is green and the "H" for Headdy is big, you have full energy. When the light is flashing red, you're gonna lose a turn if you're hit one or two more times (so be very careful!). Collect food or hit the

Use your head to bounce the basketballs into the baskets during the Intermission Bonus Game.

Sleepy Head (three Zs) in HeadCase to rest up and restore your energy. If an enemy hits you while you're sleeping, you'll be rudely awakened even if your energy is totally replenished.

✦ **INTERMISSION BONUS GAME:** If you find a Headcase with a B symbol, hit it to enter the bonus game. By shooting the required number of baskets you can earn a secret number. By collecting all four of the random secret numbers, and entering them in the system after the end of the credits, you'll get to battle against one more boss. Unfortunately, we don't have any details on this boss. Whatever you do, don't hit the A button during the bonus game or you'll cancel it and lose a chance to earn a secret number in the code. I can't imagine why, in a game that is so incredibly well designed, that a "feature" would exist that would cause you to lose a chance sim-

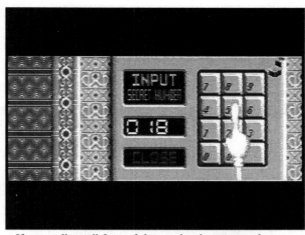

If you collect all four of the randomly-generated secret code numbers, you can enter them after the credits.

ply by slipping and hitting the A button. I could understand hitting Start to Pause, then having the option of giving up. Oh well, it's the only thing I could find wrong with this game, so I have to rant and rave a little about it. During the bonus game, stand in front of either ball launcher and wait for a ball to be launched straight up, then jump and hit it up toward the top row of baskets. With a little practice you'll get the timing down on when to hit the ball. You can continue to hit the ball back into the air unless it hits the ground (which makes it turn blue). You can hit the bombs with your head, but if they hit the ground at your feet you'll receive damage. The bottom row of baskets has a "death" basket with a key symbol (looks kinda like an infinity symbol — two zeros). If you hit the "death" basket you'll lose one of your ball launchers. Once you lose both the bonus game will end. By shooting for the top baskets with one ball at a time, you'll decrease your chances of hitting the "death" basket. The top row has a basketball icon basket, which increases the number of balls being launched for a short time. There's also a Slow icon on the top row that will slow down the movement of the baskets, making it easier to aim. There's no time limit, so take it easy and work to avoid hitting the "death" basket. There are four code numbers to earn, beginning with 5 baskets and increasing by 5 each time you play the bonus round.

Stage 0 and Stage 1

✦ You'll begin with "The Getaway", which is considered Stage 0. On most stages you can spot a sign along the way that will tell you what stage you're on, but this one doesn't have any. A Robo-Collector will appear from the left. He can't hurt you, but he'll grab all of your friends if you let him. Stand directly below him, hold up on the control pad, and hit the attack button (B) rapidly to hit him. His body will flash with each direct hit. You'll have to press the button very quickly to destroy the Robo-Collector before he walks off the screen. If you succeed in destroying him, you'll receive a Secret Bonus Point. Check the end of this chapter for more information on Secret Bonus Points. When the Yellow Baron appears (the plane), watch for his bombs to drop from right to left, then back to the right. If you stand still you'll only get hit once or twice, but with a little evasive maneuvering you should be able to walk between the blasts.

- **Scene 1-1 (Trouble Bruin):** The second boss you get to face is Trouble Bruin. You'll learn to recognize this kitty in his many different forms throughout the game. His first pattern is easy enough. You can only hit him once during cycle of his pattern. He'll begin by sucking in a bunch of white energy balls. Move to his left, about one-third of the way from the left side of the screen, and duck to avoid the balls. When he stops sucking them in, move to the far left and take one hit as he runs into the wall and bounces back to the right. Move left or right to avoid the falling energy balls that fall, then quickly move up to him while he's still panting and hit him in the head. If you hit him at the right time, his head will flash. You only need to hit him twice to defeat him. If you have plenty of energy, just walk through the energy balls to make sure you hit him before he begins to repeat his pattern.

As all of the energy balls fall through the floor, run up to Trouble Bruin and get in a hit or two.

Stage 2

- **Scene 2-1 (Practice Area):** It isn't required that you enter each of the three practice rooms, but doing so will make the later stages easier to survive, and you'll receive a Secret Bonus Point for each room you complete.
- **Meet Headcase (2-1):** In the first room you'll meet HeadCase. This is the perfect opportunity to become familiar with the various heads available to Headdy. It may seem confusing at first with so many heads to choose from, but after a few plays you'll know exactly which one to choose for the tasks ahead. You must time your hit on HeadCase the moment you see the head you want appear. Headcase will have anywhere from one to four different heads available. To make this room easy to finish, first select the Empty Head (looks like a glass window), which will make you invincible. You can hit the enemies, or stand still and wait until your head begins to flash. When the next HeadCase appears, select the War Head (eight bullets in a circle) to fire rapidly in all directions. You can kneel at the center of the screen and shoot everyone before they have a chance to hit you. Next, select the Vacuum Head (lips) and rapidly press the attack (B) button to suck all enemies in. When the War Head appears again, hit it and finish the remaining time with little effort.

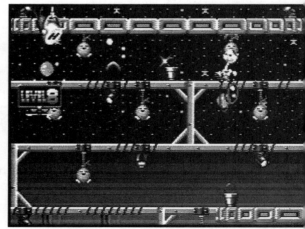

Learning to jump from one HangMan to another is a valuable skill to master.

- **Meet HangMan (2-1):** The second practice room will teach you the climbing skills necessary to survive the tougher stages later in the game. Hit the attack (B) button to shoot your head at HangMan, then let go of the button to pull yourself up above him. When you reach Level 6 you'll have to jump from one HangMan to the next without stopping on a platform, so be ready to shoot your head toward a HangMan as you fall from the first. This may seem tough at first, but that's why it's called the practice room, and you'll be needing that practice a lot later.

* **Meet Beau (2-1):** The third and final practice room teaches you the value of Beau. He flies around and points to the target you can hit. During bosses he'll appear and point out the weak spot of the boss. During this practice he'll start off slow, but by the end he really flies fast. Try to pay attention to where Beau is pointing, and avoid looking at the spheres as they open. By the time the sphere opens and you react, the sphere will be closing, so Beau will give you that moments notice required to react in a timely manner.

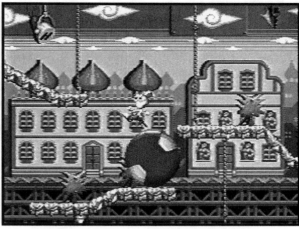
Hit this red ball to the left, then climb on it
and jump to the left for an extra life.

* **Scene 2-2 (Toys N The Hood):** If you watch the demo before starting a game you can see this scene well played almost completely through. Use HangMan to climb to higher platforms, then attack the enemies rapidly to knock them out, or off the ledge. In the first area, go to the bottom right and jump over the hole to enter the wall and find a banana (energy). When you reach the red ball above next to a HeadCase with a bonus round B symbol, hit the red ball to the left once, then stand on it and jump to the ledge on the left. Go left to find a 1-Up (Extra Life!). As you progress to the right you'll have to cancel any heads you have and grab the HangMan below the big red ball to start it rolling. It will crush a few enemies below. To the right of where the red ball is released you'll see a banana, which you can climb up to from below or suck in by hitting the Vacuum Head in the HeadCase to the left. To the right of where the rolling red ball lands is a HeadCase with three choices. It doesn't matter which you choose. Climb up and go right, then hold left as you drop off to grab 500 points in the left

wall. Hit the cage below to knock it to the right until it drops into the pit, then face off with the boss. Hit the boss each time he lands, but avoid getting cornered (run under him before reaching either wall). He'll pull you towards him the first time he stops, then push you away the second, so be ready to resist. After eight hits he'll go down in flames and the creatures in the cage will pop up. Stay to the left as you defeat the boss and hit the mule and old man for one Secret Bonus Point each (see the complete list at the end of this chapter). Hit the Sleepy Head in HeadCase and rest up, then select Spike Head and climb up the walls in the next area. There's a secret passage in the left wall, but after dropping down to the lower floor be sure to jump over the pink brick or you'll miss the final 500

Hit the boss while he's bouncing, then run under him
between bounces to avoid being cornered.

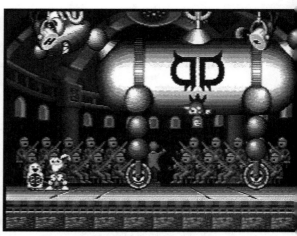

If you use the Spike Head and destroy this snake,
you'll collect a Secret Bonus Point.

Try to freeze Mad Dog,
then furiously attack his tail.

points. Hit the Spike Head in HeadCase again, then climb back up and go right. A snake boss come
out that will give you a Secret Bonus Point if you destroy it. Knock all of the snake's body armor off
then hit the Ticker Head (two glass windows) to freeze the boss when his head is reachable. Run up
to him and rapidly hit his head until the Ticker Head wears off, then go back to HeadCase and hit i
again to repeat the pattern until the snake is defeated. Go right to find the exit.

✵ **Scene 2-3 (Mad Dog and Headdy):** Here are more of those amazing graphics that has earned Treasur
a following of fans. A huge mechanical dog falls from the ceiling, then rotates and bounces before jump
ing back up off the screen. The target is his tail, which you can reach most of the time by standing
directly below it and rapidly attacking upward. The dog faces to the left and does a dance, then leap
up and drops back down facing right with a dangerous object in his mouth, which he'll gladly drop so
you can have it. HeadCase will have the Ticker Head (two glass windows), which will freeze the boss
The trick is to freeze the boss at a moment when you can reach his tail. If you can't reach the tail, can
cel the head with A and hit HeadCase again until you can reach. A second HeadCase will have a Supe
Head and a Slammer Head (hammer). Either will help. A third HeadCase may appear with a Head Trip
(lemon), which you always want to avoid. Keep
hitting that tail until the boss explodes.

Stage 3

✵ **Scene 3-1 (Down Under):** Prepare for more
incredibly cool graphics. Stay away from the bottom edge of the platforms when they're rotating.
Let Headdy slide down the platform to grab the
banana, then run back up before you fall off (use
the same strategy on the extra life ahead). Near
the end you'll have to destroy three floating hel-
mets that drop bombs. Watch their shadow to
judge their location. The best strategy is to stay
near the center and avoid them as they fly by,

Stand still and let the rotating platform
slide you down to this extra life.

During the Backstage Battle (Scene 3-2) you won't be able to control much, so concentrate on the boss.

You can attack the puppeteer or the puppet at any time during this battle.

then jump and attack when they're to the sides. The next boss will grab you from the far right of the third platform ahead (you'll see him peeking through a window in the background.

★ **Scene 3-2 (Backstage Battle):** Trouble Bruin is back, and this time he'll take you on a wild ride backstage. You can't escape until he's defeated, so enjoy the ride and do your best to hit him often. When HeadCase appears, do your best to get the War Head (bullets in a circle). The directional arrows tell you when obstacles are coming up, so try to follow them the best you can. Even if you every one of them you should still have enough energy to survive until the end.

★ **Stage 3-3 (The Green Room):** Grab the Sleepy Head from HeadCase to recharge your energy, then hit the Liberty Head (letter "B") to play the bonus game. The boss for this stage is a puppeteer and his puppet. You can try to destroy either one first. Destroying the puppeteer first will gain you a Secret Bonus Point (see section at the end of this chapter), but destroying the puppet first is easier. Stay to the right of both characters to avoid the puppets spinning cane, which he'll only throw to the left. Rapidly hit the puppet until he stars swinging, then dodge him until he stops swinging. If you destroy the puppet first, the puppeteer will swing his strings in circles, and if the tip of them hit you, you'll be pulled

into his control for a few seconds. Keep jumping and you should avoid his strings easily. If you destroy the puppeteer first, then puppet will drop bouncing fireballs from his hat, which you must jump over or duck under to avoid.

★ **Stage 3-4 (Clothes Encounters):** No reason to waste time on another level when you have the opportunity to fight *another* boss! This wooden dancer has three costume changes, beginning with a dragon. He'll breathe fire while walking from side to side. Watch for Beau to point out the current target, then attack it. When HeadCase appears, try (very hard) to get the War Head (circle of bullets), then stand back and aim your bullets at the targets. If you can't get the War Head, use jump attacks to hit the targets. Once you knock off each part of the costume, the boss will

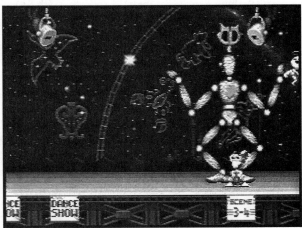

Knock the costume off the wooden dancer, then rapidly attack his heart before he jumps back to wardrobe.

be vulnerable for a few seconds. Stand directly below him and shoot your head straight up to hit his heart rapidly. Once he disappears you won't be able to attack his heart until you remove the next costume, which is a ballet dress. Try to get the Super Head from HeadCase, so you'll be able to reach the ballerina while she's jumping and dancing around. If you destroy the wooden dancer during this part of the battle, you won't have to face him when he returns as a robot. If you do face the robot costume, try to get the War Head from HeadCase. If you're desperate, you can use the Sleepy Head from HeadCase to regain energy, but if you get hit before regaining energy you'll be rudely awakened.

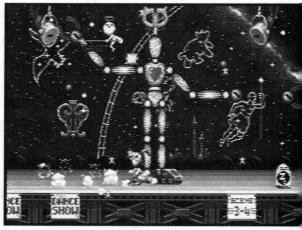

The War Head is always the best weapon to use against any costume of the wooden dancer.

Stage 4

✸ **Scene 4-1 (Terminate Her Too):** Hit the first "Hit Me" switch twice, then go right to the next switch. Hit the second switch twice. Hit the third switch once while standing on the wheel. Hold down and press jump to jump down through the floor above HangMan. When you try to grab the HangMan below the "Danger" sign, the background will rotate around. Get the War Head from the next HeadCase and rush to face the boss on the right. With the War Head you should blast down his energy quickly, then hit him a few more times in the head. When the crosshairs both stop, be sure not to be standing in front of them. Go right and hit the Vacuum Head from Headcase to collect nearby points, then hit the Slammer Head to hit the platforms ahead more quickly. Use the Vacuum Head again at the next HeadCase to grab a banana (energy) and points. Go right and grab the HangMan under the "Danger" sign to rotate the background back to normal. Stand in front of the "Shoot" sign and shoot the bouncing yellow guys into the pole on the right, then go right and climb to the platform above using the

HangMan. Use the Sleepy Head if your energy isn't full, then go left and hit four more yellow guys into the top pole. When they turn blue, jump to them to reach the extra life on the left. Go to the right and fight the Super Tank. To defeat him you must stand near him when he's all the way to the right, then hit a cannonball diagonally up into the spikes above him so it falls as he moves forward and hits him in the head. It only takes one cannonball to destroy him. If you lose any energy during this battle, you can return to HeadCase (left) to use the Sleepy Head. Go right and grab HangMan to rotate the background. Use the Vacuum Head at the next HeadCase to grab nearby bonus points, then select the Slammer Head and hit the lamp on the right to make it swing. Once it gets swinging

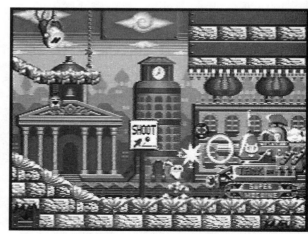

Stand near Super Tank when he's to the right, then hit a cannonball up and right diagonally into the spikes.

high enough, jump aboard and jump off on the top platform. Go down to hit the "Hit Me" switch below, which reverses the conveyor belts and makes the next enemy more vulnerable. Go right and hit the three blue platforms at the top to make them extend out to a solid platform with points and a banana. Continue to the right, hitting the "Hit Me" switches to make the enemies easier to destroy.

* **Stage 4-2 (Mad Mechs):** Hit the Liberty Head at the HeadCase to play the bonus game. You can choose to use the Pin Head (shrink ray) and walk under the plungers to the right, or select the Slammer Head and climb above for a few points. We suggest the Slammer Head and higher path, since it's a bit safer. Over the third conveyor elevator is a glass ball you can stand on, then jump to the right to the next HeadCase. Select the

If you can spare a little energy, jump off near the extra life and hold right to reach it, then hold left to go back.

Slammer Head and grab the points below, then climb back up and go right. At the third HeadCase (near the bottom of the area), go to the right to find an extra life placed out of reach. If you can spare some energy, you can grab the extra life by falling off the left side of the platform above it. When you fall off the bottom of the screen you'll lose a little energy and you'll bounce back up. Hold right to reach the extra life, then hold left to go back to the last platform. If you go to the right after getting the extra

life you'll need a Slammer Head to climb up. Go back to HeadCase and select the Slammer Head, then jump on the rising conveyor elevator to the right and hit the hammer blocks with your head as you ride up. Jump through the hole you've made and climb above for points, then go right to the next area.

* **Stage 4-3 (Mad Mechs 2):** Use the Sleepy Head at the first HeadCase to rest up and restore your energy. Go down to walk across the glass balls below, then continue to the upper right until you see the next HeadCase. Grab the War Head and go right, then climb up using the HangMans.

* **Stage 4-4 (Heathernapped):** Hit the Bino at the beginning of this stage for a Secret Bonus Point (see the end of this chapter for more information), then go right to finish the stage (oooh! Wickedly tough one, eh?).

Stage 4-3: Jump across the glass balls. Get the War Head from HeadCase. Go to the right and climb up.

Scene 5

* **Stage 5-1 (Go Headdy Go):** Get the Liberty Head from HeadCase to play the Bonus Round. You'll have two more chances after this Bonus Round to get all four passcode numbers. Get the Slammer Head from HeadCase and jump to the cool 3D tower.

Stage 5-2 (Stair Wars): You have to climb up quickly while avoiding and attacking Trouble Bruin (the cat). He'll pull large chunks of the tower out from under you, so keep climbing to the top. When Trouble Bruin approaches you, try to get above him and jump while shooting your head down to hit him, then quickly move up a step before he hits you back. This battle lasts a long time, and there's not any more you can do but climb for your life.

Stage 5-3 (Towering Internal): Pop the first two balloons and do your best to climb quickly while avoiding them. A few floors up is the first mini-boss. It looks like two arms made of basketballs. They'll spin around the center pole while moving up and down. Rush under one arm and attack it rapidly before it starts moving, then try to concentrate on that one arm to destroy it

Stage 5-2: Climb quickly while waiting for Trouble Bruin to float over and fight like a cat.

first, making the second easier to deal with. When the arms are spinning around the pole, stand in place and jump or duck to avoid them, getting in hits whenever possible. As you climb up the next two floors watch for bombs that shoot from windows in the background toward you. The next boss is a helmet in a ball. He uses the ball for protection, especially when you're armed with a special head. Stand to the right side and jump each time the ball rolls by. Most of the time the ball will roll around the floor, open, close, then roll around again. When it begins hopping, get the Ticker Head from HeadCase as

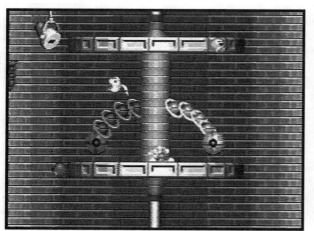

Try to concentrate on destroying one arm before the other on Stage 5-3, making the final arm easier to battle.

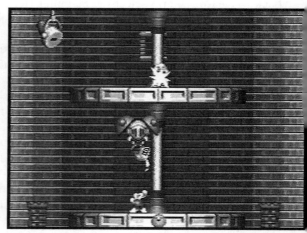

Fighting the rolling helmet in a ball is the toughest part of Stage 5-3. Freeze him in the air, then attack rapidly.

the helmet is bouncing, then run under him and attack rapidly. You'll need to do this three or four times before destroying him, which is the toughest part of this scene. The Protector Head (looks like a target) will damage the helmet while he's bouncing, but he'll stop bouncing as soon as possible when you have this head. When he's defeated, climb up and grab a banana, then prepare for another tough boss.

Stage 5-4 (Spinderella): This boss seems very tough at first, especially when he starts spinning the floor around and you end up on the back side of the area, with your controls reversed. The weak spot

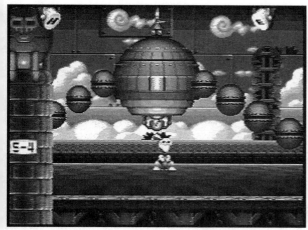

Wait for Spinderella to lock its arms into the floor...   ...then run around and attack the tank on his back.

on the boss is the tank on his back, which you can only walk around and hit when he locks his hands onto the ground. Once his arms form, he'll hit the floor with each arm twice before grabbing the floor. Walk to the left and right to avoid the arms as they come down (just take a few steps each direction as the arms land). Once the arms lock on to the floor, quickly run around to the back side of the boss and hit the tank. When you're on the front side of the floor this is fairly easy, but once he spins you around to the back side it's tougher to judge where the tank is located. Walk around until his hands are at the front center of the screen, then attack upward. The boss will flash if you're standing in the right spot. He'll spin you around to the opposite side of the screen after each two times locking his hands to the floor. As long as you dodge his arms and the spikes, you can take all the time you want.

Scene 6

✦ Scene 6-1 (Flying Game): How cool! Just about the time you start thinking you've had enough platform gaming to last a lifetime, Dynamite Headdy becomes a side-scrolling shoot-em-up (at least for a while). You can choose one of three planes. The yellow biplane lets you spray bullets left or right, while the bird and rocket only face to the right. Since you're heading to the right, we suggest you grab the rocket. It has a laser cannon that works pretty good for the first part of this stage. When the Battle Ship appears, shoot the cannons first to destroy his firepower, then attack the crane that is holding the Battle Ship up. Keep moving up and down to avoid the bullets and planes that attack.

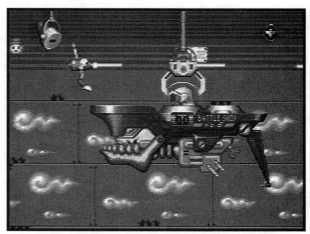

Destroy the cannons on the Battle Ship so he can't shoot you, then destroy the crane that holds him up.

✦ Scene 6-2 (Fly Hard): This part of the game is reminiscent of the arcade classic Scramble. You must avoid the zig-zagging passage walls while attacking Trouble Bruin. Shoot the yellow wall cannons immediately each time they appear to avoid taking damage. You can only hit Trouble

Bruin when he's on the closer tracks, so the rest of the time concentrate on avoiding anything that flies your way.

✦ **Scene 6-3 (Fly Hard 2):** This scene is even more like the arcade classic Scramble. The walls take you on a passage that has deep dives and steep climbs. The general strategy is to avoid the walls at all costs, since they drain energy quickly. There aren't any safer paths or shortcuts, so do your best to avoid touching anything. Near the end of this stage you'll see purple creatures climbing up and down across your path. Stay to the left until you can see a few of them, then rush through so the most damage you'll take is one hit.

✦ **Scene 6-4 (Baby Face):** We suggest the yellow plane for this boss, since you can hide up near the top of the screen and still shoot him, plus you can shoot him from the right side of the screen. Whenever possible, try to fly even with the head so you can hit him with all three bullets. The baby face will eventually split apart, then an older head appears from inside. When the second head appears (teenager), stay to the far left and be ready to fly forward the moment you see a finger appear at the bottom of the screen. Maneuver the plane in between the yellow bolts that shoot from the finger, then be prepared to maneuver again as the finger sinks and shoots up again. During the third stage (middle-aged man) your biggest hindrance is a stack of boxes, which won't hurt you but will make dodging bullets much tougher since you can't see them or yourself very well. The final head is an old man, but he doesn't last for long. He'll grab you and laugh, but you'll still get the key and end this stage.

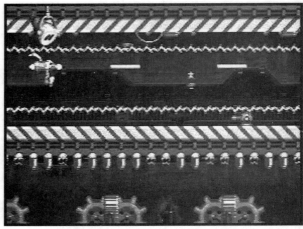

Scene 6-3 is a long and winding passage where touching the walls can crash your plane quickly.

Use the yellow plane to shoot the head from the front or back while hiding in the top corners.

Stage 7

✦ **Scene 7-1 (Headdy Wonderland):** It's back to platform madness, and this next boss is almost impossible to beat. Grab the Liberty Head from HeadCase if you still need to collect any passcodes (there are four altogether), then go to the right. There are two Special Bonus Points in this area (see the section at the end of this chapter for more information). The first mini-boss is easy. Heather is at the top of the screen, and she'll throw keys into the back of the robot to mess it up. The robot always jumps towards you, but he can't hurt you with his feet. Stick near his feet to guide him left or right. You want him to stop with his back toward Heather so she can throw a key in (otherwise she won't even try). He'll

Stay near the feet of the first boss, then run through his legs when he stops jumping to avoid his arms.

If you can get his back toward Heather, she'll be kind enough to throw a key into his moving parts.

bounce 2-5 times before stopping, so you'll have to guess when to make him turn from side to side. When he does stop, quickly run toward his back to avoid his arm as it thrusts forward. Once you get the hang of this boss, and stick close to his feet waiting to run between his legs before he hits you, you should be able to easily defeat him without getting hurt. That's good, because you're going to need all your energy for the second boss.

✦ **Scene 7-1 (main boss):** The second boss looks very similar to the first robot, but he's *much* tougher to beat. Stay near the sides of the screen to avoid the boss. When he starts hopping around, run under him to get as far away as possible. You want to encourage him to reach his arms out towards the edge of the screen, so he can grab onto HeadCase. Once he gets HeadCase, you must carefully get the Empty Head from him (it looks like a glass window). The Empty Head makes you invincible, and that's the only way to battle this boss. The biggest danger is hitting the Head Trip (looks like a lemon), which will give you a humongous head and make you extremely vulnerable to attacks. Once you do get the invincibility, stand directly below the head of the boss and wait for him to move *both* hands to the sides of his head, then hit his head rapidly once or twice. Get the Empty Head again to refresh it, being

The main boss of Stage 7 is very tough. It's crucial to get the Empty Head for invincibility...

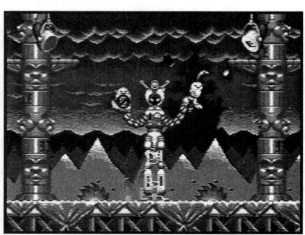

...then wait for him to move both arms out of the way and smack him in the face. Refresh your Empty Head often!

extremely careful to avoid the Head Trip. If you do get the Head Trip, move away from the boss as much as possible. HeadCase will cycle through the three heads as Bomb Head, then Empty Head, then Head Trip. It took us a long time to beat this boss, and even once we did Headdy was down to one single hit of energy. We did, however, get the Head Trip once during this battle, so don't give up too quickly.

Stage 8

⚡ **Scene 8-1 (The Rocket Tier):** You'll have a choice of two heads from HeadCase. You can choose to use the Pin Head (shrinking) to hide out in the small holes in the floor, or grab the Spike Head and press the attack button rapidly to stay up near the ceiling as the large rockets shoot by. The rockets keep coming, preceded by a siren sound. The first two holes in the floor are deep enough to hide in even without the Pin Head, but after that you'll have to choose the Pin Head to stick to the floor, or the Spike Head to stick to the ceiling. With Pin Head you'll run very slowly, and as you get further into the stage you'll have to run a further distance between holes in the floor, so you're best off using the Spike Head and getting used to it. You must jump and shoot your head to stick in the ceiling, then rapidly press the attack button while hold-

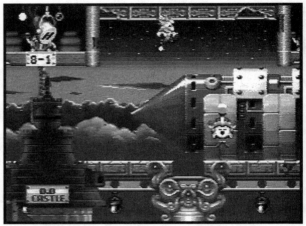

Use the Spike Head to stick near the ceiling while the huge rockets pass by below.

ing up to stay above the path of the rockets. It's critical to refresh your head from HeadCase often to avoid having your head expire while you're hanging over or hiding under a rocket.

⚡ **Scene 8-2 (Illegal Weapon 3):** Grab the Pin Head from HeadCase and drop into the hole in the floor, then check out the area to see what's happening. The rockets from the right will shoot across, just like the last scene. The helmet in the tower is controlling them, so you must knock him out to stop them. Use the Spike Head to run up to the tower and hit it, then leap to the ceiling above as the rocket launches. You head should last for two rocket launches, but you might want to play it safe and refresh your head between every attack.

⚡ **Scene 8-3 (Fun Forgiven):** Get the bonus room Liberty Head from HeadCase at the top-right, then grab the Slammer Head. Hit the jumping jack critter on the right while he's over the down arrow blocks to make him and the blocks drop. Fall into the chamber below when the jumping jack critter is to the right side, then hit him to freeze him and jump on his head so you can eas-

Hit the tower on Scene 8-2 to knock the helmet out, jumping to the ceiling with Spike Head between rockets.

ily attack the wolf in the chair on the top-right. When the wolf is destroyed, jump to the ledge where he was sitting and hit the motor on the right a few times to make the buzzsaw stop. Drop down below and hit the other buzzsaw motor, then grab HangMan to leap across the spikes. Drop to the bottom floor where two blocks are on wheels. Jump and hit the top block so the two blocks form steps, then jump on the bottom block and immediately jump up to the top block before the blocks crush you against the wall. As the blocks reach the left wall, jump over and grab the banana, then jump back to the blocks (you can make it back before the blocks get away, but take your time if you're feeling nervous). Drop into the next chamber and use the same techniques to hit the top block to form steps. Go to the right to meet the boss for the scene.

Hit the top block so the two blocks form steps, then use them to climb to the top.

✦ **(8-3 boss):** The boss is a sun surrounded by several power-up items. The 2, 4, and barely legible 6 balls will take that many hit points away from the boss. The HangMan is dangerous, because it will cause you to jump up towards the boss. The HeadCase has a useful Sleepy Head if you need to rest, but you'll need to pick a side of the screen and get the Sleepy Head as the boss moves away to avoid being rudely awakened while trying to recover your energy. The Heart ball will revive the energy of the boss, so try to avoid it. Avoid letting the boss corner you while trying to hit the 2, 4 or 6 balls. You'll need to add up about 25 hits to knock the boss apart. When the circle of power-up items enlarges, try to jump between any two items, and back through them as they come back toward the boss. The 2 ball is the easiest to hit, followed by the 4, so don't get greedy aiming for the 6 ball surrounded by riskier heart and HeadCase items unless you're feeling confident. Once you take out 25 hit points, the boss will explode, then the rays of the sun will spin around the boss and eventually sling into the floor, bouncing across to the left before returning to the face of the sun. The pattern here is easy. Stay below the sun and rapidly attack upward to hit the face, then as the rays are swinging in a wide circle move

Hit the 2, 4 and 6 balls into the boss to remove that number of hit points. Avoid being cornered.

During the second phase, jump over the rays of the sun as they bounce along the floor, right to left.

✦ to the left side of the screen and jump to the right as it comes bouncing your way. You can also use the Sleepy Head to restore your energy, but use the same strategy before of picking a corner and getting the head as the boss is moving away. When the boss is defeated he'll fall to the ground, and you can easily push him away by walking into him.

✦ **(8-3 continued, after boss):** If you check the area around this room you'll notice extra lives and points hidden in the walls. You can get them easily with little risk. Get the Spike Head from HeadCase and climb up the corridor on the left side. The Heady-eating plants will eat your head if you try to hit them high, so duck down and destroy them. Go to the right until you enter the large room with the HangMans that spin around on boards in the wall. Stand over the first HangMan and hold down while jumping to fall through the floor. There's a scarecrow below the you can land on (it's very slightly to the right of the HangMan, so guide Headdy a little to the right so you'll land on him). Jump into the wall on the left to enter and find points and, to the far left, an extra life and a banana. Go back to the right and jump to the scarecrow, then leap across to the center platform between the two long rows of spikes. Jump down through the floor and go left to find another extra life.

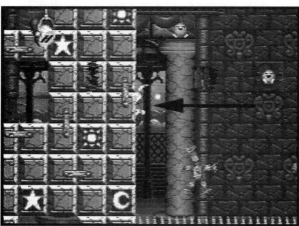

Drop below the first HangMan and enter the wall
on the left to reach points, a banana, and an extra life.

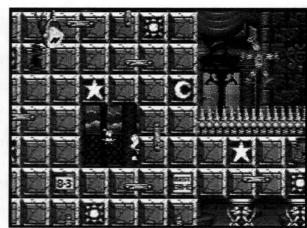

Go into the floor at the bottom-center of the room,
then go left to find another extra life.

✦ **AWESOME SECRET! (8-3):** If you collect the two extra lives we just pointed out, then die, you can build up your lives (you'll gain two, and only lose one each time). It's important to feel comfortable with what you've been through so far on this scene, including the sun boss, since you'll have to through it again each time.

✦ **(8-3 continued):** From the platform at the bottom of the large room, between the two large beds of spike, you can also jump down through the floor and go right to find a banana if you're energy is low, but if it isn't there's more hidden stuff in the walls to find, and you can still grab that same banana on your way out of the wall. From the middle platform, jump to the scarecrow on the right to land on his shoulders, then jump straight up so you can see the HangMans above. There is two at the top, and one below it in the center. Watch the top-left HangMan and get a feel for its timing, then jump to it about halfway into its appearance. As you spring up to the first HangMan, you must then drop off and shoot your head to the upper-right to grab the top-right HangMan that was visible from the scarecrow, then fall slightly to the right to land on the scarecrow below nearest the right wall. Jump into the wall, but be careful not to fall through the floor. The block directly below the banana (with a star) is hollow, and you'll drop straight down into the bottom floor. Try to shoot your head up to the banana as you're falling through the star block. Go left to get back to the center of the room, then climb to the upper-right to exit this scene. It might be easier to get back to the scarecrow near the right wall, then use the HangMans from there to reach the top-right ledge.

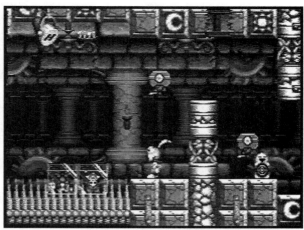

Scene 8-4 (Vice Versa): This stage is fairly straightforward. If you can't move to the right, Hit one of the floating blue buttons to flip the screen upside down. When you see the two creatures trapped in ice blocks (with the word "Shoot" flashing on them), hit them so they will land on the spikes when you flip the screen, and you'll be able to cross the spikes by jumping across them. Do the same with the next ice block. For the three ice blocks, you want them to form steps up tot he door when it opens as you flip the screen, so place one of the blocks in the

Line the ice blocks up so when the room flips over the blocks will allow you to cross the spikes.

hole in the floor, then move the other block on top of it. Use the Sleepy Head if you need it from HeadCase, then use the Empty Head (invincibility) for the beginning of the boss. The boss is a floating ship, and the only weapons you have are the three purple balls in the room. Push two of the balls (we picked the largest and smallest) into the area on the right so they'll stay out of your way, then use the remaining ball against the boss. Place the ball near the center of the room, then as the boss approaches hit the flip switch so the ball will land on the boss as the room flips. Repeat until he's defeated.

Scene 8-4 (Twin Freaks): A walking robot is the boss of this scene, and he doesn't waste any time making his appearance. When you flip the screen, the boss will go from green to red. When he's red, he'll walk much faster and he won't launch any flying creatures, but you won't be able to attack him.When he's green, he'll walk much slower, and you'll be able to hit him in the face. The following are step-by-step instructions, which will be easier to use if you have a friend read them to you while you play. If not, you'll have to memorize them or pause the game often to read the next part. As the boss walks towards you, attack him as quickly and rapidly as possible while avoiding the spikes in the

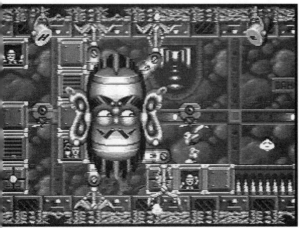

You can only hit the green face, which moves much slower than the red face.

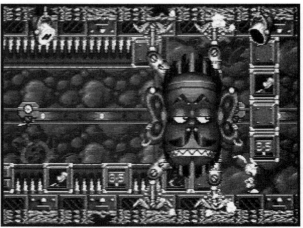

The key to survival is flipping the screen at the right time and taking every opportunity to hit the boss.

floor. When you reach the first flip switch, hit it as the boss is near it, then quickly hit the next three switches as soon as you can. Get one or two more hits on the boss, then hit the next switch at the last possible moment. Go to the right, avoiding the next switch, walking fast to stay ahead of the boss. As you climb the steps past the skipped switch, be ready to make a jump to a higher ledge ahead so you can get a Slammer Head from HeadCase. Hit the next switch to turn the boss green, then keep going right while getting in as many hits as possible. These really count, since the Slammer head increases your strength. Hit the next switch so you can avoid the wide bed of spikes on the floor (making it the ceiling), then skip the next switch so you don't flip over into that bed of spikes. Hit the next switch which is located directly next to a wall. Hit the next two switches quickly (the boss will be back to green after the second). Hit the boss rapidly. You should be able to finish him off in this area.

Stage 9

✤ **Scene 9-1 (Fatal Contraption):** Trouble Bruin will chase you up a long climb. You can't attack the car until you reach the top floor, so don't worry about him. Grab the Slammer Head from HeadCase and use it to break through the blocks on the left. Jump to the next floor up, at the center of the screen and hit the left of the two green up arrows to move the platform up. Jump up to the next floor left as soon as possible and hit whichever green up arrow isn't being weighted down by the wooden face. The spikes that move from left to right along the red wires are very difficult to avoid, but they don't cause much damage. As soon as you can, jump up to the top of the wall at the center, then run to the right and jump up to the next floor before the rising platform crushes you up against the spikes. Run to the left and jump up to the next floor before the rising platform crushes you, then go to the center and stay on the rising platform. Move left or right to avoid the spikes, which luckily don't move. Stay near the center, then go to the left of the 500 point item. You can grab the next two 500 point items safely, but be careful not to touch any part of the spikes. If you grab the Pin Head from HeadCase you can go up the right side and collect two extra lives, but the small tanks make the path risky. As long as you grab one of the extra lives you'll break even, starting over at the bottom. We suggest playing it safe and grabbing the Slammer Head from HeadCase, then go up the left side, hitting the platforms with

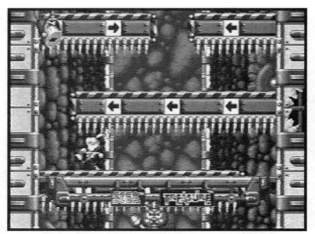

It's important to stay ahead of the rising platform by jumping up to the next floor as soon as possible.

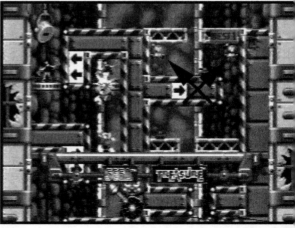

Near the top you can risk going for two extra lives with the Pin Head, or use the Slammer Head and play it safe.

the dancing ladies up quickly. When you reach the next barrier you must hit the next two Slammer blocks quickly before your head wears out, or run to the right and hit the "Shoot" block. Above is the stage where Trouble Bruin will attack. It looks scary, but when you realize you're not controlling Headdy you'll feel better knowing you don't have to fight the kitty now.

Scene 9-2 (Far Trek): Chances are your energy will be at a critical point as you enter this scene, so be sure to grab the banana at the very beginning before Trouble Bruin can catch you. The cat will try to jump on you and grab you, while his walking robot machine chases and attacks at the same time! You can't harm the cat or his machine. The beams from the machine are easy enough to avoid, but when the cat puts his bear hug on you, you're helpless in avoiding the

Keep moving and jumping to avoid Trouble Bruin's bear hug and the beams of the contraption.

beams. Keep moving rapidly left and right, and jump a lot as the cat gets near you to avoid his hug.

Scene 9-3 (Finale Analysis): Oh no! It's the final boss! If you think those other bosses were tough, wait until you see this one! Somehow the programmers thought it would be cute to place a small crystal ball in the bosses hand that would flash colors, and the attack that followed would correspond to the color in the ball. Well, it could take you a few dozen lives before you even realized the colors in the ball were changing, then another few dozen lives to figure out what the colors correspond to. That's why we're here to help you!

Your head will be surrounded with head icons before each attack by the boss. Hit Start to pause the game as the color is in the ball. Then decide which head to use (see next page) and grab it as you unpause the game. The only tricky color is the "flashing" ball, which is hard to spot since you'll see a solid color when you pause the game, and since the ball always flashes solid yellow before showing any of the solid colors or flashing signal.

The key to beating the boss is watching the signal in his crystal ball, then choosing your head accordingly.

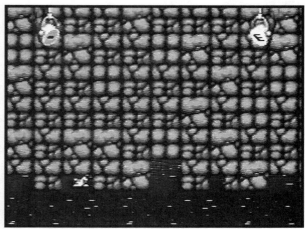

The orange ball signals the roof will be falling, and the Pin Head will make it easier to avoid.

The only time you can hit the boss is during the moment the head icons surround your head.

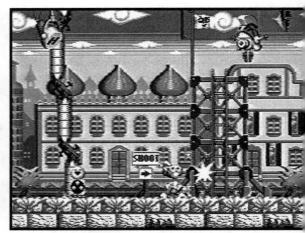

After 17 hits the boss is defeated and you'll be treated to an extremely long ending sequence.

✴ Look at the color of the orb in the bosses hand, then choose your weapon accordingly.

> **ORANGE:** Roof is going to fall — use Pin Head and position under one of the holes as the roof comes crashing down.
>
> **BLUE:** Boss will shoot electric balls — use Pin Head and stand close (under bosses cape)
>
> **FLASHING:** Big laser - use Pin Head.
>
> **GREEN:** Spike missiles — use Pin Head and stand close (under bosses cape), or use Slammer Head and destroy all spikes.
>
> **PINK:** Little enemies - use either shooting head (War Head or Pig Head).

✴ The only time you can hit the boss is when the head icons are spinning around your head. This make it extremely difficult, because you have to avoid hitting one of the icons when you're attacking him You'll also only be able to get in one hit per round, making this a long battle. The moment the bos reappears after an attack, stand next to him and hit him once with your head to make sure you're stand ing close enough, then the moment the icons appear, shoot your head through two of them to hit the boss. Pause, decide which icon you want to grab, then unpause and grab it. It takes 17 (!!!) hits to destroy the boss. On a positive note, the ending sequence is even longer than the last battle. If you're curious about the passcode requested at the end of the credits, see the Bonus Round section at the beginning of this chapter.

Awesome Secrets

✴ **Stage Select:** From the first title screen hit Start to reach the screen where the Options can be chosen Press C, A, Left, Right, B. You should hear a sound, indicating the trick worked. Press Start to begin the game and you'll see a Stage Select where you can choose any stage in the entire game.

✴ **Secret Bonus Points:** Throughout each stage of each scene are hidden Secret Bonus Points that give you extra points at the end of the scene if you can find them. When you *do* find one, you'll hear a "Secret Bonus Point" voice. Chances are you've figured out a few, but some of these were impossible In case you want to give it a try, here's a complete list of every Secret Bonus Point in the game.

✴ **SCENE 1:** Destroy the Robo-Collector that grabs your friends before he leaves the screen (1-1).

SCENE 2:

✸ Clear each of the practice rooms (Hangman, Headcase, Beau) for a Secret Bonus Point from each one (2-1).

✸ Hit the tower to knock off the soldier on the bottom floor (if you hit him first, you won't get the point) (2-2).

✸ After beating the dancing boss, a cage rises up from the ground. Defeat the old man and his mule for one point each (a total of two points) (2-2).

✸ When you reach Headcase, select the Spike Head icon and climb up the first passage to fight a snake worth 1 bonus point (2-3).

✸ Defeat Bino during the fight with the boss (2-4).

SCENE 3:

✸ Defeat the Smiley Ball that rolls out of the second box on the third rotating platform (3-1).

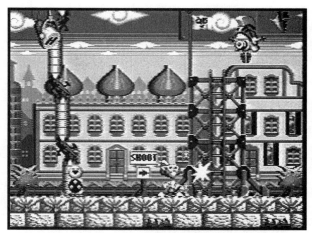

Hitting the soldier will gain you some points, but knocking him off the tower from below is a Secret Bonus Point.

✸ Defeat the special floating cat while enjoying the wild ride backstage with Trouble Bruin. The special floating cat will look similar to the floating bears that Trouble Bruin releases, only he looks different. Since you spend most of this stage feeling totally out of control, you may not be able to catch this point (3-2).

✸ Defeat the puppeteer (the top guy) before defeating his puppet (the bottom guy) (3-3).

✸ Defeat Bino during fight with boss (3-4).

SCENE 4:

✸ Hit the first "Hit Me" switch 20 times (4-1).

✸ Destroy Supertanks bouncing bullet (4-1).

✸ Destroy the purple statue that blocks the fountain (4-1).

✸ Destroy all boxes in the level (4-2).

✸ Destroy a fan (4-3).

✸ Destroy the other fan (4-3).

✸ Defeat Bino during the fight with the boss (4-4).

SCENE 5:

✸ Climb the tower twice while fighting Trouble Bruin (5-2).

✸ Defeat arms boss without losing energy (5-3).

✸ Defeat running Bino during fight with boss (5-4).

SCENE 6:

✸ Get Smiley in Headcase before getting a plane at the very beginning of the stage (6-1).

✸ Destroy rocket with cow in it (6-1).

✸ Defeat Bino after old man's head opens (6-4).

SCENE 7:

✸ Destroy the special cow. He's the first black cow after the HeadCase (7-1).

Destroy the special black cow after the HeadCase on Stage 7-1 for a Secret Bonus Point.

- Destroy funny-looking bird. He's in a tree to the right of the HeadCase (7-1).
- Defeat Bino in bosses hand (7-1).

SCENE 8:
- Collect all items (8-1).
- Destroy falling knight after battle (8-2).
- Hit heart that surrounds the boss 3 times in a row (8-3).
- Hit second to last "don't shoot" sign (above the exit). All others will give you a Head Trip (8-3).
- Destroy 3 bullets from enemy (8-4).
- Defeat Bino during fight with boss (8-5).

SCENE 9:
- Destroy one rock statue (9-1).
- Destroy all of the blocks with Slammer Head (9-1).
- Don't let the cat grab you more than three times (9-2).
- Destroy all rising spikes with Slammer Head (9-3).

Shoot this sign over the exit of stage 8-3
to see a smiley face and collect a Secret Bonus Point.

EARTHWORM JIM

CATEGORY: Platform
PLAYERS: 1

DEVELOPER: Shiny Entertainment
PUBLISHER: Playmates

Introduction

Earthworm Jim is the mega-hyped game by Shiny Entertainment, and it deserves all the hype. Besides having one of the coolest characters around, *Earthworm Jim* is a challenging and fun platform game—and it has good music, too. And if you ever get bored (or frustrated, as is the case), just let go of the controller to see the hilarious animations. The difficulty ranges from Practice to Difficult, but don't expect to beat the game easily, even on Practice or Normal.

One of the best-selling games in recent history is the critically-acclaimed Earthworm Jim!

Basic Strategies

❋ Earthworm Jim has the ability to fire in many different directions, but unlike most games, there is no projectile, just a huge muzzle flash. It's important to know that even though an enemy isn't in the direct line of fire, it can still be hit. Hold down the fire button and wiggle the control pad in the general direction for the best results. Jim can also fire a huge megablast that destroys nearly anything it hits, but you have to get the gun icon with the electricity around it to do so. Jim can also use his head like a whip. He can only whip his head in seven directions: up, left, up-left, right, up-right, down-left, and down-right. You can get extra ammo and extra energy by getting the various power-ups for each one. The small blue energy balls give you four percent of your energy back, while the bigger red ones fill you up all the way.

❋ There are some basic moves in *Earthworm Jim* that soon become a critical aspect to beating the game: the jump, the head-swing, and the helicopter move.

❋ The Up-and-Over Jump: This jump is mainly used to reach platforms above you and to avoid certain enemy attacks. Simply press the jump button to jump straight up and use the control pad to move Jim left or right.

❋ The Long Jump: This jump allows Jim to leap over dangerous areas and small land-based enemies. To do this jump, just start running left or right and then press the jump button.

❋ The Head-Swing: Jim literally uses his head for this one. With this move, Jim can latch onto certain spots and swing across to other areas of the level. Some of these spots are obvious (such as a hook in the middle of nowhere) and some aren't (like the moose antler in level one). All of these spots, however, can be identified by a sparkle.

✦ The Helicopter Move: This move can be used to get across large pits or to float down from high areas to collect power-ups. Jump in the air (or fall) and start to press the jump button repeatedly. It helps to have a control pad with a rapid-fire option. If you don't have one, plan on resting your thumb a lot.

Level 1: New Junk City

✦ This level is a big junkyard. Use this level to get used to the controls and perfect Jim's jumps and head swing. There is no time limit so you can practice as long as you like.

✦ Start out by going right. Shoot the crow until it explodes and latch onto the chain. About halfway across a very ugly dog will try and ravage the lower half of your body. Destroy it and continue on. When you get off the platform, jump up and you'll see a chain above you. This chain will be important later on.

✦ Next you'll come up to a refrigerator hanging by a chain. Go even further and you'll see a tree trunk and a cow. Either shoot or whip the fridge to bring it crashing down onto the tree trunk. The trunk will catapult the cow to who knows where. Afterwards a sign will flash on the screen saying "Cow Launched." This part probably has no relevance to the game, but you have to do this to continue on. There will be another crow to get rid of afterwards.

✦ After killing the crow there will be a large pile of tires that you have to get across. Instead of walking, the tires will make you bounce around. Move yourself across with the control pad until you reach a column of tires. Use the jump button to bounce higher and negotiate the column up to the top. When you reach the top, bounce to the left onto the small platform. Jump up the two other platforms and shoot the dog above you before latching onto the trolley to the left. Latch onto the trolley and let it take you to the left (you'll collect some energy along the way).

✦ Right before the trolley drops, do an up-and-over jump to the left. If you go far enough, you'll see a moose head. With a well timed head whip, you can latch onto the moose's antler on the right. Do it correctly, and you'll land on the chain you saw at the beginning of the stage. Go left and up on the platform you come across. Above you is a series of trolleys that you have to scale to get up. Jump onto the first trolley. When it reaches the middle of its chain, jump to the next trolley. Do this on each trolley, and you'll make it to the top with no problems.

✦ After getting off the trolleys, go left and kill the two dogs you come across. Follow the path and

Latch onto the moose head's antlers for a shortcut out of this stage.

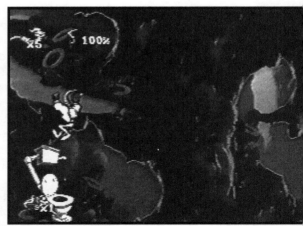

Flush yourself down the toilet and instantly be teleported to the end of this level.

grab the gun. Drop down and you'll see a toilet to the left. Jump into it. The toilet will teleport you to another part of the stage. You'll end up below ground standing on a platform with a gun on it. Grab the gun and jump onto the platform on the right. Jump off the right edge of the platform and whip your head left to latch onto the hook that is underneath. You'll swing to the left collecting guns. Continue going left (you can walk through the wall) and get the gun that's on the other side of the wall. Then jump to the platform to the left that leads to a 1-up. If you need any energy, just drop down directly below the 1-up and you'll get two energy balls. Make your way up and you'll come across the first mini-boss of this stage.

Taking the trash out shouldn't be this hard.

* The first mini-boss is a trashcan with wheels that can take on a humanoid form with the tires acting as arms and legs. To defeat the boss, get about three inches away from it and whip it with your head. It will drop a French horn on you after a couple of seconds. Shoot the horn away and continue to blast the boss. It will then try to nail you with an anvil. You can shoot this away so you can concentrate your fire power on the boss. After you shoot the anvil, the boss will transform into a vehicle. It resembles a soap-box racing car a kid would build (only it has six wheels). When it gets close, use an up-and-over jump to clear it and head to the opposite side of the screen. If you try a long jump, the boss can hit you. If he does, he'll knock you way up into the air, then hit you again as you come down. Continue this process and you should make quick work of this boss.

* After defeating the boss, climb up and latch onto the hook at the top of the screen. Swing left to get a huge energy boost. Then go right and you'll come up on another stone ladder. Again, use the helicopter move at the top to get your gun refilled. Helicopter to the far left to get energy and to get to another "Continue" spot. Make sure you get this continue because to the right is the second (and last) boss of level 1.

* This boss resembles a disgruntled construction worker, only fatter and more disgusting. You can't harm him by directly shooting him. Instead, use the wooden boxes that are dropped on the ground. When the box lands, use your head to whip it across the ground and onto a spring at the right side of the screen.

The spring will shoot the box up and it will hit the boss. After the boss is hit, he will begin to belch out fish at you (obviously manners aren't at the top of his list). Go to the far left until the fishes reach you, then run underneath them to the right. The magnet that drops the boxes alternates between the boxes and French horns. When the magnet appears with the horn, make sure you have enough room to move out of the way. You'll have to do some tricky maneuvering to avoid the horns and the fishes. After hitting him with two or three boxes, the boss will move to the center of the screen. When a box drops onto the ground, whip it twice to get it close to the spring. When the boss moves back to the right, time your third whip in order to knock the box up to hit him. After the box hits him, he'll start to belch the fish

Use the spring on the right of the screen to launch boxes into this fish hurling boss.

out again, except this time he'll move back and forth. Avoid all the fish by staying to the far right next to the spring (but watch out for the horns!). Continue the pattern to defeat this boss.

Race With Psy-Crow

- ✻ In between each stage, you have to race this bounty hunter who wants your suit. Along the way are meteors, turbo boosts, electric force fields, and lots of blue balls (ahem).
- ✻ Meteors: Avoid these. If you hit one, you stop dead in your tracks allowing Psy-Crow to catch up to you and possibly pass you up.
- ✻ Turbo Boosts: These hurl you through the space tunnel at an amazing speed. Use these to leave Psy-Crow behind, but be careful. In the later stages, he starts to grab them also.
- ✻ Electric Force Fields: Collect these and use them to smash through the meteors and knock Psy-Crow back some. They only last temporarily so be sure to get as many as possible.
- ✻ Blue Bonus Balls: Collect fifty or more before the race ends and you get an extra continue. The races aren't very hard, but they can get tricky. If by chance Psy-Crow beats you, you have to fight him on the planet's surface. Avoid his hook gun and blast at him. When you hit him, he'll be stunned for a couple of seconds. Use this time to whip him with your head. Keep this up and sooner or later, he'll fly away.

Level 2: What the Heck?

- ✻ Jim must have done something very bad to be sent to this place. This level is filled with hidden spots that shoot fire out at you, so be on the lookout.
- ✻ At the beginning of the stage, jump up to collect a gun. Follow the path until you come upon a floating demon. It's a good idea to kill these as soon as you see them; if you don't, they start to gang up on you as you go along. Keep following the path (you'll meet up with a couple of more demons along the way) until you come to a point where you can go up or right. Go right first to collect a gun and some energy, then go up. When you come across a bar that you can hang onto, jump onto it then drop down. Go to the left to collect a gun then head right, following the path. There is a spot on the ground that looks like a small volcano. If you walk over it, it'll make a disgusting sound and send a stream of fire at you. Simply jump over the volcano to avoid any more headaches. Follow the path and kill the demon at the top. Get the energy ball and keep following the path until you come to a platform that's about head high (that's Jim's

Use this hook to swing to the left...

...then turn around and swing back to the right for the gun.

head, not yours). Jump on the platform to avoid the fire bellowing out of the ground. Grab the energy and slide down.

✤ When you get to the bottom of the slide, there will be a hook stationed right above you. To the right of the hook is a gun. Here is one point where all that swinging practice you did in Level 1 comes in. Go to the right of the hook and latch onto it. When you disconnect, immediately push the control pad in the opposite direction you're facing and whip your head again to re-attach yourself to the hook. You'll swing back to the right and get the gun. If you need more practice with this swinging technique, do it here. It will help you out tremendously later on in the game.

✤ After getting the gun, continue on to the right and go down the slide. The slide ends in a pit that will make you lose a life so be careful. Use the momentum of the slide to help you across the pit. Jump back to the right onto the platform. Do a long jump (that doesn't need to be so long) onto the next platform to the right to get a gun and an energy ball. Go back across the pit and continue to the left. There will be three demons to kill and some energy at the end of the path. After you get the energy, jump onto the platform above you and jump to the right. Grab the continue and jump on the platform next to you. Use the hook to swing across to the chain. Move along the chain to the left and you'll see a green crystal below you that is spinning in one place.

Running on this crystal will take you up to a higher level. Be sure not to fall off.

✤ The secret to the crystal is to ride it like a logger would do. To do this, drop from the chain onto the left side of the crystal. Tap the control pad to the right two or three times, then hold it down when you feel confident you won't walk off the other side. If you time the walk right, you will be walking on the crystal in much the same way a logger does a log. The crystal will take you up to the next part of the stage.

✤ When the crystal stops going up, there will be a platform to the left with a 1-up underneath it and a hook to the right that you can latch onto. Swing to the right and land on the platform there. Latch back onto the hook and swing left. You'll land in an alcove that contains the 1-up. If you've done this quick enough, the crystal should still be in a reachable place (when you get off the crystal, it slowly heads back down). If it is, use it again to get back up. If it isn't, then make your way back around to the crystal (it doesn't take that long).

✤ When you reach the platform again, go up to the chain and to the left. Drop down next to the wheel that has a chain wrapped around it. This wheel is used to open the gate to the left. Hit the

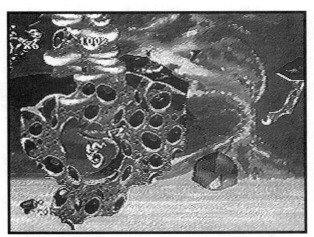

Use the hook on the right to get this extra man.

wheel with your head about two times and the gate will be open far enough to go under. If you continue left, you'll find another wheel and a lawyer that will start to throw legal documents at you. Down and to the right of the wheel is a hook that is underneath the walkway. Position yourself correctly so that you

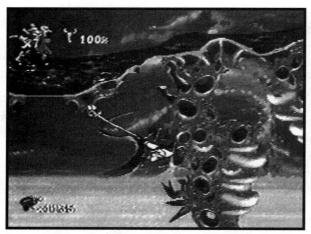

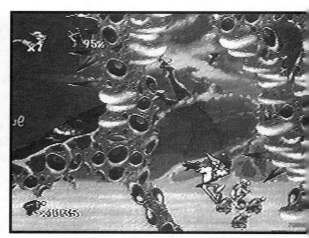

Push down and drop right
through the platform to reach this hook.

Don't leave this extra man behind,
because you'll need it later on.

can kneel down and latch onto the hook. You'll swing through the ground and wind up below the walkway. If you use this route instead of continuing to the left, you get to skip one of the bosses of this stage. Use the hook again to swing to the right through the wall. There is energy and a 1-up here. Walk through the wall to the left and touch the "Continue."

As you start to go to the left, Evil the Cat will through a bomb that will make stalactites fall. Run along the path until you run into a wall then quickly start to run the other way until you reach the continue again. Wait for a couple of more seconds until the stalactites stop falling. Follow the path back up again and go up when you run out of walkway. Make your way up until you see two hooks. Use these hooks to help you continue your way to the chain that is extended across the screen. At the beginning of the chain at the top of the screen there is an invisible hook. You can see the sparkle that it emits if you look carefully. Swing on this hook to collect the various power-ups that line the chain. Be on the look-out for another invisible hook at the other end of the chain. This will help you get the other items that you miss.

Drop down on the far right of the chain and go to the right and you'll come across two green crystals like you encountered before. Unlike the other crystal, however, you don't need to run on this one to make it

go. Jump on the left crystal first and let it take you up (avoid the fire spitting out of the wall). When it reaches the top of the rock structure, jump over the structure to the left to get the 1-up. You'll fall through the rock and land back at the bottom. Now get on the crystal on the right and ride it up (again, avoiding the fire from the walls). Follow the path until you come to a ledge that has a small pit of spikes to the right of it. Right underneath the ledge is a 'Continue' spot. Kill the demons that lurk in this area and touch the continue. Make your way right until you get another wheel that opens a gate. If you have a mega plasma blast, it's a good idea to shoot the lawyer at the bottom before opening the gate. If you don't have one then this next part will take some timing. Use your head to whip the wheel three times at about one

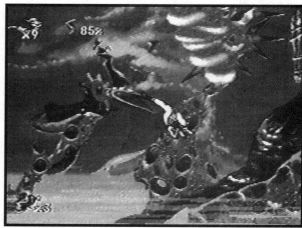

Whip this wheel three times in one-second intervals
to open the gate on the right.

second intervals. Then jump off and go under the gate. This is easier if the lawyer is dead because he can really get on your nerves (just like in real life).

✳ Go under the gate and go up. Use the hook to the upper left to swing across. At the peak of your swing, whip your head again to latch onto another hook. If you miss, go right and repeat the gate process again. Killing the lawyer the first time really saves a lot of headache if you keep messing up. If you don't miss, you'll swing to a small ledge. Climb up and kill the two demons that are there. Once on the ledge, jump along the small ledges to the right. There will be some demons to kill along the way. If you need energy, there is some under the small platforms that are risky to get. The best way to get them is to walk off the

ledge and point the control pad up and in the opposite direction you fell. This will grab the energy and grab onto the ledge so you won't fall all the way down. Continue on all the way to the right and you'll get to another green crystal. Treat this like you did the first one (ride it logger style). This takes you to Evil the Cat's lair.

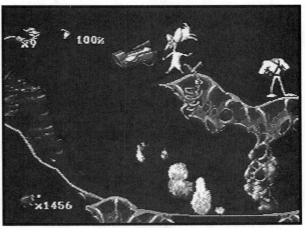
Whoa! Jim sure is skinny without his suit.

✳ This is the first time you see Jim out of his suit. He is indeed just an earthworm. There is a ledge that has both your suit (which is waving at you) and Evil the Cat (who is shooting at you). Evil fires fire at the top of the platform you are standing on. The fire then trails down the path to get to you. Simply jump over the fire to avoid it. The trick here is to jump over enough of Evil's shots so that they hit the platform he is standing on. Sometimes, Evil stops to lick himself (he is a cat after all) so you'll have to taunt him by jumping up and down in front of him. The platform that Evil is standing on will melt each time a shot hits it. If it's hit with enough shots, the platform will collapse and Evil will run away. Slime your way over to the right and you'll find your suit, eagerly pointing at the open spot that your head once occupied. Jump on the suit to become the kick-butt earthworm you once were.

✳ Continue to the right to face Evil for the last time. The background is dark and Evil is black when he attacks. The only things you can see are his beady little eyes. Focus on these every time he attacks. Every time you hit him, two streams of flame trail toward you along the ground from both sides at different intervals. Time your jumps carefully and keep your eyes peeled for Evil; he attacks swiftly after the flames leave. The easiest way to hit Evil as

Look for Evil's beady eyes, then blow them away.

he appears is to stare at the center of the screen and use peripheral vision to blast the first thing that moves (which will be Evil). Like all cats, Evil has nine lives. Each time you hit him, the number of lives wasted appears on his chest. When this number reaches nine, he flies away for good and you fly off on your rocket.

Level 3: Down the Tubes

⚡ There isn't much to this stage. The enemies are enough to worry about, so the stage is easy to negotiate; just go where the tubes take you. There are, however, parts of the level where you have to pilot a bubble ship under the water to get to the next part of the stage.

⚡ At the beginning, follow the tubes right. The main enemy is a floating sponge creature that is very weak. One shot will destroy them. The next enemy is a drone cat that looks more like a gorilla. The only way to get by these nasties is to hang from the small oval bubble that is at the top of the tube. While hanging, press up on the control pad to lift your bottom up so the drone cat can't grab you. If he does, he'll proceed to beat the stuffing out of you and take off lots of precious energy. After the cat goes under you, drop down and proceed right. You'll face more sponges and cats along the way so be on the lookout. As you travel along the tubes, look along the oval bubbles at the top. These usually contain either energy or extra ammo. When you run out of tubes, you'll enter a room that has a platform at the far end of the wall. Get the energy and ammo there and latch onto the post in front of you and swing across to the other side. If you keep going left, you'll run across a room that has a hamster locked up in a tube. Go back to the right and latch onto the next post you come across. You'll swing up into a tube that takes you up.

Whip this switch to release the hamster below.

⚡ Go left into a room that has a switch. Shoot the sponges and whip the switch. This opens the hamster cage. Keep going left and latch onto the post at the end of the tube. Swing across and jump back to the right to get a major energy boost. Then get on the hamster and hold down any button to make him chomp the little creatures along the way.

⚡ When the hamster stops, you'll end up directly under a mega-gun power-up and a tube that leads up. Jump up to get the power-up and you'll be sucked into the tube that leads to an airship capsule.

⚡ While in the capsule, use the "Jump" button to control the air jets that make the capsule move. The longer

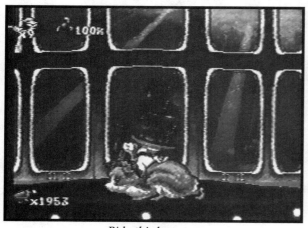

Ride this hamster
Through the forthcoming enemies.

Make sure you guide this capsule carefully
— once it cracks, you're history.

you hold the button down, the faster you go. Go directly to the right and go into the tunnel of rock. Stop when you get to a junction of cables then go down. You'll reach a landing platform where you'll exit the capsule and enter the next part of the stage. Go right and touch the "Continue," then follow the tubes up and right. There is a part of the tube that is blocked off. Head back to the left and go up the second tube that leads up. Go to the left and whip the switch that is there. Head right and avoid the two drone cats by hanging from the oval bubbles. After the cats, keep going right and drop down the tube at the end of the corridor. Go all the way right and you'll get to another air capsule.

✦ After you launch off in the capsule, go right and then down until you reach a metal structure sticking out of the rock. These give you more time (in this case, it fills it up to 30). To refill your time, you need to touch the metal stem that's on the left side of the capsule to the tip of the filling station. Make sure you reach each of these filling stations because time is very precious. Stick to the right wall of rock and head down. Get the mega-gun along the way and refill your time at the second filling station further down. Go right and keep to the bottom. This will take you to the next filling station. After leaving the filling station, keep to the wall of rock on the right. Follow this wall and it'll take you to the next part of the stage.

✦ After you drop down from the capsule, head right until you reach one of those small creatures similar to the ones that the hamster ate. I hope you have enough energy (at least 25 percent) because there is no hamster and no way to avoid this guy. Let him grab you and he'll slam you on the ground and throw you to the right.

✦ When you recover, you'll be in a small alcove that has a tube to the left that leads up. Don't go up the tube. Instead, jump up through the rock ceiling and you'll be sucked up into a tube that way. Go right and you'll enter a large tube. At the left edge of the tube, there is a platform that looks like it is too high to jump to. Jump up below the platform anyway and you'll be sucked up onto the platform. There is a mega energy ball here that should restore the energy you lost from the kitten guard. Go to the far right, and you'll fly off to the next stage.

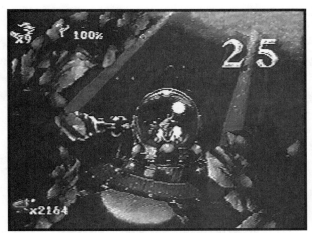

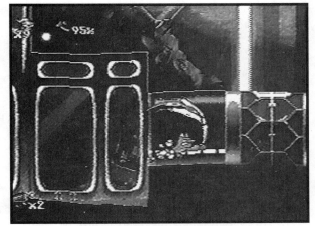
Carefully move to these refilling valves to obtain more time.

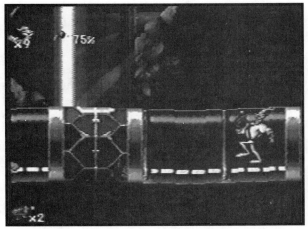
Don't bother trying to kill this guy.

Use this hidden passage to obtain an extra man.

Tube Race

✵ This is an extension of the last stage. The major portion of this stage is in the air capsule, and the way to the stopping point can be tricky.

✵ Head right and use controlled jumps to make it past the two kitten guards. Be sure not to get caught by the first guard. If you do, then he'll slam you on the ground and toss you to the next guard, who'll take his turn pounding on you. These two can take off up to forty percent of your energy alone. Continue to the right; there is a platform at the end of the tunnel that has a post you can grab onto.

✵ Swing across to the right and grab on to what appears to be an invisible ledge. This is a secret cave that has an energy boost in it. Getting this would be a good idea if you got nabbed by the kitten guards at the beginning. Drop down from here and go to the bottom. Head right to switch open the hamster cage. Get on the hamster and chomp the guards on your way to the air capsule. When you get off the hamster, jump from the ledge to grab the energy, then jump down to get the continue and ammo. Go left and jump up into the capsule.

✵ This is the last (and toughest) of the water mazes. Go to the left and connect to the filling station. This will boost your time up to 99, so be sure not to miss it; this is the last filling station you'll have. When you're finished having your time filled up, go down and to the right. Follow the lower wall of rock. There is really only one way to go, but there are lots of tricky twists and turns. You must be quick; a minute and a half isn't as long as it seems. You'll know when you're getting near the end because you'll start to see flashing lights along the walls.

✵ Probably the toughest object of this part of the stage is not bumping into the walls. Even though you have to hurry, don't go too fast because once you bump into one wall, you'll ricochet into others. When you reach the end, drop down and head to the right. Kill off the last three sponges and go into the next room to find Goldfish Bob. Either shoot him, whip him, or simply touch him and he'll fall off onto the floor.

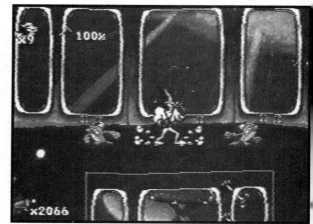

If you touch either of these kittens, you'll lose massive amounts of energy.

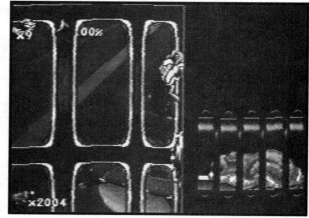

Go in here if you were damaged by the kittens.

Goldfish Bob is the easiest boss in the game. Simply touch him and he's dead.

Level 4: Snot a Problem

🪱 This stage is a bungee-cord battle between Jim and Major Mucus. There are three rounds, each progressively harder than the previous one. The way to win is to break the other guy's cord (or in Mucus' case, snot line). To do this, bang your opponent into the wall. When you reach the bottom of the pit, you'll notice an eye peeping out from the goo. Avoid this eye at all costs. This is actually a tongue set out to snare earthworms for lunch. If it's able to chomp you, you automatically lose one life.

🪱 Round 1: Use this round to get use to the controls. You can control yourself to a great extent horizontally, but only control yourself slightly vertically. You can also do a shoulder rush; use this move to knock Mucus into the wall. Mucus is easy this round so you can take your time.

🪱 Round 2: This round isn't that difficult either. The best way to defeat Mucus is to slam into him at the beginning of the round to get him closer to the wall. When you reach the bottom, you'll spring up before he will. As you're going up, get as close to the wall as you can without hitting it. Mucus will follow you up. As he gets near, move away from the wall and start to bash Mucus into the wall. This should make short work of him this round if you repeat this pattern.

🪱 Round 3: This round is tough. Keep using the same method against Mucus as used in Round 2. Sometimes, however, when you start to bang Mucus into the wall, he'll start to spin violently, letting slime fly off himself. When he does this, stay away; this is his method of attack and it is devastating if you happen to get caught near a wall. Wait until he stops spinning, then resume the pattern all over again.

🪱 There are times when it seems you are in a no-win situation. You are at the bottom of the pit waiting to sling back up, but the slime creature is near you, Mucus is on one side of you, and the wall is on the other. In cases like this, it's best to hit the wall. When you do, you'll be knocked up a little bit. The monster will miss you and you'll shoot back up with only a few scratches.

Get into this position and slam Mucus into the wall to tear his snot cord.

Don't try to touch Mucus when he is spinning — it's "snot" good for you (giggle, snort).

Level 5

🪱 This level is the lab of Professor Monkey-for-a-head. It's filled with electrodes and failed experiments. The main problem with this stage is the enemies because they like to gang up on you. As soon as you see one of the bad guys, kill it because doing so will save a lot of headache (and energy).

Go right at the start and shoot the green brain that's flying around. Shoot it once and it bursts open letting out three worm-like creatures. These larva bounce around and really get annoying. It takes one hit each to dispatch them. After killing the brain, go left and latch onto the hook; swing onto the black sphere and very quickly jump to get the power-up. If you wait too long, you'll get zapped by electricity. Head right and kill the two pink brains that are jumping along the ground. Along the way are a series of electrodes, three of which have electricity running through them. Jump on the lowest electrode to the far left. This

is the only one that isn't electrified and can be used as a starting point for the other three. Time your jumps to avoid getting electrocuted along the electrodes. As you jump off the last electrode, latch onto the hook that is to the right and swing onto the chain. Drop off from the chain and kill the green brain. Then jump onto the black sphere to the right and quickly jump up onto the platform with the red target on it.

Shoot this target to get the escalators to move.

Shoot the target and go back down collecting the energy as you go. Head back to the beginning and go up where you see the escalator going up. Ride the escalator and kill the green brain when you get to the top. Head left and up onto the platform above, and then go right (there are two brains to kill along the way; one green, the other pink).

The next part of the stage is a series of black spheres that must be negotiated quickly to avoid getting hurt. First jump onto the first sphere to the right of the platform you're on. The next sphere is to the right and down a little. As you jump from this sphere, you'll see two spheres just above you; land in between these two to get to the third sphere. Follow the spheres counter-clockwise until you reach the top sphere. Jump to the right to get the ammo and quickly jump back to the right and latch onto the hook that is beyond the sphere. You'll land on another sphere, so quickly latch onto the hook that is up and to the left of that sphere. Go up the stairs and jump on them from above. Head right, kill the green brain, and grab the continue spot. Continue right until you end up in a spherical cage.

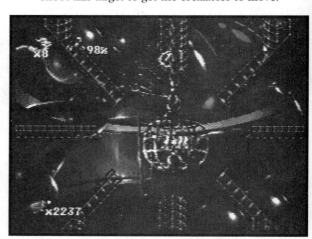

Get ready to shoot in all directions while travelling along in this cage.

The cage will take you to a spot where there are eight tracks pointing at you. From these tracks come little cell-like organisms, three at a time. They travel fast, but luckily they also travel in a pattern. The way to beat this part is to shoot the cells as they come off the tracks. The track order for the first set is: left track, upper-left track, upper-right track. Shoot in this pattern and you'll come out okay. The cage will then take you all around the lab to collect energy and ammo. It then stops at a second set of eight tracks, similar to the first set. The pattern for this set is: left track, upper-left track, right track, upper-right track. There have been a couple of occasions (though they are rare) when this pattern is broken. Still, this pattern will work the best. Once you've finished with this area, the cage takes you to another part of the level and drops you down a shaft with sharp metal things protruding from both walls. Helicopter down to collect all the power-ups and get the continue at the bottom.

✵ Jump off the platform, following the pattern of the energy balls until you land on a black sphere. Jump from that sphere onto the sphere to the right where the four guns are. Then leap from that one onto the third sphere to the right. Jump straight up and latch onto the hook; swing across to the platform and kill the pink brain.

✵ Go up and you'll see Professor Monkey-for-a-head (monkey side down). Shoot him quickly so he can't open up the compartment above you. If he does, little eyeballs with wings come out to attack you. Make your way left until you see the Professor again. Shoot him quickly again and he'll climb away again. Climb the stairs and make your way right, using the eyeball compartment as a stepping-stone. Jump onto the platform to the right and kill the two pink brains. Head up and to the left to meet the Prof for one last time. Repeat what you did the other times and go left. Use the hook to swing left and kill the pink brain on the platform you land on. Go up and swing on the hook to the right, reattach yourself to the hook and swing back to the left. If you hit the right spot, you should be teleported to a secret room.

Meet Professor Monkey-for-a-head.
He gets annoyingly fast.

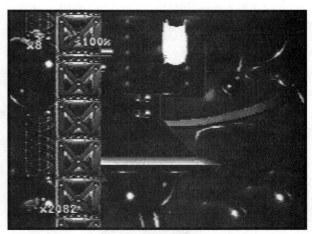

Look for this area
to enter the secret dark room.

Secret Room: Afraid of the Dark!

✵ This secret stage is pitch-black except for the beams of light that radiate from certain slots. The main enemy here is a beady pair of eyes (at least that's all you can see). All you have to do to get anywhere is to follow the lights. The object is to find the door marked "EXIT" so you can proceed to the next dark room.

✵ The first room is easy to get around in. Head right until you come to the first light. Then jump to the left onto the next lit platform. Jump to the left and climb up. Though you can't see it, you'll be on a chain that you can go across. When you reach the end, you'll fall. Point the control pad right so you'll fall right. Keep negotiating the terrain until you reach the door with the "EXIT" sign on it.

✵ At the second room, head right until you run into something. Make your way up and jump to the left to get to the light. Make your way left, jumping from platform to platform until you jump into a wall. At this point you'll have to jump up to get to the next light. Do a long jump to the right from this platform. Continue doing this until you make it to the "EXIT."

✵ In room three, head right. You'll see a 1-up, but you can't get to it from here. Go up and left, following the lights. Once you can't go any farther left, turn and go right until you reach the "EXIT" door. Jump over the door and go to the far right. You'll drop down to the 1-up. Make your way back up to the "EXIT" door from here and continue on.

⚡ In the fourth dark room, go all the way to the right until you come to a lit platform. To the left is a creature with the beady eyes. Look carefully and you'll soon see a sparkle, indicating that there is a hook there. Kill the creature and swing across. Be ready to latch onto another hook right after you detach from the first one. You'll swing from the second hook all the way to the "EXIT" door.

⚡ In the last room, there are no lights. Just go right until you come across a huge pair of eyes. Jim will give a surprised yelp (followed by his own pair of large eyes). Quickly run to the left until you reach a dead end (and hopefully not your dead end). Wait for the eyes to get near, then do a long jump to clear them. Quickly start running to the right until you come to a sphere with three lights coming out of it. This will teleport you back to the Professor's lab.

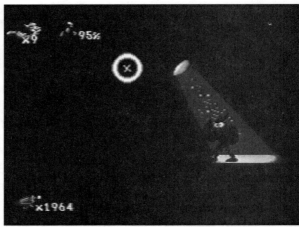

Look for this sparkle while in the dark room to find the hook leading out.

⚡ You'll wind up at the last place you were before you entered the dark rooms. Make your way to the right and you'll see a red pedestal. Jump over it and get the gun, then jump on the pedestal. You will be teleported to another part of the level.

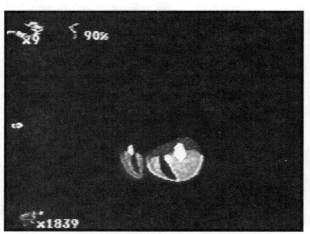

As soon as you see these eyes, start running to the left.

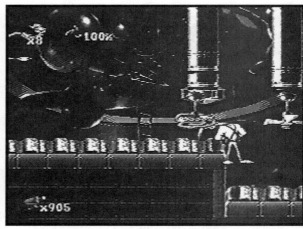

Jim gets whipped out of his suit when you get hit by a fan.

⚡ This part of the level is filled with annoying conveyor belts. Remember to kill the enemies as soon as you come across them. Go all the way down and to the left to get the energy. Then continue to the right until you come across a fan spinning horizontally. Run into the fan and Jim is whipped out of the suit. You walk along the upper track while the suit goes along on the conveyor belt below. Wait for your suit when you reach the end of the track. Jump into the neck to acquire the suit again then go back to the left of the track you were walking across.

⚡ To get under the fans, tap the control pad to inch your way through. If you try and run through them, you'll get sucked out again. Make your way left until you come across a series of hooks placed one on top of each other. Here's where some of that swinging practice helps out. Latch onto the first hook and swing, then when you let go, immediately turn the other direction and latch onto the hook higher up. Repeat this process to make your way up. At the top of the hook ladder, go right to collect some power-ups and a 1-up. Go back down and to the right and jump on the platform that has the "Continue" spot on it. Go up the stairs and kill the green brain. Latch onto the hook that's up and to the left and swing across. Go to the end of the conveyor belt to get more energy and ammo.

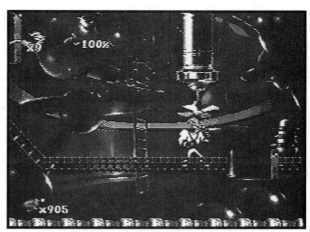

Walk slowly under the fan to avoid getting hit.

✦ Go back until you come across a second horizontal fan. Let the fan whip you out of your suit again and follow the same instructions here as you did earlier. Along the way, a green brain will come after you. You'll have to wait until you get your suit before you can kill him so avoid the brain while you're an ordinary worm. The conveyor belt will drop off at the end, but there is a hook to latch onto to swing to another conveyor belt. Kill the green brain and keep going to the right. There is another hook at the end of this conveyor belt as well so be ready. This hook leads to yet another conveyor belt. Go all the way to the right and up one conveyor belt. This one takes you to the left and to a chain. Grab onto the chain and proceed left. Drop off onto the next conveyor belt. When you reach the end of this one, don't jump onto the chain. Instead, jump to the left and latch onto the hook that's on the platform above you. You'll swing across onto a small platform. Use this platform to jump up over to the right. Continue going right and jump onto the red pedestal that takes you to the next part of the stage.

Stand directly under the monkey and shoot up to kill him.

✦ When you reappear, head right and then down at the end of the platform. Go left and you'll run into a conveyor belt. There is a chain above the belt that Professor Monkey-for-a-head has decided to occupy. He starts to throw stuff at you constantly. To get rid of him, walk along the conveyor belt until you are directly underneath him, then shoot him from below. He should run away. It's now safer to climb along the chain than to continue on the conveyor belt. Get rid of the various brains as you make your way to the left. Head down then to the right and you'll come across another conveyor belt/chain setup that you were just at. The

Hit this faucet valve to release power-ups, but don't get too greedy.

Professor is here as well. Use the same technique to get rid of him. Head all the way right and use the platforms there to go up.

✦ This next part can get pretty hairy. All you have to do is to follow the path that the platforms make for you to get to the next "Continue" spot. However, along the way, there are a lot of compartments that release those eyeballs with wings. Try not to stay in one spot for too long. It's also a good idea to clear the screen of bad guys about every five to ten seconds so they can't gang up on you. Once you get past this area, you'll come across another conveyor belt/chain setup like before. Get rid of the Professor as before and get on the chain for safety. Go left and you'll run across a red wheel connected to half a black sphere. If you whip the wheel, the sphere will release an item that will travel along the conveyor belt for you to get. At first these items are helpful ones like energy balls, extra ammo, etc. After a while, however, the items start to turn into creatures, so don't be greedy. Continue left and go down to reach the next "Continue." Use the chain to the right to go across, and be sure to avoid the electricity that's coming from the electrodes. Go all the way right and you'll come to the boss of this stage.

✦ The boss of this stage is really strange. It has a barrel for a body, a chicken for the head, and two robotic chicken legs. It also has what looks like a grappling hook attached to the front of it. In the center of the room is a chain that runs from left to right. Above the center of the chain is a dispenser. To the right of the dispenser is a red target. If you whip the target, a cellular organism (like from the beginning of this stage) falls out. This time, though, they are your weapons to defeat the chicken boss. The chicken boss attacks by either laying eggs that travel on the ground or sending exploding feathers after you. It also gets on the chain and travels across it. When it does, you can walk under it to get to the opposite side. What you want to do is to catch the boss when it's on the ground under the dispenser. You can then whip the target and send a cell crashing onto it. When the boss is hit, it breaks apart for a couple of seconds then rebuilds itself. If it's on the ground, then you can get a rhythm going that will trap the boss in that one place until it disappears. If you can't get that lucky, then you have to do it the tedious way. Avoid its feathers and eggs and wait for the right moment to hit the target. This takes longer but has the same results. After you hit it with enough cells, the boss flies away, and you go on to fight it again. Except this time, you're falling down a corridor.

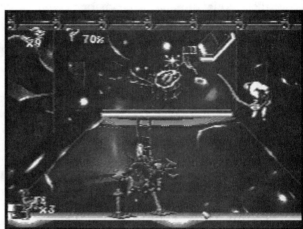
Wait for the chicken to go under the dispenser, then whip away.

✦ In this battle, you're falling down a very long corridor with spikes lining the walls. The boss is flying after you and trying to ram you. The best way to beat the boss is to play "keep away." Avoid the boss as it charges and shoot it. As before, when it gets hit, it breaks apart and rebuilds itself after a couple of seconds. Try and keep it in one spot by constantly shooting it when it tries to move. After you shoot it, it will shoot up a bomb. If you can

Avoid the walls and blast away at the falling chicken.

keep it from moving, the bombs will hit the boss as well. If it manages to get away, just repeat the pattern and you'll defeat this boss with little effort.

Level 6: For Pete's Sake

✣ This level is the most frustrating level of the game. Not only do you have to make it safely to the end, but you also have to help a small innocent looking puppy get safely to the end. This is easier said than done. Space ships, unipuses, and meteor showers are a few of the nasties that try to rain on your parade, and whatever you do, you can't let anything happen to Pete. Pete has an alter ego like the Hulk. If Pete is so much as breathed on wrong, he mutates into a two-eyed, many-toothed, purple, earthworm-man-gling monstrosity. Instead of trying to explain what to do on every platform that comes up on this level (and there are a lot of them), I'll explain the basic moves needed to make it somewhat safely to the end. I'll also give some tips on how to make this walk-in-the-park from Hell a little easier.

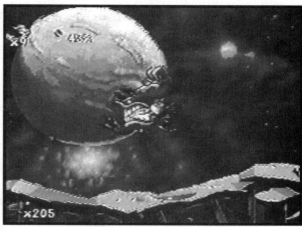
This is what happens when little Pete gets big.

✣ Stop: To make Pete stop, just shoot him with your gun. This move is used most often to stop Pete from continuing on while you are busy with all the hazards.

✣ Jump: Whip Pete with Jim's head to make him leap into the air. Use this move to help Pete get across the crevices between the platforms.

✣ The "Paddle-Ball": This is essentially a jump within a jump. Start off by whipping Pete into the air. Jump after him and whip him again before he hits the ground (much in the same way that you keep a paddle ball moving). This move is the most useful as it allows you to keep Pete off the ground out of harm's way.

SITUATION #1: SPACE SHIPS

✣ The space ships are not out to harm Pete; they're out to harm *you*. They cast a force field around you and hold you in one spot while Pete moves on his merry way towards some unseen danger. It is imperative to get rid of the ships as quickly as possible by shooting them. In some instances it is necessary to stop Pete as well so he can't go on. The ship can't get you if you are jumping, but they can and will try and get you when you land, so be cautious.

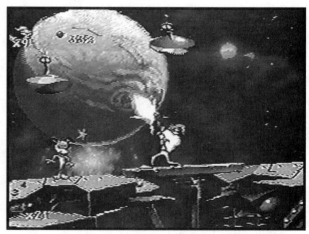
Pete won't get hit by the space ships, but make sure they don't hit you.

SITUATION #2: UNIPUSES

✣ The unipuses are those vine-like arms that protrude from the ground. They try and whip you around as well as try to grab Pete. As Pete approaches a unipus, shoot it first to make it duck down into its hole, then whip

Pete so he'll leap over the unipus. There are times when you whip Pete across a crevice and there is a unipus on the next ledge that Pete is heading toward. Simply shoot the unipus so Pete can land in safety.

SITUATION #3: METEOR SHOWERS

The meteor showers are meant to drain Jim's suit of its energy, but with a little fancy shooting, you should come out of it with hardly a scratch. The meteors range from small pebbles to large boulders and come from the top right of the screen. The small pebbles can't hurt you, but the larger rocks can. Wait until the larger rocks start to fall then start shooting the meteors from the sky like oversized clay pigeons. The simplest thing to do is to move the control pad back and forth in a circular motion from right to up while firing. You may start to run low on ammo, but there are usually some guns afterward that you can use to refill the blaster.

Hold Pete down while you fend off Meteors.

SITUATION #4: THE SEE-SAWS

The best way to get past the see-saws are to avoid them altogether. Use the paddle-ball technique to get over the see-saws. This is much easier than trying to negotiate them on foot. If the right part of the see-saw is up and Pete tries to walk across it, he'll fall down a pit, thus causing Jim great bodily harm. If you jump on the upper-most part of the see-saw while Pete is on the lower-most part, he'll spring into the air. If there are three see-saws in a row, it is harder to do the paddle-ball move than if there were just one or two. Simply get Pete onto the first see-saw, then paddle-ball him across the rest of the way.

SITUATION #5: SPRING LOADED PLATFORMS

Most of the time, all you have to do is step on the platforms to lower them to the ground so Pete can walk across. Some of them are so high, however, that even if you jump on them, they are still too high for Pete to get on. To handle this situation, make Pete jump so that he lands on the far left edge of the platform, then jump up on the platform yourself. To get off the platform, you can either have Pete jump off (by whipping him), or you can jump off first. If you jump off first, the platform will shoot back up and send Pete into the air. He'll land safely so don't worry about anything happening to him.

A spring.

SITUATION #6: THE HOOKS

✦ There are two spots in this stage where Pete is picked up by a hook and carried across part of the stage. When this happens, nothing can harm him. Unfortunately, there are plenty of things that can harm you. For example, after the first hook grabs Pete, there is a rolling cement mixer on the right. If one of these hit you, you bounce away from it, sometimes off of a ledge.

SITUATION #7: END OF STAGE LONG JUMP

✦ Don't jump until the screen scrolls all the way to the other side of this jump.

✦ At the end of the stage, a second hook will pick Pete up and carry him across a wide pit. You have to perform a very long jump in order to get across. Don't jump right away though because if Pete hasn't let the screen scroll to the next platform, you can't make it across; this will lead to a loss of life and being sent back into the stage some.

✦ You'll know you've reached the end of the stage when you come across an old road sign with a skull on it. Pete then goes into his dog house and waves at you. You'll fly away on your rocket, collecting the extra ammo at the end of the screen as you leave.

A hook.

Finally, little Pete has found his hole.

Level 7: Intestinal Distress

✦ This level resembles the inside of an intestinal tract (hence the name). The main enemies are floating fish and the sponge enemies like in Level 3. The main problem, however, comes from these big boulders (or gallstones as the case may be) that drop from nowhere. These stones roll down the platforms you're walking on, or simply drop on you.

✦ Start the level off by entering the tube to the left. This tube will shoot you up into the air onto a higher platform. Head right along the platform until you come up on two fish. Destroy the fish and inch forward. You should see a boulder come rolling down from the right very quickly (it won't hit you though). After you see a boulder disappear, quickly move right to the end of the path; jump up to the left and go to the upper most edge of the platform. Duck down here to avoid the boulders that are trailing down from above. After a boulder passes by, jump up to the next platform to the left. Get the energy at the end of this platform and jump up onto the chain above. You'll grab some ammo while gong across the chain and meet up with a fish that is in your way. At the end of the chain, drop down to the platform below and enter the tube to the right, it'll suck you to the top.

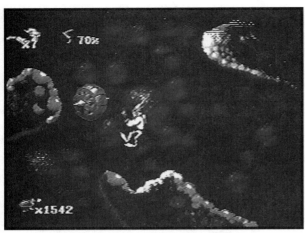

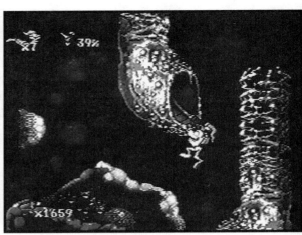

Avoid these stones with spikes at all costs.

These tubes really suck.

- When you exit the tube, destroy the two groups of sponges on the platform and head left. The path you're walking on comes to a drop at the end. Drop down here and you'll land on a platform below that heads right. Follow this path to the end and watch out for falling rocks. Proceed to the platform above. On the first platform, kill the sponge and quickly stand on the left edge of the platform to let a rock pass over you, then jump to the next platform. Do the same for the second platform. On the third platform, you'll need to stand in the middle to avoid the rocks that go by; jump to the safe spot to the left and wait for another rock to pass by. As soon as a rock goes by, jump to the next platform so that you are hanging on to the ledge. As you are pulling yourself up, another rock will fly over head. Make your way right to the tube. There are three tubes in a row that you have to maneuver through. Enter the first tube and it'll shoot

you up. While airborne, position yourself so that you'll land on the ledge of the next tube. Climb up and enter the second tube. Repeat this for the third tube except when you exit the third tube, move right and land on the chain above.

- Travel across the chain to the right and drop down at the end. Follow the path to a hook suspended in the air. There is another hook off the screen to the left, so be ready to latch onto it when you disconnect from the first hook. Move left along the path until the point where the path turns upward to the right. just before that point, there is a hook beneath the platform. Get in line with the hook and latch onto it to get the mega guns there. After disconnecting, immediately turn around and reconnect to the hook to get back on the ledge. Stand at the turning point of the plat-

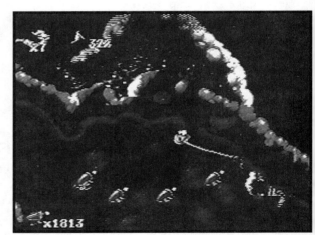

Use this hook to obtain these power-ups.

form again and watch the pattern of the rocks falling. Find the spot where there is the greatest amount of space between the bounce of the rocks. This is the spot you want to aim for while traveling up the platform to head to the right. At the end of the platform, there is a "Continue."

- After touching the continue, jump off the ledge. When you start to go down from your jump, start to helicopter down the rest of the way so you can reach the platform (and be sure not to over-shoot it either). Do a long jump from this point and do the same thing for the next ledge. Don't worry about over shooting this one, more than likely you'll have to grab for the ledge to make it up.

✺ Follow the path to a pit of spikes. Aim your jump towards the hook that is on the ceiling above the middle of the spikes and swing across.

✺ You'll more than likely get hit a couple of times on this next part. You have to go up a series of platforms while rocks are cascading down upon you. Don't worry about avoiding the rocks, just make it through as quick as possible. To make it to the first platform from the path you're on, you have to go all the way left. This will take you up high enough to jump to the next platform. Proceed up until you come across another pit of spikes. This time, the hook is at the beginning of the pit, so you can use it to make it across to a chain stationed above the spikes. Travel along the chain and drop down at the end. Fall off the platform and enter the tube at the bottom.

✺ The tube will send you up to a path that is partially covered by a wall. The path does have three "windows" along the way so you can see where you are. At the third "window" there is a fish so be sure to kill it. Continue to follow the path and you'll reach the lair of Doc Duodenum.

✺ The Doc is constantly jumping back and forth. To defeat him, simply go to the opposite side of the screen than where he lands and shoot him until he dies. The tricky part is that you can't let him get too close because he'll start to spit bile at you from his orifices. He does change the arc of his jump so be alert when he jumps. Don't try and shoot him with too many shots at one time either; just hit him with a short burst when he lands. He'll then jump again, and he's very fast. After defeating Duodenum, you'll fly away to the last level.

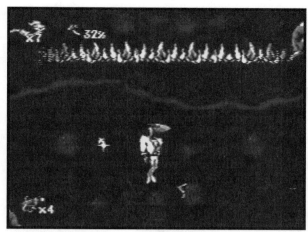

Use the helicopter at the peak of your jump to reach the next platform.

This boss is really gross. Take your time and don't let him get too close.

Level 8: Buttville — Use Your Head

✺ A controller with a rapid-fire option would be nice at this point. In this stage you have to guide yourself down a dangerous path that has spikes lining the walls. Keep in mind that you constantly have to helicopter throughout this stage to maneuver around all the obstacles.

✺ You start off on a platform that's above the pit you have to drop down. Jump either left or right and begin to helicopter down. There is a fork in the pathway that will allow you to go either left or right. The right path is easier, but the left path is more rewarding. The left path is a narrow passage way, and if you make the mistake of hitting one of the walls, you'll bounce back and forth between the walls and take severe damage. The right passage is an open area with some mounds of spikes spread out along the way.

✦ If you take the right passage, there will be a hook to latch onto before continuing on. When your head is just above, let go of the jump button and latch onto the hook. You'll swing right, over a bunch of spikes, and onto a floor that has some power-ups on it. Grab these and jump back to the left and continue to helicopter down. Keep avoiding the spikes on the way down and move in between the spike mounds to collect the various power-ups along the way.

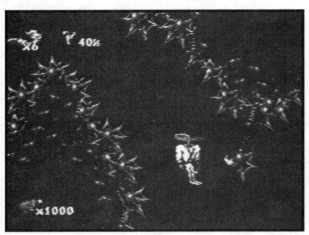
Use this hook to reach the extra man to the right.

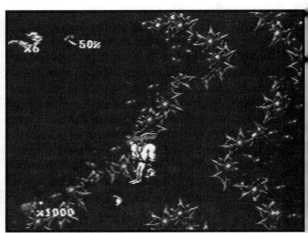
Be sure to take the left path at this split. It is much easier.

✦ When you reach the bottom, you'll come to another fork in the path. This time, take the left path to reach the end of the stage quicker. The right path is another tricky path that is narrow and full of spikes. If you have a slow motion option, now would be a good time to use it. When you reach the bottom, do a long jump over the pillar of spikes to the right, get the two 1-ups that are there, land you'll be teleported to the next part of the level.

Buttville: Part II

✦ This is the final stage. There are a variety of enemies in this stage, ranging from tiny flies to the evil Queen Pulsating, Bloated, Festering, Sweaty, Pus-filled, Malformed, Slug for a Butt. Tread carefully, because one false move could mean the end of ol' Jim.

✦ To start the level off, go right and jump up onto the vines that are hanging from the ceiling (you can hang onto these). Move over to the right a little bit then drop down onto the platform beneath you. Go to the left and get the mega-gun, then head right and jump on the next set of vines. There are two rows of items under the vines. Going across the vines from the left will get the top row of items; going across from the right will get the bottom row of items.

✦ After getting the items, go right and you'll see a ladder of hooks with two mega-guns underneath the platform. Use the bottom hook to swing down

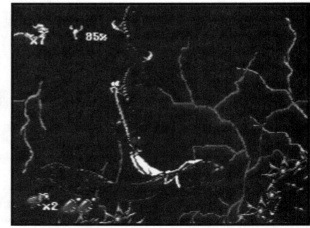
Use this hook to get the guns below the platform.

under the platform to get the guns. Go up the ladder of hooks and get on the platform on the left. Head left and you'll come across a blue bee-hive. One mega blast will take care of it. Try and get it before it releases any bugs. Keep going left and get rid of the next hive. Go left still and get the extra ammo. Head back to the right. When the ground slopes up, jump up and you should see a hook. Latch onto it and swing right, then latch onto the other hook to swing further right onto a platform with energy next to it. Continue right and kill the bee-hive there then stop.

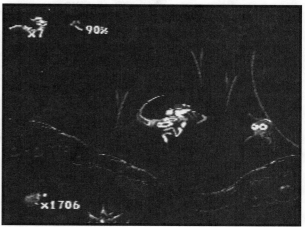

Wait for this creature to pop its head out before you try to whip it. It'll kill you with one hit if you touch it.

✶ Next to the hive is a pair of eyes. Wait where you are and in a couple seconds, a nasty looking monster will stick its head out. These monsters can kill you with one bite, but you can kill them with one whip of your head. After killing the creature, go right and drop down. You might want to helicopter down because it's safer and you can collect the items easier on the way down. When you reach the bottom, go right. As you go, little green creatures will appear and try to attack you with their tongue. You can use your head to whip them into submission, but they do come back. It's better you just avoid them. Continue right and go up until you can't go up any more. As you head right, you might see something fly across the background. This is the cow that you launched in the first stage (just something I thought I'd tell ya). Continue right do a long jump over the pillar of spikes and helicopter down the rest of the way to avoid the other spikes and get the power-ups. Head right and jump on what looks like a basketball. You can't stay on these for too long because you will begin to slide off. If you want to stay on longer, do small jumps by tapping on the jump button. Walk off of the basketball to the right and you'll fall to a platform that has a "Continue" spot on it.

✶ Next to the continue is a hook. Latch onto it and swing to the right under the platform (the spikes can't hurt you while your swinging). You'll see another hook ladder. Go up and swing right when

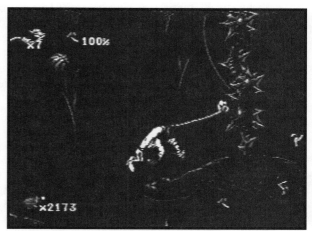

Swing to the right using this hook. Don't worry about the spikes below; they won't hurt you.

you reach the top. Go right (avoid the little green thing and the hive) and jump over the spikes.

✶ Begin to helicopter your way down and to the right. Along the way you'll collect some energy and at the bottom you'll grab onto a basketball. Up and two the left, there is another basketball with another pair of eyes like before. When it pokes its head out, kill it with your head like before and get on that basketball platform (do the small jumps to stay on it). Look for the next platform in the upper right part of the screen. Get rid of that creature the same way. The third creature is a little harder to get, but it's easier (and safer) to kill it, instead of trying to avoid it. After killing the third creature, go right along the basketball platforms.

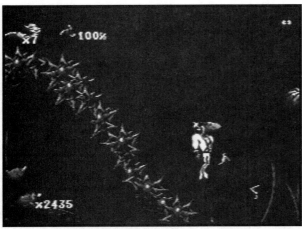
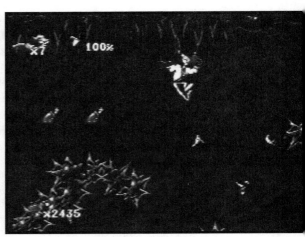

Use your helicopter move again to hover gently down.
Be sure to power-ups along the way.

Don't miss these hooks
or you'll and on the spikes below.

✦ After the last platform, there will be some vines hanging from the ceiling. Climb along the vines until you reach the end. Below you should be a hook; fall and latch onto the hook and swing right. You'll land on a large blue tubular structure. Touch the "Continue" there before proceeding.

✦ After getting the continue, go right and stop when you see the basketball platform. Jump straight up and you should see those eyes again. Handle this like before and jump on it. The next platform has nothing on it so you can jump safely to it. The third platform has a creature on it so handle it in the same fashion as the others. Jump up and start looking to the left a little bit. You should see a sparkle in that general area. Latch onto it and swing left; when you let go, re-latch onto it and swing right. You should swing far right and land on some moving rocks. This is a mini-boss of this level and is very easy to take care of.

✦ If you read the manual thoroughly, you'll notice that this boss is actually the tail end of the evil Queen. Go to the far left of the screen next to the spikes on the wall (but don't touch them). You'll be below and to the left of the tail. Jump up next to the tail and use your whip. Just keep doing this as quick as possible and you should get by very quickly. If you take too long, the moving rocks underneath your feet will start to turn into moving mounds of spikes. After you have destroyed the tail, the rocks will disappear and you'll fall down to the next part of the level.

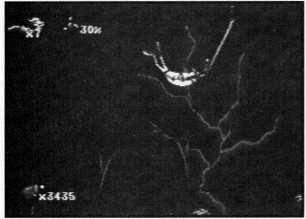
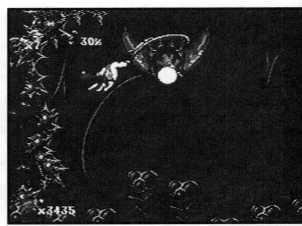

Look for the sparkly to find the hidden hook you
must use to easily reach the first boss in this level.

"Destroy the tail end of the queen by jumping up
and whipping it with your head."

After you drop, go right to get energy if you need it. Head left to the "Continue" and proceed forward. Get the extra ammo after that and get rid of the hive. Jump off the platform to the left and get the mega gun, then land on the basketball platform to the left. Jump onto the next platform and wait for the green elevator to circle around to you. Jump on it and it'll take you up and around to the left. At the 11 o'clock spot of its journey, there will be another green elevator. Jump on this one and get ready to do battle with the evil Queen. The evil Queen will be located in the center of the screen as you revolve around her on the elevator. The best spots to shoot her at are at the three, twelve, nine, and six o'clock spots of the elevator's rotation. Use all the megablasts, then start shooting in short bursts to keep her from sending her bug

Don't fall off this platform or you'll land on the spikes and more than likely die.

minions after you. When you are just about to be underneath her, start to whip your head. This takes off additional energy. Continue this pattern and you should make short work of the Queen. The Queen can't hurt you directly, but the bugs she tries to send after you can knock you off the elevator and down onto the spikes below. Those spikes will kill you.

After you defeat the Queen, sit back and enjoy the funny ending animation. You are rewarded by finally being able to see Princess What's-Her-Name. Oh, and remember that cow? Uh, never mind....

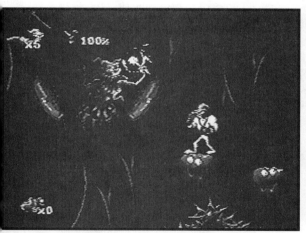

You are now fighting the boss with the longest name in video game history: The Evil Queen Pulsating, Bloated, Festering, Sweaty, Pus-filled, Malformed, Slug for a Butt.

Does Jim get the Princess?

ECCO: THE TIDES OF TIME

PLATFORM: Action/Puzzle DEVELOPER: Novotrade
PLAYERS: 1 PUBLISHER: Sega of America

Introduction

Don't be confused by the title—this game is really *Ecco II*, the sequel to 1993's extremely original (and difficult) action/puzzle game in which you controlled a dolphin. This game has more levels than *Ecco I* (over 40 in all), more music, more graphics, and the same wicked difficulty level. It also has a few new wrinkles, such as the ability to "morph" into birds, sharks, and even a school of fish. Nifty!

Ignore the confusing title–this is an excellent sequel to *Ecco the Dolphin*.

Basic Strategies

✺ Use your Sonar to call up Ecco's map frequently. As the levels get more complicated, it's important to keep track of where you've been and where you're going—which is almost impossible to do without the map to guide you along.

✺ Whenever there's a Barrier Glyph blocking your way, you need to find the Key Glyph that gives you ability to pass the Barrier by shooting it with Sonar. Finding these Glyphs is the key to getting through the game. Find and remember the locations of fish and air bubbles on each level to restore your energy. It's usually taking too much damage, not running out of air, that kills you.

Home Bay

✺ Talk to your dolphin friends, who butter you up by complimenting your amazing powers and overall excellence. When you tire of getting your butt kissed, swim to the right to find a current. Swim down and right, against the current, and follow the tunnel until you bump into a mirror image of yourself. Talk to the mirror image and he mentions teleport rings. Swim upward and into the teleport ring.

No, not Siamese dolphins–it's your mirror image telling you about the mysterious teleport rings.

Teleporting

* We find that the easiest way of getting through all the 3D teleport sequences is to simply press B and C constantly. This makes Ecco swim fast and charge through any enemies in his way. Steering is a bit difficult, but once you get the hang of it, you'll cruise through the rings.

* It's easy to swim through the underwater rings, but jumping through the rings in the air is trickier. Jump through the lower rings by pressing C; jump through the higher rings by pressing B to leap *way* out of the water.

Crystal Springs

* Talk to the dolphin next to you and follow him down and left to a sparkling Glyph. (It's a Puzzle Glyph.) Now search out the other three Glyphs around the edge of the level. You need to shoot these Glyphs until they shake free and start sinking toward the Puzzle Glyph in the lower-left corner. The trick here is to shoot each Glyph when it's close to you, let it bounce away and then toward you, and shoot it again. Repeat this until the Glyph breaks free. When all the Glyphs are united into a single Glyph, shoot it. The Glyph gives you a song to shoot through the stone wall on the far right side of the level.

Blast the Glyphs loose and steer them into the lower-left corner of the level.

Fault Zone

* Swim along the tunnel and use your Sonar-charge to eliminate the crabs along the tunnel. About halfway through the tunnel, the screen starts shaking and you lose the powers that the Asterite gave you in *Ecco I*. Dang! Continue swimming along the tunnel until you run into a mirror-image dolphin. Talk to him and he tells you what you already know: your nifty powers are gone. Swim to the right, through the tunnel, to the next level.

Two Tides

* Swim down and to the far left to find the Pulsar. Get it and try it out. Wicked cool, eh? Now swim to the far right, then down, and follow the tunnel left through the falling rocks to the Glyph. Shoot it to get the key. Go back to the right and up. Get some air, then go down and left to the Barrier Glyph. Shoot it out of the way, then swim down and right to another Glyph. Shoot it for another key. Swim right, up, and around.

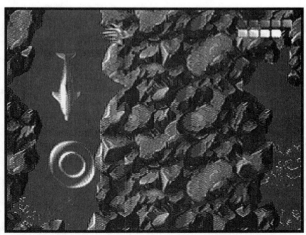

You encounter the Pulsar power-up for the first time in the Two Tides level. It is way cool.

• Go down and left again and look for a turtle swimming near the current on the far left side of the level. Wait for the turtle to swim above the current and touch it to make it go into its shell. Now follow the turtle downward to the bottom. Shoot through the second Glyph and swim right to find Trellia, a huge dolphin that's your great-great-something or other from the future. Talk to her and she tells you about the evil Vortex Future. You automatically touch her to be sent into the future.

• Talk to Trellia in the future. She quickly tells you what to do, then leaves. Swim left through the green kelp. (The green stuff slows you down, so you need to use the B and C buttons.) Keep going left along the bottom to find the Pulsar. Now go up to the surface. Take a breath, then swim right and up into the water tube. Go all the way to the top, swim quickly to the right, and jump out of the tube. You'll (hopefully) get caught by a flying dolphin on the way down. Let the dolphin carry you to the right and to the second pool. (The first pool is empty, but the second one has a Glyph inside.) Shoot the Glyph and it sucks up all the loose rocks scattered around the level. Jump out of the pool and back into the ocean.

• Swim to the lower-left side of the level and shoot the Glyph in the small tunnel. It says "The Glyph that is a door is only open for a short time." Now you must hurry to the far right side of the level, swim past the Cracked Glyph that's normally blocking your way, and touch a second Glyph behind it. A timer appears near your air and health meters to show how much time you have left before the Cracked Glyph closes. If the Glyph closes while you're on the right side of it, you must

Trellia is a big ol' dolphin from the future who brings bad news about the Vortex Queen.

The Cracked Glyph doesn't stay open for long, so quickly swim past it.

shoot your way out, come back and get the charge again, and escape before the Glyph closes.

• Now go up the water tube on the far right and jump left into the nearby tube. You want to land in the large junction in the middle of the tube. Swim up, shoot the Glyph out of the way, and continue upward to the next level.

Skyway

This is a very easy and short level. From the start, swim up and left and touch the Glyph. Go down and left and shoot the Cracked Glyph open. Now swim to the far left and talk to the futuristic dolphin about how the ocean "feels and thinks." Yeah, whatever. Search around for the Key Glyph on the left and touch it to get its power. Now go to the far right and swim up into the water tube. Shoot the Glyph out of your way and swim up to the next level.

Sky Tides

✳ This level is kinda tough. You have to stay in the water tube while avoiding the empty spaces. If you fall out of the tube, you plummet to earth and get to restart the level. Use your speed and speedy jumps to go from one side of screen (one tube) to another. The screen scrolls upward at first, then eventually starts scrolling up and right diagonally. Stay in the bottom tube first, then move up to the higher one. The last section of the tube has you swimming past whirlpools. If you get touched by a whirlpool, you fall out of the tube and have to start from the beginning. Use the C button, *not* the B button, to get past them.

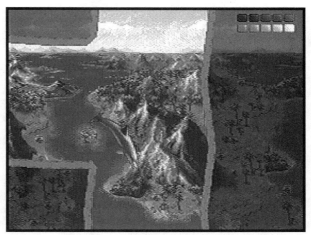

Use power jumps to leap from one water tube to another. Don't drop off the bottom of the screen!

Tube of Medusa

✳ Here's what makes this level so frustrating: if you fall off the bottom of the screen, you have to go all the way back to Skyway. Aargh! Medusa is hard to avoid—nearly impossible, really. The trick is that you have to outrun the Medusa—speeding up the tube without stopping so that you leave it behind. It seems like the only way to do this is in the left-hand tube. When you reach the top of the tube, jump up the next tubes, again without stopping, to keep the Medusa below you. Once you're past the Medusas, you can slowly swim to the top. The final jump to the exit tube is tough, but makeable. Swim right to the arrow and the next level.

The Tubes of Medusa is just quite possibly the most difficult level in the game. Patience is the key!

Skylands

✳ Swim along the bottom of the level to find a Glyph that says "Sing to the bubbles in the sky and they will make you fly." Good idea. Swim to the far left side of the level and use the Sonar to see the first bubble in the air. Swim quickly through the water, leap into the air, and shoot the bubble to get thrust upward to a second bubble. Shoot it to get flung to the right and into a pool. There's a third bubble above the pool that leads to a fourth and fifth. The timing of your shots needs to be perfect to send you up the bubbles to the second pool. Continue hopping up the bubbles until you reach the last pool (which is after a group of three bubbles). Now you need to hitch rides on the flying dolphins to reach the exit. Press C to jump from one dolphin to the next.

Fin to Feather

* Swim right and jump out of the water to the ocean below. Swim down and shoot the Glyph for a message about the Metasphere. Swim right and up, then touch the Metasphere while jumping out of the water to morph into a bird. Neat! Fly upward and over to the right. Watch out for falling rocks in the air and attacking predator gulls. If you hit one, you drop back into the water and become a dolphin again. The trick we found is to stay close to the right wall. When you get close to the top of the wall, two gulls attack. Dodge them both with quick (C button) moves and fly to the right. Now, if you get attacked, you should drop into the water on the right side of wall. Swim down and left into the teleport ring.

Stay close to the cliff wall to dodge the attacking eagles.

Teleporting

* This 3D sequence has long strings of seaweed to avoid. If you fail in this sequence, you're sent back to Fin to Feather to try again. Aargh! As with the first 3D level, the only hard rings to get are the ones *high* in the air. The others are quite easy.

Eagle's Bay

* Swim up to the surface and hit the Metasphere to morph into a gull. Now fly to the far left and drop into the corridor to touch the Glyph. Now return to the right. Fly to the far right and drop down to the next Glyph. Shoot it out of the way and swim to the arrow to the next level. The only real challenge in the level is avoiding the eagles in the air.

Asterite's Cave

* Swim to the left to find the shattered lower half of a Glyph. You need to reunite it with the upper half. Swim up and right to find it. You can push it with your nose or shoot it with your Sonar beam. When the halves are back together, shoot the Glyph to get power. Swim up and blast the Glyph out of the way. It cracks open and closes quickly, so swim through it immediately.

* Now swim up the water tube and catch a ride right and over the rock wall on a flying dolphin. Swim down to the white worm. Lure the worm to the right and over to the wall of rocks. Shoot the worm into the wall to destroy it. Now swim down and

Reunite the halves of the shattered Glyph to get the power you need to progress through the level.

reunite the two halves of another broken Glyph. Shoot the repaired Glyph, then shoot away the Barrier Glyph and swim into the presence of the Asterite. Talk to it and it shows you its memory of being attacked by the Vortex Queen. When it's done, swim to the top of the Asterite and over it. Wait for a space to appear in the curling Asterite and swim downward while staying in the space. This is a tricky little maneuver! Touch the Metasphere at the bottom to teleport into a new area.

• Talk to the mother orca and her baby. Being the hero that you are, you need to save her babies (four of them in all). The first two are in the opening area and easy to find. Swim down and right along the ledge. You'll hear a whistle when the baby starts following you. Return the baby to its mommy and you hear another sound.

• The other two orcas are deeper down in the level. Swim to the far right side of the surface and jump over the wall, then go downward to find them. You don't have to go too deep to find them both. When you've brought all four orcas back to the mother, you're rewarded with a special power that you need to finish this level. She whistles three times, and one of the babies starts swimming to the right. Follow it as it takes you to the far right, jumps over the wall, and swims all the way down and right to where there's usually a wall of round boulders blocking your way. The boulders are gone, allowing you to swim to the right and finish the level. If you screw up and lose the baby along the way, you need to return to the mother and talk to her again. You must keep the baby on the screen.

Four Islands

Swim down and right and talk to the dolphin. He tells you that Blackfin and Tara are below and can help you find the exit. Swim downward and talk to the dolphin Blackfin (but not before collecting the Pulsar weapon nearby). Blackfin says "Follow me, Ecco." Keep up with the bugger as he swims a blazing path through the level. As with the baby orca in the last level, if you fail to keep up and lose Blackfin off the screen, you need to return to where you first found him and try again until you succeed. The hardest part is the four big jumps on

Shoot the white worm into the rock wall to break it down and open a path to deeper water.

Find the four orcas scattered around the level and bring them back to their mother.

Blackfin is a tough act to follow. Use your speed swimming to keep up.

the surface of the water about halfway through Blackfin's path. If you make it all the way—which is made much easier by the Pulsar—Blackfin gives you a song to break the stone. Use it to bust through the walls and swim downward to the next dolphin, Tara. Look for the turtle, bump into it, and follow its shell through the current to reach her.

✦ Following Tara is much easier than following Blackfin. Keep using the Pulsar and following as she leads you into a seemingly solid wall. Follow her through the wall to enter the next level.

Sea of Darkness

✦ This level is shrouded in darkness, and the only way to light it up (briefly) is by shooting a Sonar beam. From the start of the level, swim up, left, and down to touch the Key Glyph. Now go up and right through the narrow tunnel. There's a Barrier Glyph below. Swim up and right along the tunnel to find another Key Glyph. You've probably noticed the aliens swimming in the water—the same nasty suckers from the final levels of *Ecco I*!

✦ While here, swim downward and talk to the mother orca. She's missing her kid. The baby orca is directly below her, but the current pushing up is too strong for you to swim against. Instead, swim left and around to the Barrier Glyph.

✦ There's a swirling circle of stars just below the Barrier Glyph. Shoot this with your Sonar to move it to the baby orca on the right. The star circle eats through the rocks trapping the orca inside. You have to make this quick, or the circle disappears and you have to go left to try again.

✦ Rescue the orca and take him up to his mom. She shows you her memories of the Asterite's death. Swim right past the reunited orcas to the next level.

Move the circle of stars into the rock wall
before it disappears and you have to try again.

Vents of Medusa

✦ There are two ways through this level: the easy way and the hard way. First, the easy way: From the start of the level, swim far to the right, touch the Key Glyph, and then shoot the Glyph for a message ("This way is very hard, but not insoluble"). Swim back to the far left, then swim upward and touch the Metasphere to turn into a Medusa (jellyfish). Use the B and C buttons to swim upward; press B for a big thrust upward, and C for a small one. There are a few dolphins along the way, shooting to the left, so avoid the shots. Keep going until you reach the surface of the water and become a dolphin again. Swim to the right, shoot the Barrier Glyph, and jump out of the water to fly to the next level.

✦ Now the hard way: From the start of the level,

Okay, so maybe morphing into a jellyfish
isn't all that exciting–at least it's different.

swim far to the right, touch the Key Glyph, and then shoot the Glyph for a message ("This way is very hard, but not insoluble"). Swim back to the left and up into the first tunnel you reach. Follow this Medusa-filled tunnel all the way up to the surface of the water. There aren't any air pockets along the path, so you need to swim quickly and constantly. When you reach the surface, swim to the right, shoot the Barrier Glyph, and jump out of the water to fly to the next level.

Gateway

✦ Swim downward and shoot the Key Glyph for a message about the "Magic Arm." What does this mean, you ask? Swim down and right to find the Magic Arm—a small creature with a long arm. Now here's the secret to the Arm. If you use your Sonar-charge (B then A) to shoot the arm repeatedly, a small group of bubbles comes out of the arm. Grab the bubbles and shoot the arm again. If you collect four groups of bubbles, you get a special power during the 3D sequence: your Sonar beams home in on the enemies. This isn't particularly necessary, but it's a neat secret. When you're done collecting bubbles, or just want to move on, swim to the teleport circle and go through it.

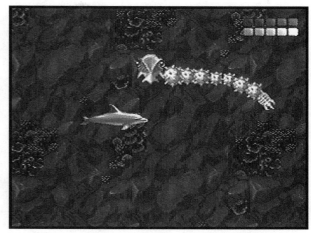

There's a bizarre trick related to the Magic Arm creature that makes the 3D sequence a little easier.

✦ The 3D sequence is filled with jellyfish (Medusas). Use the charging methods to destroy the Medusas and get through the rings. You appear in a non-password level called the Sea of Green.

Sea of Green

✦ Swim right and jump over the green palm into the water below. Now swim down and right toward the Key Glyph. A dolphin guarding the Glyph won't let you past until you give him a fish. Swim to the far left to find a small blue fish in the water. Use your Sonar to guide the fish to the dolphin. He eats the fish and leaves the Glyph. Touch the Glyph to get its power, then swim to the surface and jump over the rocks to the right. Shoot the Barrier Glyph out of the way, swim downward, and swim left to the Pulsar weapon.

✦ Swim to the left, using the Pulsar to clear the way, until you see a rock sliding down into the current. Follow the rock to the bottom. Swim up and right to the next rock and follow it down against the current. Go to the far right and swim down to the next level.

Look for the tiny blue fish and steer him to the hungry dolphin.

Moray Abyss

✴ This level is one *long* cavern going straight down. Avoid the large conch shell sinking down the screen by moving to the lower-right corner of the screen and swimming downward. There are yellow serpents on both sides of the cavern, but these are easy to kill. It's the red serpent inside the shell that you want to avoid; one touch from it means instant death. If you stay in the lower-right corner, the red serpent should only slither down the left side of the screen, leaving you safe. (The serpent looks out of his shell just before it crashes into either side of the cavern.)

✴ When the shell reaches the bottom of the Abyss, it smashes into the ground. *Quickly* swim as close to the shell as possible and blast it rapidly with Sonar beams. If you're quick enough, you can destroy the shell before the red serpent has a chance to emerge.

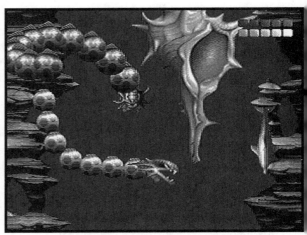

The yellow serpents hurt, but the red serpent kills you with one touch. Avoid it!

✴ Two globes come out of the shell. These are what's left of the Asterite. Talk to them and they tell you to "Find...globes." Swim back to the top of the Abyss and into the teleport circle on the left.

✴ The circle on the right is where you start. Swim left to the left side of the channel. Use Sonar to find an Asterite globe. Shoot the globe with your sonar and it starts circling around you. Now swim down to find a second globe and shoot it. Return to the teleportation circle and go through. Swim down and give the globes to the Asterite.

✴ Go back through the circle. Swim down to the bottom, and right, and shoot the Barrier Glyph out of the way. Retrieve the next two globes and go back to the Asterite to give them away. Go through the circle again. Swim down and right to the next Barrier Glyph. Shoot it and swim past it into the next level.

The Eye

✴ The teleport circle takes you back to the chamber of the Asterite. Use your sonar to locate the first two Asterite globes (to the right of where you start), shoot them to pick them up, and return them to the Asterite. Return to The Eye. Swim right into the chamber with Barrier Glyphs in all directions and a teleport circle in the middle. Use the circle and then return to The Eye. Swim straight up and shoot the short, fat Milestone Glyph to save your progress.

✴ Swim down and left and shoot the Glyph out of the way. Get the Pulsar. Swim down and left for the first globe, then back up and left to the second one. Return them to the Asterite and come back to The Eye.

✴ Swim up and left and shoot through the Glyph. Get the globes, take them to the Asterite, and

Collect the Asterite globes and take them back to the Asterite to rebuild it.

return to The Eye. Swim straight down and shoot the Barrier Glyph on the left. The first globe is straight down, but the second is at the very bottom. Make the Asterite trip and give it the globes.

🐬 • Swim down again and shoot the Glyph on the right. Go down to the sea floor for two globes. Take them to the Asterite and return. Swim up and left, then go left and shoot the Barrier Glyph. One of the two globes in this area is very close to the surface of the water. Get them both, take them to the Asterite, and return.

🐬 • Swim up and right and shoot past the Glyph. There's a teleport circle here, but ignore it. Get the globes and go through the other circle to the Asterite. Give it the globes and it tells you that the Vortex Queen followed you back to Earth. Duh. Return to The Eye. Swim to the right and shoot the Glyph. Collect two globes, take them to the Asterite, and return. Swim down and right and shoot past the Glyph. Collect two globes and take them to the Asterite for more Vortex Queen info. Return to The Eye. Swim far to the right and shoot past the Glyph. Collect two globes, take them to the Asterite, and return. (Yes, that's the 28th time we've used that sentence.) Swim down and into the right-hand tunnel. Follow the tunnel to the Glyph, shoot past it, and swim right to the exit.

Big Water

🐬 Swim down and left to get the first globe. Go left and talk to the whale. He tells you that "The leader can help you." Swim to the whale on the far left side of the level and talk to him. He breaks through the wall of rocks to open up the way to the second Asterite globe. Pick it up and swim down to get air from the bubbling rocks below the leader. Go into the circle to teleport to the Asterite chamber and give it the globes. Go back to Big Water, shoot the Glyph, and swim left to the next level.

The "leader" will smash through the wall of rocks in front of the Asterite globe.

Deep Ridge

🐬 From the start of the level, swim up and right, then to the right for two globes. Go back to the left and take the globes to the Asterite. Return to the Ridge and swim up and right. Jump over the rocks on the surface to find the next two globes. Make an Asterite trip and return. Swim up and right again and go across the surface until you find two globes inside a small cave. It doesn't seem like you can enter the cave, but you can. Jump onto the right side of the cave and then swim through the rocks on the top to enter the cave. Return the globes to the Asterite and come back to the Ridge. Swim up and right, and across the surface to the right, for two more globes.

🐬 Take the globes to the Asterite and return. Swim

Swim into this cave through the seemingly solid roof to get the globes inside.

down and right a short distance to two globes. Make an Asterite trip and return. Swim down and right through the narrow tunnel until you find the teleport circle. (You can also go up and right to the surface, swim all the way to the far right, then swim down and left to the circle.) Enter the circle and immediately come back to the Ridge.

✹ From the circle, swim almost directly to the right for two globes. Take them to the Asterite and return. Swim left and get the Pulsar. Continue swimming left, down, and right to find two globes. Go right and get air before swimming back to the circle, because this is a long trip. Take the globes to the Asterite and return. Go left, down, and right through the tunnel again for the final two globes. Thank God! Take them to the Asterite, which tells you that the Vortex Queen has the final pair of globes in the Vortex Future, among other things. After you've absorbed all the information, return to the Ridge. Swim up and right and look for the exit arrow pointing the way to the next level.

The Hungry Ones

✹ Turn around and shoot the Key Glyph for a handy hint: "Sometimes to escape your enemy you must become your enemy." Swim left along the bottom and get the Pulsar weapon. Swim upward and touch the Metasphere to turn into a shark. Press C to swim fast and B to charge and bite. You need to swim fast to maintain your air supply. Keep going all the way to the far left. Swim down into the current and touch another Metasphere to become Ecco again. Swim down to the bottom, then through the tunnel to a dolphin. Charge through the rocks in the way. Touch the next Metasphere to become a shark again. The dolphin attacks you, but don't hurt him. Just swim past. Go down and right through the tunnels, avoiding the dolphins and swimming fast to maintain your air supply. The exit arrow is in the lower-right corner, below your starting point next to the Key Glyph.

When you morph into the shark, keep swimming fast to maintain your air supply.

Secret Cave

✹ Swim down and right to find the Magic Arm. Do the arm-shooting trick you did before, then go up and right into the teleport circle.

✹ This 3D sequence has lots of sharks. Charge through them and swim through the rings to finish surprisingly fast.

Lunar Bay

✹ If you get caught by one of the aliens, you're taken to a strange level where you become an alien (!) and have to swim through a small maze of walls moving back and forth. Finish the maze and you return to the beginning of Lunar Bay.

✹ From the start, swim to the right, jump the rock on the surface, and go down. Swim left to get the Pulsar

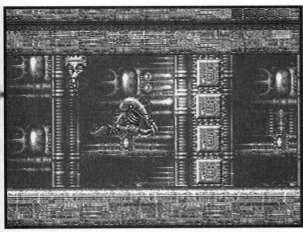

The most surreal sequence in *Ecco II* has you morphing into an alien (!) and swimming through a maze.

These two aliens grab you and carry you by force into the Vortex Future. Uncool.

weapon. Continue swimming to the bottom. A group of round spheres is blocking your path. Go all the way to the far left and shoot the Key Glyph. It sucks away the spheres. Go right and down through the shaft to the next area.

✸ Swim down and left to find a Key Glyph that also sucks away spheres. (There's an invincible Glyph just above.) Shoot the Key, then swim to the far right along the bottom. Look for a Glyph with an alien guarding it. Swim to the Glyph. You're grabbed from behind by two aliens and carried to the Vortex Future!

Vortex Future

✸ From the start of the level, swim up and right into the tunnel. Go right to the first downward-leading water tube and take it. At the bottom, go left and drop down the shaft. Go left and drop down the next shaft to slide down and right. When you hit the ground, go left and touch the Key Glyph. Return to the right and keep going right until you're sucked up into a shaft. Shoot the Glyph in the middle of the shaft to become invincible (for a few seconds, anyway).

✸ At the top of the shaft, go right and jump up into the tube. Swim to the top of the tube and go right. Jump up and left onto the slope leading up. Use a spin jump (tap the C button twice quickly and press Up on the control pad) for extra height. Go upward until you see a tube on the right. Jump into the tube and swim right to a wall. Shoot through the wall with your sonar. Drop out of the tube and shoot the Milestone Glyph when you land. (If you have to restart the level from this point, go left and shoot the Key Glyph to regain your power to blast through walls.)

✸ From the Milestone, go right and down the tube. Shoot the sphere to make it smash through the wall blocking your way. (Note that when you shoot the sphere, it flies in the direction that you shot it from. This is important to remember later

When you shoot the giant sphere, it moves in the direction you shot it from.

on in the level.) Drop out of the tube and slide left into the next tube. Now swim right and jump across a series of tubes. Don't fall off the bottom of the screen or you have to restart.

* Keep going right until you reach a wall. Shoot to the right and the sphere breaks through the wall for you. Drop into the shaft and let the wind suck you upward. At the top of the shaft, go into the left tube and shoot the Milestone Glyph. Swim right and jump right into the next tube.

* From here, you need to jump "up" the tubes to reach the Milestone Glyph at the top. Here's how: swim near the bottom of the tube you're in, holding the C button for speed. Just before you pop out of the tube, angle upward and hit B for a speed burst. You should fly upward and into the next tube. Use this method to "climb" the tubes and get to the Milestone Glyph.

* After you shoot the Milestone, slide left down the ledge, then go left through the tube. Drop to the bottom of the shaft and shoot the Glyph for temporary invulnerability. Jump up into the next tube. At the top, jump up and right into the next tube. You'll reach a wall. Shoot through it and drop into the shaft. Let the wind suck you upward and land in the right tube. Jump up to the left tube and slide left. Jump over the gap and touch the final Key Glyph. Return to the right and go to the tube that was previously blocked by a wall. (Use the sonar to look for the exit arrow.) Swim to the next level.

Black Clouds

* Swim to the right and down into the tube, then go left into the tunnel. Drop down to the next platform and slide right to the Key Glyph. Shoot it and it sucks away a wall elsewhere in the level. Go left and drop off the ledge. Hug the right wall to land on a ledge below. Drop left again and hug the wall again. This time, you land next to an electric beam.

* Go to the right, past the beam, and shoot the blobs. Keep going to the right until you reach the end of the ledge. Drop down and you fall into shaft that sucks you up and down. You want to get into the narrow tunnel on the left side of the shaft. Slide to the end of the shaft and shoot the Glyph for invincibility.

Drop down the left side of the level
to land next to an electric beam.

* Return to the right and drop into the shaft again. This time, go all the way to the bottom, then go right into a small water-filled room with a Key Glyph. Shoot it to suck away more wall parts.

* Return left to the shaft. Let it suck you up to the water tube high on the right. Drop down the shaft on the right side of the pipe. Go right and shoot the Key Glyph inside the water-filled room. Return left to the shaft and let it suck you up to the tube on the left. Now go up and left and retrace your path back to the beginning of the level.

* From the beginning (again), go right and up the first tube. At the top, jump up and right and look for a ledge on the left. Jump to the ledge, then slide to the far left and shoot the Glyph. Return to the right and drop onto the hill. There's another tube at the top of the hill, but go past it and continue to the right. Keep going until you fall into a pipe next to two balls blocking a tunnel. (There's a Pulsar in the water-filled room above the balls.) Swim to the bottom of the pipe to find a sphere. Shoot the sphere from above to move it upward. Guide it into the balls to destroy them. Go left into the tunnel and slide down to the next water tube. Drop into the tube and swim down and right to finish the level.

Gravitorbox

One of the toughest jumps in the game is in the Gravitorbox level. Nasty!

❖ From the start, swim right and drop out of the tube, then slide down and left into a water-filled room. Swim down and right and get the Pulsar. Return to the top of the room and jump up the hill. Slide down the right side of the hill and jump into the water tube on the right before you fall off the bottom of the screen.

❖ Swim against the current to the first lower tube and swim into it. Now swim out the bottom of the tube and "fly" two pipes to the right. Stay close to the pipes or you fall off the bottom of the screen. Enter the third tube when you reach it. Now swim up and left into the next pipe. The current is strong, so you need to quickly dash up into the pipe before the current pushes you past it. If you miss, you need to go back around to the third pipe from the left and try again.

❖ Now comes a very difficult jump. You need to speed up in the pipe—without dropping into the current—jump straight out of the water, and land on the tilted ledge above. There's no real trick to this except skill. Try speeding up on the right side of the pipe and jumping to the left. As soon as you land on the hill, jump up and left until you reach a tunnel. Slide down and left, then go left into the water-filled pipe and touch the Key Glyph.

❖ Return to the right and jump to the right, up the hill. Keep going up and right until you reach a tube on the left. Jump into the tube and swim to the left. Slide out of the tube and quickly jump into the next tube on the left before you fall downward. (If you fall, you have to go back around.) Swim left, shoot out the wall, drop into the shaft, and go up and left to finish the level.

Globe Holder

❖ Remember the Crystal Springs level, where you shot the Glyphs to shake them loose? You need to use a similar technique here. Stay on the far left side of the giant Globe and shoot it to move it to the right. Wait for the Globe to rebound to the left, then shoot it again to move it even farther to the right. Keep moving it until it snaps loose from both connectors. Now quickly shoot the Globe to smash it into the sides of the room. If the Globe reconnects, you need to shoot it loose again.

❖ The Globe's connectors eventually explode, and it starts bouncing around the room, trying to squash you into the wall. (It won't bounce if you stay too close to it, however; you need to move far enough away to lure it into attacking.) Use your B and C buttons to speed away from the Globe and avoid being crushed. After it smashes six times into the

Shoot the giant globe to shake it loose of the connectors.

wall, shoot the Globe and it leaves behind the final two globes of the Asterite. Touch the globes to tele-port to a new level.

✦ Swim left and jump over the wall, then swim down and left, following the tunnel. There's a teleport circle in the lower-right corner. Touch it, swim down to the Asterite, and give it the final two globes. The Asterite gives you power to kill the Vortex Queen. Swim up and into the teleport circle to yet another location.

Dark Sea

✦ A group of dolphins are scattered throughout this level, helping you against the aliens. (Don't let an alien grab you, or you'll be taken into a bizarre sub-level where you *become* an alien and need to swim through a short maze.) Swim to the right and jump over the wall. Note that the Asterite's power makes it so you don't need air anymore. Yee-ha! Go down-ward to find a Milestone Glyph and a tunnel blocked off by a wall of spiky bubbles.

✦ Swim left to the Glyph and shoot it to remove the spiky bubbles. Return to the right and to the tun-nel. Swim down into it, then go left. Shoot the alien and go down into the next room. Shoot the Glyph on the bottom for invincibility. Return up and right to the tunnel into this area. Swim down and right to the Glyph. Shoot it and star sparks come out. Neat. Return left and go down, then right again to another Glyph. This one sucks away the bubbles blocking the next area. Swim left and down the tunnel that the balls were blocking.

✦ Oh, great! A level where the screen continuously scrolls! If you played *Ecco I*, you've probably start-ed screaming, because the forced-scroll level at the end of that game was *extremely* tough. This one isn't half as bad, but it's still a toughie. If you shot the star Glyph, you'll see stars throughout this level to "guide" you, but use our directions instead.

✦ From the start, the screen scrolls: right, up, right (quickly swim to the right side of the screen), down, left. Down, right (to a Glyph), up, left (stay on the left side of the screen), down. Left (stay along the bottom), up, up/right, right, left. Up/left,

Several dolphins help you out in this level by keeping the aliens busy.

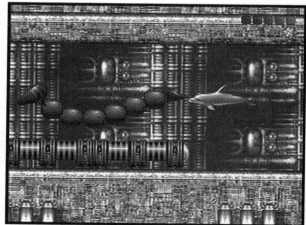
The forced-scroll level was one of the hardest levels in *Ecco I,* and it's almost as hard in *Ecco II.*

up, left, down, up/right (stay on the right side of screen). Left (to the Glyph), up/right, down, left, down/right (swim quickly to the bottom of screen). Right, left, down, right, down/right. Right (slow scroll). That's it!

Vortex Queen

Wait for the Queen to start spitting, then swim down and hit her with a few sonar blasts.

✦ The Vortex Queen has three attacks: an arm that shoots out of her mouth and grabs you, a vacuum attack that sucks you into her mouth, and a laser that extends across the screen. The laser absorbs sonar blasts and slows down Ecco for a short time if it hits him. (It also makes him glow blue to show that you were zapped.) If the Queen "eats" you, you have to play through a short alien sub-level; when you finish it, the Queen spits you out and you get to try again.

✦ The key to defeating the Vortex Queen is patience. Compared to the rest of the game, beating the Queen is cake. Stay in the upper-left or upper-right corner of the screen and wait for the laser beam and arm attacks. When the Queen starts spitting a bunch of crap out of her mouth, swim downward and hit her with sonar blasts, then retreat to the upper-left or upper-right. It takes 12 hits to destroy the Queen. After eight hits, the Queen stops attacking with her arm, making your job even easier.

✦ When the Queen dies, you get treated to a spiffy animation sequence, and what seems like the ending of the game, complete with programmer credits presented by a group of three dolphins. But is the game really over yet? Nuh-uh! When the dolphins are done talking, swim to the right, underneath the currents, to the teleport ring.

✦ Here's the final 3D teleporting sequence of the game, with a combination of all the enemies from earlier sequences. Just use those trusty B and C buttons to swim quickly and ram your enemies!

Epilogue

Put symbols on all of the boxes to make them disappear.

✦ Swim downward and talk to the Asterite, which says that you must go to Atlantis and destroy the time machine to make everything okay again. Swim up and left into the teleport ring to appear in—that's right—Atlantis!

✦ Swim left and down to a 4X4 group of blocks with symbols on them. When you charge into a row or column of blocks, you toggle them on and off. For example, if there's a row of blocks with no symbols, and you ram it, all the blocks get symbols. (This is making sense, ain't it?) The goal is to get symbols on all the blocks. One way to do this is to ram the 2nd and 4th columns, then the 1st and 3rd rows. When all the blocks get symbols, then turn into a single block. Use this block to swim straight down against the current. When you reach the bottom, go right and get the Pulsar.

✦ Swim back up and right to the corridor to the right of where the blocks were. Swim right and then upward to the surface of the water. Jump left out of the water and slide across the ledge, and continue going left until you find a pushable block on the far left.

- Push the block to the right and follow it downward as it breaks through a wall in your way. Now swim to the right to touch the Glyph. (Use your Sonar to see it.) There's a dolphin in your way who wants a fish. Go back to the left to find a small blue fish and use your Sonar to push it to the dolphin. He eats it and splits. Touch the Key Glyph.

- Swim down and left until you find a pushable block. Push it left and follow it down as it breaks through a wall. Now swim down and right until you find a narrow, current-filled tunnel leading back up to where you started the level. Swim right into the tunnel and swim downward to the Barrier Glyph. Shoot it out of the way.

- Swim left into the narrow tunnel. Now you need to pass a series of six blocks moving up and down. Don't get crushed against the top or bottom of the tunnel or you get to play through the level all over again. Continue to the left until you swim into the next level.

Fish City

- At the start of the level, you hit a Metasphere that turns you into a school of fish. Now you need to swim through the level while avoiding the constant attacks of several hungry dolphins who eat all the fish in the school! As you encounter other schools of fish, you can add their fish to your school. Keep swimming in a generally eastward direction, always avoiding tunnels with currents. This isn't a particularly difficult "maze;" just keep heading to the right whenever possible. Never swim in a straight line—keep zig-zagging back and forth to keep the dolphins from eating your fish too quickly. As long as you keep getting new fish to replace the ones that are eaten, you'll be okay.

Keep picking up fish to replace the ones that get eaten away by the attacking dolphins.

City of Forever

- There are two walls in this level—near the beginning and near the end—that you can't open up or smash through. These walls only open when a Vortex Larva (a large, clear, blue swimming creature that looks like a turtle) swims into them. You need to follow behind a Larva, wait for the wall to open up, and slip past it before it slams shut again. The trick is not to get too close to the Larva, or it turns around and attacks you. Use your Sonar to locate the Larvas.

- Here's the path you need to take through this level. From the start, go left, down, left, down, and right to the wall. Go down, left, down, left to the wall. Go up and look for the falling brick. Push the brick left, down, right, and follow it down through the current. Now go right, up to the top, right, and

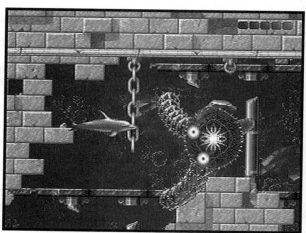

The Vortex larva are very aggressive and swim very fast. Stay at a safe distance.

down into the teleport circle. Now you get to see the *real* ending sequence, with a fireworks display and a secret password (if you finished the game without using the cheat mode below).

So what's the deal with the secret password? Believe it or not, the secret password doesn't do anything! We even called up the playtesters at Sega of America, and they couldn't figure out what the password does. (One tester's theory is that this password will do something cool when you enter it into *Ecco 3*, whenever that comes out.) According to *Ecco 2's* producer, Mark Griffin, the password keeps track of how long it took you to get through the game, how many times you died, etc., so it might be used in some kind of contest. For now, just be proud you finished the game!

The secret password. What does it mean? Absolutely nothing–at least, it doesn't seem to.

Awesome Secrets

DEBUG MODE: Pause the game while Ecco is turning and press A, B, C, B, C, A, C, A, B. You call up a debug menu that lets you skip to any stage, turn on invincibility, and more. Keep in mind that the game keeps track of whether you've cheated or not. Try finishing the game with the cheat mode and see the message you get!

PASSWORDS: Use these passwords to skip to any level in the game.

Crystal Springs: OVYKBYEB
Fault Zone: AYGVOGZA
Two Tides: IMGMSZYA
Skyway: YUMNPLDB
Sky Tides: YCBYHNDB
Tube of Medusa: YQEFUHZA
Skylands: EQLXZAFB
Fin to Feather: SVDUTAXA
Eagle's Bay: KXCVYJGB
Asterite's Cave: AGLDSMAB
Four Islands: ECAMWHFB
Sea of Darkness: KLKCHTZA
Vents of Medusa: UIDMNWAB
Gateway: OBYSGYGB
Moray Abyss: YUCXYRAB
The Eye: GXZSHSTE
Big Water: QGLXJLJA
Deep Ridge: QHDEMIRD
The Hungry Ones: ONEESBME

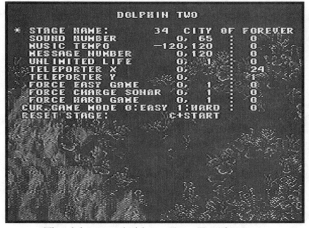

The debug mode blows *Ecco II* wide open, but the game knows if you're using it to cheat.

Secret Cave: AUYMLRRE
Lunar Bay: OLLAPSRE
Black Clouds: AYICWLNE
Gravitorbox: SLIWEYJE
Globe Holder: WNYPLZIE
Dark Sea: OSCCEPDA
Vortex Queen: UHYZSSAA
Epilogue: UXURCHBA
Fish City: CGJDXGCA
City of Forever: IXTRWUHA
Secret Password: IXHZOJAA

HEART OF THE ALIEN CD:
OUT OF THIS WORLD PARTS I AND II

CATEGORY: Adventure	DEVELOPER: Delphine Software
PLAYERS: 1	PUBLISHER: Virgin Interactive Entertainment

Introduction

Out of This World was one of the coolest action/adventure games of 1993, and *Heart of the Alien* is the long-awaited sequel. It uses the same super-smooth polygon graphics as the original, and even fills in some of the plot holes from the first adventure. The game puts you in control of a buff alien who wields a mean whip—the same alien who befriended Lester in *Out of This World*. Your goal is to infiltrate the prison where your people are being held captive, and free them by defeating the evil warden. The puzzles aren't quite as involving as *Out of This World*, but the death sequences are better than ever. (We especially enjoy the scene where you plummet onto a bed of spikes.) This chapter has complete walk-throughs for both *Out of This World* and *Heart of the Alien*, since both games are on the CD (wasn't that nice of Virgin?).

Heart of the Alien has some of the nastiest death sequences you've ever witnessed in a video game. Ouch!

Awesome Strategies

✦ The puzzles in *Out of This World* and *Heart of the Alien* range from easy to quite tricky. We strongly suggest you use this chapter only when you're completely stuck and ready to give up. The death scenes are some of the coolest scenes in the game, and if you use this chapter to walk through the game, you would be missing out on them.

✦ Since the stages aren't labeled, the only logical way to refer to them is by passwords. Be strong. Resist the temptation to look ahead!

Part I: Out of This World

STAGE 1: LDKD

✦ When the stage begins, press Up to swim out of the pool of water and out of the reach of the tentacle monster. To the left of the pool is a vine, but first, you most go to the far right. The small black slugs on the ceiling and floor are deadly, as you're bound to find out. The safest way to destroy them is with a kick.

To the far right is a black beast (which you probably saw lurking in the background earlier on). You can't defend yourself against his attack, so you have to outsmart him. Run back to the vine, jumping over the black slugs if you didn't kill them, and leap onto it before the beast catches you. After your Tarzan-esque swing, run to the right and keep running until the pursuing beast gets blasted by an alien. The alien is unimpressed by your gesture of peace and blasts you, too. You regain consciousness in a hanging cage with a fellow prisoner.

STAGE 2: HTDC

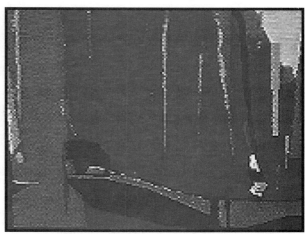

Swing from the vine like Tarzan,
then run for your life!

✦ Escape the hanging cage by pressing Left and Right to swing back and forth until it drops to the ground and crushes the alien guard. Pick up the deceased guard's flashing gun and follow your new friend to the right. Go past the first screen and into the second, then duck and shoot the approaching guard. Continue to the right one more screen. Your friend starts hacking into the security system to open the doors. More guards approach from the left, and you have to protect yourself and your buddy.

✦ There are three different shots available from the gun. The more powerful shots require more energy, and the gun runs out of juice in a hurry, so don't overdo it. Shot #1: Quickly press the A button to fire a laser beam. Shot #2: Press and hold the A button until a white orb appears on the barrel of the gun. Let go of the button and a shield forms in front of you. Shot #3: Press and hold the A button until a large white orb appears. Let go of the button and the gun fires a Super Shot that blasts through walls and enemy shields. (You don't need to use a Super Shot at the moment.)

✦ Stand near the center of the screen and put up a shield to the left, then take a step to the right and put up another shield to the left. Continue creating shields until your buddy indicates that it's time to run to the right. If you don't want to keep moving when you build up shields, you can overlap them and create multiple shields in the same location.

Swing the cage to squish the guard
then grab the gun and run.

As your friend breaks the code,
you must build shields for protection.

Ride the elevator up and
look out the window for a cool view.

Bottom Floor: Be ready to blast a guard
the moment you enter this room.

⚡ Run to the right and enter the elevator. Ride it to
the top floor and look out the window on the right
for a cool animation sequence that has no purpose
other than to make you say "Cool." Take the elevator to the bottom floor and walk left. The moment
you appear on the next screen, quickly fire the gun
to shoot a guard. Shoot again at the left to hit the
blinking white dot and disable the power line. Ride
the elevator up one floor and go left. Use a Super
Shot to blast through the wall, then quickly go left
and down through the hole before the guard gets
his door open. Run to the left and climb up to the
second ledge. Continue left, but don't shoot
through the wall. Wait for your friend to open a
hatch into an underground passage. Drop into the
passage before the guard grabs you.

Wait for your friend to open a hatch,
then jump into the next stage.

STAGE 3: CLLD

⚡ Roll slowly to the left until you see an airstream. Wait until it stops and quickly roll past it. Drop down and
roll to the right slowly until you see another airstream. Again, wait for it to stop and quickly roll past. (This
one has shorter bursts than the first airstream.) Drop down to find yourself with airstreams to the left and
right. Timing the roll to the right is tricky here, but watch the rhythm and make your move. Drop down
and roll left (no airstreams), then roll right and drop down to the next stage.

STAGE 4: LBKG

⚡ You drop into a blue room with a glowing wall in a room to the left. Walk into the room and toward the
wall to recharge to recharge the gun, then shoot Super Shots at the three walls to the right. Recharge your
gun again and go right two screens. As you go outside, you see a guard. Quickly shoot him and continue
to the right. Stop when you enter the next screen to avoid falling off the ledge. Stand at the edge and jump
to the far right to land on a lower ledge. Fire a Super Shot at the wall to the right and walk through the
hole into the next stage.

Stage 4: Shoot the left wall in the glowing room to recharge your gun.

Stage 5: The falling rocks land on the lower ledge, making the higher ledge safe to walk on.

STAGE 5: XDDJ

✱ Drop down the first hole, go right, and drop down the next hole. You land on an anvil-shaped rock. Go to the screen on the right and jump over the spikes below (the tentacles won't grab you), then continue to the next screen. Watch for falling rocks on this screen. They fall in a pattern, always in the same spots, so study the screen for the safe spots. As soon as the rocks land, run past them while they're still breaking apart. On the next screen to the right, watch the pattern of the falling rocks again, then run to the right where the two walkways join near the tentacles. Don't stand below the tentacles. Take a few steps to the left up the higher walkway (the rocks won't hit you) and shoot to the right at the tentacles. Now walk right to the next screen. Jump over the floor monsters in this area. On the next screen, shoot the tentacles and avoid the floor monsters. Be careful to avoid a hole as you enter the next screen. Jump over the hole, avoid the floor monster on the other side, and go right. Walk through to the next screen and fire a Super Shot through the wall.

STAGE 6: FXLC

✱ Return to the left until you reach the falling rocks, avoiding the floor monsters along the way. Go up the higher walkway and left to the next screen. There's a bird hanging from the ceiling. Walk left past him, then turn around and shoot him. He flies onto the next screen. Follow him. Jump off the ledge and grab onto the stalactite hanging from the ceiling, then push Up on the control pad to climb it. Jump to the next stalactite and wait for the bird to get caught by the tentacles, then quick climb to the left across the rest of the stalactites. When you jump off the screen to the left from the last stalactite, you land on top of the anvil-shaped rock.

Climb across the stalactites, quickly past the tentacles as the bird is captured.

STAGE 7: KRFK

✱ Fall off the left side of the anvil-shaped rock and fire a Super Shot at the base to crack it and cause it to tilt. Climb to the upper-right passage, then go right. Carefully jump over each hole and go to the right until you find a reservoir of water. Here comes the tricky part! Stand to the far left of the screen and fire a Super

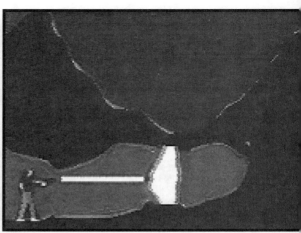

Shoot the base of the anvil-shaped rock,
then climb upward.

Fire a Super Shot to release the water,
then make a run for the far left.

Shot to the right to release the water, then race three screens to the left. As you jump on the rock covering the left hole, a jet of water shoots you upward. Walk up the passage to the right. Fire a Super Shot at the right wall and go to the next screen. Go up the stairs and jump over them to the right. Walk across the moss-covered wall. On the next screen, you see your alien friend thrown into a small passage.

STAGE 8: KLFB

✴ Run back to the left and down the stairs, then run to the right until you enter a room with three chandeliers. Go to the bottom of the stairs, duck, and fire rapidly to shoot a guard. Go back up the steps and shoot the chandelier (to release your friend). Run to the right until you're knocked to the floor by a guard. When he picks you up off the ground, press Down on the control pad and press A to kick him where it hurts. Run left and press Down to grab your gun, then shoot the guard.

✴ Go right to the next screen. Place a shield on your right, but also to the left of the center of the screen. Walk through it and place another shield to your right so that you're standing between them. Shoot the guard on the right and put up shields as necessary to protect yourself. When the guard on the right is toast, run to the right and quickly jump into the water before the other guard catches you.

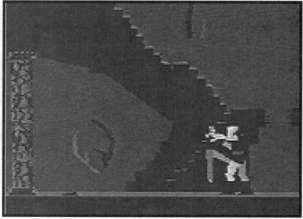

Kick the guard between the legs, then roll
and grab your gun to shoot him.

Place a shield to the left and right, then concentrate
on blasting the guard on the right.

STAGE 9: DDRX

✦ It's time to go swimming. Swim down two screens and left two screens. Go up into the left passage (avoiding the floor monster) and take a breath from the air pocket. Swim down two screens and go right. Climb out of the water carefully to avoid the floor monsters and go to the right one screen. Shoot the power line, return left, and jump back into the water. Swim up to the air pocket again, down one screen, then two screens right and up to reach the area where you began the stage.

STAGE 10: HRTB

✦ Get out of the water on the left side and run left until you reach the stairs. Stand under the electric lift and press Up. Go up the stairs and zap the guard at the top. Go right to the next room. Put up a shield next to the three doors and walk to the right until the doors open. When the guard throws a glowing grenade, step back to the left until the doors close. The grenade rebounds and kills the guard. Go through the door and fire a Super Shot at the wall to the right. Walk right to the next screen.

✦ Stand below the electric lift and press Up. Recharge the gun and go back down. Walk right to the next room, and a tricky sequence. Closely watch the glass sphere. Crouch down and wait for the glare on the bottom of the sphere to reach the center area, then shoot the sphere to make it drop. You should hear a death cry from the guard as he gets crushed by the sphere. If you didn't hear a cry, you screwed up. (It happens.) Go back three screens to the left, down the stairs, and two screens to the right. Swim across the water and continue right to see the dead guard. Continue right into the next room.

STAGE 11: BRTD

✦ Fall down the hole and blast the wall to the right with a Super Shot, then run for your life! When you reach the dead end, turn around and put up a shield. Keep creating shields and fighting off the guards until your alien friend rescues you from above.

STAGE 12: TFBB

✦ Walk to the left a few steps as your friend runs into the building, then run to the right along the path in the background. Go two screens to the right, then run into the other side of the building

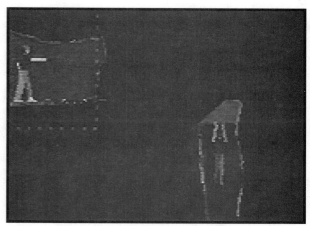

Stage 9: Shoot a Super Shot to destroy the Force Field, then return to the air pocket.

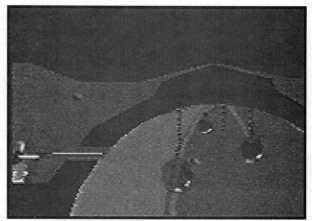

Stage 10: Kneel and aim at the green glass sphere, then fire when you see the guard's reflection.

Stage 11: At the dead end, make shields until your friend rescues you from above.

Shoot the guard on the right, then wait
for your friend to finish off the other.

Your friend will throw you across the gap,
then miss when he tries to jump.

to help your friend. Walk up to the shield until
your arm can reach through and shoot the guard
on the right. Wait for your friend to finish off the
other guard, and follow him to the right. Run into
your friend's arms and he throws you across the
gap. Unfortunately, your friend can't quite make
the jump himself. You have to save him!

✷ Stand on the edge above your friend and jump to
the left to swing into a tunnel. Stand on the right
edge of the tunnel and place shields to the left,
then step forward and fire a Super Shot to blast
through the shields of the attacking guards.
Quickly fire another shot to kill the guards.
Continue making shields and firing Super Shots
until the guards stop coming.

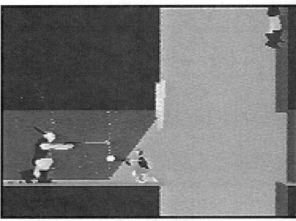

On the right edge, quickly and
repeatedly place shields and shoot.

STAGE 13: TXHF

✷ Run to the left and follow the group of guards
escaping the building. Stop running just before
you reach the door; this makes it slide open, and it
also won't crush you when it closes. Point your
gun at the guard trapped in the building. He raises his arms and hits a button to close the door.
Run to the right one screen and climb the stairs.
Jump over the stairs to the right and face left.
Place a shield to your left, step forward, and fire a
Super Shot to destroy the wall next to the guard.
He starts throwing glowing grenades that roll
down the stairs. Wait until at least five grenades
are dropped (to destroy the floor below) before
shooting the guard. Go down the hole to the left
of where the guard was, face right, and charge up

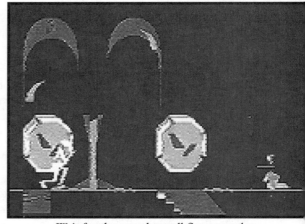

Wait for the guard to roll five grenades,
then blast him.

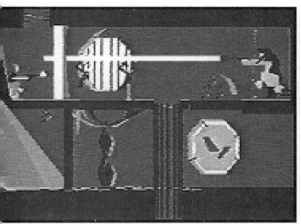

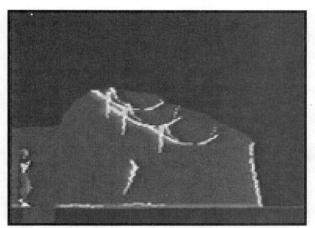

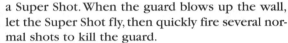

Charge up a Super Shot, then let it go
when the guard blasts the wall.

If you walk fast out of the dark room, you'll
fall into this hole early, missing the switch.

a Super Shot. When the guard blows up the wall,
let the Super Shot fly, then quickly fire several normal shots to kill the guard.

✦ Go down the shaft in the center. Blast the wall on
the right, then go back up the shaft and up the
hole at the left. Go down the stairs and drop into
the hole. Run to the right through the next screen
until the lasers stop firing. Quickly stop running
and tiptoe to the right until you appear in the next
screen. Jump over the hole and hit the lever on
the wall. Go down the hole and run to the right
while all hell breaks loose. When you reach the
dead end, push Up to ride an electric lift. Walk to
the left to activate a floor and save your friend.
Follow him to the right, up the passage, and right
to the battle vehicle.

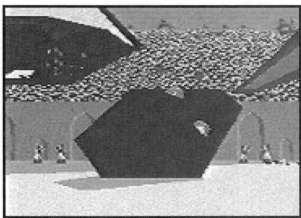

Press the buttons in the battle vehicle
to launch out of this war zone.

STAGE 14: CKJL

✦ The battle vehicle is loaded with buttons to experiment with, but you don't have time to mess around.
Press the lower button first. More buttons appear. Press the lowest-left button to make a keypad appear.
Press the button on the right side of the green light to activate the control panel and weapons. Now press
all four of the buttons in the upper-left corner, in any order. A while button starts flashing. Press it to activate the escape pods.

STAGE 15: LFCK

✦ Your pod lands in an alien bath, but the ladies are soon replaced by gun-toting guards. Run right to the
next screen, crouch down, and put up a shield to the right. The lasers from the left are harmless as long
as you stay crouched. Blast every guard that appears from the right—use some Super Shots to speed up
the job—and run to the right when the coast is clear. Your friend joins you on the next screen. Continue
to the right until the floor is shot out from underneath you. After a long fall and a rescue of sorts, you end
up on the ground while your friend fights with the bad guy. Immediately crawl to the right and the controls. When the bad guy walks towards you and reaches the middle of the room, press Up and A to pull

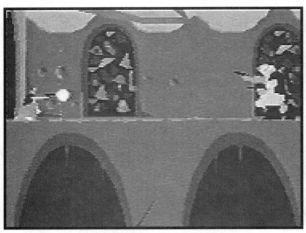

Crouch down, build shields,
and fire Super Shots at the guards.

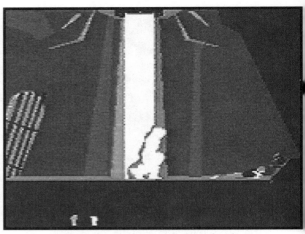

When the evil twin is below the disc
on the ceiling, throw the switch.

the lever and fry him. Hit the switch again and crawl to the left to zap up to the roof before the guards shoot you.

Part II: Heart of the Alien

STAGE 1: BDXF

✦ You start the game standing next to a cute little kitten. Walk left until you appear on the next screen and see a big (and not at all cute) black cat. Quickly turn and run right two screens, then climb up onto the rock ledge to avoid the black cat as it runs underneath you. Now you can run right to see the cat gruesomely devouring the kitten (although you'll die if you do this) or run left two screens and jump over the hole in the ledge. Continue walking left two screens to find three spore pods on the ground. Jump over each spore pod and walk left to the next screen. Get close to the end of the ledge (but not too close) and jump left. Climb onto the top ledge and walk left to the next screen.

Climb onto the rock ledge before the
black cat makes a meal out of you.

Use careful jumps to bounce over the trio of spore pods.

Grab the whip from the rock below the circling birds.

You use the whip right away to swing across the gap.

STAGE 2: XRCL

✤ Wait for the bat to dive toward the ground, then run left past it to the next screen. Your whip is on the ground with two bats flying over it. Wait for the right-hand bat to dive, then run to the whip. Press Down on the control pad to crouch and pick it up. Now you're armed and dangerous! Go right two screens to the large gap you jumped earlier. Press Up on the control pad, and the B button, to wrap the whip around the stalactite in the ceiling and swing across. Carefully walk right to the next screen and leap over the spore pods. After you jump the third pod, run to the right and don't stop running until you fall through a hole into the next stage. If you *do* stop, you're attacked and eaten by a black cat.

STAGE 3: KGDD

✤ The blue drops falling from the stalactites in the ceiling aren't water, but acid, so you need to move through them very carefully. Stand near the first stalactite and wait for two drops to fall off the second stalactite, then run just past the second stalactite and stop. Wait for drops to fall off all three stalactites in front of you and run left to the next screen.

✤ Crack your whip up and left to snag the stalactite and swing over the acid pit. Walk left two screens to an elevator. Stand on the far left side of the elevator and press Up on the control pad to move upward. As soon as you see a spray of acid on the right side of the shaft, press Down to avoid the spray, then press Up again. On the next screen, wait for an acid spray from the left side of the shaft; press Down just before you reach the valve where the acid comes out, then press Up.

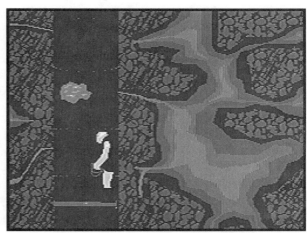

Don't zip straight up the elevator shaft or you'll be killed by a spray of acid from the wall.

✤ At the top of the elevator shaft is a recharge room. Walk to the right and enter the room to charge the whip. Walk left to leave the room and press Up to go through the blue door and into the next stage.

You need to run through here with precise timing to avoid the laser fire from the guards.

Here's another puzzle that requires brutally precise timing. Swing across at just the right moment.

STAGE 4: DGBJ

🔆 As soon as you appear on the screen, hold down the A button for a moment to quickly put up a shield. Wait for the guard's shield to disappear and blast him with a tap of the A button, or use a Super Blast to destroy his shield and shoot him before he puts up another one. Once he's dead, you can experiment a bit with your whip's new powers. Tap A to fire a laser beam; hold A for a moment, then release A to put up a shield; or hold A until a large white ball forms on the whip, then release A to fire a Super Blast. Super Blasts destroy shields and can blast through certain doors.

🔆 When you're ready to continue, walk slowly left to the next screen. Watch the guard on the right side of the screen; as soon as he fires two shots, run left *without* stopping to the next screen. If you stop, or if the guard fires more than two shots before you start running, you're dead.

🔆 You're now in a room with four doors to the left. Run to the middle of the screen, turn right, and put up two shields to block the guards that attack you from the right. Turn left and use a Super Blast to shoot through the first of the four doors. Keep turning right to put up shields and left to shoot through the doors. When you destroy the fourth and final door, run left to the next screen.

🔆 Stand at the end of the ledge and watch the guard marching back and forth below you. Wait for him to walk below you and turn to the left, then use the whip to swing across to the left. You kick the guard into the pit, and he shoots the control panel as he falls, shutting off the electric field. (If you miss the guard, you get fried by the field.) The timing of your swing is very important, so don't swing too early. Walk left to the next screen.

STAGE 5: KTLB

🔆 Walk onto the elevator and press Down on the control pad. Shoot or whip the power box to shut off the electric field at the bottom of the shaft, and go down to the next screen. On the next screen, wait for an acid spray from the left side of the shaft. Press Up and then Down to reach the bottom of the shaft and run right to the next screen. Here's the guard you kicked from behind just a few

Use the whip to open the vent and free your good buddy Lester.

screens ago. Jump over him (don't get too close or he grabs you) and walk right to the next screen. Quickly put up several shields and shoot it out with the guards. Kill them both and walk right to the next screen.

❧ Climb up to the middle ledge and put up shields as you slowly work your way to the right. When you're about halfway across the screen, crack your whip at the guard to bring the gate crashing on his head and to release Lester. Don't teleport down to the next guard immediately. Instead, go left and off the screen, then return. When you come back onto the screen, the guard should *not* be pointing his gun. Now use the teleporter and immediately put up a shield. Lester kills the guard with a well-rolled grenade. Walk right to the next screen.

❧ Walk onto the elevator and you automatically give Lester a boost into the air vent. Press Down and ride to the next screen. Shoot the power box near the bottom of the screen to shut off the electric field and ride down to the bottom of the elevator shaft.

STAGE 6: RLRB

❧ Walk carefully past the two acid sprays, one at a time, to the next screen. This screen has five sprays coming from the ceiling and floor. Wait for the right-hand floor vent to erupt, then run past it to the right side of the left-hand floor vent. Now wait for the left-hand vent to erupt and run left to the next screen.

❧ Use the whip to swing across the gap and walk left to the next screen. Use the whip again to swing across the room with the legs of the guard. The evil mutha drops out of the ceiling and falls into the spikes. Cool! Walk left to the next screen. Wait for both tentacles to withdraw into the ceiling and for both floor vents to erupt, then run left to the next screen. (You can also whip the first tentacle to destroy it.) Walk underneath the teleporter and press Up on the control pad. Relax and enjoy the nifty animation sequence.

Swinging across the pit using the guard's legs is the most amusing (and satisfying) moment in the game.

STAGE 7: RJLG

❧ Walk left one screen. Shoot the control panel to disable it and stand to the left side of the grate in the background. Whip upward to cause a stack of crates to fall to the ground. (If you don't whip the crates down, they smash you when you try to walk past them.) Walk left to the next screen. The three blue lights in the middle of the screen are spikes that skewer you if you try to walk past them. Get a running start and jump over the floor plate below the spikes. Walk left to the next screen. Put up several shields and kill the guard. Walk left to the next screen.

❧ There's a snake hiding in the skull just to the right of the electric door. Get a running start and jump over the skull to avoid the snake. Walk left to the next screen. Put up shields and kill the guard. Walk

Don't get crushed by the stack of crates.

left to the next screen. Walk into the recharge
room on the left to fill up your whip, then go
through the door on the back wall to the next
stage. Here comes the longest and toughest section of the game!

STAGE 8: LKHC

✳ Run right two screens and stop between the first
two of the three electric fields. The second and
third fields go on and off at regular intervals, so
move slowly past them to the next screen. Use the
teleporter to move up to the guard and the door.
Put up several shields, then use a Super Blast to
shoot through the door. Kill the guard and use the
teleporter at the top of the screen. Walk left into
the recharge room to give your whip a boost of
juice. Go down one screen and right one screen.
Quickly put up shields and kill the guard. Make
sure you're facing to the right before going down
the teleporter to the next screen.

✳ Quickly put up shields to the right and kill the
guard. Walk right one screen and use a Super Blast
to kill the tentacle creature in the ceiling. (There's
no real reason to do this other than it's fun.) Walk
left two screens. Quickly put up shields and use
the teleporter to move above the guard. Walk left,
use the teleporter to move down again, and shoot
the guard from behind. Use a Super Blast to disable the glowing dial that the guard was standing
next to and walk left to the next screen.

✳ Run past (or shoot) the tentacle creature and walk
left to to the next screen. Put up shields and shoot
the guard. Ignore the teleporter for now and walk
left to the next screen. Use the elevator and go
down one screen. When you reach the bottom,
walk left to the next screen. Get a running start
and jump across the hole. Walk left to the next
screen and prepare to run across the spraying
vents. if you start running when the middle vent is
spraying, you'll make it through easily. Now use a
Super Blast to destroy the strange machine.

STAGE 9: CXLD

✳ Walk left past the machine to the next screen. Use
a Super Blast to destroy the huge and hard-to-see
black tentacle in the ceiling. Stand over the bomb
timer (which looks like a glowing pyramid) and
press Down on the control pad to pick it up. Run
right two screens and don't stop running until

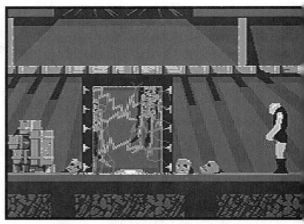

There's a snake hiding in the skull next
to the electric door. Don't get bitten!

Five steaming vents–they're equally
hard to run across in either direction.

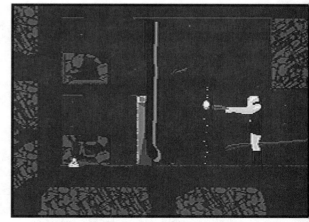

That glowing pyramid is a bomb timer.
That large black thing is a deadly creature.

you're past the spraying vents. Walk right to the next screen and jump across the hole. Walk right to the elevator and ride it upward. Walk right to the teleporter and use it.

STAGE 10: TBBL

✦ Walk left one screen. Run left past the bats to the next screen. Run left two screens to the teleporter and use it. Put up shields and kill the guard. Walk left one screen and pick up the bomb. Walk right one screen and down one screen, then walk left to the electric fields. Use the whip to swing to the left and walk left to the power generator.

STAGE 11: HLCJ

✦ Walk up to the generator and press the A, B, and C buttons on the control pad at the same time to activate the bomb. (Sure would've been nice if the instruction manual mentioned how to do this!) Walk right to the next screen and wait until you see and hear the bomb go off. Swing across to the right and walk right three screens to the bats. Stop on the left side of the screen and time your run to the right. (Wait for the bats to fly to the top of the screen before starting your run.) Use the teleporter to go down.

STAGE 12: FFTR

✦ Put up a shield to your left and run right to the next screen. Avoid the tentacle creature and move

Drop the bomb next to the generator and move onto the next screen before you're caught in the blast.

right two screens to the next teleporter. Use it, quickly put up a shield to your right, and walk left to the next screen.

STAGE 13: GCDT

✦ Use the teleporter, put up shields, destroy the door with a Super Blast, and shoot the guard. Go up the teleporter and use the recharge room. Go down one screen and left two screens. Put up shields and kill the guard, then use the teleporter.

STAGE 14: LTKX

✦ Walk left two screens and go through the door. Go left and a crate falls on your head, knocking you to the ground. Walk left and pick up the whip. Unfortunately, it's now broken, and can't shoot lasers or make shields. Walk through the door to the chamber of the prison warden.

STAGE 15: CDJR

✦ Walk left to the edge of the screen and the warden pops you with a sucker punch. As soon as you stand up, whip upward to drop a crate on the warden's head. Walk left to the next screen. Whip to the left to hit the warden, take a step to the left, and whip the warden a second time. Take two steps to the left and whip upward to drop anoth-

Crack your whip above the warden to drop a crate on his head, which stuns him for a few moments.

er crate on the warden's head. He's got to be hurtin'! Walk left to the next screen.

⚡ Whip the warden three times to move him onto the platform on the left side of the screen. Stand in front of the switches on the wall and press Down on the control pad to open the platform. And that's it! Sit back and watch the nifty ending sequence. (Why'd they have to kill off Lester, though?)

Drive the warden onto the platform and then throw the switch to drop him into the jaws of the black cat.

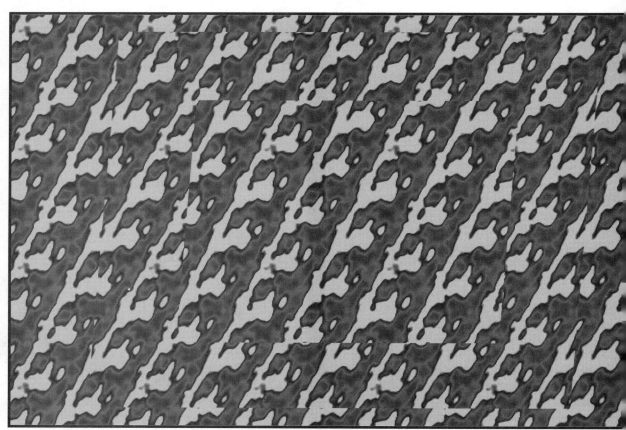

"Distortion Bars" by J. Douglas Arnold
This stereogram is what I consider a "happy little accident". I started with the pattern, played around with different distortion techniques, and ended up with an odd but cool image. See page 325 for more 3D information.

THE LION KING

CATEGORY: Platform   DEVELOPER: Disney Software/Virgin Interactive
PLAYERS: 1   PUBLISHER: Virgin Games

Introduction

Virgin does it again! Disney has always demanded that games based on their characters be top-quality in all aspects, and Virgin has fulfilled that demand with each of their Disney co-productions. The Lion King features great graphics, animation, music, and (most importantly) gameplay. As with past productions, such as The Jungle Book and Aladdin, this latest creation also has some flashback gameplay from some of the best video games in history. You're likely to recognize levels that will remind you of Donkey Kong and Kaboom!, among others. The game follows the movie fairly closely, beginning with life as little Simba, and eventually ending with the battle against the older Simba and his evil uncle, Scar.

Gameplay is never compromised
when Virgin and Disney join forces!

Basic Strategies

- **Controls:** The slick color manual (a rarity in the Genesis market) will give you a great breakdown of the controls. In case you've lost the manual, or are renting this game, we'll give you the basics. Use Up and Down on the control pad to scroll the screen, allowing you to see a little more in that direction. All of the following controls can be modified in the Options screen, but if you didn't change them, this is what they'll be: A to roar, B to slash (as adult Simba), C to jump/pounce. Press down diagonally while moving to roll. As adult Simba, press Slash and Jump simultaneously to maul or flip enemies (you can also use the X, Y, and Z buttons if you have a 6-button controller). During the bonus rounds, press any button besides Start to make Pumbaa belch (causing all of the bugs to disappear), and hit C to make Timon jump.

- **Jumping:** If you make a jump from standing still, you'll only jump about half as far as if you jump after taking a step.

The rolling attack works well against enemies
that are too dangerous to pounce, like porcupines!

Bonus Rounds

✦ You'll get a bonus round if you find one of the Bonus Round Bugs during a stage. This bug has a yellow X on it's back. You'll enter one of two bonus rounds: The Bug Toss or The Bug Hunt.

✦ **BUG TOSS**: The Bug Toss bonus round is very reminiscent of the classic video game Kaboom! Timon runs back and forth along the top of the screen dropping bugs. Most bugs drop quickly, but some drop slowly. The trick is to avoid getting confused by the slow-moving bugs. When you see a bug moving slowly, ignore it and concentrate on the next bug or two, then grab the slow bug. You'll get bonuses depending on how long you last. The only bugs you can't grab are the spiders (black). Make sure you grab all the

The Bug Toss will give you long-time game fanatics flashbacks of the Atari 2600 classic *Kaboom!*

rest. If you know for sure that you can't grab every bug on the screen, quickly hit the roar button to remove all of the bugs from the screen and start fresh. You only have one roar per bonus round.

✦ **BUG HUNT**: The only rule here is to grab as many bugs as you can while avoiding the spiders and bombardier beetles. There's a clock to beat, so move quickly, but carefully.

Stage 1: Pridelands

✦ **There is no time limit,** so don't feel rushed to get to the end. Exploring the area will net you plenty of tasty bugs that will increase your energy and roar power. There's also a fake wall (read on to find it) that hides an extra life and a continue.

✦ **Enemies:** The chameleons will hit you with their tongues as you approach. Pounce on them to take them out easily. The Bombardier Beetles are dark in color, and will raise their wings when you pounce on them — move away quickly because they explode after raising their wings. The porcupines cannot be pounced unless they are on their backs. Roar at them or pounce them to flip them onto their backs.

✦ There's an African Red Bug (increases Simba's total health) that looks out of reach on the far left of the second floor. If you hold down on the control pad, you'll be able to see the red ladybug. From the point directly above the red ladybug, go to the left and drop straight down from the side of the ledge, then leap to the right to the next stone. As you jump to the ledge with the red ladybug you must make a short jump by tapping the jump button once quickly. If you hold the jump button down too long, you'll jump too high and land on the ledge above the red ladybug.

Enter the wall here to find a hidden area with a Circle of Life (continue) and a 1Up (extra life).

There's a **Circle of Life** (continue) and a **1Up** (extra life) in the right wall. When you reach the third floor up (directly below the top floor), go to the right wall and jump up. Simba will grab the top of the stone in the wall, then you can press Up to climb up onto it and go through the wall. Below inside the wall is a porcupine guarding a 1Up. Land to the left of it, then growl to flip it over. Roll into the wall on the right to reach the area below. Another porcupine guards a ledge here. Land on the right side of the porcupine, then go down on the right side of the ledge to find the Circle of Life.

Search the top left area to find lots of bugs. There aren't any spiders, so grab everything you see because it's all good stuff. Be sure to find the **bonus round bug** with the yellow X on it's back

Search the top-left area of this stage for lots of bugs, including this bonus round beetle with a yellow X.

in the top-left corner. Once you find the continue marker you'll have to face a hyena.

BOSS: The hyena will try to pounce you, and he's invincible while he's active. Once he stops and breaths heavily, quickly pounce on him once and bounce away from him, then wait for him to get tired again. Don't let him corner you, and run under him when he's leaping into the air.

Stage 2: Can't Wait to be King

Grabbing the tails on the rhinos is very tricky, since Simba tends to miss grabbing it often. Since there's no time limit, spend some time practicing on the first rhino until you're comfortable with making the grab.

The trees are filled with monkeys that will throw Simba in various directions. The pink monkeys will change their direction if you roar at them. From the beginning of this stage, jump onto the head of the

rhino to reach the monkeys above. They'll throw you to the giraffes, which tilt their heads after a second or two. Quickly jump across the heads of the giraffes before they dump you into the water below. When you reach the next island, roar at the pink money once to turn him toward the left, then climb up and roar at the higher pink money to make him face toward the right. Launch off the head of the rhino and the monkeys will throw you to a giraffe, and you'll land on an ostrich.

Ostrich: This part can be tricky thanks to a confusing double jump required in some areas. There are two ostrich areas like this, and the second area doesn't have the added advantage of arrows to clue you in on upcoming obstacles. Therefore, it's important to pay attention to the trees and pink rhinos while playing the first area.

The ostrich ride has a tricky double-jump that's bound to give Simba a headache.

If you see a pink rhino, you must jump, and if there's a nest in the tree, you have to jump again while in the air to clear the nest (the double jump, marked by two up arrows in the first area). If you see any nests in the tree, you must duck to avoid them (marked by a down arrow in the first area). The double jump is the only tough part of the ostrich run, since you must time the second jump at the right moment, when you're at the highest point of jumping with the ostrich.

Be sure to make a leap for this Circle of Life before leaping to the giraffe head above the 1Up.

* **After the first ostrich run** you'll have to deal with more rhino tails. There are four rhinos that will allow you to safely cross the first water area, but there's an easier way to get across. Make a running jump across the water, jumping from the very edge of the land, and you'll always grab the tail of the third rhino. When you reach the next small island, you'll find a **1Up.** If you lose a life

after grabbing the 1Up, you'll be able to grab it the next time you pass through. As long as you grab it each time, you'll never run out of lives. Some of the other 1Ups, including the next two in this stage won't reappear after you lose a life (unless you use a continue). From the small island you must reach the top nest of the tree to jump over to the giraffe on the right. Jump up to the second nest, stand on the right edge of the nest, then leap over to the left and grab the purple rhino facing forward at the top of the screen. You can grab onto the nostril on the right of this purple rhino. Once you grab it, push up to climb onto his nose. There's only two steps you can take on his nose, so move carefully. Before leaping to the giraffe, leap to the left to grab a **Circle of Life** (continue), and land on the nose of the purple rhino next to it. Leap back to the last purple rhino, then from the left side of his nose take one step to the right and leap for the giraffe.

* **You'll land on the second (and last) ostrich,** but this time you won't have arrows to help you. Read the tips above from the first ostrich run for clues on when to jump or duck. Here's the pattern: single jump, duck, single jump, single jump, duck, double jump, duck, duck, single jump, double jump.

* **The tricky monkeys:** There are two islands with lots of monkeys, and the path that the monkeys must throw you through will eventually have you flying between islands a few times. Begin by hitting the continue marker, then roar at the pink monkey to the right of the marker. Go to the rhino on the right and let him launch you up to grab a **1Up.** Launch off the left rhino to reach the second island to the right. When you land, you'll be next to a pink monkey. Roar to

Roar at the monkeys to make them turn as we've instructed and you'll be thrown to the end of this stage.

make him face to the left, then jump down to the ground. Go to the left to find a 1Up and floating logs in the water. Grab the 1Up and jump left to each log as it is rising to reach the first island. Launch off the first rhino and, after being thrown many times, you'll land on a nest in a tree on the first island.

Don't fall to the ground, or you'll have to start over again from the left rhino. Leap to the nest above and roar to make him face right. There's a Blue Beetle to the right that you can leap to, which will increase Simba's total roar. Drop down to the bottom and roar at the pink monkey near the right rhino to make him face left. Go back to the left rhino and launch again to reach the end of the stage.

Stage 3: The Elephant Graveyard

This romp through the bones of unfortunate elephants begins with a battle against two hyenas. Use the same strategy as the boss of the first stage. Once you knock one of the hyenas out, the second will be

a breeze. Beware of many collapsing bones in this area — try to stop on areas where the surface below looks solid. The vultures always begin below you, but once they fly above you they are very difficult to pounce. Try to pounce them the moment you see them rising from the ground. If they're above you, stand still and wait for them to swoop down, then leap straight up and pounce them.

After fighting the first two hyenas, go to the far left to grab a patterned beetle, then go back to the right and fall to the area below. To the far left of this floor is a Bombardier Beetle, which will decrease your life if grabbed. Be careful when dropping into area where you can't see — it's easy to drop to your death in this area. You can look down by standing still and holding down on your control pad — look before you leap. After fighting the third hyena (he's alone), stand below the spot with the Plain Beetle and leap to the left to grab the ledge above. Climb up to grab the **bonus round beetle** (it has a yellow X on its back), then drop back down and go right along the bones hanging near the ceiling. Continue following the obvious paths ahead, and use the roll attack to get through any walls of bones that block your way. You're leaping skills will be put to the test when you must climb up narrow passages by jumping back and forth between the walls. There's an **extra life** under a slide, and the only way to it is a risky fall before you reach the slide. A safer bet is the **Circle of Life** just a few screens ahead. When you see it, go to the left edge of the bone above it and hang down, then drop to it. After grabbing it, leap to the trampo-

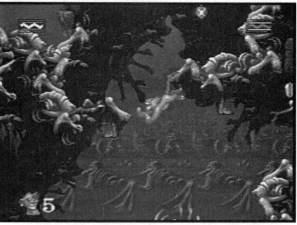

Make this leap to reach the bonus round beetle, then you'll be able to play the bonus round, of course.

You might take a hit falling for this Circle of Life, but it's well worth the continue you'll earn to lose a little health.

line to the right. You'll have to battle two hyenas ahead, with the same pattern that worked with the first two hyenas of this stage. They're the only thing between you and the end of this stage.

Stage 4: The Stampede

✸ Here's a very cool stage that's totally different than the rest. Everything is running toward you on the screen, leaping over the "camera" that provides your view. Move left or right to avoid the stampeding wildebeests. When you see a rock flash at the bottom of the screen, move left or right to avoid it, or jump immediately after the fourth flash to clear it. The question mark (?) flashing means random rock will appear. Jump on the fourth flash of the question mark to be sure to avoid whatever rocks appear.

Make your jump on the fourth flash of the rock to jump over it safely.

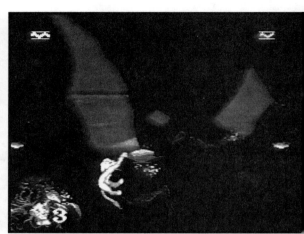

In Simba's Exile, take your time making the jumps across these rocks to avoid falling into danger.

Stage 5: Simba's Exile

✸ This stage is almost as easy as the first. The only challenging elements are large boulders that chase you down the passages leading to the right. Also be sure to master the rolling attack so you can quickly get past the porcupines. Near the first checkpoint is a tricky area with lots of rocks to hang from and climb across. Take your time making the jumps from rock to rock to avoid falling.

Stage 6: Hakuna Matata

✸ Head for the right whenever possible. Pounce the frogs and spiders the moment you see them. There's a one-up directly before the first checkpoint that's in plain sight and will reappear if you lose a life later. When you get to the checkpoint, go right and keep heading right down each waterfall junction to take a shortcut to the waterfall with logs. Climbing up the waterfall using the logs is very challenging. Try to stick to the slower-moving logs near the center whenever possible. There's a **1Up** on the right side of the waterfall. When you reach the top of the waterfall, go left to grab the bonus round beetle, then head to the right and roll down through the sloped ledges.

After you hit the second checkpoint, you'll meet **the boss.** This ape munches on a banana while throwing coconuts your way over his shoulder. He will stand up and slam the ground with his fists, which is the only time you can safely pounce him, then he'll climb up to a higher ledge. Make your jump so you're in the air at the moment he his hitting the ground with his fists. If you try to hit him at any time other than when he slams his fist on the ground, you'll get back-handed. If you want to get this battle over quickly, simply roll into the coconuts to knock them back into the gorilla.

Roll into the coconuts to launch them at the ape,
or pounce him as he slams his fist into the ground.

Stage 7: Simba's Destiny

The adult Simba has new moves, including better pouncing and a mauling/wrestling move. Use his claws to slash your way through vines. The main enemy on this level is the cheetah. Hold down and slash rapidly to hit them while protecting yourself if they decide to jump over you. Attempting the other moves just makes you more vulnerable to getting attacked. Monkeys are everywhere, and they often sit on the edge of a ledge, making it difficult for you to jump for that ledge. Use your growl to knock them out of the way.

There's a **Circle of Life** (continue) near the halfway mark. Here's how to find it: there's a group of vines near the beginning wear several cheetahs come out from. Slash all of them with your claws, then go forward. There's a boulder held up by vines that will roll when you release it. Follow the boulder and use it to climb up to the ledge above, then jump over to the higher platform to the left. As you go left you'll find a plain beetle (energy). Below this platform is a barely visible Circle of Life, which can be reached with a proper jump from the edge of the ledge below. If you release the boulder held up by the vines, you'll have a place to land at the end of the jump.

Knock the boulder down from the vines,
then leap for the Circle of Life and land on the boulder.

Another cheetah-infested vine area is ahead. Just beyond it is a boulder hanging from above that will drop and chase you as you walk past it. Just move as quickly as possible.

Stage 8: Be Prepared

✦ Duck and slash to defeat each cheetah as you see him. If you run past them, they'll follow and eventually gang up on you. There's a hidden room in a wall on this stage. To find it, go to the right until you make a longer-than-most fall down a wall (there's a carcass directly next to the wall, which you can walk left into). Inside the wall is a blue beetle (increases Simba's total roar).

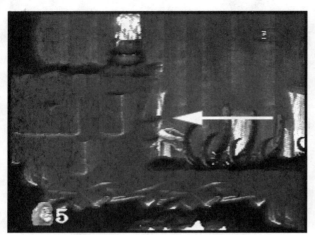

Walk into this wall to find a hidden area with a blue beetle to increase Simba's total roar.

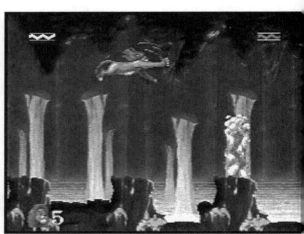

This room seems like a dead end, but the stalactites on the ceiling can be used to bust through the floor.

✦ Near the halfway mark of this stage is a room that seems to be a dead end. There are items viewable below, lava geysers, and high walls on each side that can't be climbed. The secret is in the stalactites on the ceiling. Stand on the lava geyser between lava blasts and jump to hit the stalactites down. There are two stalactites, each above a separate block leading to a separate path. You'll see a tempting 1Up and several bugs below the path on the right, but the left path is the only path that leads to a valuable checkpoint.

✦ After hitting the checkpoint, go to the left and drop to land on a floating log in the lava. As you float to the left, jump and slash to hit each bat the moment you can reach it (before it flies toward you). The **1Up** is a tough jump, but worth the risk if you hit that checkpoint only a few screens back. You'll reach a platform with a hyena and a cheetah to fight. The log will continue to float below, and you must move quickly through these two short battles to catch up with the log or you'll be stranded on this platform. There's a 1Up to the left of the platform to grab on your way back to the log (worth jumping for even if you miss the log). When you reach the next platforms, climb to the top and quickly run to the left, drop, and run back to the right to drop before a boulder rolls over you. As you ride the next log, you'll see two cheetahs above. The log will hit the wall and stop, allowing you to remain standing on it until it's safe to jump up and battle the cheetahs. After the next checkpoint you'll enter a room

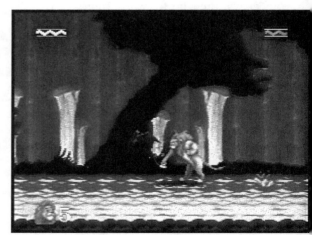

As you float on the log in the lava, jump and slash to hit each bat the moment you see them.

When you leap to the platform to fight the hyena and cheetah, don't waste any time getting back to the log.

Stand on the geysers after they shoot to avoid the falling rocks, then wait for a block to fall that will launch you.

with four lava geysers. Wait for the first geyser to shoot, then jump to stand on the geyser. Rocks fall from the ceiling in between each geyser burst, and the only safe spot is directly on top of any of the four geysers. After the rocks fall and the next geyser shoots, jump to it, and continue this pattern. When you reach the left side of the room, stick to the left two geysers. Eventually a block will drop and plug up the second geyser, and you'll be able to stand on it safely. Then another block will land on the first (far left) geyser. Stand on it and you'll be launched to the next stage.

Stage 9: Simba's Return

※ Defeat all of the hyena's on this stage to take back Pride Rock and face the final boss, Scar. There's a **1Up** on this stage near the beginning. Go to the right into the second cave, defeat the three hyenas in this room, then go to the top-left corner of the room to enter another cave. In this room is a 1Up to

the right. Go back out to the last room, then drop down and enter the cave on the right. In this room, go to the far right into the wall to find a hidden African Red Bug (increases Simba's total health and fills it up). Go back out to the last room, then enter the cave on the left to get back to the first room of this stage. Go right and enter the cave on the far right. Climb up and defeat the hyena, then enter the cave on the right. Defeat the hyena and climb up, then go right, drop down, defeat another hyena, and enter the cave. Defeat the hyenas below, then enter the cave at the top-right corner. Drop down to the left and defeat the three hyenas, then enter the third cave on the bottom floor where you battled the hyenas. Defeat the two hyenas and enter the cave to the left. Defeat the hyena and climb up the cliff

Work your way through the maze of caves while defeating all of the hyenas to claim Pride Rock.

on the left to defeat another hyena. Enter the cave to the top-left. Defeat the four (!) hyenas and grab the plain beetle to add some energy to your health. The moment you defeat the final hyena, you'll be off to the next stage.

Stage 10: Pride Rock

* It's time to cut some new scars for Scar. Stand up to him and slash like crazy with your sharp claws to hit him as rapidly as possible. Take a step forward each time he takes a step back. When you corner him, you can make hits more rapidly, but he'll eventually jump over you to continue the battle. If you want, back up before he jumps over to avoid being hit by him when he leaps, or duck and slash until he makes the leap. When he's about to give up, he'll breath heavy (pant), then make a run for it. It takes at least 100 hits (!!!) just to get through this first battle. This is only the first of three battles necessary to defeat him. Go to the left to chase after him, defeating the hyenas along the way.

* Lightning strikes the ground in several places, causing temporary fires that will burn out if you wait a moment. The flames at the bottom of the screen are only there for decoration, so don't feel rushed to move upward. When you reach a ledge to the upper-left of this area you'll meet Scar for the second battle. Use the same strategy as before. This time it takes about 175 hits to chase him away (what was Virgin thinking?!). After Scar runs away, you can grab a patterned beetle (full health) by climbing up the small steps on the cliff directly above where you just battled

Battling Scar is extremely boring. Move toward him slowly and use hundreds of rapid slashes to slice him up.

Scar. If you have plenty of energy, you might want to chance fighting the two hyenas to the right first, then come back for the beetle. Continue to the right, past the next two hyenas, and head upward. There's lots of lightning along this final run, starting fires on nearly every platform. Wait for the fire to burn out, then make your move. When you reach the final ledge at the top-left, you'll meet up with Scar for the final battle. The exact same strategy will work here, but you're in for a long and boring battle with well over 200 hits before he finally falls off the cliff, and Simba reclaims the kingdom.

MADDEN NFL '95

CATEGORY: Sports
PLAYERS: 1-4 (Simultaneous)

DEVELOPER: Electronic Arts
PUBLISHER: Electronic Arts

Introduction

After years of small adjustments and minor improvements, *Madden NFL '95* undergoes its most substantial facelift ever. Windowless passing modes, two-point conversions, and a host of new offenses and defensive plays are just some of the changes in store for Madden gamers.

With John Madden's jump from CBS to Fox, EA took the opportunity to work in a promo mug (!) for Fox Sports.

Basic Strategies

PICKING A TEAM

✼ The real key to domination is always the running back. *Madden* is almost entirely an offensive-minded football game, and if you don't have a good running back, you won't be able to take advantage of many of

the best offensive plays in the game. When choosing a team to pummel the opposition, the first thing to do is to pick a running back with a combination of speed and strength. Always remember that speed is the most important statistic in *Madden* running backs. Make sure that your running back is in the HB1 position, since this is the position that carries the ball in most of the running plays. HB1 also runs some of the best receiving routes for running backs. The strongest choices are Emmitt Smith (22) of Dallas, Barry Sanders (25) of Detroit, and Barry Foster (25) of Pittsburgh, and Gary Brown (33) of Houston.

✼ Why is the running back so important? There are a variety of reasons. The *Madden* game engines over the years have never been a good at covering running backs out of the backfield. Unless your

The running game is vitally important to your success in *Madden*. Here, Emmitt Smith prepares to bust a move.

opponent has the perfect coverage or reads your play perfectly, the running back is wide open 90% of the time if you know how to run the offensive plays correctly. Running backs are also more dangerous than receivers after the catch (in most cases). Rarely do receivers have the tackle-breaking ability of a good bruising running back. Backs are not only dangerous runners, but can do even more damage if they catch a ball in the middle of a secondary.

✯. After you find a team with a good back, the next thing to do is to make sure that you have speed throughout the secondary. *Madden '95* is a game geared towards long bombs and catch-and-run passes. If you don't have an able secondary, you will get burned often. Allowing easy big plays is not the way to win games. Make sure your cornerbacks (CB) and safeties (SS/FS) have speed of at least 11, preferably 12. Without this minimum, you will be forced to dedicate your defense against the pass, which will leave you defenseless against the run and short pass routes. Good secondaries allow you to have more freedom with your defense. It will allow you to blitz the opposing team more while still keeping decent coverage on receivers. Teams with a good back and good secondary are Dallas, Pittsburgh, Houston, and Philadelphia. Philadelphia is a bit unique because your quarterback makes another good runner.

✯. The next item to check is receivers. You don't need several great receivers; in fact, you don't even need *one* great receiver, although it's a nice luxury to have. Just make sure you have at least one receiver that can consistently catch and has decent speed of at least 10. I consider a statistic of 8 in the catching category to be a reliable receiver. Anything above that is just icing on the cake. Make sure this receiver is in the WR1 or WR2 slot so he will be on the field in every play. It doesn't do any good to have him in the WR3 or WR4 slots because those slots aren't used in every formation.

✯. Finally, the last item to check is to make sure you have a fairly accurate quarterback. Accuracy is the only really important statistic, and it would be wise to pick a QB with accuracy of at least 10 or above. If you don't have an accurate quarterback, you will be missing wide-open receivers all day. Most quarterbacks pass this test, however, and shouldn't really be a problem. A QB with good accuracy will throw bombs well, and keep INTs low, as long as dumb passes aren't thrown.

Offensive Strategies

✯. *Madden '95* is an offensive-minded football game. As stated above, I believe the best mixture to produce a yardage-eating offensive machine is to have a great running back, one consistent receiver, and an accurate QB. In addition to having great players, you must also formulate great plays. Here are some strategies that can be used to perfect these great plays.

PICKING UP AND EXPLOITING BLITZES

✯. Blitzing is a high-risk, high-reward style of defense. Blitzes can cause a lot of offensive disruption, especially if you don't know how to exploit this attack style of defense. *Madden '95* blitzing has its technical flaws, which also make it very hard to read. Normally during a blitz, blitzing linebackers inch up towards the line of scrimmage so they can overwhelm the offensive line as quickly as possible. Not so with *Madden '95*. Blitzing players sit idly by in their formation until the snap of the ball that unleashes them at the quarterback. It makes blitzes nearly impossible to read, but it also makes the computer blitzes very ineffective.

Blitzes don't work properly in *Madden '95*, which makes them hard to read but also not very effective.

The most effective blitz plays are those done by a human opponent. Most human opponents' favorite ways to blitz is to take a defensive player and move him to the outside of the offensive line. This can work pretty well sometimes, but there are all sorts of ways to make your opponent never want to take that high-risk defensive approach again. The best thing to do is to recognize which player he is using to blitz. If he is using a linebacker to blitz, throw to a running back (most of their routes are covered by linebackers) or throw to a receiver that will be crossing the middle of the field. If the player takes a safety, throw deep to the receiver on the side of the field the blitzing safety left vacant.

If you aren't doing particularly well at exploiting holes in the defense as a result of blitzes, improve your pass-protection scheme. Try putting your motion receiver in front of the player that is ready to blitz you. If that's not enough, go to some plays that implement maximum pass protection. These are the plays that only have three receivers running pass routes. Often pass plays will run receivers other than your three active receivers as decoys to get your primary wide-outs open. I will list some of these plays later.

RECOGNIZING ZONE DEFENSE

One of the most basic keys to successful passing in *Madden '95* is recognizing zone defenses. Because this new version of *Madden* actually moves defenders to cover your motion man—something that none of the previous versions have done before—it is very easy to distinguish zone defense from man-to-man defense.

To recognize zone defense, just move your motion receiver by pressing the control pad Left or Right. If a defender follows, you know that the pass-coverage scheme, or at least most of it, is man-to-man coverage. That is, each receiver that goes downfield will be covered by a single defender in the secondary. If no one moves opposite your motion man, a zone defense is being played.

FLOODING THE ZONE

"Flooding the zone" is a popular way of exploiting the zone brand of defense. The basic premise of this offensive strategy is to send so many receivers in one area of a zone at the same time that it is physically impossible for the one assigned defender of that zone to cover them all. Often he will get help from defenders covering the adjacent zones, but it's usually not enough help, and it's not on time. With luck, you'll get a 3-on-2 matchup favoring your receivers. You can even get 4-on-1, but one of the four receivers is a decoy that you can't throw to. The defender doesn't know that, of course, until it's too late. Be sure to move the motion receiver to the side of the flood to complete the offensive tidal wave.

Sending all your receivers into the same area of the field is called "flooding the zone."

To learn how to execute the "flooding" of a zone, read ahead for good flood plays in each formation and how to run them.

FLIPPING PLAYS

Make use of the ability to "flip" your plays. Flipping your plays to the correct side can make a difference between a 3-yard loss and a 25-yard gain.

As a rule of thumb, you generally want to run your play to the side of the field that has more room for your receivers to operate. You don't want to run a play with three receivers to the "short" side of the field. The "short side" of the field can easily be explained running a play to the same side of the field that the ball is on. For instance, if the ball is on the left hash mark, the short side is the left side. If you run a lot of receivers on the short side of the field, they can get jammed up, which will cause them to break their routes. It also makes things easier to the defender because they won't have as much field to cover.

⚡ Running sweeps and toss plays are also not recommended, especially if you have a speedy running back. If you have a fast running back, you need as much lateral room to run to burn defenders so that you can turn the corner for big gains.

⚡ Another way to take advantage of play-flipping is to find out which side of your opponent's defense is weaker. Some teams may have a linebacker with the speed of lightning on the left, while on the right, the LBs are slow as molasses. Take advantage of these matchups by flipping your running plays or receivers away from the good defenders.

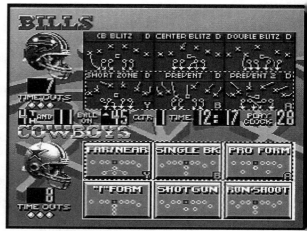

Learn when to flip your plays to run them on the side of the field with more space.

OFFENSIVE PLAYS

⚡ Now that I have given you some offensive strategies, below are some of the best plays in each offensive formation.

FAR FORMATION

⚡ A well balanced formation. Possesses a healthy mix of good running and pass plays. Lots of good plays to defeat zone coverages.

⚡ HB TOSS SWEEP: One of the better running plays in the game. This toss play is a quick hitting outside run that utilizes a large number of blockers in a great scheme. This is a good running play even against a defense loaded against the run.

⚡ FB SCREEN: One of the audibles out of this formation. Throw to the fullback out of the backfield and exploit zone defenses.

⚡ WEAK FLOOD: This play obviously uses the zone flooding technique. The fullback and halfback both run to the weak side (side of OL without the tight end). Be sure to move the motion receiver just to the left of the offensive line. This will generally occupy the linebackers with your receivers

Far Formation. A well-balanced formation (and part of a complete breakfast). Great against the zone D.

while your running backs are left wide open in the flooded zone.

⚡ STRONG FLOOD: Roughly the same thing as the weak flood, except run to the side with the tight end. This play is more suited to get wide receivers open where as the weak flood is good to get backs open.

⚡ GOAL LINE: Obviously for short yardage. The only pass plays in this formation are pretty good ones.

⚡ PLAY ACTION: This play isn't good because of the supposed "play-action fake." It really doesn't fool anyone into thinking the HB has the ball as the name "PLAY ACTION" implies. What it does do, however, is make a nice, wide pass to the left when the defense will usually be pinched inside to defend against the run. What's even better is that this pass route is run by the good HB1 I told you earlier to make sure you have on your team. (You did do that, right?) Hike the ball and immediately hold down the button for a bullet pass to the running back moving straight left from the backfield.

✳ QB SNEAK: A great play to get one or two yards. My favorite on the goal line. Just hike the ball and pound the C button to make your QB fight for some hard-earned short yardage. Sometimes interesting things can happen if you run this play against DIME and NICKLE defenses. I've seen some QB SNEAKs up the middle for 7-9 yards.

✳ HB LEAD LEFT/RIGHT: Bread-and-butter short yardage running plays.

I FORMATION

✳ Strong running formation, but the running plays aren't very good, and there is only one really good pass play.

✳ QUICK SLANT: A great pass versus zones.

✳ HB COUNTER: The recommended running play for this formation.

I Formation. It's a running formation which unfortunately doesn't have very good running plays.

Near Formation. Not as good as the Far Formation, but a decent formation nonetheless.

NEAR FORMATION

✳ Not as good as the FAR formation, but still pretty good. Good mix of pass and running plays.

✳ STRONG FLOOD: A good zone-flooding play to the right of the field. Throw to either of the backs out of the backfield.

✳ HB TOSS: See the Audibles below for this formation.

✳ HB LEAD: Good running play for a consistent 3-5 yards.

PRO FORM FORMATION

✳ Perhaps the best formation. Provides a variety of protection schemes, great passes out of the backfield, and a variety of very effective running plays. A good formation to give the QB throwing time against a blitz.

Pro Form Formation. The best formation in the game, with great passing *and* running plays.

- ✦ CIRCLE PASS: Great pass to HB1. Can lead to big gains. Try moving the motion receiver to the left to clear out linebackers while your running back catches the ball underneath for an easy gain.
- ✦ HB SWEEP: An excellent outside running play. A great blocking scheme. Follow the blocks well and chances for a good gain are high. Don't run this if you have a slow running back.
- ✦ ALL STREAK: An interesting passing play that sends your running back deep immediately. It gives you the unique chance of letting you throw a bomb, and letting the running back catch it in stride while traveling downfield. If your back has good speed and strength, there is a good chance you will score. The passes to the wideouts are very effective if your receivers are burners.
- ✦ QUICK POST: Use against blitzes. Both backs pick up blitzing players on either side of the quarterback. The routes are tailor-made for quick throws.
- ✦ OFF TACKLE: Another well-blocked running play. Use it when you need those sure 3 to 4 yard gains. This generally will not spring you for big plays.

RUN AND SHOOT FORMATION
- ✦ If you have a great offensive line at pass blocking, it's a good formation. If you don't, I wouldn't recommend it too much. Has a lot of great passing plays and anti-blitz plays.
- ✦ FLOOD LEFT: Another effective zone flood play. Pass to the running back. This one will have to be executed quickly since you only have five offensive linemen for protection. No running back or tight end for assistance. If you use a wide receiver for blocking, it will ruin the zone flood.
- ✦ HB COUNTER: A surprisingly good running play despite the blocking. This one can go for some moderate gains. It will fail miserably if there is a half-decent run defense used against this play due to lack of blockers. Rarely do people play run defense against a Run and Shoot formation, however.

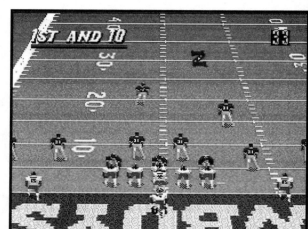

Run and Shoot Formation. A pass formation all the way, with mondo receivers.

- ✦ HB TOSS: Another good outside running play. The toss makes it effective, but don't expect blocking support. Can do some damage against DIME and NICKLE zone defenses.
- ✦ PA PASS: Great deep pass to your wide receivers. Your offensive line better have good pass-protection ratings, however.
- ✦ DEEP POST: Great pass play with lots of options. Generally you will have one or two guys open on this one due to the way the routes are run.

SINGLE BACK FORMATION
- ✦ A formation that is very strong in the run and pass. Also has some great maximum protection schemes. Has a great variety of all types of plays. A good formation to operate out of.
- ✦ WR SCREEN: Good anti-blitz play, and some nice deep passes.

Single Back Formation. Another good formation that provides plenty of protection for the QB.

- CIRCLE PASS: If it's a CIRCLE PASS, it has to be good. Move the motion receiver to the left of the offensive line to clear out the linebackers, then pass to the running back out of the backfield.
- PA STREAKS: Good play for bombs to speedy receivers. A good maximum protection play also. Burn a blitzing team badly with this one. Throw to your fastest receiver.
- HB TOSS: The best running play out of this formation. A good outside play that doesn't necessarily need a speedy running back to execute. For those of you who don't emphasize getting a fast running back, this is a good play for you. If you have a fast running back, let the fireworks begin.
- HB DIVE: One of the better plays in the game in short yardage situations.

SHOTGUN FORMATION

- If you need more time to pass, this is the formation to operate out of. The running plays are weak, but if you like passing downfield, you should feel right at home.
- HAIL MARY: Implies that you should only use it when the game is in the desperation stage. I disagree—it's a great deep ball, especially if you have speedy receivers.
- HB TOSS: Best running play in formation.

Shotgun Formation. Used to be very popular in real-life football, but isn't seen as much any more.

Defensive Strategies

- It's hard to teach defense, and harder still to learn it. *Madden* can make playing defense frustrating because of the numerous flaws in the defensive plays. Earlier I listed ways to take advantage of these flaws when playing offense. It's always easy to exploit flaws, but harder to cover them up. For each strategy I listed in offense, I will explain the best counter to it. Understand that because of the way that the game operates, you will be at a disadvantage. I hope you picked a team with a good secondary like I suggested, because without it, things will be rough. Try to learn timing on getting those hands up.

BLITZING EFFECTIVELY

- If your defensive zones are getting chewed up and spit out, and your defensive backs are getting burned deep because the quarterback has time to eat lunch before throwing the ball, it's time to blitz. You can blitz without being burned if you know how to do it. Having a good secondary will help your cause a lot. Because a steady diet of blitzing is almost essential in *Madden '95*, it is imperative that you get a fast secondary.
- The first rule in blitzing effectively is to use as few computer blitzes as possible. Many of them are just worthless, and take too long to get to the quarterback. The only thing it accomplishes is leaving yourself open to big plays. Find your fastest safety or linebacker, and use him as your blitzer. To make a blitz effective, you must disguise it so that the (human) opponent will not know to throw to your vacated spot. (Of course, the computer opponent is an idiot. You could line up your entire secondary on the line of scrimmage, and it wouldn't know the difference.)
- Outside blitzes are generally the most effective. Set up as close as you can to the line of scrimmage on the side of the field that doesn't have a tight end or wide receiver that can slow you down. Of course, a smart human player will see this and will want to throw do the vacated spot. This is where the trickery begins.

Immediately after the ball is hiked, run back to the place that you vacated. If you took a safety from the deep middle, run back and cover deep middle receivers. If you took a middle linebacker, run back and cover that part of the field. How does this make blitzing effective? Now your opponent can no longer be sure that if you are lined up on the line of scrimmage that you will indeed blitz. The opponent must take into account that you can, and will, fake the blitz and cover the man that he might think will be left open. This confusion can make it so that even a good offensive player will not be able to burn you. A bad offensive player will throw you a good number of interception chances.

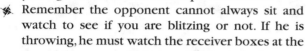
Line up on the outside of the line and blitz as soon as the ball is snapped.

🏈 Remember the opponent cannot always sit and watch to see if you are blitzing or not. If he is throwing, he must watch the receiver boxes at the top of the screen. Unless your opponent is very good, you will create confusion, turnovers, and sacks. I generally prefer using safeties on the blitz because they are fast, and you can generally get back to your coverage assignment about the same time that the receiver does. When you do blitz, there is no particular art to it. Just charge right in, and be sure to dive. If you are blitzing on the same side of the field of a running back assigned to pass-protection or a wide receiver is in your path, you will generally get knocked down. Don't give up if this happens, as your man will generally get up quickly.

CONTROLLING FLOODS IN THE ZONE
🏈 It's difficult to control this defensive problem, because the solutions can result in other problems. Of course, a fast secondary that can react after the ball has been thrown helps things tremendously. If you have trouble with an opponent using a flood technique, you might try taking a safety and bringing him to the problem area. Most zone floods are usually short to medium size passes. Taking a safety that covers deep passes will not usually hurt you. When the opponent hikes the ball, move the safety to the area of the field where there is a large concentration of receivers. Sometimes it will be obvious when the motion receiver is lined up on the side of the field with the running backs. Move the safety in this area and "roam" around, going to anywhere in that zone that the ball is thrown to. A fast safety should be able to get very close to the receiver that it is thrown to, and should get a good number of opportunities at an interception or two. Using a blitzer to hold up a running back or receiver is a little more risky, but usually effective as well.

DEFENSIVE PLAYS
🏈 Because so much of defense is reacting to what the offense does, there are no plays that I can say are just great defensive plays you should use. I will list a few defensive plays I like to use, and will elaborate somewhat on them.

GOAL LINE FORMATION
🏈 Of course a good inside run defense, but can get burned to the outside for big gains if you aren't careful. If you have a fast secondary it can actually be a great pass defense also. The five-man front provides great run stoppage and pass pressure, while the fast defensive backs are capable of covering the receivers.
🏈 MAN LEFT 1: Good run and pass coverage if you have fast defensive backs.
🏈 MAN RIGHT 1: Same as above.

LEFT: As a good run-stopping strategy, try using this play to tell the defensive line to stop runs to the left side. This will generally clog the center as well. Then take control of the linebacker on the line of scrimmage on the right and protect that area against a possible run coming that way. By doing this, you have strong run defense against the left, good run stoppage on the center, and a good chance of stopping runs on the right. You can of course flip it on the right. If the offense is on the right hash mark, pick the LEFT defense because there is more running room that way, and you can guard the right side, where the field is shorter.

Goal Line Formation. The name tells you where it's used (although we're using it on the 30 in this screen shot).

4-3 FORMATION
- A good all-around formation. Good if you have above-average pass rushers up front.
- MEDIUM ZONE: One of my favorite zone defenses, a good balanced zone.
- SHORT ZONE 2: Great zone against annoying short passes, Try blitzing a linebacker out of this formation.
- MAD TIGER BLITZ: A good blitz to stop the run. If the opponent passes, all short routes should be wide open.

4-3 Formation. If you have above-average pass rushers, use this defense for best results.

3-4 Formation. A solid defense against the short passing game, but weak against the run.

3-4 FORMATION
- Good against short passes due to the four linebackers. Runs will be more effective, and the pass rush will be diminished.
- SHORT ZONE: Good defense that utilizes the use of the 3-4, to stop those short passes.
- MONSTER BLITZ: Good against the run, and won't leave you naked against the pass.
- JAM MIDDLE: If you are getting pounded by the running game, this should stop it. Will leave you open to short passes and outside runs.

NICKEL FORMATION

✴ Mostly offers zone defense, and I recommend this pass defense over the DIME, unless your opponent is throwing deep nearly every down. NICKEL will give you good medium pass defense.

✴ CIRCLE ZONE: One of my favorite zones, this saturates the medium passes. No run support by linebackers. If a running back gets past the line, he's going to get at least five yards.

✴ BUMP AND RUN: If you have fast defensive backs, use this defense against the pass. It provides good run support because the linebackers are free to help against the run.

✴ SAFETY CHEAT: I like this play because the defensive linemen "stunt." They cross one another and can make an offensive line blow assignments. You can get added defensive pressure without using a blitz as a result.

DIME FORMATION

✴ If long bombs are killing you, go to this defense. Otherwise, I don't recommend it, even against medium passes.

✴ SHORT ZONE: A short zone in a DIME formation will basically cover medium length passes.

✴ CENTER BLITZ: Good at stopping run, but middle of field will be wide-open

✴ PREVENT 2: Never use this defense unless your ahead substantially with time ticking down. This is the best prevent play because the defensive linemen stunt and can give you a little more pass rush.

SPECIAL TEAMS

✴ FAKES: I don't recommend fakes because they don't put your best players on the field for a key play. If you need that 4th and 1 or 4th and 3, use a good play you know how to execute well. Usually the element of surprise isn't worth passing the ball with your punter.

✴ KICK-OFFS: I recommend kicking to the sides of the field, rather than down the middle. *Madden 95's* kick-return blockers don't set up as well when you kick it to the left or right as opposed to the center.

BLOCKING KICKS

✴ Blocking punts is nearly impossible, but blocking field goals and extra points are another story. The

Nickle Formation. A zone defense for pass protection, and safer to use than the Dime.

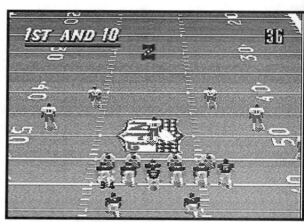

Dime Formation. To be used only against long passes, and even then, it's too vulnerable for your own good.

Block that kick!

most consistent way to block a kick is to take one of your fast men positioned behind the line. Take him and line him up on the outside of the line, then try to line up a direct diagonal path between you and the holder. At the snap, charge and dive at the last second. If you succeed, you will generally tackle the holder. There is no exact science to it. You must experiment and find your fastest man, and the strength of your opponent's offensive line will also have quite a bit to do with it. For some reason, it is much easier to block kicks from the right side of the line. Don't bother with the PUNT BLOCK play, just set up a PUNT RETURN. The only time I would recommend trying the PUNT BLOCK play is if your opponent is backed up in the end zone. Because he is backed up deep, the punter can't set up as far back as usual, making it easier for you to get to him.

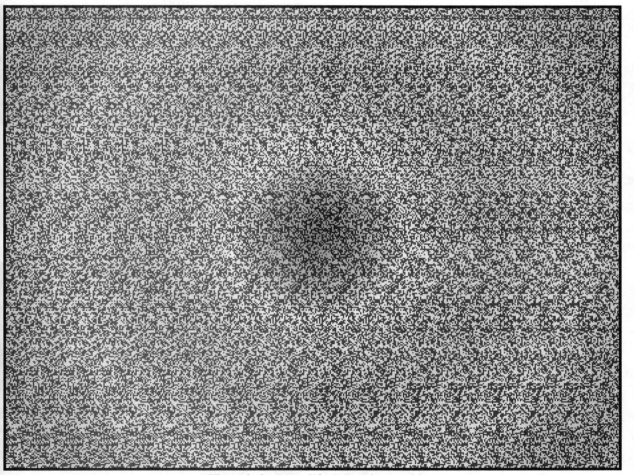

"Through the Funnel" by J. Douglas Arnold
This stereogram began as an experiment in colors, where the colors would disappear when the 3D effect was viewed. Since color would have doubled the price of this book, try to enjoy it without. See page 325 for more 3D information.

MICKEY MANIA

CATEGORY: Platform   DEVELOPER: Travelers Tales
PLAYERS: 1   PUBLISHER: Sony Imagesoft

Introduction

This chapter covers both the cartridge and CD versions of *Mickey Mania*. If you have a Sega CD you must buy that version, otherwise you'll miss out on several excellent comments from Mickey Mouse and an extra bonus level near the end of the game. Regardless of what version you buy, you'll be playing one of the most amazing games available for the Genesis. Traveler's Tales has accomplished many eye-popping graphic tricks, which include a 3D rotating tower and incredibly smooth animation. Mickey travels through several of his most popular movies, beginning with *Steamboat Willie* and ending with a final battle in *The Prince and the Pauper.* Be prepared to be amazed and entertained — 16-bit doesn't get any better than this!

Nearly every Mickey Mouse game has been above and beyond the average game, but this one is the best yet!

Basic Strategies

✦. Both the cartridge and CD versions of Mickey Mania play the same, except for an extra level near the end that we'll point out. All of the following strategies and tips apply for both versions of the game.
Controls: A or C to jump, B to throw.

✦. You have a limited number of **marbles,** and you won't find too many laying around, so don't waste them.

✦. The **hand** in the upper-left corner shows how many more hits Mickey can take before losing a turn. Collect **stars** to add more hits to Mickey's strength.

✦. Walk by the **rockets** to launch them and record your position in the game so you can restart there with your next life.

✦. When throwing marbles at the **weasels** in the last stages, don't throw too fast or your marble will pass through them and be wasted. As soon as their feet hit the ground you can hit them with another marble.

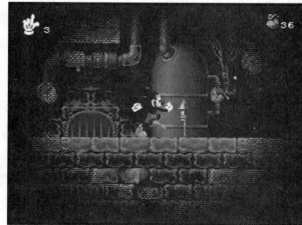

Walk by a rocket to record a checkpoint so you can start at that position if you lose a life.

Scene 1: Steamboat Willie

✦ Dodge the musical notes and jump on the bottle to launch a cork into the goats mouth. Wait for the steam in the whistles to stop before running past them. Jump on the cat to pop a hole in the floor so you can find a **hidden area** with stars. Push the crates to the left and climb back up to the whistles.

Continue to the right until you see a crane picking up crates. Jump on a crate and wait for the crane to carry you safely across the water.

✦ **Stage 1-2:** Avoid the swinging balls while collecting the marbles. Jump up to the windows of the house, then leap to and bounce off the **bird** to reach the stars above. Go right across the clothesline, then leap to the first window below. On the left side of this building is a small sign Mickey can jump to, then jump up to the windows above. In order to lower the **bridge** to the right you must **ring the bells** on the top left and right windows of the building. Leap over the **bully** when crossing the bridge, then turn toward him and throw marbles to knock him out. Bounce on his stomach to climb the crates on the upper-right. From these crates be sure to bounce of the birds back to reach the higher group of windows in the next building. Watch for the crates to fall from above, then jump to the next window when safe. Beyond the last window is a pair of Mickey's ears (an **extra life**). Jump on the crate with the up arrow for a ride, then leap to each of the crates hanging on the right. Move quickly to avoid falling with the crates.

✦ **The Boss** is a group of four gears. Each gear takes for hits by a marble or by pouncing. Pounce on the lower two and use the spring to launch up and shoot marbles at the higher gears. You can push the springs around, but you should be able to shoot the gears from wherever they drop. The crates will drop several bombs before dropping a spring. Concentrate on dodging the bombs, since there's no time limit, and you should be able to survive this boss easily and save Steamboat Willie.

Ring the bells on the top left and right windows
to lower the bridge next to the bully.

Hit each one of the four gears
with a pounce or a marble.

Scene 2: The Mad Doctor

✦ You can shoot marbles at the **bats,** but you're better off saving them for later. Ducking the bats is easy enough. Inside watch out for **skeletons.** The skeletons that fall from the ceiling and crouch only need one marble hit or one pounce before they shatter apart. The skeletons that come walking for you require three marbles or pounces. The bones from both skeletons will damage you, so dodge them as they fall. Watch for knives on the back wall below a hanging skull. Walk slowly up to them to make them drop to the ground, then you can safely walk past them.

✴. **Stage 2-2:** The bats will take two hits, while the swinging skeleton **spiders** only require one hit. Knock the spider off the rope, then grab it for a ride to the other side of the pit. While dodging the burning embers from the fireplace grab the rope and swing, then leap to the left to collect two stars. Don't waste too much energy trying to get all of the marbles over the fireplace. Climb into the pipe to exit.

✴. **Stage 2-3:** The **gurney ride** requires a little memory to know when to duck and when to jump. There's a tricky **1-Up** (Mickey ears) right at the beginning, but avoiding the blades can be tricky. Make your leap the moment you see the blades to grab the ears, then land on the gurney and quickly leap again to avoid falling into the lava pit. You can make each of the leaps from the gurney as its sinking into the lava, so don't feel pressured to jump off too early. The pattern is as follows: Duck or jump the first three sawblades, jump to the next gurney, jump over spikes, jump to next gurney, duck under saw-

blades, jump over two sets of spikes, jump to next gurney, jump over rising sawblades, jump to next gurney, avoid the next sawblades and leap to the exit.

✴. **Stage 2-4:** This **tower** has one of the coolest effects in the game. Keep walking to the left while throwing marbles at bats the moment you see them appear around the corner. You must keep moving because many of the platforms collapse. After dropping down and heading to the right you'll have a few barrels following behind you that are moving too fast. Jump back over at least one of them to avoid being run over, then continue to the right. There's another barrel to jump below.

✴. **Stage 2-5:** In the laboratory watch for more skeletons. The rest of this stage is familiar enemies and obstacles.

✴. **Stage 2-6:** Ride the **elevator** up while throwing marbles at skeletons and dodging their bones. When a skeleton lands on the top of the elevator stand at the center to avoid the bones. When you reach the top don't enter the door! Get off the elevator, then get back on and you can ride up to another floor with lots of marbles and stars. You'll be in the dark, but there are hidden platforms directly below each star. At the top-right is an **extra life** (Mickey ears), and Mad Doctor Mickey will make an appearance before sending you to the next round.

✴. **Stage 2-7:** You must mix chemicals into the **beaker** by pushing the beaker below a pump, then climb up and jump on the pump to put the chemical in the beaker. You must pump each one of the chemicals into the beaker. You can't

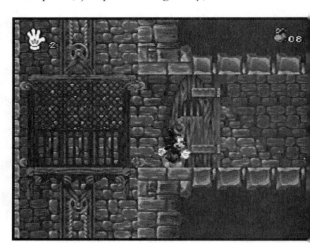

When you reach the top floor in the elevator, take a step out then get back in to reach another floor with goodies!

Push the beaker below a pump, then climb up and pump the chemical into the beaker.

put too much of any chemical in the beaker, so don't worry about hitting the pump twice. After filling the beaker push it all the way to the right onto the burner and hit the button to the upper-right until the beaker explodes. If you kill the bats in this area they'll come back each time you go down to push the beaker. Drop down and go right to meet the boss.

Pounce the Mad Doctor, then make a run for the platform on the far side of the room while dodging his bombs.

✦ **The Mad Doctor:** After the door slams shut go to the right to see the doc. Don't grab the stars above until you need them. There's a rocket to the right that will save your position in this room in case you die. The moment the doctor opens his cape quickly run to the left and jump to avoid the first bomb he throws, then jump on the small platform. When he approaches jump and pounce on his head, then run to the right to avoid the bombs he drops. Jump on the platform to the right. Repeat the pattern of pouncing and running until he's defeated (nine hits).

Scene 3: Moose Hunters

✦ Watch for falling branches and boulders. The moment you see Pluto turn and point to the left be prepared to jump over a rushing moose.

✦ **Stage 3-2:** Here's a really cool 3D effect. The most important part of this stage is collecting the **apples** to keep your speed up. Try to jump over every rock and water stream you see. If you hold down the jump button you'll keep jumping the moment you land. There's an even number of apples on the far left and far right sides, so stick to one or the other and you'll collect enough to reach the finish line.

Collecting apples is the key to speed and the key to outrunning the moose behind you!

Scene 4: The Lonesome Ghost

✦ There are three pits inside the house. If you can clear the first two, stay to the left or right on the third and you'll collect a **1-Up.**

✦ **Stage 4-2:** Take your time in the dark to watch for ghosts. All of the **metal stairs** will flatten out as you walk up them, so be ready to slide back. Wait for the ghosts to disappear, then make your move. Use the rotating platforms to reach the stars by making the side closest to the star rise up, then run across and jump. There's a **1-Up** in the top-left corner that can be reached with the same technique. There are stars above the three pipes blowing their lids. You can reach the stars by rapidly jumping as the lid gets blown. As you climb up the next passage you'll have to leap from lid to lid as they open. There's a star in the upper-right corner of the passage. The exit is to the left, but you'll have to cross a **collapsing bridge** haunted by three ghosts to get there. Jump rapidly as you cross the bridge to keep from falling. It's better to get hit by the ghosts once or twice instead of dropping below and climbing back up.

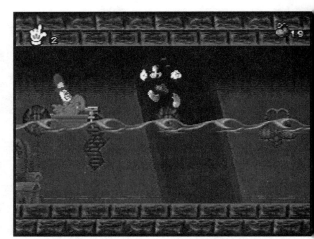

Stay on the barrels to avoid drowning in the water, but don't move too fast or the ghost will get you.

✦ **Stage 4-3:** Jump on the **barrel** and control it to stay above the water and behind the ghost in the boat. Stay on the barrel as it's sinking, then make your jump to the second barrel the moment the ghost speeds ahead. Take the third barrel all the way to the left, then keep jumping to stay out of the water while you wait for it to drain. As soon as the water hits bottom, jump left to hit the next area and a **rocket** checkpoint. Climb the steps and go right. As you walk past the stretching posters (as featured in Disneyland's Haunted House), push the table to the right while avoiding the ghosts and their hats. You have to push the table all the way to the right so you can reach the stairs upward. The star above is reachable, but you have to jump from the swinging rope at just the right moment. At the end of this room is a rising platform with many ghosts. Take your time to run over or under the ghosts as the platform moves.

Scene 5: Mickey and the Beanstalk

✦ Stay off the roots that connect the clumps of mud (they won't hold Mickey's weight). Dodge the seeds and the bugs in the next area. You can jump on the back of the bugs. Use the green apple to collect the stars (push it left to reach the first star). Push the **flowerpot** into the waterdrops to the far right until it grows a flower, then push it all the way to the left to jump to the mushroom. You can't kill the mosquitos, but you can stun them for a second with a pounce or a marble. Jump off the leaves as soon as they start sinking. From the final leaf make the jump from the very edge to reach the ledge above.

Push the flowerpot into the waterdrops to make it grow, then push it to the left to reach the mushroom.

✦ **Stage 5-2:** As you head underground jump from the backs of the **beetles** to reach the marbles and stars above. Watch for falling **cocoons** that break into two little bugs. You'll cross a small bridge that blocks the passage below. Go right and head up the hill, stopping to dodge the first cocoon, then walk quickly to dodge the rest. Hit the button, then go back down the hill to enter

Bounce off the back of the beetle as he flies up
and hit the switch on the wall above...

...go back to the left down two steps, then bounce off
the backs of the butterflies to reach the ledge above.

the darkened passage. Go left and hit the light switch, then rush to the right and jump on the ladybug
for a quick ride out of the cave.

✦ **Stage 5-3:** There's a bonus stage hidden in this area! Don't shoot any of the butterflies. Jump on the
magic beans to make them grow so you can leap to the next ledge. Climb to the top where a light
blue beetle paces back and forth. There's a **switch** on the wall above the beetle, which you can only
reach by jumping on the back of the beetle as he flies upward. Hit that switch, then go back to the left
down two of the giant steps and jump to the green butterfly, then hold the jump button and bounce
off the orange butterfly to reach a ledge with **four stars,** a **1-Up,** and a **big question mark** (?).

✦ **HIDDEN STAGE — THE BAND CONCERT:** If you can survive the climb to the top of the tornado you'll
find Band Leader Mickey and collect an **extra continue.** There's no time limit, so don't rush or you're
bound to fall and end the stage quickly. Watch the next box carefully, then make the jump to it when
safe. The boxes move in a pattern from side to side. If it comes down close and then rises, it will come
back down again soon.

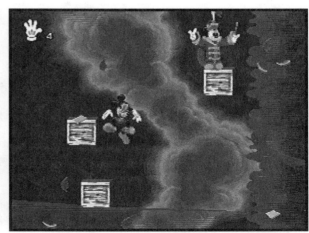

...on the ledge collect four stars and an extra life,
then jump into the question mark (?)...

...TAKE YOUR TIME climbing up the boxes
in the tornado of the bonus stage.

- **Stage 5-3** (continued after switch for hidden stage): Go inside the passage and hit the **rocket** checkpoint, then bounce off the beetle to collect a star. You can knock the beetles out by hitting them with a marble as they are flying up. You must climb the **huge rope** to reach the next area. Climb up to the left of the rope as far as you can, then leap across to the right. As you reach the top you'll see lots of marbles and a star on each side of the rope. Make the leap from the top of the rope, but be careful not to jump from too high or you'll go into the next area.
- **Stage 5-4:** Mickey has to dodge more mosquitos and beetles. When you see the clear Jell-O, push it to the right so you can reach the jar above. Most of the jars have marbles hidden in them, so fall in and walk both ways to collect them.

Climb to the top left of a braid,
then jump right to the next braid up.

Scene 6: The Prince and the Pauper

- Push the crate to the right, then when you see the weasel duck and throw marbles until you defeat him. Keep pushing the crate under the stairs to collect three marbles and a star. Push the crate back to the left all the way to climb up to the **chandelier.** Walk left and right on the chandelier until it swings far enough to reach the next chandelier. Continue until you reach the stairs to the far right. At the top of the stairs hit the light switch and the **rocket** checkpoint. Stand below the bookshelf of the first **weasel** and jump while throwing marbles to knock him out. If you hop on the first book to the left it will bounce you up. By timing the jump correctly you can leap up to a star on the far left wall. Knock out the second weasel, then jump over the third to attack him safely from behind. There are two sparkling books that are connected to each other, If you jump on the left book it will sink while the right book rises. When the right book is at the top, jump to it and throw one or two marbles at the

weasel before you sink too far. Continue to the right, knocking out the weasels as you go (try to jump over them as often as possible) and go down the stairs. As you walk past the vases in the next area walk quickly to avoid getting hit by them as they fall. We always run out of marbles in this area, and if you do just make a run for the far left where Pauper Mickey is waiting.

- **Stage 6-2:** Immediately go to the right, dodging the embers from the fireplace, and hit the rocket checkpoint. Go back to the left and climb up while knocking out the weasels. After hitting the third weasel you must push a **small hanging platform** to the left until the rope is aligned with the left side of the window at the top of the screen. Climb up on the left side and hit the switch, then jump across to the right using the

Move the small hanging platform to align with the left
side of the top window, then make the jump across it.

hanging platform. Collect the marbles and star, then jump to the black platforms and keep leaping across to the right until you fall below to the exit.

$ **Stage 6-3:** Quickly jump on the black pump until the **duck innertube** is filled, then jump on it to float up with the water. Go right and be sure to collect every marble you can reach while knocking out the weasels. As long as you collect every marble you'll have enough to knock out every weasel. Jump on the **moving platform** and be ready to jump up to avoid the spikes. When the platform reaches the right side of the track, make a leap to the right. After hitting the **checkpoint** go down, then move quickly across the collapsing platforms above the firepits. When you reach the left wall past the firepits, move *quickly* down the passage before the walls close up and smash you. Go to the far right and climb the incline (the falling arrows won't hurt you). To the right of the weasel push the rock to the left onto the button to keep the platforms above from disappearing. When you jump to the **hanging platform** above it will move into the path of the spears. Jump to the platform on the right, then jump back over to the hanging platform as it moves above the spears. Leap across to the right to find Prince Mickey.

Push the rock onto the button to make a platform appear above. (is that Minnie on the bench?!)

Scene 7: Pete's Tower

$ Quickly climb up the tower while avoiding the spiked balls. Don't be afraid to stop for a moment and time the jump over the spiked ball.

$ **Stage 7-2:** The climb up inside the tower is very difficult. Keep jumping rapidly the whole time you're climbing, and throw marbles while jumping to hit the weasels. You can also bounce off the heads of

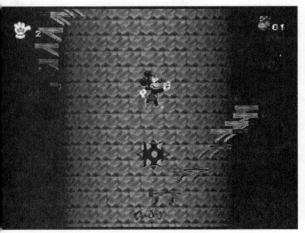

Time your jumps over the barrels as they land in between bounces.

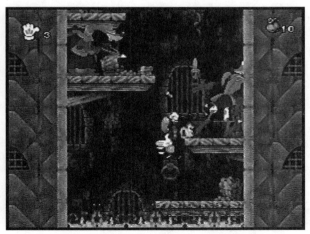

Keep jumping rapidly while throwing marbles as you make the climb up the inside of the tower.

If you're playing the Sega CD version you'll get to fight Pete twice! Oh joy! Marbles won't hurt him.

Grab the pencil on the far left or right, then fight your way to the other side for the next pencil.

the weasels to reach the platform above. At the top go right for a rocket checkpoint, then keep going right past a few dozen weasels (!!!) to reach the exit.

- ⚡ **SEGA CD ONLY — FIRST BATTLE WITH PETE:** This stage only appears on the Sega CD version, so if you're playing the cartridge you can skip to the final battle below. Go to the right and collect all of the marbles. You can't hurt Pete with the marbles, so save them. Go back to the far left and collect the pencil to see the Mad Doctor Mickey help you beat up on Pete. Pete will whistle for his weasels to attack. Wait for the two weasels below to go to the left, then hop down and rapidly throw marbles to knock both of them out. Go to the right ledge but don't grab the swing yet. If you throw marbles to the right you can hit the weasels safely. Watch you marble bag at the top-right of the screen. If you hit a weasel you won't lose a marble. Go to the far right for another pencil, then back and forth for four more pencils. The Prince and the Pauper Mickeys are the second to last, then Steamboat Willie will lift him up to the final room.

Mad Doctor Mickey will be the first to help you defeat Pete when you collect a pencil.

When the Prince and the Pauper Mickey's help you you'll only have to make one more trip to the other side.

Dodge the metal stars and Pete's knife,
then push the spikes to the middle where Pete lands.

During the second phase duck under Pete's knife
then jump on it to reach the switch above...

THE FINAL BATTLE — PETE: Dodge the falling metal stars, duck under the knife when Pete throws it, then push the spikes under Pete as he lands. The spikes should be lined up with the center area of the window in the background. Be sure to get away from the spikes before Pete lands on them or he'll land on you too. After five hits a swinging ball will lower with a switch on the left. Duck one of Pete's knives, then jump on it while it's still stuck in the wall and hit the switch. As Pete leaps into the air, run to the right and repeat the pattern. After six hits you'll finish the game and see the ending sequence.

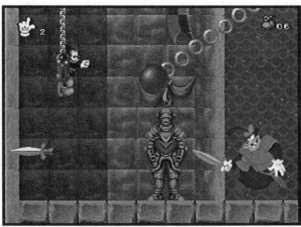

...when Pete jumps into the air
quickly run under him to the other switch.

Awesome Secrets!

LEVEL SELECT (cartridge version): Go to the Options screen and select sound test. Select music to "continue". Select sound fx to "appear". Select speech to "think". Go to exit (don't select it yet) and hold the directional pad to the left for about five seconds until you hear a sound effect. Select exit and start game to reach the level select. Notice that the first letters in the code spell "C-A-T".

LEVEL SELECT (CD version): Go to the Options screen and select sound test. Select music to "continue". Select sound fx to "appear". Select speech to "take that". Go to exit (don't select it yet) and hold the directional pad to the left for about five seconds until you hear a sound effect. Select exit and start game to reach the level select. Notice that the first letters in the code spell "C-A-T".

MORTAL KOMBAT II

CATEGORY: Fighting	DEVELOPER: Probe Limited
PLAYERS: 1-2 (Simultaneous)	PUBLISHER: Acclaim Entertainment

Introduction

It's the sequel to the most notorious fighting game of all time, it has a $10 million promotion campaign behind it, and it has all the blood and guts of the coin-op original—although the Super NES version does, too, no doubt a result of the uncensored Genesis *MK I* cart outselling the censored Super NES *MK I* by a huge margin. (Just goes to show that the once-mighty Nintendo will do whatever it takes to become #1 again!) Read on to learn every special move, fatality, and hidden secret.

You know that they sold $50 million worth of *MK II* cartridges during the first week of release?

Basic Strategies and Stage Fatalities

- Certain fatalities will not work unless you are standing a specific distance away from your dazed opponent when you press the necessary buttons. If you can't perform a particular finishing move—and you've satisfied all the other requirements—then you may need to either move closer to your opponent or farther away. Look at our pictures to get a rough idea of where you should be standing to get the desired move to happen; when all else fails, experiment with different distances.

- While some players avoid pressing the BLOCK button unless it's absolutely necessary, beginners should try holding the BLOCK button when executing tricky moves like Scorpion's "Toasty!" fatality or several of Jax's finishing moves. Holding BLOCK will prevent your character from jumping or moving horizontally while you manipulate the directional pad, which makes certain moves easier to perform. Just be sure to release the BLOCK button when you press the final punch or kick button in the sequence.

- To perform a Babality or Friendship move, you must not press HIGH PUNCH or LOW PUNCH

Some fatalities don't work unless you stand a certain distance away from your opponent.

Don't press the punch buttons during the round you want to do a Babality or Friendship.

The Dead Pool fatality is the same move for all twelve characters in the game.

during the round in which you expect to do the move. If you press a punch button during the winning round, your Babality or Friendship move will not work.

✹ The "Pit II/Kombat Tomb" fatalities will only work on those two stages. Do the move on "The Pit II" stage and you'll uppercut him or her right off the bridge; do the same move on the "Kombat Tomb" stage and you'll uppercut him or her into the spikes that point down from the ceiling. To make a character slide off the spikes and drop to the floor, press and hold Down on both controllers immediately after the fatal uppercut.

✹ To knock an opponent into the acid waters of the "Dead Pool" stage, stand right next to him or her when the words "Finish Him/Her" appear on the screen, hold the directional pad Down, hold LOW PUNCH+LOW KICK and press HIGH PUNCH to uppercut your opponent off the bridge. This move is the same for all twelve characters.

Basic Combos

✹ Jump Kick/Sweep: If you're fighting against the computer, you can usually follow up a jump kick with a foot sweep. Keep sweeping until they jump away and then do another jump kick.

✹ Sweep/Throw: After hitting a human opponent with a sweep, you can sometimes follow up with a throw, even if the human's blocking down and back. This also works with a few other moves, such as the jump kick or roundhouse.

✹ Jump Kick/Hop Kick: Jump kick your opponent low and immediately do a hop kick. This works very well with the ninjas and Shang Tsung.

✹ Jump Kick/Missile Weapon: Jump kick your opponent low and immediately shoot a missile weapon. It's important to kick the enemy low and deep so you can land on the ground quickly and fire the missile.

Baraka

✹ Baraka was the leader of the band that attacked Liu Kang's Shaolin Temple, murdering Liu Kang's brothers. Impressed by Baraka's brutality, Shao Khan recruited him into his evil army. Use Baraka's Blade Fury to catch opponents who always try to jump kick. The

Baraka ventilates himself with a
flurry of Blade Fury slices.

Baraka launches a Blue Bolt at his evil twin. (Well,
they're both evil, but you know what we mean.)

Blue Bolt is a good way to hold somebody at bay but it doesn't do much damage. The Blade Slice gives
your close attacks an extra reach that is good against characters like Jax. Once you get used to Baraka's
unique kicking and punching style, you'll find that he's good for deep attacks that are quite bloody.
Remember that both of his finishing moves require a little distance from your stunned opponent.

- Backhand: HIGH PUNCH (in close).
- Blade Fury: Back, Back, Back, LOW PUNCH.
- Blade Slice: Hold Back, press HIGH PUNCH.
- Blue Bolt: Rotate pad Down/Back, HIGH PUNCH.
- Double Kick: HIGH KICK, HIGH KICK (in close).
- Babality: Forward, Forward, Forward, HIGH KICK.
- Friendship: Up, Forward, Forward, HIGH KICK.
- Pit II/Kombat Tomb Fatality: Forward, Forward, Down, HIGH KICK.
- Head Chop Fatality: Back, Back, Back, HIGH PUNCH.
- Stab Fatality: Back, Forward, Down, Forward, LOW PUNCH.

The oh-so-cliche Head Chop fatality. Man, they were
cuttin' people's heads off in games ten years ago...

Baraka gently lifts Johnny Cage into the air
and lets him slide down onto his twin blades.

✽ Combo #1: Jump Kick/Blue Bolt. Jump kick your opponent low and immediately do the Blue Bolt. After starting the jump kick, keep the control pad pointed Down, so you can quickly do the quarter-circle motion right after you hit.

✽ Combo #2: Jump Kick/Blade Fury. Jump kick your opponent low and immediately do the Blade Fury. Start the three Back motion right before you hit, then quickly press LOW PUNCH. If you don't connect with the Blade Fury, you're left vulnerable to attack.

Jax

✽ Major Jackson Briggs enters the tournament for the first time this year to save a fallen comrade. As leader of Sonya's Elite Special Forces team, he hears her distress call and enters the Outworld, where he thinks she may still be alive. Jax is a good close-combat warrior. Both the Gotcha Grab and Multi-Slam do a lot of damage, but you have to be in close to execute them. The best move in his arsenal is also the most subtle: the in-close Hammer Punch. It temporarily stuns your opponent, allowing for a big-damage follow-up move.

✽ Back Breaker: Press BLOCK while close to opponent in mid-air.

✽ Earthquake: Hold LOW KICK for three seconds, then release.

✽ Energy Wave: Rotate pad Forward/Down/Back, HIGH KICK.

✽ Gotcha Grab: Forward, Forward, LOW PUNCH.

✽ Multi-Slam: Press HIGH PUNCH repeatedly while throwing your opponent.

✽ Babality: Down, Up, Down, Up, LOW KICK.

✽ Friendship: Down, Down, Up, Up, LOW KICK.

✽ Pit II/Kombat Tomb Fatality: Up, Up, Down, LOW KICK.

✽ Arm Rip Fatality: BLOCK, BLOCK, BLOCK, BLOCK, LOW PUNCH.

✽ Head Pop Fatality: Hold LOW PUNCH, press Forward, Forward, Forward, and release.

✽ Combo #1: Overhead Hammer/Uppercut. The Hammer stuns the opponent momentarily. Follow it up with an uppercut or Gotcha Grab. (You can't do consecutive Hammers.)

✽ Combo #2: Jump Kick/Energy Wave. Jump kick your opponent low and immediately do the Energy Wave.

The earth shakes as Jax delivers an Earthquake.

"Gotcha!" says Jax as he executes a Gotcha Grab and puts his giant fist in his opponent's face.

The Arm Rip fatality is just plain brutal. Even we, lovers of gore that we are, were a bit disgusted.

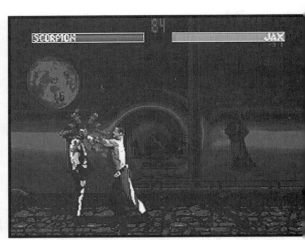

Pop goes the brainpan as Jax crushes Scorpion's head.

After starting the jump kick, keep the control pad Down/Toward, so you can quickly do the half-circle motion right after you hit.

⚡ Combo #3: Jump Kick/Gotcha Grab. Jump kick your opponent low and immediately do the Gotcha Grab. Start the two Forward motion right before you hit, then quickly press LOW PUNCH. Jax grabs nothing bu air if you aren't quick enough.

⚡ Combo #4: Jump Kick/Back Breaker. Jump kick your opponent low and immediately do the Back Breaker Be sure to kick low and deep. As soon as you press the kick button, press BLOCK to execute the Breaker

Johnny Cage

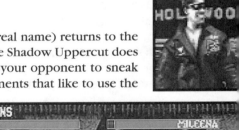

⚡ Always on the lookout for a new movie, John Carlton (Cage's real name) returns to the tournament to find the sequel to his first *MK* movie. Though the Shadow Uppercut does extra damage, you have to be in close, leaving room open for your opponent to sneak in for major damage. Use the High Green Ball to pick off opponents that like to use the

The painful-looking Ball Breaker is one of Johnny Cage's signature moves.

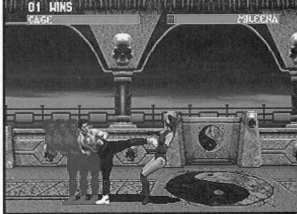

Often imitated, never duplicated: Johnny Cage's Shadow Kick.

jump kick a lot. The Shadow kick doesn't have much of a range so use it for emphasis on a combo, not as a starting point.

✦ Ball Breaker: Hold LOW PUNCH, press BLOCK.

✦ Green Ball: Rotate pad Back/Down/Forward, LOW PUNCH. The arc on the Green Ball makes it hard to judge, since it looks almost exactly like the High Green Ball. Good for hitting opponents from across the screen. It can also be used when your opponent is jumping away or toward you for a jump kick.

✦ High Green Ball: Rotate pad Forward/Down/Back, HIGH PUNCH. It's just like the Green Ball, except it arcs higher (duh). Very useful for hitting opponents in any stage of a jump. Mix up Green Balls and High Green Balls to keep your opponent guessing,

✦ Shadow Kick: Back, Forward, LOW KICK. This is an excellent move as part of a combo or as a counter-attack. When a slow opponent sweeps you, block and quickly do the Shadow Kick. This hits most of the time, except on fast sweepers like Kitana and Mileena. The only other time to use the Kick is when you anticipate your opponent will stand. Hide your evil intentions by walking back and forth without blocking, then do the Kick when they make a move. Sometimes Cage does a Red Shadow Kick, which leaves a red Shadow and makes a zapping noise. This is a random occurrence and there's no way to produce a Red Shadow Kick every time. (Could this be a parody of the mysterious Red Fireball that Ken sometimes throws in *Street Fighter II*?)

✦ Shadow Uppercut: Back, Down, Back, HIGH PUNCH. This move takes off less damage than you might

You can knock off one head or three heads with the Head Punch fatality.

Words cannot adequately describe this horrific screen shot. (At least not the ones we know.)

think, but it's still very handy for nailing an opponent jumping toward or away from you, since it hits them every time. You can also use it after jumping near an opponent, to strike them as they make a move. Counter-attacking against the Uppercut is easy, since Cage hangs in the air for such a long time, so use it sparingly.

✦ Babality: Back, Back, Back, HIGH KICK.

✦ Friendship: Down, Down, Down, HIGH KICK.

✦ Pit II/Kombat Tomb Fatality: Down, Down, Down, HIGH KICK.

✦ Head Punch Fatality: Forward, Forward, Forward, Down, Up. (Hold Down+LOW PUNCH+BLOCK+ LOW KICK during the first punch to knock off three heads.)

✦ Torso Fatality: Down, Down, Forward, Forward, LOW PUNCH.

✦ Combo #1: Jump Kick/Shadow Kick. Jump kick your opponent low and immediately do the Shadow Kick. if your opponent is jumping toward you, do a hop kick followed by the Shadow Kick.

✦ Combo #2: Jump Kick/Shadow Uppercut. Jump kick your opponent low and immediately do the Shadow Uppercut. You must kick low and deep and do the Uppercut as quickly as possible or it won't connect. This combo is easiest when your opponent is close to the corner.

- ✤. Combo #3: Jump Kick/Green Ball. Jump kick your opponent low and immediately do the Green Ball. After starting the jump kick, keep the control pad held away, so you can quickly do the half-circle motion right after you hit.
- ✤. Combo #4: Ball Breaker/Turn-Around Kick/Shadow Kick. Hit your opponent with the Ball Breaker, jump over the opponent, and kick them low as you turn to face the other direction. Follow up with a Shadow Kick or Shadow Uppercut.

Kitana

- ✤. Kitana is Shao Khan's personal assassin, though some suspect that she has been disloyal to the laws of Chaos and the tribe of Shao Khan. In order to find out if she is worthy, Khan has asked her twin sister Mileena to watch her every move. Use Kitana's speed to her advantage, especially when playing against the boss characters Kintaro and Shao Khan. Try the Fan Lift/Air Attack/Fan Throw for an easy Killer Kombo.
- ✤. Air Attack: Rotate pad Forward/Down/Back, HIGH PUNCH.
- ✤. Elbow: HIGH PUNCH (in close).
- ✤. Fan Lift: Back, Back, Back, HIGH PUNCH.
- ✤. Fan Slice: Hold Back, press HIGH PUNCH.
- ✤. Fan Throw: Forward, Forward, HIGH PUNCH+LOW PUNCH.
- ✤. Babality: Down, Down, Down, LOW KICK.
- ✤. Friendship: Down, Down, Down, Up, LOW KICK.
- ✤. Pit II/Kombat Tomb Fatality: Forward, Down, Forward, HIGH KICK.
- ✤. Fan Fatality: BLOCK, BLOCK, BLOCK, HIGH KICK.
- ✤. Kiss of Death Fatality: Hold LOW KICK, press Forward, Forward, Down, Forward, and release.
- ✤. Combo #1: Jump Kick/Fan Throw. Jump kick your opponent low and immediately do the Fan Throw. Start the two Forward motion right before you kick, then press both PUNCH buttons. If you're fighting the computer and its blocks your jump kick, the Fan Throw usually hits.
- ✤. Combo #2: Jump Kick/Fan Throw/Hop Kick. Jump kick your opponent low and immediately do the Fan Throw. Start the two Forward motion right before you kick, then press both PUNCH buttons. If you connect on the first jump kick and get the Fan out fast, you can also hop kick the opponent as he's falling down.

Kitana sure does like her fans. Here's the Fan Lift...

And here's the Fan Throw. Impressive, no?

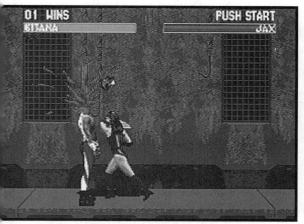

Yet another head-choppin' fatality move.   Kitana gives Baraka a smooch he'll never forget.

⚜ Combo #3: Fan Lift/Jump Kick/Fan Throw/Hop Kick-Air Attack. Catch the opponent with the Fan Lift and wait until he's near the top of the lift. Walk forward as far as you can and do a jump kick to catch the opponent as he's falling down. Immediately do the Fan Throw and follow up with a hop kick or Air Attack. If your opponent is fairly close to you or near the corner, you can do a regular jump kick instead of a hop kick for the last move. This combo works very well against Kintaro and Shao Kahn.

⚜ Combo #4: Fan Life/Jump Kick/Fan Throw/Uppercut. Your opponent must be near the corner to use this combo. Catch the opponent with the Fan Lift and wait until he's near the top of the lift. Walk forward as far as you can and do a jump kick to catch the opponent as he's falling down. Immediately do the Fan Throw and follow with an Uppercut as the opponent is falling.

Kung Lao

⚜ As a fellow member of the White Lotus Society, Kung Lao enters Shao Khan's tournament with Liu Kang. His motivation stems from a 500-year-old grudge against Goro, who killed off members of Kung Lao's family. Kung Lao's Whirlwind Spin works like an uppercut, bringing Toasty to the screen. One advantage to the Hat Throw is your ability to control the direction in case your opponent tries to duck or jump. Usually the Teleport doesn't bring you close enough to your opponent to allow a surprise uppercut, but back them into a corner and you'll be able to nail them with an uppercut right after you land from the warp.

⚜ Air Kick: Jump, then hold Down and press HIGH KICK in midair. The Air Kick works well on opponent who rely on missile weapons; wait until the opponent fires a missile and then do the Kick. Another tactic is to do a series of low punches on the opponent, jump back, and do the Air Kick as you hit the top of the jump. A third method is to use the Air Kick just after jumping off the ground. The Kick doesn't travel as far, but doesn't leave you as open to a counter-attack.

⚜ Hat Throw: Back, Forward, LOW PUNCH. The ability to control the direction of the hat in the air makes this a great long distance attack. Press Up or Down on the pad to control the flight of the hat. it can be used to hit a jumping opponent or an opponent ducking on the ground. Definitely an effective move against players who duck without blocking.

⚜ Headbutt: HIGH PUNCH (in close).

⚜ Teleport: Down, Up (quickly). The advantage of the Teleport is the ability to punch and kick when com-

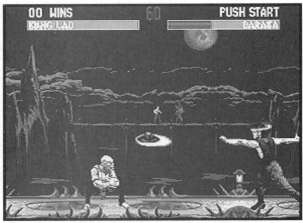

Kung Lao is blatantly ripped off from the little-seen
action-horror movie *Big Trouble in Little China*.

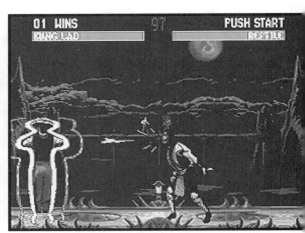

Kung Lao goes for a Whirlwind Spin.

ing up. If you kick as Kung Lao comes up from the Teleport, this usually strikes the opponent before they
can do anything. The Teleport leaves you open for a jump kick, missile, or uppercut, so use it carefully.

- Whirlwind Spin: Up, Up, LOW KICK. Once this move is executed, the only way to hit Kung Lao is with a
  missile weapon or Jax's Earthquake. This makes it a good defensive move when performed quickly.
  Anticipate when an opponent is going to jump at you and execute the Spin. There's a small period of time
  in which Kung Lao speeds up and slows down where he's vulnerable to regular attacks. To maintain the
  Spin, press LOW KICK rapidly.
- Babality: Back, Back, Forward, Forward, HIGH KICK.
- Friendship: Back, Back, Back, Down, HIGH KICK.
- Pit II/Kombat Tomb Fatality: Forward, Forward, Forward, HIGH PUNCH.
- Hat Throw Fatality: Hold LOW PUNCH, press Back, Back, Forward (press Up just before the hat reaches
  your opponent to aim for his or her neck).
- Slice Fatality: Forward, Forward, Forward, Forward, LOW KICK.
- Combo #1: Jump Kick/Hat Throw. Jump kick your opponent low and immediate do the Hat Throw. be
  sure to guide the hat to hit the falling opponent.

Yes, it's *another* decapitation fatality.

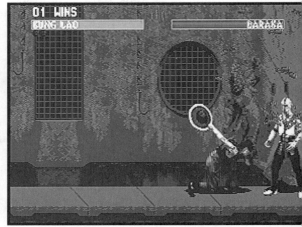

Baraka goes to pieces thanks to a
well-placed swipe of Kung Lao's hat.

- Combo #2: Hop Kick/Air Kick. If your opponent jumps at you, do a hop kick quickly followed by the Air Kick. This is a very fast combo.
- Combo #3: Jump Kick/Whirlwind Spin. Jump kick your opponent in the corner and execute the Spin. be sure to kick low and start the Spin immediately by pressing Up and LOW KICK rapidly.
- Combo #4: Whirlwind Spin/Jump Kick. If your opponent is hit with the Spin as it's slowing down, Kung Lao recovers fast enough to do a jump kick, Air Kick, or Hat Throw.

Liu Kang

- Returning home after the first Shaolin Tournament, Liu Kang finds his brothers have been mysteriously murdered and his home destroyed. He re-enters Shao Khan's second tournament to avenge his brothers' deaths, assuming that the murderer must be a member of Shao Khan's evil tribe. The warrior of the White Lotus society has expanded his range of moves, including crouching and jumping fireballs. Keep charging the bicycle kick to surprise your opponents when they drop their guard. Take advantage of Liu Kang's special moves when attempting Babalities and Friendships; two of them involve only the kick buttons.
- Bicycle Kick: Hold LOW KICK for three to five seconds, then release. Like the Flying Kick, the Bicycle Kick is a handy surprise move. Keep your finger (or thumb) on LOW KICK throughout the round so you can unleash it when necessary. And like the Flying Kick, don't use it when far away from your opponent or when they're standing and blocking. It's best used when your opponent jumps toward or away from you. If you are thrown or jump kicked, use the Bicycle Kick as you stand up to catch the opponent off guard. Make sure you release LOW KICK while standing on the ground; otherwise, the move doesn't work.
- Fireball: Forward, Forward, HIGH PUNCH. This is a good follow-up to a jump kick since it can be launched very quickly. it can also be done in the air to knock jumping opponents out of the sky. You can also toss an aerial Fireball to avoid a missile weapon; if you're jumping and your opponent launches a missile weapon, do the Fireball while in the air to stay above it.
- Flying Kick: Forward, Forward, HIGH KICK. The Flying Kick is a good surprise attack. While walking toward your opponent, tap the control pad toward him and then press HIGH KICK when he's about to make a move. The Flying Kick is also a good jump kick follow-up. If your opponent jumps away from you

"I want to ride my bicycle," sez Liu Kang
just before unleashing the Bicycle Kick.

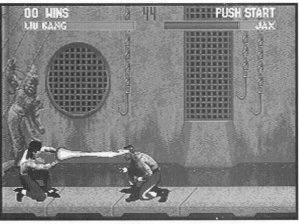

Here is the Low Fireball, although it looks more
like a big bolt of fire in this screen shot. Sorry.

The Dragon fatality is one of the most impressive fatalities in the game: hard to do, but very cool to watch.

Of course, you can always wimp out and execute the wimpy-by-comparison Uppercut fatality.

or just in front of you, use the Flying Kick to knock him out of the air. Never use the Flying Kick to fly across the screen at a blocking opponent; he can follow up his block with a devastating uppercut.

- Forearm: HIGH PUNCH (in close).
- Low Fireball: Forward, Forward, LOW PUNCH. Your opponent can't simply duck to avoid the Low Fireball; they must block or jump. This is most effective at long range or close range and is very hard to counter. The Low Fireball is also a good defensive move, since Liu Kang is low to the ground. The only way to hit Liu Kang when he's shooting a Low Fireball is with a late jump kick. Use the Low Fireball to counter an enemy's missile weapon; his missile flies over your head, but yours slams right into him.
- Babality: Down, Down, Forward, Back, LOW KICK.
- Friendship: Forward, Back, Back, Back, LOW KICK.
- Pit II/Kombat Tomb Fatality: Back, Forward, Forward, LOW KICK.
- Dragon Fatality: Down, Forward, Back, Back, HIGH KICK.
- Uppercut Fatality: Rotate pad 360 degrees counterclockwise.
- Combo #1: Jump Kick/Flying Kick. Jump kick your opponent low and immediately do the Flying Kick. Start the two Forward motion right before you hit, then quickly press HIGH KICK. If you do the Flying Kick too fast, you fly right over your opponent, so make sure you're on the ground.
- Combo #2: Hop Punch/Fireball: Hop punch your opponent in the air and immediately do the Fireball. Start the two Forward motion right before you hit, then quickly press HIGH PUNCH. Follow this up with a Low Fireball, which they have to block.
- Combo #3: Jump Kick/Bicycle Kick. Jump kick your opponent low and immediately do the Bicycle Kick. be sure to charge the Kick for a few seconds before you jump kick. Wait until you land on the ground before releasing LOW KICK, or the Bicycle Kick won't happen.
- Combo #4: Jump Kick/Fireball. Jump kick your opponent and immediate do a Fireball. Start the two Forward motion right before you hit, then quickly press HIGH PUNCH. If you're fighting the computer, you can follow the Fireball with a Low Fireball. Against a human, use the Bicycle Kick after the Fireball.

Mileena

✵ Along with her sister Kitana, Mileena is one of Shao Khan's personal assassins. She is in the tournament to watch her sister who is suspected of dissension from the forces of chaos. Use the Ground Roll/Air Kick combo to surprise opponents from both ends, and keep the Sai charged for added flourish. You'll have to be a step away from your opponent to do the Stab Fatality, but the Inhale Fatality should be triggered while you are touching the enemy.

We could say many naughty things about this screen shot showing a Ground Roll, but we shall resist (barely).

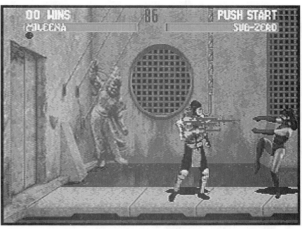

Mileena tries to put Sub-Zero's eyes out with a Sai Throw.

✵ Elbow: HIGH PUNCH (in close).

✵ Ground Roll: Back, Back, Down, HIGH KICK.

✵ Sai Throw: Hold HIGH PUNCH for two to three seconds, then release.

✵ Teleport Kick: Forward, Forward, LOW KICK.

✵ Babality: Down, Down, Down, HIGH KICK.

✵ Friendship: Down, Down, Down, Up, HIGH KICK.

Breathe in...and out...Mileena gets fatal.

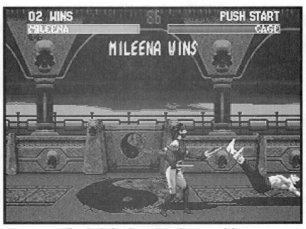

The Stab fatality wins the award for most blood-letting fatality in *MK II*.

- Pit II/Kombat Tomb Fatality: Forward, Down, Forward, LOW KICK.
- Inhale Fatality: Hold HIGH KICK for two to three seconds, then release.
- Stab Fatality: Forward, Back, Forward, LOW PUNCH.
- Combo #1: Jump Kick/Sai Throw. Jump kick your opponent low and immediately do the Sai Throw. You need to charge the move before you jump. Immediately after hitting with the jump kick, release HIGH PUNCH.
- Combo #2: Hop Kick/Sai Throw/Teleport Kick. Hop kick your opponent as they jump towards you and immediate do the Sai Throw. Release HIGH PUNCH as soon as your hop kick connects. After the Sai Throw hits, do the Teleport Kick.
- Combo #3: Jump Kick/Ground Roll. Jump kick your opponent low and immediately do the Ground Roll. Start the two Back motion right before you hit.

Rayden

- The Thunder God returns to the tournament, warning the other contestants of Shao Khan's evil intentions. Why Rayden bothers with the tournament is cause for speculation, considering that he's a God and should have no problem with Shao Khan. Keep the Electrocution charging to surprise your opponents close in, especially when they try to throw you. Rayden's fatalities take practice, because you have to start charging them before the "Finish" appears on screen. This practice is worth it, because the exploding uppercut is one of the most spectacular fatalities in the game.
- Electrocution: Hold HIGH PUNCH for three to four seconds, then release (in close).
- Flying Attack: Back, Back, Forward.
- Lightning: Rotate pad Down/Forward, LOW PUNCH.
- Mini Uppercut: HIGH PUNCH (in close).
- Teleport: Down, Up (quickly).
- Babality: Down, Down, Up, HIGH KICK.
- Friendship: Down, Back, Forward, HIGH KICK.
- Pit II/Kombat Tomb Fatality: Up, Up, Up, HIGH PUNCH.
- Shock Fatality: Hold LOW KICK for five seconds, then release; when Rayden starts to shock his opponent, press BLOCK+LOW KICK repeatedly to explode.

Electrocution!

Teleport!

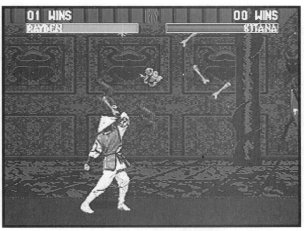

Shock fatality!

Uppercut fatality!
(Very uninspired captions!)

- Uppercut Fatality: Hold HIGH PUNCH for ten seconds, then release (you need to start charging this move before the words "Finish Him/Her" appear on the screen).
- Combo #1: Jump Kick/Flying Attack. Jump kick your opponent low and immediately do the Flying Attack.
- Combo #2: Hop Kick-Punch/Flying Attack. Hop kick or hop punch your opponent in the air and immediately do the Flying Attack.
- Combo #3: Jump Kick/Lightning. Jump kick your opponent low and immediately do the Lightning. After starting the jump kick, keep the joystick in the Down position, so you can quickly do the quarter-circle motion right after you hit.
- Combo #4: Electrocution/Two Punches/Flying Attack. As Rayden lets go of the opponent after the Electrocution, punch twice to pop the opponent in the air. Follow up with the Flying Attack.

Reptile

- Reptile acts as Shang Tsung's personal bodyguard, so you know he must be an awesome fighter. His human form hides a scaly body; he's thought to be the only remaining member of a race that has been extinct for over one million years. Reptile's Power Ball can be used to keep your opponents off-guard, but remember that it leaves you wide open to any kind of projectile attack. The Acid Spit is quick, but doesn't do much damage; use it to pick people out of the air. The Invisible Slice Fatality is very hard to do, but just think of it as a two-part fatality like Sub-Zero's Deep Freeze.
- Acid Spit: Forward, Forward, HIGH PUNCH.
- Backhand: HIGH PUNCH (in close).
- Invisibility: Up, Up, Down, HIGH PUNCH.
- Power Ball: Back, Back, HIGH PUNCH+LOW PUNCH.
- Slide: Hold Back, press LOW PUNCH+BLOCK+LOW KICK.
- Babality: Down, Back, Back, LOW KICK.
- Friendship: Back, Back, Down, LOW KICK.
- Pit II/Kombat Tomb Fatality: Down, Forward, Forward, BLOCK.
- Invisible Slice Fatality: Forward, Forward, Down, HIGH KICK. (This fatality can only be executed when Reptile is invisible.)

Reptile shows absolutely no manners by letting loose with an Acid Spit.

Reptile slides into Liu Kang's footsies to send him flying.

- Tongue Fatality: Back, Back, Down, LOW PUNCH.
- Combo #1: Jump Kick/Acid Spit. Jump kick your opponent low and immediately do the Acid Spit. Start the two Forward motion right before you hit, then quickly press HIGH PUNCH.
- Combo #2: Power Ball/Two Punches/Hop Kick/Slide. Do the Power Ball move on your opponent. If it hits, do two high punches as the opponent comes at you, then do a hop kick. You need to be in the right place for the high punches to land. After the kick, complete the combo with a Slide.

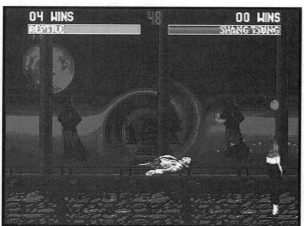

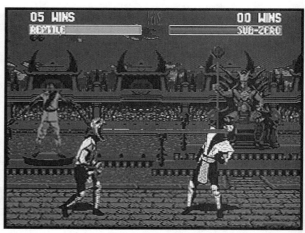

The Invisible Slice fatality is one of the more bizarre finishing moves.

At least this decapitation fatality is at least somewhat original.

Scorpion

- Seeking revenge on Sub-Zero for dooming him to an eternity in hell, Scorpion returns to the tournament to try to kill him one last time. Scorpion's new Air Throw works well for opponents that jump around a lot. The Toasty Fatality is good for beginners because

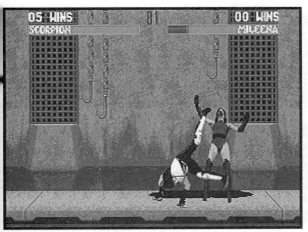

Scorpion shows off his flexibility with the Leg Grab.

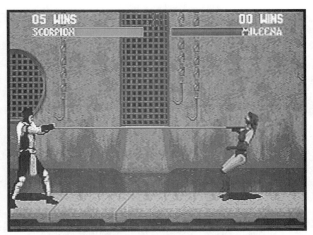

"Get over here!" The Spear produces the most recognizable sound bite in the game.

it can be executed from any position on the screen. The Slice Fatality is also nice because of its extra-bloody panache.

- *$.* Air Throw: Press BLOCK while close to opponent in mid-air.
- *$.* Leg Grab: Rotate pad Forward/Down/Back, LOW KICK.
- *$.* Spear: Back, Back, LOW PUNCH.
- *$.* Teleport Punch: Rotate pad Down/Back, HIGH PUNCH.
- *$.* Babality: Down, Back, Back, HIGH KICK.
- *$.* Friendship: Back, Back, Down, HIGH KICK.
- *$.* Pit II/Kombat Tomb Fatality: Down, Forward, Forward, BLOCK.
- *$.* Fire Fatality: Up, Up, HIGH PUNCH.
- *$.* Slice Fatality: Hold HIGH PUNCH, press Down, Forward, Forward, Forward, then release.
- *$.* Toasty Fatality: Down, Down, Up, Up, HIGH PUNCH.
- *$.* Combo #1: Jump Kick/Spear. Jump kick your opponent low and immediately do the Spear. Start the two Back motion right before you hit, then quickly press LOW PUNCH.

Beavis can't say it any more, but we can: Fire! Fire! Fire!

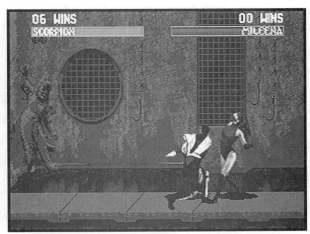

Scorpion swings and connects with an intensine-shredding Slice fatality. (Nice visual image, huh?)

- Combo #2: Jump Kick/Leg Grab. Jump kick your opponent low and immediately do the Leg Grab. After starting the jump kick, keep the control pad in the toward position, so you can quickly do the half-circle motion right after you hit.
- Combo #3: Jump Kick/Air Throw. Jump kick your opponent low and deep, then immediately do the Air Throw by repeatedly pressing BLOCK.
- Combo #4: Teleport Punch/Spear. Teleport Punch your opponent and immediately Spear. This works best if you catch the opponent in the air with the Teleport Punch, making it easier to Spear them before they hit the ground.
- Combo #5: Teleport Punch/Leg Grab. Teleport Punch your opponent and immediately do the Leg Grab. This works best if you catch the opponent in the air with the Teleport Punch, making it easier to Leg Grab them before they hit the ground.

Scorpion's third fatality: Toasty!

- Combo #6: Turn-Around Kick/Teleport Punch/Spear. Do a turn-around kick on your opponent and immediately do the Teleport Punch. If you connect on the Teleport Punch, throw the Spear and finish with an uppercut.

Shang Tsung

- After losing the first tournament to Liu Kang, Shang Tsung's life is spared by Shao Khan—but only after he promises to lure the contestants back for a second battle. Shao Khan restores Shang Tsung's youth so that he can fight again. Shang Tsung is the expert player's favorite; with his morphing powers, he can do every move in the game. Along with his three awesome fatalities, his flaming skulls pack quite a punch. Use Shang Tsung if you really want to master *Mortal Kombat II*.
- Elbow: HIGH PUNCH (in close).
- Flaming Skulls: Back, Back, HIGH PUNCH.
- 2 Flaming Skulls: Back, Back, Forward, HIGH PUNCH.
- 3 Flaming Skulls: Back, Back, Forward, Forward, HIGH PUNCH. If you can catch your opponent in the air with the first Flaming Skull, there's a good chance that the other two will hit. Do the 3 Skulls before your opponent jumps toward or away from you.
- Babality: Back, Forward, Down, HIGH KICK.
- Friendship: Back, Back, Down, Forward, HIGH KICK.
- Pit II/Kombat Tomb Fatality: Down, Down, Up, Down.
- Inner Ear Fatality: Hold HIGH KICK for two to three seconds, then release.

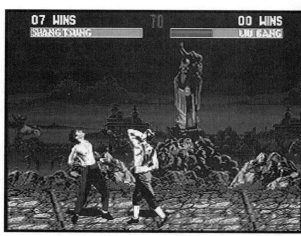

Shang Tsung staggers Liu Kang with a whiff of his armpit odor.

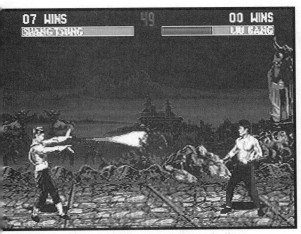

Is this the 1, 2, or 3 Flaming Skulls
move? We have no idea.

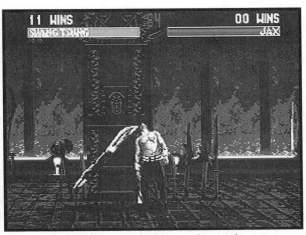

The Inner Ear fatality is a darn sight
more painful than an inner ear infection.

- Kintaro Morph Fatality: Hold LOW PUNCH for entire round (at least 25 seconds), release button one step in front of your opponent.
- Life Force Fatality: Up, Down, Up, LOW KICK.
- Baraka Morph: Down, Down, LOW KICK.
- Jax Morph: Down, Forward, Back, HIGH KICK.
- Johnny Cage Morph: Back, Back, Down, LOW PUNCH.
- Kitana Morph: BLOCK, BLOCK, BLOCK.
- Kung Lao Morph: Back, Down, Back, HIGH KICK.
- Liu Kang Morph: Back, Forward, Forward, BLOCK.
- Mileena Morph: Hold HIGH PUNCH for three seconds, then release.
- Rayden Morph: Down, Back, Forward, LOW KICK.
- Reptile Morph: Up, DOWN+HIGH PUNCH.
- Scorpion Morph: Up, Up.
- Sub-Zero Morph: Forward, Down, Forward, HIGH PUNCH.

The damn impressive Kintaro Morph fatality.

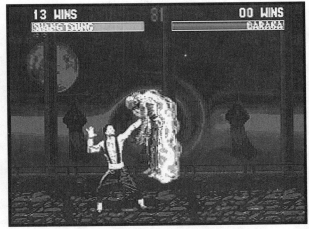

Shang Tsung's third, and extremely cool,
fatality is the Life Force move.

✯ Combo #1: Jump Kick/Flaming Skull. Jump kick your opponent low and immediately do one Flaming Skull. Start the two Back motion right before you kick, then press HIGH PUNCH. This is difficult, as Shang Tsung's Skulls travel slowly. More than than one Skull after the jump kick is possible, but extremely difficult.

Sub-Zero

✯ Thought dead, Sub-Zero returns to the tournament to assassinate Shang Tsung. Does he realize that Scorpion is after him? Sub-Zero's Ground Freeze is one of the best moves in the game. Just remember that if an opponent is moving away from you when you do the Ground freeze, they'll fall backwards, making it harder to nail the uppercut. You can still freeze yourself if you do a Double Ice Backfire (i.e., re-freeze a frozen opponent), but if you've done a Ground Freeze, all other freezes are disabled. To do the Ice Ball Fatality, you have to be as far away from your enemy as possible to get it to work.

✯ Backhand: HIGH PUNCH (in close).

✯ Freeze: Rotate pad Down/Forward, LOW PUNCH.

✯ Ground Freeze: Rotate pad Down/Back, LOW KICK.

✯ Slide: Hold Back, press LOW PUNCH+BLOCK+LOW KICK.

✯ Babality: Down, Back, Back, HIGH KICK.

✯ Friendship: Back, Back, Down, HIGH KICK.

✯ Pit II/Kombat Tomb Fatality: Down, Forward, Forward, BLOCK.

✯ Deep-Freeze Fatality: Forward, Forward, Down, HIGH KICK to freeze, then press Forward, Down, Forward, Forward, HIGH PUNCH (in close).

✯ Ice Ball Fatality: Hold LOW PUNCH, press Back, Back, Down, Forward.

✯ Combo #1: Jump Kick/Slide. Jump kick your opponent low and immediately do the Slide. If you don't kick low and deep enough, the Slide won't connect against a human opponent, although it's almost always effective against the computer.

✯ Combo #2: Jump Kick/Hop Kick/Slide. Jump kick your opponent low and immediately do a hop kick followed by a Slide. Most effective when your opponent is frozen.

Sub-Zero's universally hated Freeze move.

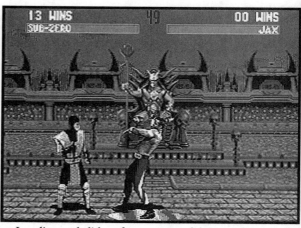

Jax slips and slides after a successful Ground Freeze.

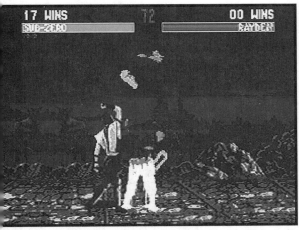

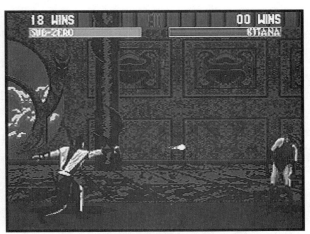

The Deep-Freeze fatality seems \inspired by the "altered" fatality from the Super NES version of the original *MK*.

The Ice Ball fatality looks even cooler after the Ice Ball connects with its victim.

✦ Combo #3: Jump Kick/Ground Freeze/Uppercut/ Slide. Jump kick your opponent low and immediately do the Ground Freeze. Keep them deep, or they will land beyond the range of the Ground Freeze. If they slip, hit them with the uppercut and then do the Slide.

Hidden Characters

✦ Jade: To fight Jade, you must reach the stage just before the question-mark stage in a one-player game. While fighting on this stage, you must win one round using only the LOW KICK button—pressing any other button during the round will disqualify you from reaching Jade in that round. If you fulfill these requirements, you will be transported through the portal to do battle with Jade in Goro's Lair.

✦ Noob Saibot: Play until the "Battle" counter reaches 25. You get a special congratulatory message and are warped to the Blue Portal to do battle with Noob Saibot, an all-black shadow Ninja. ("Noob" is *MK II* pro-

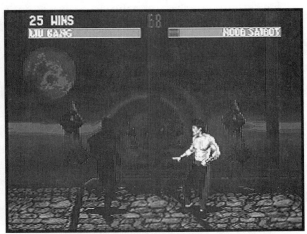

To get to Jade, you need to reach the stage just before the question mark stage.

Noob Saibot has a goofy name which is the last name of two *MK II* programmers spelled backwards.

grammer Ed Boon's last name spelled backwards; "Saibot" is the reversed surname of *MK II* artist John Tobias.)

Where there's smoke, there's, uh, Smoke.

- Smoke: To fight the ninja Smoke, you must fight on The Portal stage in either a one- or two-player game. During the battle, watch for *MK II* sound designer Dan Forden to appear in the lower-right corner of the screen; he's the guy who pops up and sings "Toasty!" at certain times, usually after a player has connected with a particularly vicious uppercut. While Forden is on the screen, hold the control pad Down and press the START button. If your timing is right, you'll be sent through the portal to face Smoke in the Blue Portal.

Awesome Secrets

- TEST MODES: At the title screen, select OPTIONS. At the options screen, move the cursor to DONE! and then move the control pad Left, Down, Left, Right, Down, Right, Left, Left, Right, Right. A new option called Test Modes appears. Here's what the various Test Modes items do.
- No Damage to P1, No Damage to P2, 1 Hit Kills P1, 1 Hit Kills P2: Pretty bloody obvious what these do!
- Free Play: Gives you infinite credits.
- Background: Lets you play on a single background for the entire game, even when encountering secret characters. Here's a quick chart of numbers and backgrounds.

Get into the Test Modes to activate various cool cheats.

Number	Background
1	Dead Pool
2	Kombat Tomb
3	Wasteland
4	The Tower
5	Living Forest
6	The Armory
7	The Pit II
8	The Portal
9	Kahn's Arena
10	The Blue Portal

- Battleplan: Lets you determine where you start on the battle plan. 14 lets you start at Kintaro; 15 lets you start at Shao Kahn.

- Soak Test: Tells the computer to fight itself.
- Fatalities, Friendship, Babalities: Lets you decide which finishing move the winner of the Soak Test match will use on his vanquished opponent.
- Oooh, Nasty!: Lets you do the extremely bizarre Fergality finishing move (see below).
- Activating the Test Modes does something else interesting. Normally, when you land a really juicy uppercut, Dan "Toasty!" Forden pops up in the lower-right corner of the screen. With the Test Modes activated, a picture of the programmer—as drawn by his six-year-old brother(!)—appears in the lower-right corner. Check it out....
- FERGALITY: Activate the Test Modes, set the Background to 6 (The Armory), and turn on Oooh, Nasty! Start a one- or two-player battle as Rayden and win two rounds. When you're prompted to "Finish Him/Her," press Back, Back, Back, START.

Fergality? Huh?!

Your opponent is turned into Fergus McGovern (an employee of Probe Limited, and the same guy whose head flew in front of the moon in Mortal Kombat I). Nice bod, Fergus!

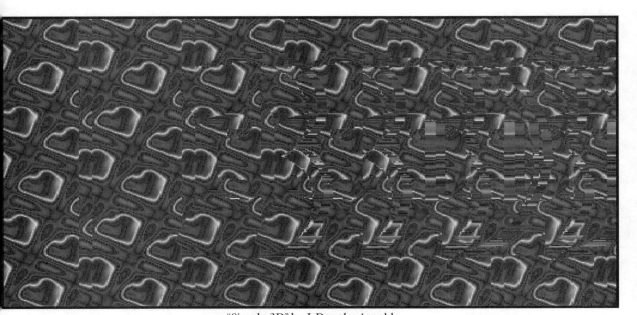

"Simple 3D" by J. Douglas Arnold
This stereogram is a simple text example. See page 325 for more 3D information.

NBA JAM

CATEGORY: Sports	DEVELOPER: Iguana Entertainment
PLAYERS: 1-4 (Simultaneous)	PUBLISHER: Acclaim Entertainment

Introduction

NBA Jam is the first game to be officially sanctioned by the National Basketball Association. That means real players and real teams in rim-rockin' two-on-two action. The Genesis version of *NBA Jam* is an exceptional conversion of the coin-op original, with all the same strategies and a few new secrets. Along with all the Genesis tips and tricks, this chapter also has secrets for the coin-op versions of *NBA Jam* and *NBA Jam Tournament Edition*. Enjoy!

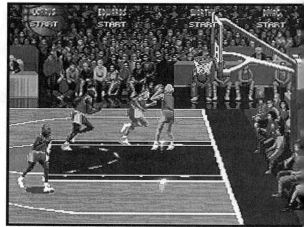

If you liked the coin-op version of *NBA Jam*, you're gonna love the Genesis version.

Basic Moves

- ✦ Pass: Press the PASS button. Press TURBO and PASS to throw a safer, quicker pass. It's safer to pass to an on-screen teammate; passes to off-screen players have a higher chance of being picked off.
- ✦ Shoot: Press and hold the SHOOT button to make your player jump, then release it while the player is airborne. Your shot will be more accurate if you release the button at the peak of a jump. You can also press the SHOOT button twice for a quick-release shot; your accuracy won't suffer, but you stand a much greater of having this type of shot blocked. Always follow your shot in to give yourself better rebounding position in case the shot misses.
- ✦ Head Fake: Tap the SHOOT button once. A computer-controlled teammate will shoot if you do this while he has the ball.
- ✦ Dunk: Hold SHOOT while running near an unobstructed basket. Hold TURBO and SHOOT for a "super dunk." (See the "Super Dunks" section below.)
- ✦ Lay-Up: Hold SHOOT for a short time while running toward the basket.
- ✦ Hook Shot: Tap the SHOOT button while running

Release the SHOOT button at the peak of the jump for the most accurate shot.

Shoot the ball while running vertically to release a hook shot.

Throw elbows before you shoot to knock your opponent silly.

vertically (straight up or down on the screen). Hold TURBO and tap SHOOT while running vertically to launch a high-arcing hook shot. Both of these shots have a higher chance of scoring than a standard jump shot, and they're also harder to block—just like in the real game.

- Throw Elbows: Tap TURBO twice. This is helpful if you're a smaller player who has just grabbed an offensive rebound; throwing elbows in the paint can clear a path for an easy dunk. The computer will occasionally throw elbows automatically while rebounding, and the head fake may also include an automatic elbow throw.
- Steal: Tap the STEAL button to knock the ball away from an opponent.
- Knockdown: Hold the TURBO button and tap STEAL to knock your opponent down! You can even do this while you're in possession of the ball. If you are knocked down, hit your buttons to get up quickly.
- Block: Hold the SHOOT button to jump. Hold TURBO and SHOOT to jump higher.
- Rebound: This is automatic if you're close enough; otherwise, press SHOOT and point the control pad toward the ball.
- Alley-Oop: Easier to do with two-player teams. The player without the ball moves under the basket and holds SHOOT (to jump); meanwhile, the ball handler presses TURBO and PASS to throw to the jumping player quickly.

Offensive Strategies

- To win the tip-off, tap the SHOOT button as fast as you can. Whoever taps the SHOOT button the most wins the tip.
- Taking a shot while an opponent is nearby reduces your shooting percentage by 15%. If an opponent is jumping to attempt a block, your shooting percentage decreases even more; if your opponent jumps higher than the point at which you released the ball, it's 5% lower for each on-screen pixel of differential.

Tap the SHOOT button as fast as possible to win the tip-off.

Go for the dunk, draw the attention of the defense, and pass the ball to your teammate for the easy three.

Burn time off the clock to preserve a lead against the computer opponent.

✴ Remember that you can pass to your teammate while in the air for a jump shot or a dunk. For example, you can go for a dunk and draw the attention of both defensive players, then pass off to your teammate, who has a wide-open three-point shot.

✴ Try to set a screen when you're going for a shot. There seems to be a pattern with the computer in which you can usually go three-fourths of the way downcourt and have a screen for the three-point shot if you let your computer teammate run ahead of you.

✴ Avoid taking three-point shots from a 45-degree angle; instead, take them from the top of the arc or the sides. Shots taken at an angle have the greatest chance of missing.

✴ Head fakes work *great*. Try to mix in a few elbow throws, though, or you may be knocked down.

✴ With a lead of four points or more in a game against a computer-controlled team, you can burn seconds off the clock and prevent the lead from changing quickly. When you get the ball after a basket or a goaltend, stay at your end of the court; just hold your position and wait as long as you can. The computer players will stay in position and do nothing until the shot clock counts down below five, then they'll come at you and force you to do something. With the shot clock at six, quickly pass to your open teammate or take the shot yourself. Even if you miss, you should have a decent shot at the rebound; then you can get the ball, pass back to the player in the backcourt and milk the clock again. This trick works best in the fourth quarter.

✴ Here's another strategy involving the clock: If you're near the end of a quarter, wait until there are three seconds or less on the clock before you put up the desperate three-pointer. The computer drastically increases the chances of your shot going on. Note that this trick doesn't work if Computer Assistance is turned off (see "Awesome Secrets" below). Speaking of the clock, you need at least 6/10ths of a second to take a shot.

✴ During the last minute of each quarter, the losing

Wait until the clock gets under three seconds before shooting the buzzer-beating three-pointer.

team's speed is slightly increased. To counter this advantage, pass the ball around frequently before going for a shot or dunk.

✦ When a player takes a shot and the computer calculates the percentage of the shot, the computer will increase your shooting percentage by one for each point that you're behind in the game. Similarly, if your team is ahead, it will subtract one percent for each point you're ahead. For example, if you're losing by ten points and you take a shot that has a 75% chance of scoring, the computer increases your percentage for the shot to 85%. You can disable this feature by turning Computer Assistance off at the options screen.

He's On Fire!

✦ When a player scores three consecutive shots without any opponent scoring in between, he is said to be "on fire." During this time, the player has unlimited Turbo power, can goaltend to his heart's content without being called, and has a much better chance of making any shot inside the halfcourt line. Players can really open up a lead by launching three-point shots one after another while on fire. You stay on fire until the other team scores or until the fire wears off (which usually doesn't happen until you've scored between 30 and 35 points).

He's on fire! A player on fire can make just about every shot and can goaltend at will.

Use strategic goaltending to stop a player from going on fire or to give yourself a chance to go on fire.

✦ If you're "heating up"—you've made two shots in a row and need a third to go on fire—work in the back of the court, goaltend any lay-ups or three-pointers, and steal or rebound the ball whenever possible. Getting called for goaltending an opponent's shot will not keep you from heating up, since the goaltending doesn't end your hot streak. This strategy also helps when you're on fire and trying to stay that way, since you can get away with shameless goaltending. If an opponent is called for goaltending one of your shots while you're heating up, the shot won't count in the three-shot total you need to go on fire—but it won't end your hot streak, either.

✦ When an opponent is on fire, you need to score to cool him off. Try to knock down the player on fire to give your teammate enough time to shoot without being goaltended. Or, get your teammate to knock him down while you shoot. It's best to go for a lay-up when an opponent is on fire, since he won't be able to knock you down and lay-ups are difficult to goaltend.

Super Dunks

- There are over 50 different dunks in *NBA Jam*. The dunks are divided into ten "sets"—each set consisting of between one and ten different jams—and each player has between one and ten sets of dunks available to him. Look at your player's "Dunks" rating on the attributes screen: the higher the bar, the more sets of dunks that the player can perform.

- Below are ten of the more common dunks in the game, along with fairly reliable methods of performing each one. Keep in mind that some of these dunks may not be available to your player, and that the type of dunk executed depends entirely on where the player is positioned when he starts the dunk. A shift of a single pixel may mean the difference between two completely different dunks. And remember that you must be moving to dunk!

The Easy Jam can be done by every player in the game, even the shortest dudes.

- Easy Jam: Hold the SHOOT button while close to the basket.

- "Look Out!" (360-Degree Dunk): Hold SHOOT while near the second tick on the key.

- Two-Handed Jam: From close and above the basket, hold SHOOT.

- Tomahawk Jam 1: From close and below the basket, hold TURBO and SHOOT.

- Tomahawk Jam 2: From the middle of the key, hold TURBO and SHOOT.

- Tomahawk Jam 3 (Windmill): From three-quarters of the length of the key (near the bottom of the circle), hold TURBO and SHOOT.

The Cannonball Slam is a fiery display of dunking ability.

- Cannonball Slam (Fireball): From the top of the circle, hold TURBO and SHOOT.

- High 720-Degree Slam (a.k.a. "Tarzan Yell" Slam or "Helicopter Rotor" Slam): From a corner of the key—or from outside the key and near the third tick mark—hold TURBO and SHOOT.

- Weird Slam: From outside the key and near the second or third tick, hold TURBO and SHOOT.

- Dunk and Hang on the Rim: From outside the key and near the third tick, hold TURBO and SHOOT.

- If you see that your teammate is open while you're on the way to the rim for a dunk, press PASS to feed the ball to your teammate for an easy three. This strategy is highly recommended if you're doing an Easy Jam with an opponent nearby.

Go for a power slam in the fourth quarter to smash the backboard in a lovely display.

❖ Performing any of the special dunks in the fourth quarter or during any overtime periods causes the backboard to shatter in a spectacular display.

❖ Try to avoid dunking near the end of the quarter. If you put up a jump shot and the buzzer sounds while the ball is in midair, you can still make the shot count. But if time expires as you're sailing to the rim for a jam, you made a "bad decision."

Defensive Strategies

❖ To reject a dunking player, it's best to wait until the dunker has reached the peak of his leap before you jump to block. For example, if Barkley starts a cannonball dunk, wait until he's coming down before you press TURBO and SHOOT. Also make sure that you're in front of the player and near the basket.

❖ Another way to reject a dunking player is to knock him down (see "Basic Moves") if it's a low dunk like an "Easy Jam." Lay-ups are considered stronger than dunks because you can't be knocked down.

❖ To block a shot, you need to jump at the same time you believe the shooter will jump. A common technique is to allow your opponent to shoot while you're in his face (but not jumping), then go for the rebound.

❖ It is possible to block a three-point attempt at the buzzer; immediately after the ball is passed inbounds, press TURBO and SHOOT and point toward the shooter.

❖ Stealing is slightly less of a science. Here are three techniques: 1) Stick close to the player with the ball and tap STEAL repeatedly. 2) Knock down the opposing player until he drops the ball. Especially effective against computer players. 3) Let a player shoot while you're near the basket, and jump before the ball gets there. You may or may not get busted for goaltending.

❖ Conserve your TURBO power for when you need it, instead of wasting it to chase players all over the court. Use it only to keep up with a fast player, to knock down an opponent, or for a Super Dunk.

❖ A helpful strategy involving knockdowns is to shove down the offensive player without the ball, which eliminates the possibility of a pass to him.

it's possible to block dunks, but you need to time your jump perfectly.

Knock down the player with the ball to steal it away...

Or knock down the player who *doesn't* have the ball.

This is very effective when a player is going for a dunk and his teammate is out at the three-point line waiting for the pass.

✴ Here are two time-tested rebounding techniques. 1) Press SHOOT to jump toward the ball *after* it has hit the rim or board. 2) Knock down opposing players near the ball so you can grab the ball off the floor. Remember that if you're close enough to the ball, your player automatically jumps for the rebound.

Awesome Secrets!

✴ The following secret codes should be performed at the "match-up" screen before the tip-off, when the announcer says "Tonight's match-up."

✴ Juice Mode: This code speeds up the game considerably. It's also the default mode for any game you play after defeating all 27 teams to become the Grand Champion. Tap the A button 13 times at the match-up screen, then hold down buttons B and C. Once you've activated Juice Mode, there doesn't seem to be any way to disable it again without switching off the Genesis.

✴ Powerup Defense: Press the A button five times. Now you can goaltend without being called for it.

✴ Powerup Dunks: Probably one of the best powerups in the game, this trick lets you dunk from anywhere inside the half-court line, and also lets your player make any of the 50-plus dunks. Press the B button 13 times while rotating the pad in a clockwise direction, On the thirteenth tap, hold the button until tip-off (this is tricky).

Use the "Dunks" code and you can jam & slam from the half-court line!

✴ Powerup Fire: Press the B button seven times, then press and hold B, C, and Up until tip-off. This sets your player on fire for the entire game. You have unlimited Turbo power, can goaltend without being called, and make almost any shot from inside the half-court line. Unlike being on fire in a normal game, this cheat does not wear off when your opponent scores.

✴ Powerup Intercept: Rotate the control pad 360 degrees and press the B button 14 times.

✴ Powerup Turbo: This code gives your player unlimited Turbo power for the entire game. Press the A button 13 times, then hold down A, B, and C.

✴ Shot Percentage: Press the A button, then press and hold A, B, and Down on the control pad. With this option, a number between 5% and 99% appears on the screen whenever anyone takes a shot (not a dunk). This number represents the chance of the shot going in. The percentages are based on several factors, including the player's "hot spots." Each player has two hot spots on the floor from which his shooting percentage can be a full 99%—if you shoot from a location that's farther away from one of the hot spots, the percentage is reduced. With some experimentation—and

Use the "Shot Percentage" code to see if you're taking shots from your hot spots.

cooperation from other players looking for hot spots—you may be able to find where your player's hot spots are by keeping an eye on the percentage.

Special Guest Players

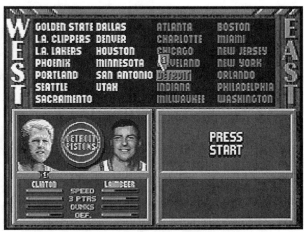

Bill Clinton, but no Rush Limbaugh?

✹ As in the original arcade game, the Genesis version of *NBA Jam* includes hidden "special guests" that can be accessed by entering special sets of initials. When the game asks if you want to enter initials for record keeping, choose YES and follow the instructions for each player listed below.

✹ Asif "Chow-Chow" Chaudhri: Associate Producer of *NBA Jam* for Acclaim. Enter the initials CAR as follows: Input C and A, then highlight R, hold the START button down, and press the C button.

✹ Bill Clinton: The President of these here United States of America. Enter the initials ARK as follows: Input A and R, then highlight K, hold the START button down, and press the A button.

✹ George "P-Funk" Clinton: The "Godfather of Funk" and the leader of the legendary funk band Parliament/Funkadelic. Enter the initials DIS as follows: Input D and I, then highlight S, hold the START button down, and press the C button.

✹ Sal DiVita: An artist who worked on the *NBA Jam* coin-op. Enter the initials SAL as follows: Input S and A, then highlight L, hold the START button down, and press the C button.

✹ Dan "Weasel" Feinstein: Executive Producer of Acclaim's home versions of *NBA Jam.* Enter the initials SAX as follows: Input S and A, then highlight X, hold the START button down, and press the C button.

✹ Al Gore: The Vice-President of the U.S. of A. Enter the initials NET as follows: Input N and E, then highlight T, hold the START button down, and press the B button.

Why didn't they keep in all the secret characters from the coin-op? Hmmm?

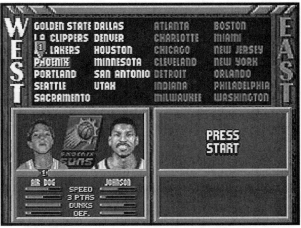

All you have to do to get into a game is be the son of a really powerful Acclaim executive.

🏀 Eric "Kabuki" Kuby: An analyst/tester for *NBA Jam*. Enter the initials QB[SPACE] as follows: Input Q and B, the highlight the space character, hold the START button down, and press the A button.

🏀 Warren Moon: Starting quarterback for the NFL's Minnesota Vikings. Enter the initials UW[SPACE] as follows: Input U and W, then highlight the space character, hold the START button down, and press the A button.

🏀 Tom "Scruff" Rademacher: An analyst/tester for Acclaim's *NBA Jam*. Enter the initials ROD as follows: Input R and O, then highlight D, hold the START button down, and press the B button.

🏀 Jamie Rivett: A programmer who contributed to the *NBA Jam* coin-op. Enter the initials RJR as follows: Input R and J, then highlight R, hold the START button down, and press the B button.

🏀 Eric "Air Dog" Samulski: The son of Paul Samulski, Acclaim's VP of product development. Enter the initials AIR as follows: Input A and I, then highlight R, hold the START button down, and press the A button.

🏀 Mark Turmell: The main designer and programmer of Midway's *NBA Jam* coin-op. Enter the initials MJT as follows: Input M and J, then highlight T, hold the START button down, and press the A button.

NBA Jam Coin-Op Secrets

🏀 There are two slightly different versions of the original *NBA Jam* coin-op: Version 2.0 and Version 3.0. Here's a simple test to see which version you're playing: Play a game with the initials MJT and birthdate of March 22. The long-haired guy who appears as your player in Mark Turmell, lead designer of *NBA Jam*. If Turmell appears in a purple Los Angeles Lakers uniform, you're playing a Version 2.0 machine; if he's wearing a jersey that corresponds to the color of your team (red for Chicago, green for Seattle, etc.), you're playing a newer 3.0 machine.

Here's a bonus screen shot from the coin-op version of NBA Jam. Check out Kerri Hoskins going for the slam!

🏀 These secret codes should be performed at the "match-up" screen before the tip-off, when the announcer says "Tonight's match-up..." and says the names of the two teams.

🏀 Big Head: Hold the joystick Up and hold the TURBO and PASS buttons at the match-up screen; continue to hold until the court appears. This gives your player a head that's three times larger than normal, which makes it easier to see the detail of the characters' digitized faces. Your arcade owner may have set up the *NBA Jam* machine with the Big Head feature turned permanently on. If this is the case, performing the trick will turn the Big Heads off.

🏀 Computer Assistance Off: Tap TURBO ten times at the match-up screen to disable Computer Assistance. This only works on Version 3.0 machines, and only in four-player games, three-player games, or two-player games where the players are on opposite teams.

🏀 Assistance Off and Big Head Combo: Tap TURBO eight times, then hold down TURBO and PASS and hold the joystick Up.

🏀 Assistance Off and Intercept Combo: Tap TURBO seven times, then hold down the TURBO, PASS, and SHOOT buttons, then hold the joystick Down.

🏀 Powerup Defense: Tap PASS or SHOOT exactly eight times at the match-up screen.

🏀 Defense and Big Head Combo: Tap TURBO six times, hold down TURBO and STEAL, then hold the joystick Up.

✦ Defense and Intercept Combo: Tap SHOOT seven times, then hold Down on the joystick and hold down all three buttons.

✦ Powerup Intercept: Hold the joystick DOWN and hold down all three buttons. This gives your player extra intercept power.

✦ Powerup Offense: Tap PASS or SHOOT exactly 21 times. This gives you extra offensive power.

✦ Shooting Percentage: Rotate the joystick—being sure to touch all eight directions at least once—and tap any button or combination of buttons 21 times. The easiest way to register all 21 buttons is to tap all three buttons simultaneously seven times. On Version 2.0 of NBA jam, the screen display the message "Shot % display activated" when you perform this trick. The message on a 3.0 machine is "Shot % display activated—Learning Mode 2." It's currently unknown how to access Learning Mode 1 (or 3).

✦ Tank Game: At the match-up screen, hold the joystick Down and hold down all three buttons for Player 1 and 2. Player 1 now enters a hidden tank game! The joystick controls the tank's movements, the TURBO button makes your tank move faster, and the SHOOT button lets you fire at enemy tanks. If your tank gets hit too many times, the message "You are dead!" appears on the screen. Destroyed tanks make the sound of a shattering backboard. If Player 1 destroys ten tanks or survives for 60 seconds, the game says "All players powerup!" and the game begins with all power-ups in place: Big Head, Defense, Offense, Intercept, and Shot Percentage.

✦ Version 2.0 machines may end the game at this screen. 2.0 machines can also end the game if the messages "All players powerup!" or "You survived!" appear. Version 3.0 machines don't end the game at this point. You also don't get a "You survived!" message. Instead, you just get the "All players powerup!" message.

NBA Jam Coin-Op Special Guests

GUEST NAME	INITIALS	BIRTHDATE	GUEST NAME	INITIALS	BIRTHDATE
Carlton	JMC	8/5	Newcomer	JRN	6/18
DiVita	SAL	2/1	Oursler	SNO	1/3
Goskie	TWG	12/7	Petro	GNP	10/8
Hey	JWH	9/20	Rivett	RJR	1/17
Howard	HOW	7/15	Scott	TON	7/3
Liptak	SL_	6/24	Turmell	MJT	3/22
Morris Jr.	WIL	1/1			

NBA Jam Tournament Edition Secrets

✦ These secret codes should be performed at the "match-up" screen before the tip-off, when the announcer says "Tonight's match-up..." and says the names of the two teams.

✦ Baby Size Players: Hold the joystick Down and Right, then press TURBO, SHOOT, PASS, TURBO, SHOOT, PASS, TURBO, SHOOT, PASS. All the players on the screen (and the ref) get real small.

✦ Big Head #1: Hold the joystick Up and hold TURBO, SHOOT, and PASS. Your player's head is slightly larger than normal.

✦ Huge Head: Hold the joystick Up and hold the TURBO button. While holding, press the PASS button five times. On the fifth press, keep holding Up, TURBO, and PASS until the tip-off. Your player's head takes on amazing proportions.

✦ Max Power: Hold the joystick Down and hold TURBO, SHOOT, PASS, and START until the game begins.

- Your Power rating is maxed out, which means you can drive through and around players, and *can't be* knocked down.
- Quick Hands: Hold the joystick Down and press SHOOT five times. After the fifth press, keep holding down and SHOOT until the game starts. Now it's easier for you to steal the ball, and your opponent can't steal from you.
- Powerup Goaltend: Press any button or combination of buttons 24 times. You must finish pressing the buttons before the screen starts to shrink. Now you can goaltend your opponents' shots and get away with it about 70% of the time.
- Shot Percentage: Rotate the joystick 360 degrees and hit the TURBO, SHOOT, and PASS buttons simultaneously seven times. This trick only works in conjunction with the Tournament Mode.
- Team Swap: At the halftime substitution screen, hold the joystick Right and hold the PASS button until the words TEAM SWAP ENABLED appear. Now use the PASS button to switch to a different team, the TURBO button to swap players, and the SHOOT button to enter your selection.
- Tournament Mode: Hold the joystick Right and hold down the TURBO, SHOOT, and PASS buttons until tipoff. The Tournament Mode is activated, and cancels out secret power-ups, guest characters, and other special abilities. (Harmless power-ups such as the Baby Size Players and Huge Head still work.)

NBA Jam Tournament Edition Special Guests

- Be sure to check out the codes for *Mortal Kombat* creators Ed Boon and John Tobias; their bodies crackle with arcs of electricity, just like Raiden! Also note that the Charles Barkley code may not work on all machines; Sir Charles was removed from early versions of the *Tournament Edition* but restored to more recent versions.

GUEST NAME	INITIALS	BIRTHDATE	GUEST NAME	INITIALS	BIRTHDATE
Air Morris	WIL	1/1	Green	JDG	5/31
Barker	PCB	5/9	Hay	JWH	9/20
Barkley	BRK	2/20	Heager	JEH	7/13
Beran	SAB	8/29	Heitsch	WMN	11/11
Boon	EJB	2/22	Hoskins	KER	10/10
Booty	MVB	4/18	Jarvis	EPJ	1/27
Brown	DEE	11/29	Kemp	KMP	11/26
Carlton	JMC	8/5	Kinkead	DIE	1/1
Coleman	DC_	6/21	Lasko	AML	8/31
Cox	PGC	4/11	Linhoff	JFL	4/16
Dabelstein	DOZ	12/31	Liptak	SL_	6/24
Davies	RJD	9/3	Loffredo	ML_	5/25
Davis	WBD	8/17	Lowes	JML	11/4
Deal	LTD	4/30	Macika	REM	3/26
Dillon	JPD	6/3	Malone	KRL	7/24
DiVita	SAL	2/1	Martinez	MAM	8/7
Ewing	PAT	8/5	Mednick	CMM	7/2
Forden	DWF	9/28	Mourning	ZO_	2/8
Gay	RMG	8/11	Newcomer	JRN	6/18
Gentile	JPG	1/23	Olajuwon	HAK	1/21
Goskie	TWG	12/7	Olivia	LOR	2/20
Granner	CG_	12/4	Oursler	SNO	1/3

GUEST NAME	INITIALS	BIRTHDATE		GUEST NAME	INITIALS	BIRTHDATE
enacho	MDP	1/13		Skiles	JMS	7/29
etro	GNP	10/8		Thomas	ZEK	4/30
ippen	PIP	9/25		Tobias	TOB	8/24
ontarelli	VJB	4/11		Tsui	JYT	11/28
ivett	RJR	1/17		Turmell	MJT	3/22
obinson	ROB	8/6		Vogel	VOG	6/27
harpe	ROG	8/1		Webber	WEB	3/1
impson	JMS	2/22		Wilkins	DOM	4/16

Kerri Hoskins, Playboy Playmate and one-half
of the *NBA Jam* cheerleading squad.

Lorraine Olivia, Playboy Playmate and the other half of
the *NBA Jam* cheerleading squad. Baby got back!

NBA LIVE '95

CATEGORY: Sports
PLAYERS: 1-4 (Simultaneous)

DEVELOPER: Hitman Productions
PUBLISHER: Electronic Arts

Introduction

Of all the games in the EA Sports series, the basketball games were always the weakest. They just didn't have the excitement or the feel of real basketball—that is, until *NBA Live '95*. Hitman Productions has started from scratch and designed a game that's fast and furious—almost like a five-on-five version of the classic *NBA Jam*. The view of the court is similar to the one used in *FIFA International Soccer*, the animation is smooth, and the sound effects are incredible. Because *NBA Live '95* is so much like real basketball, all the strategies used in the real game work in this game. For that reason, we'll just focus on basic strategies.

NBA Live '95 is the best 5-on-5 basketball game on the market, complete with monster dunks.

Basic Strategies

PLAYER POSITIONS

✴ Point Guard: The point guard is usually the smallest player on the field, and is the "field general." He dibutes the ball and calls the plays for the entire team. The point guard has the best hands and dribblin skills on the team, so he's the guy who brings the ball up the court. On defense, the point guard hovers around the three-point line, looking to steal a pass or to strip the ball from the opponent's point guard. The best point guards can shoot the three and pass the ball with equal amounts of skill.

✴ Shooting Guard: Shooting guards are almost exclusively used as three-point weapons, roaming around the line and waiting for the open shot. Shooting guards are taller than point guards, but not usually big enough to drive in and score against the opponent's forwards or centers, so they have to stay outside if they want to rack up the points.

✴ Center: The center is the tallest player on the team—usually at least a freakish seven feet in height. On offense, he wanders in and out of the

The point guard distributes the ball and shoots the three-pointer with equal skill.

The shooting guard's main
specialty is the three-point shot.

The small forward can dribble and shoot like
the shooting guard, and drive like the power forward.

key (the rectangular area underneath the basket).
When he gets the ball, he tries to make a move on
the opposing center so as to get an easy dunk or
lay-up. Centers don't generally dribble the ball—
they just catch and shoot (or pass). Centers also
have poor long-range shooting skills. Take care not
to pass the pass to the center until he's taken his
position under the hoop. On defense, the center's
skills are in blocking and rebounding. When the
center gets the rebound, he looks to quickly pas
the ball to a streaking guard or forward and start
the fast break.

✯ SMALL FORWARD: The small forward is a combination of the shooting guard and the power forward. He doesn't have the strength or power of
the power forward, but he's faster and a better
shooter. The "small" in small forward doesn't necessarily mean height; most small forwards are 6' 6"

The power forward is a strong rebounder
and likes to take it inside for power slams.

or taller. On offense, small forwards can shoot the three and drive for the slam, but it's important to estab-
lish the long jump shot early so that the forward can get the opportunities to go inside.

✯ POWER FORWARD: Power forwards are big and buff—second only to the center in sheer size. On
offense, power forwards look for inside shots and slam dunks—they don't shoot outside. On defense,
power forwards look for blocks and rebounds, just like the center.

Offense

✯ The best way to score is to shoot off screens. A screen is when you use a player on your own team to
block your defensive player so that you have an open shot. This is especially effective with the point and
shooting guards, who are the best three-point shooters on the team.

✯ Take advantage of the turbo button for an extra burst of speed to get around your defensive player and drive strong to the basket. Turbo boosts are also effective on fast breaks to make sure you stay ahead of any defensive players charging in for the block.

Defense

✦ Blocking is easier in this game than the previous EA basketball games; even big guys like Shaq can get snuffed if they try to shoot with someone right in their face.

✦ Stealing in *NBA Live '95* is attempted automatically whenever you move close to the man with the ball, but this usually doesn't result in much. You can, however, use the turbo boost to try and push the man with the ball out of bounds so you get the ball on the turnover. The computer sometimes uses this technique against you when you try to shoot, so use it right back.

✦ There are two ways to play defense: stick with a single man and let the computer run the rest of the defense, or switch from man to man as the ball is passed around. If you stay with one man, you can practice double-teaming the man with the ball, which is a risky defensive strategy, but an effective one if your player is fast enough.

NHL '95

CATEGORY: Sports
PLAYERS: 1-4 (Simultaneous)
DEVELOPER: High Score Productions/Visual Concepts
PUBLISHER: Electronic Arts

Introduction

The hockey season may have been screwed up completely by the NHL players' strike (what's up with all this salary cap B.S., anyway?), but *NHL '95* is a great way for hockey fans to get their fix. It's a redesigned version of EA's previous hockey games, with a higher vertical viewpoint of the rink and a couple of new moves, with more animations than ever. It's fun!

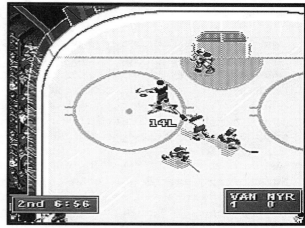

NHL '95 has a higher view of the action than the previous NHL Hockey games.

Basic Strategies

* PASSING: The key to success in hockey is quick and accurate passing. Skillful passing means that you hold onto the puck longer, keeping it away from the opponent and giving yourself more shots on goal. You may be tempted to try a lot of single-player breakaways, but a better strategy is to make a pass to one of your wingmen, putting the defense under more pressure, instead of trying to do everything yourself.

* SHOOTING: Most goal-scoring in NHL '95 is done through one of three techniques: the back pass, the one-timer, and the goalie fake-out. The back pass is a new addition to NHL '95, and the way it works is simple; you just drop the puck to a player skating near to you and behind you, and he blasts it at the goal. It's almost a variation on the one-timer shot.

* The one-timer shot works thusly: Get the puck (duh). Skate down the ice on either side of the rink. As you reach the face-off circle near the goal, pass the puck back to the middle. If the pass is timed correctly, there will be one of your players skating into the puck's path. Quickly tap the shoot button for a quick slap shot.

Passing is power in NHL '95. Learn to pass quickly and accurately to increase your scoring chances.

Faking out the goalie is the toughest way to score. You need to make the goalie commit himself by diving, and then shoot the puck in the opposite direction. Try this: skate directly at the goalie and then turn slightly to the left as if you're going to shoot. Just as you reach the crease, turn right and wrist shot the puck in the opposite direction. This technique works only in a one-on-one situation, and even then it's hard to pull off, but it's very satisfying.

DEFENSE: There are three ways to get the puck when you're on defense: body checking, stick stealing, and holding. Stick stealing is tougher, because it requires precise timing, but it's safer, because there's no chance of a penalty. Body checking is more effective, but also risks drawing a penalty. Holding is the least effective method of the three, because it's easily seen by the refs and doesn't always get the puck clear.

MANUAL GOALIE CONTROL: Only expert players should attempt manual goalie control, and only then when you're playing a very good computer or human opponent. With manual control, you can make quick passes and get counter-attacks started faster than with the computer goalie. The most important thing to do is to make sure you don't overcommit. Don't dive or lunge too early, or you leave a wide-open goal for the opponent. Stay on your feet as long as possible, and maneuver to give the attacking player the least amount of goal to shoot at.

One-timers are the best shots on goal in *NHL '95*.

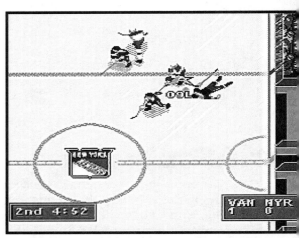

There's nothing quite as satisfying in *NHL '95* as a good, hard, body-slammin' check.

PANIC!

CATEGORY: Point-and-Click
PLAYERS: 1

DEVELOPER: Sega of Japan
PUBLISHER: Data East

Introduction

We gotta hand it to Data East: Not only did they come up with one of the most memorable (and grotesque) print ads in recent history—with a guy laughing so hard that milk is spraying from his nose—they also had the good sense not to mess with some of the more "offensive" animations in this hysterically funny game, released in Japan a couple years back under the name *Switch*. This chapter ain't funny, but it does show you what happens when you press each and every one of the 1,000+ buttons in the game. Oh, by the way, ignore the MA-17 rating given to *Panic!* by the humorless dweebs at the V.R.C.—there's nothing here that most people haven't seen or heard by the age of five.

Basic Strategies

When you destroy all 30 monuments, or press one of the "restart" buttons (see below), you're sent back to Level 1A, but you don't lose your saved game. (Destroying all the monuments also earns you a brief animation sequence.) All of the levels and gags you've seen so far are still indicated in the save. To get a perfect score of 100% levels and 100% gags, you literally have to press *every* button, including the ones that destroy monuments or send you back to the start.

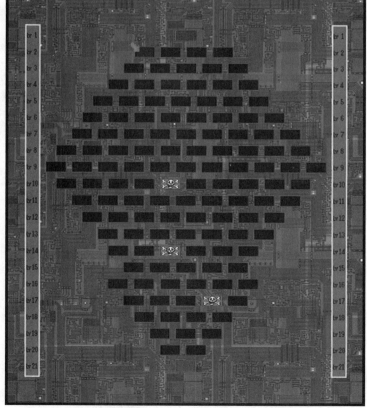

Refer to the level map frequently to find out which levels you still need to explore and which you've already explored.

Monuments and Where To Destroy Them

- Level 6H: Bullet Train
- Level 7A: Golden Gate Bridge
- Level 7C: The Opera
- Level 8C: The Smiths' House
- Level 8I: Versailles Palace
- Level 9C: Taj Mahal
- Level 9E: White House
- Level 9F: Pyramid
- Level 9G: Buckingham Palace
- Level 9K: Luxury Liner
- Level 10B: Leaning Tower of Pisa
- Level 10C: British Parliament Building
- Level 10G: Roman Coliseum
- Level 10J: Industrial Complex
- Level 11C: Dam
- Level 11D: Tribal Tent
- Level 11F: New York
- Level 11H: Great Image of Buddha
- Level 12B: Great Wall of China
- Level 12E: Igloo
- Level 12H: Mount Rushmore
- Level 13C: Eiffel Tower
- Level 13D: The Kremlin
- Level 14E: Raft House
- Level 14F: Arc de Triomphe
- Level 15B: The Statue of Liberty
- Level 15D: Himeji Castle
- Level 16D: Stick's House
- Level 16E: Sagrada Familia
- Level 17A: Temple of Seva

Golden Gate Bridge

Leaning Tower of Pisa

Mount Rushmore

Button Label Legend

✦ Letter/number combination (e.g., 14D): Indicates the level you're sent to when you press the button.
✦ M: Indicates a booby-trapped button that destroys one of the 30 monuments.
✦ R: Indicates a "restart" button that sends you back to Level 1A.
✦ W: Indicates that you win the game when you press the button.
✦ Unlabeled buttons: These show wacky animations when you press them.

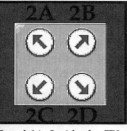

Level 1A: Inside the TV

Level 2A: Outside
the Elevator

Level 2B:
Cigarette
Vending
Machine

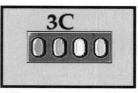

Level 2C:
Vacuum Cleaner

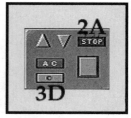

Level 2D:
Facsimile Machine

Level 3A: Inside
the Elevator

Level 3B:
Frankenstein

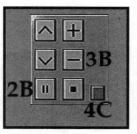

Level 3C:
Control Room

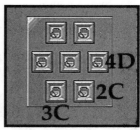

Level 3D: Statue
with Many Hands

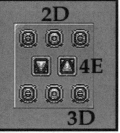

Level 3E: Green
Monster

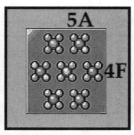

Level 4A: Lawnmower

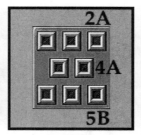

Level 4B:
Giant Television

Level 4C:
Umbrella

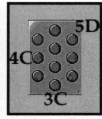

Level 4D: Hallway
with Doors

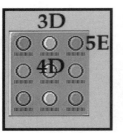

Level 4E:
Movie Camera

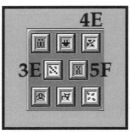

Level 4F: Living Room

Level 5A:
Mona Lisa

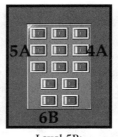

Level 5B:
Light Bulbs

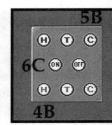

Level 5C:
Hairdryer

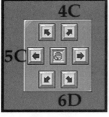

Level 5D:
Genie's Lamp

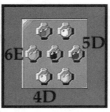

Level 5E:
Blender

Level 5F: Metal Pig

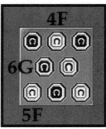

Level 5G:
Flying Horse

Level 6A: Blob

Level 6B: Spacesuits

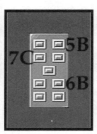

Level 6C:
35mm Camera

Level 6D: Toilet

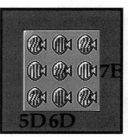

Level 6E: Speedboat

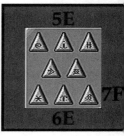

Level 6F:
UFO Above a Field

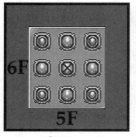

Level 6G: Parachute

Level 6H:
Nuclear Test Site

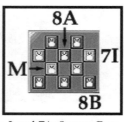

Level 7A: Snowy Day

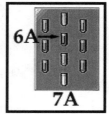

Level 7B:
Test Tubes

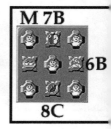

Level 7C:
Row of Houses

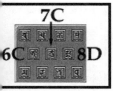

Level 7D: Spider

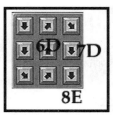

Level 7E:
Batting Practice

Level 7F: Tubes
Press the tubes to fill up the entire screen and see all the gags,
then press the middle tubes until you're sent to Level 7E.
(This is perhaps the most boring level in the game.)

Level 7G:
Ice Monolith

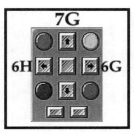

Level 7H: Biplane

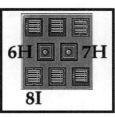

Level 7I:
Giant Battery

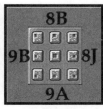

Level 8A:
Stone Face

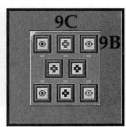

Level 8B: The Thinker

Level 8C:
Video Game

Level 8D:
Burning Building

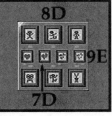

Level 8E:
Strange Statue

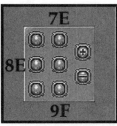

Level 8F: Small Room

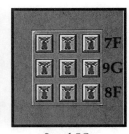

Level 8G:
Merry-Go-Round

Level 8H:
Inside an
Elevator (Dog)

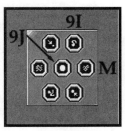

Level 8I: Blob (Dog)

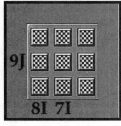

Level 8J: Chessboard

Level 9A:
Flying Bike

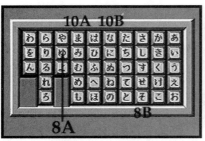

Level 9B: Japanese Computer

Level 9C:
Forest Monolith

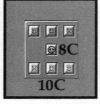

Level 9D:
Floating Sphere

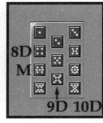

Level 9E:
Star Projector

Level 9F:
Conveyor Belt

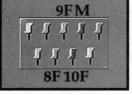

Level 9G: Gas Station

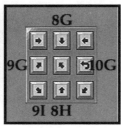

Level 9H:
Movie Theater

Level 9I: Giant
Television (Dog)

Level 9J: Test
Tubes (Dog)

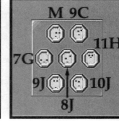

Level 9K:
Desert Monolith

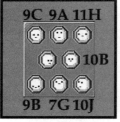

Level 10A:
Beach Monolith

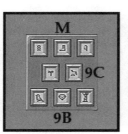

Level 10B:
Dinosaur Skeleton

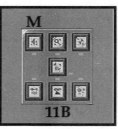

Level 10C:
Mermaid Statue

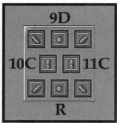

Level 10D:
Dentist's Chair

Level 10F:
Flashlight

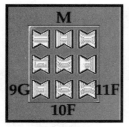

Level 10G:
Yellow Car

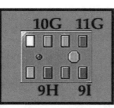

Level 10H:
Soda Machine

Level 10I:
Inside Another
Elevator (Dog)

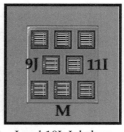

Level 10J: Jukebox

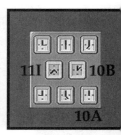

Level 11A: Clocks

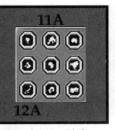

11A
12A

Level 11B: Globe

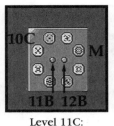

10C
M
11B 12B

Level 11C:
"The Fly" Chamber

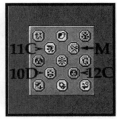

11C
M
10D
12C

Level 11D: Strange
Musical Instrument

12D
11D

Level 11E: More
Conveyor Belts

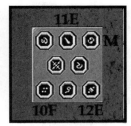

11E
M
10F
12E

Level 11F:
Trophy Room

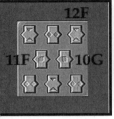

12F
11F
10G

Level 11G:
More Tubes

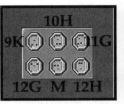

10H
9K
11G
12G M 12H

Level 11H:
Underwater Monolith

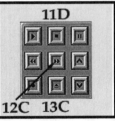

11H
12H

Level 11I:
Small Chest

11A

12H

Level 12A: Spaceship

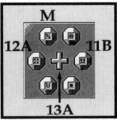

M
12A
11B
13A

Level 12B:
Personal Helicopter

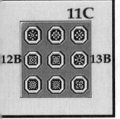

11C
12B
13B

Level 12C: Black Dot

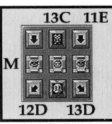

11D
12C 13C

Level 12D: Mega-CD
Title Screen

13C 11E
M
12D 13D

Level 12E:
Grassy Field

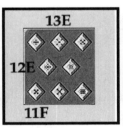

13E
12E
11F

Level 12F:
Subway Car

11G
12F
13F

Level 12G:
Bubble Machine

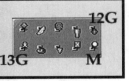

12G
13G
M

Level 12H:
X-Ray Machine

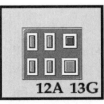

12A 13G

Level 13A:
Film Projector

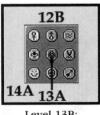

12B
14A 13A

Level 13B:
Basketball Player

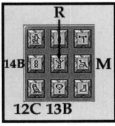

R
14B
M
12C 13B

Level 13C: Pyramid

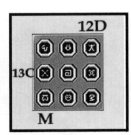

12D
13C
M

Level 13D:
Headless Babies

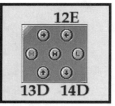

Level 13E:
Jacket Closet

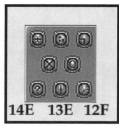

Level 13F:
Satellite Dish

Level 13G: Outside
Another Elevator
Pressing the two buttons
in different combinations
causes different gags and
sends you to different levels. Try these three combos
for starters: top button
twice; top, bottom, top;
bottom, bottom, top.

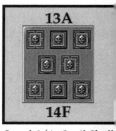

Level 14A: Snail Shell

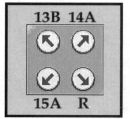

Level 14B:
Inside the TV Again

Level 14D:
Robot Sumo
Wrestler

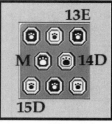

Level 14E: Moped

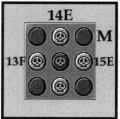

Level 14F: Cannons

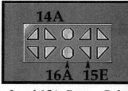

Level 15A: Button Belt

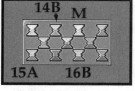

Level 15B: Chorus

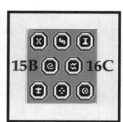

Level 15C: Bus Stop

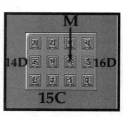

Level 15D:
Headless Animals

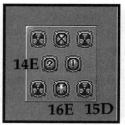

Level 15E:
Refrigerator

Level 16A:
Outside Yet
Another Elevator

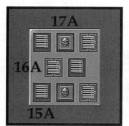

Level 16B: Another
Giant Television

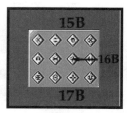

Level 16C:
Hovercycle

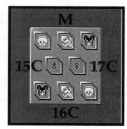

Level 16D:
Microwave Oven

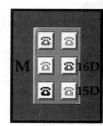

Level 16E:
Phone Booth

Level 16F:
Inside Yet
Another
Elevator

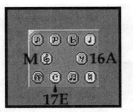

Level 17A:
Animal Treadmill

Level 17B:
Diving Suit

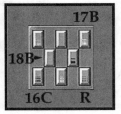

Level 17C:
Pipe Organ

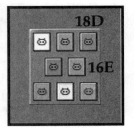

Level 17E:
Coal Engine

Level 18A:
What, *Another* Elevator?
Pressing the two buttons
in different combinations
causes different gags and
sends you to different levels. Try these three com-
bos for starters: top button twice; top, bottom,
top; bottom, bottom, top.

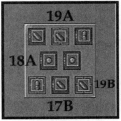

Level 18B: Bed

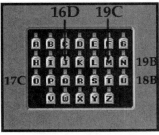

Level 18C: Typewriter

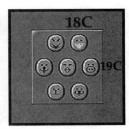

Level 18D:
Washing Machines

Level 19A:
Entering the Network
There are no buttons
here; you automatically
go to Level 20A.

Level 19B:
Entering the Network
There are no buttons
here; you automatically
go to Level 20B.

Level 19C:
Entering the Network
There are no buttons
here; you automatically
go to Level 20B.

Level 20A: Computer
Network Server

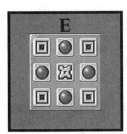

Level 20B: Computer
Network Server

Awesome Sega Genesis Secrets 5

SONIC & KNUCKLES

CATEGORY: Platform   DEVELOPER: Sega

PLAYERS: 1   PUBLISHER: Sega of America

Introduction

The original *Sonic the Hedgehog* was a ground-breaking game, with innovative gameplay and the coolest graphics in 16-bits anywhere. Each sequel has introduced new characters, new obstacles, and a few interesting tweaks in the gameplay. *Sonic & Knuckles* is the logical next step, with the amazing innovation of having what Sega is calling "Lock-On Technology". This new feature allows you to plug *Sonic & Knuckles* into your Genesis, then plug any other Genesis cartridge into the top of the *Sonic & Knuckles* cartridge. Enter the "secret code" (A+B+C+Start) and most games will only let you play an incredibly tough bonus round (the bonus round from *Sonic 3* where you run along the surface of a globe collecting blue spheres and avoiding red spheres). However, if you plug in *Sonic 2* or *Sonic 3,*

Sonic returns with a new "friend", Knuckles,
in the first cartridge to feature Lock-On Technology.

you'll be able to play those games using the Knuckles character. And since Knuckles can climb walls and break through blocks, you'll be able to enter a new area or two and fight a boss you didn't even know was there before. Without the Lock-On Technology, you'll still find a huge adventure in *Sonic & Knuckles,* with eight complicated levels, most with two acts each.

Basic Strategies

✦ **CONTROLS:** One of the greatest features in Sonic games, since the original, is the design of the controls. The A, B, and C buttons all do the exact same thing, so you don't have to worry about hitting the wrong button at the wrong time. However, with this latest installment there are new moves to perform, still accomplished with any of the three buttons. For Sonic you can now blast forward with a short burst of energy when you have the Flame Shield, and you can double jump if you have the Lightning Shield. Press A, B, or C to jump, then quickly press either of the buttons again to burst forward. Sonic can pounce enemies when they have the

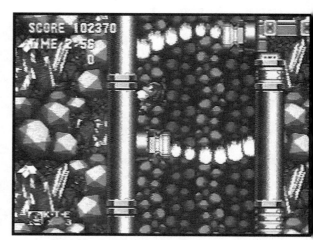

Knuckles is "The Man"! He can climb walls,
float down, and bust through walls with his fists!

bubble shield and performs the same move. Knuckles can do much more (maybe they should have put his name first in the title!). For starters, he can glide down slowly (kinda like Bubsy — hey, we ain't afraid to say it). Just press A, B, or C while in the air to put your arms out and float down. Another useful trick is Knuckles ability to climb walls. Jump into a wall and press any of the three button to grab the wall, then climb up. When you reach the top of the wall, just keep pressing up and Knuckles will climb to the floor above. As if that weren't enough, Knuckles can bust through walls with his fists (hmmm... maybe *that's* why they call him "Knuckles"!). By busting through these walls, Knuckles is able to enter areas that Sonic can't enter in any way, which takes us to the next point...

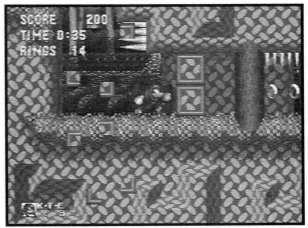

Knuckles can bust through walls with his fist, allowing him to enter areas that Sonic can't.

✱ There are **separate paths for Sonic and Knuckles** throughout most of the game. Both characters begin at the same point, but since Knuckles can climb, he'll be able to reach the higher platforms more easily. And since Sonic can't bust through walls, Knuckles will be able to enter areas that Sonic has no way of reaching. In each stage we will point out how the paths vary, what to look for in each area, and where most of the hidden stuff is (we might not have found *everything,* but we found more than enough to finish the game). There are a few areas where the paths cross before splitting again, until after Stage 4, when both characters take total-ly different paths. Which you end up with is a lengthy adventure with Sonic, and a similar but differ-ent adventure with Knuckles. By using the Lock-On Technology to plug Knuckles into Sonic 2 and Sonic 3, you'll also find those games to provide totally new challenges. Plugging in nearly any other cartridge, including Sonic 1 and Sonic Spinball, will simply make a bonus round appear (after you press A+B+C) which is very tough to complete. You can choose between using Sonic or Knuckles in these bonus stages by pressing any button before pressing Start (the colors of the stars will change from blue for Sonic to red for Knuckles). If you do manage to collect all of the blue spheres, you'll get to see a screen with Sonic surrounded by the gems. Not worth the effort, but the main reason for this fea-ture is the amount of practice necessary to com-plete the tougher bonus stages during the game, which takes us to the next point...

✱ **The seven emeralds** can be collected one-by-one as you finish Special Stages. To enter a Special Stage you must find one of the well-hid-den large gold rings, then jump into it. Inside is a Special Stage straight out of Sonic 3, only now it becomes necessary to jump over red spheres to reach other blue spheres (except for the first emerald). To add fuel to the fire, the Special Stages become more complicated with each one you complete, making the collection of all seven emeralds as close to impossible as you can get. Your first goal should be completing the game

Finding the Special Stages is challenging enough. Finishing the tougher Special Stages is way too hard!

with Sonic or Knuckles, then go back and attempt collecting all of the emeralds (if you dare). Once all of the seven emeralds are collected, you'll become **Super Sonic** or **Super Knuckles,** you'll be invincible to enemies, and you'll be able to move quickly across the ground until all of your rings are gone. As a bonus, it's possible to plug Sonic 3 on to Sonic & Knuckles, then collect all of the emeralds in *both* games to become Hyper Sonic or Hyper Knuckles. If you're reflexes and searching abilities are fine-tuned enough to collect all of the emeralds, you'll have an easier time at the bosses, whom probably won't be a problem to beat without the Super or Hyper powers, since you're *that* good a player anyways. Kinda ironic, eh? Either way, you're best off beginning with Sonic 3 and collecting the easier emeralds so you can at least have Super powers.

If you plug Sonic 3 into Sonic & Knuckles, you'll be able to use the battery save on the Sonic 3 cartridge!

⚡ **RINGS: The most important thing to remember during any Sonic game? Always carry at least one ring!** As long as you have one ring you'll be safe from enemies taking your lives away. Anytime you get hit, your first priority (before running, fighting, anything!) is to grab at least one of the rings that flies from your body. You'll be invincible for a few seconds after getting hit, so walk through whatever you have to in order to reach that one ring. You'll collect an extra life for each 100 rings you grab. Even if you get hit and lose all of your rings, you can still build back up to 100 again. Many stages contain 200-300 rings, making it possible to earn up to three extra lives (and that's not including the bonus stages!). Collect 50 rings during a bonus round and you'll get a continue.

⚡ **SAVING:** What? You say you didn't know you could save in *Sonic & Knuckles?* Well, there's no battery built into the game, but there is a way to save. What you must do is plug **Sonic 3** into **Sonic & Knuckles,** then play all the way through Sonic 3 using either Sonic or Knuckles. When you complete *Sonic 3,* which is fairly easy with Knuckles since he can fly and climb, you'll go straight from the final boss in *Sonic 3* to the first stage in *Sonic & Knuckles.* Any time you run out of continues, you're game is automatically saved and can be continued from that stage, in either game, the next time you begin.

Bonus Stages

⚡ Jumping into the giant gold rings will take you to the Special Stage, which is the only way to collect an emerald, but there are two bonus stages that are a great way to **earn extra lives, coins and continues.** Since earning extra lives and continues is a critical requirement to conquering this game, mastering these bonus stages becomes essential. You must have at least 20 rings to make the ring of stars above a checkpoint post appear (the manual says 50 rings are required, but don't believe them!). Jump into the ring of stars to enter the bonus round. The choice of which bonus round you enter seems to be random (we tried really hard to find a pattern in the number of rings we were carrying, but couldn't fine one). Collect 50 rings during any bonus round to earn an extra continue!

⚡ **Slot Machine Stage:** One bonus round resembles the **Vegas-style** rounds from previous Sonic games, where you do your best to bounce off bumpers into a slot at the center of the screen, which activates the three jackpot wheels. If you can get three of a kind in the wheels, you'll earn extra rings (or lose them if the wheels land on Robotnik). The outside walls that surround the Slot Machine stage has colored blocks. Each time you hit a block, it will change its color. After turning red, the blocks will turn into "Goal" blocks, which aren't really your goal, but the only way you'll be sucked out of this bonus stage. Try to avoid them as long as you can while attempting to collect as many rings as possible. Collecting 50 of the rings that surround the wheels is very easy, and by far the easiest way to collect a **continue!**

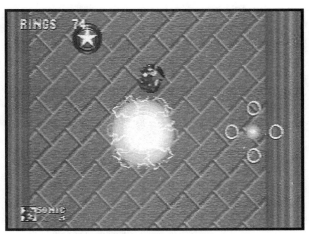

On the Glowing Magnetic Spheres stage, use Left and Right to aim, then launch Sonic upward.

- **Glowing Magnetic Spheres Stage:** The other bonus stage begins on a **large white sphere** that you'll spin around. Most players end up falling to the exit beam at the bottom of the screen quickly. The beam will move up the screen, so you must try to climb upward as fast as possible. While on a white sphere, press left or right on the control pad to make Sonic or Knuckles change their aim. You want to aim them upward (so they spin around the ball in a vertical line), then press A, B, or C when you're at the top of the white sphere to launch up to another sphere, bumper, or flipper. If you can reach a flipper, press any of the buttons to activate the flipper and send your character to higher (and safer) goals above. As you hit the rings and small white spheres you'll earn bonuses in the form of a glass ball with a letter in it. The only glass ball to fear is the black one, which will make you drop to the exit beam. Keep an eye out for the **1-Up glass balls,** which are the only item worth dropping for, even if you are going to hit the exit beam.

- **The stage-by-stage analysis ahead** will cover the varying paths taken by Sonic and Knuckles, as well as the location of the hidden large Gold Rings for the Special Stage, where to find other valuable hidden stuff (1-Ups mostly), how to fight bosses, and how to approach the other various enemies.

Mushroom Hill Zone, Act 1

- **SONIC/KNUCKLES STRATEGIES:** The majority of the stage is the same for both characters, except for the first few screens worth. Knuckles will have more walls to bust through at the beginning. Search high and low to find plenty of rings. There's a flame shield to the left of the third one-way lift for Sonic. Knuckles can find a flame shield at the very beginning of the act on a high platform.

- **SONIC GOLD RING LOCATION (Special Stage):** Go to the right past the first one-way lift (you can use it if you want — you'll end up at the same spot). Continue to the right and use the second one-way lift. Go right along the lower path to find and use two mushrooms that work like a seesaw to reach the area above (there's a mushroom parachute to the right of the seesaw, but using it will put you in an area where the Special Stage Gold Ring can't be reached). Go right, past the Madmole, and use the swing launcher (well, what would *you* call it?!) to launch to the upper-right. When you reach the ledge, go right a few steps and enter the wall to find the Special Stage Gold Ring.

- **KNUCKLES GOLD RING LOCATION (Special Stage):** You'll go through a few walls before reaching the same one-way lift and swing launcher as Sonic (see above).

- **ENEMIES:** The Butterdroids (butterflies) will fly in circles around you, with the circle getting smaller

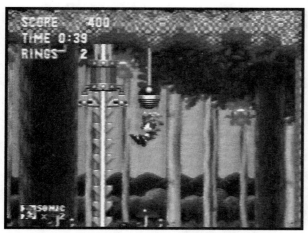

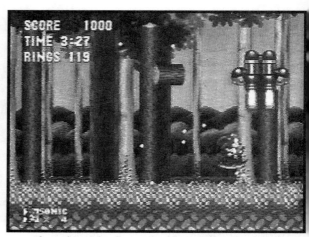

When you find this one-way lift you'll be close to finding the Special Stage for Sonic or Knuckles.

If you have the flame shield, simply stand under the lumberjack and pounce up into him.

until they hit you. Leap into them from any direction for a safe and easy hit. Be careful not to grab onto the handle of the one-way lifts when Butterdroids are near. Madmoles will pop out of their hole and throw a mushroom that knock you backward. Hit them quickly when they appear, or take cover and wait for the next appearance. The Mushmeanie is a mushroom on a spring that hops around. You must hit him once to knock off his mushroom top, then again to help the poor little forest creature inside escape. The Dragonfly is a snake-like flying creature with spikes along its body. Wait for it to head upward, then pounce its head while avoiding its tail.

💰 **BOSS:** The boss is a robotic lumberjack that chops down trees. As it chops the tree, the pieces of wood will fly your direction. If you have the flame shield, you can stand directly below the lumberjack and jump rapidly to destroy it. Without the flame shield you'll have to pounce him while avoiding the flames from the jetpack on his back. As he gets near the bottom of the tree he'll be easier to pounce, since there are no flames on the top of his head.

Mushroom Hill Zone, Act 2

💰 **SONIC STRATEGIES:** Knuckles will shoot you to the top of the area near the beginning — there's no way to avoid it. The rest of this stage is very straightforward, with lots of cool loops. Stick to the advice in the Basic Strategies at the beginning of this chapter and you should breeze through this act.

💰 **KNUCKLES STRATEGIES:** You'll bust through a wall at the beginning and find a switch on the wall. After trying to hit the switch for a few hours, give up and go on. When you pass through this area with Sonic you'll finally realize why the switch is there — Knuckles hits it and Sonic shoots up to an area above. After exiting the Special Stage, go right to leave the wall and use the first two mushrooms you see to reach a red spring on the wall above. The spring will shoot you to an area with an **extra life** and one of each shield (choose carefully — we suggest the flame shield since you can charge forward across gaps or into enemies with it). Use the spring near the top of the next one-way lift to reach an area with two more shields to choose from.

💰 **SONIC GOLD RING LOCATION (Special Stage):** You'll pass through the area where Knuckles' first Special Stage Gold Ring is located (see below). The background color changes from dark green to fall colors at this point. Continue to the right, down the hill and through several loops. When you reach the one-way lift, grab the handle but don't pull down on it yet. Jump to the right and hit the Cluckoid, then enter the wall behind him to find the Special Stage Gold Ring.

The cluckoid guards a secret passage in the wall that leads to the Special Stage Gold Ring.

✦ KNUCKLES GOLD RING LOCATIONS (Special Stage): Stick to the higher areas of the level (climb the walls whenever possible). When you find a one-way lift, use it and climb above using the springs. Go right, through the loop, and down through the next loop to find a Cluckoid (blowing rooster) by the wall above. The wall behind the Cluckoid has the first Special Stage Gold Ring. The background color will change from bright green to darker fall colors as you pass the first gold ring area. The second gold ring is straight to the right from the first ring. Go through five loops and up the wall from the last loop, then go right to find a one-way lift. The Cluckoid to the right of the one-way lift guards the entrance to the second Special Stage Gold Ring.

✦ ENEMIES: Same as Act 1, plus Cluckoid. Cluckoid will blow you backward. Duck until he's done blowing, then pounce him (there are no sharp edges).

✦ BOSS: When you reach the end of the act you'll see a radar dish sending out a signal. Don't jump into the stream of the signal or you'll take a hit. Duck down next to the radar dish and spin into it. Robotnik appears and flies off to the right. Chase him! The chase includes a run through several hurdles. Check the hurdle as you approach, then decide if you need to run under it or jump over it. While avoiding the hurdles you must also hit the bottom of Robotniks aircraft while avoiding the flames of its engine. The timer counts up to 10 minutes, so if you have plenty of

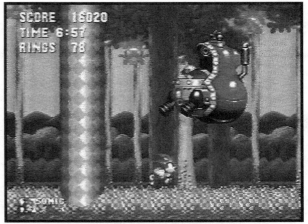

Take your time when approaching Robotnik to avoid the hurdles, then pounce up into him.

time use it wisely to grab rings if you drop them, and to time your hits safely. Also keep in mind you can perform short or high jumps, depending on how long you hold the button.

Flying Battery Zone, Act 1

✦ SONIC/KNUCKLES STRATEGIES: Sonic and Knuckles follow the same path during this act, but Knuckles can still climb to a few high ledges that Sonic can't reach. The small bumps on the ground in this act are **land mines** that explode after you step on them, so keep moving. The **turrets that shoot flames** will stop shooting flames while you're standing on them, and most of them will launch you up like a spring.

✦ Knuckles Only: From the beginning of this stage, climb the first wall you see after coming to a stop (as the platform below you falls) to grab a Lightning Shield and an Invincibility.

✦ Near the beginning of this stage are **monkey bars** that you hang on and climb across. Most of the time the last monkey bar will lower you to the next set of monkey bars. As you lower from the last one you'll be above a Technosqueek (mouse). Go left to find a flame shield and rings, then go to the right until you see the next Technosqueek (he's hanging from the ceiling). There's an **extra life** hidden in the higher part of the ceiling, to the left of the Technosqueek on the ceiling. Jump into the ceiling and you'll see the extra life icon appear.

✴ Every time we see someone having trouble with the **floating platforms** below the **bottom of the ship** (outside), they're always falling to their death because they are rushing. Take your time! Study the next floating platform to see if its moving, and how its moving, then make your jump when it's safe.

✴ Near the halfway mark (back inside the ship) are a **group of corner pipes** in the air. A few groups of metal circles pass through the corner pipes in a square formation around the room. You must jump on the metal circles and corner pipes to reach the next area on the top-left of the room. The last jump is the toughest, since the ledge is guarded by a flaming turret. Stand on the lower-left pipe corner and make the leap to the ledge as the flames are facing away from the sides, then quickly jump on top of the turret. The tank with the button to the left has enemies inside, so if you're using Knuckles stand on the right side of the button and float over the button (with Sonic you can't avoid hitting the button unless you have the flame shield).

✴ When you reach the **top of the ship** (outside the ship), you'll hang from **props** while blowing in the wind. Move up to the area just below each prop, then hold right and hit the jump button to fall to the next prop. When you reach the last prop (can't see another to the right), climb up to the prop and hold left, then jump to the next prop (you'll collect rings along the path), climb up and go right to the area above the last prop (more rings along the path), then climb to the top prop and hold right and jump to reach a ledge with an **extra life** and rings. Drop off the left side of the ledge and go to the area below. There's a sled that will shoot you out of this area, making it very confusing to figure out which direction to go. The trick is to jump over the sled

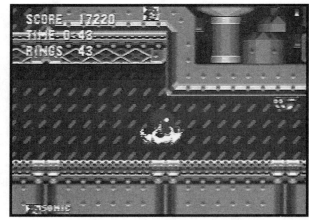
Grab this extra life in the ceiling before going outside of the airship.

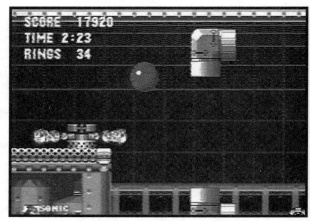
The jump to this flame turret is a tricky one. Wait until the flames are short, then try to land on it.

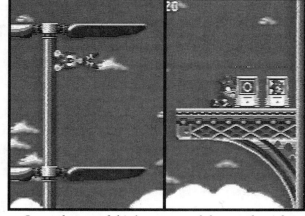
Get to the top of this last prop and drop to the right to find an extra life and rings.

and jump into the wall on the left to enter back into the ship.

- ✸ **Sonic Only:** After the next checkpoint you'll hit a button on the floor and drop a few floors. You can go left or right. The left path is a bit trickier, but more fun. Both paths lead you to the same spot.

- ✸ **Knuckles Only:** After the next checkpoint you can climb above the button that opens the floor or take the "Sonic path" below. Either path will take you to the same area eventually, which leads to the next area described.

- ✸ Bombs are lobbed up into the air on the **top deck of the ship** (back outside again). Knuckles can climb the left wall and float through the air to collect rings, but most of the rings can only be collected if Knuckles has the Lightning Shield (it attracts rings like a magnet). Go to the right wall and wait for the second group of bombs to blow a hole in the ship where you can enter back to the inside. As you enter, slow down by holding left on the control pad so you can get to the **Special Stage Gold Ring** (see below). If you don't stop and drop to the area with the Gold Ring, you'll be whisked to the boss.

- ✸ **SONIC/KNUCKLES GOLD RING LOCATION (Special Stage):** Check the paragraph above for a tip that begins with "Bombs are lobbed up...". When you enter back into the ship you must slow down so you won't shoot through the round metal cage and into the next room. As you're holding left you should stop inside the metal cage and drop to the bottom floor where you'll find five tanks with yellow buttons on top. Three of the buttons will spring you into the air, while two will explode the tank and rings will appear. Go to the left of the tanks. The floor curves up to the wall. Run up it to enter the wall and find the Special Stage Gold Ring.

- ✸ **ENEMIES:** The Blaster is a tank-like creature with a huge cannon for a nose. Approach cautiously between bullets and stomp him.

- ✸ **BOSS:** The boss appears to be another tank with a yellow button on top, but once you hit the button arms will grow. This boss is *easy!* Stand on the button until the eyes of the boss flash, then walk off the side to avoid the smashing hand. Jump back up onto the button and repeat until the boss beats the heck out of itself.

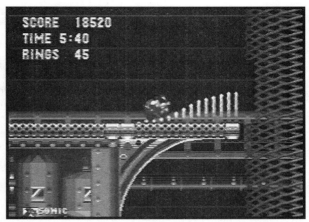

As you enter into the interior of the airship for the second time, hold left to drop through this cage...

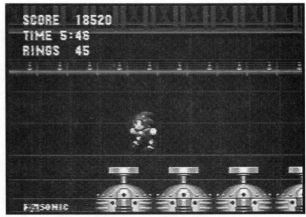

...then go left from these springs to find a hole in the wall with a Special Stage Gold Ring.

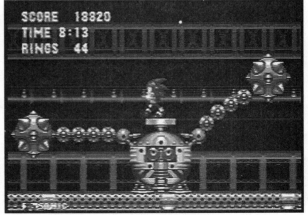

The boss looks harmless until he sprouts arms. Wait for his eyes to flash, then walk off either side.

Flying Battery Zone, Act 2

※ **SONIC/KNUCKLES STRATEGIES:** When you reach the second screw elevator, you'll be able to get off on one floor to the right, or you can ride it all the way down and go to the left. The lower path to the left is easier, and it begins with a checkpoint. The next tank with a yellow button on top is a trap with enemies inside, so float over it if you're using Knuckles. When you reach a button that opens the floor, go to the passage on the upper-left and climb the walls to find an easy path with super-fast action. If you're using Sonic you'll have to jump to the small platforms that pop out of the walls. The rest of the path to the boss is fairly easy.

※ **SONIC/KNUCKLES GOLD RING LOCATION (Special Stage):** After being carried past the second revolving round cage by a spider, continue forward until you go up a screw elevator and shoot up through a revolving round cage. Hold left while going up through the cage to enter the wall on the left. At the top of the cage you'll be standing on a solid floor, so if you're using Knuckles you can jump onto the wall on the left and climb to enter the passage with the Special Stage Gold Ring. If you're using Sonic and you miss the wall hole on the way up, you must jump onto the rising platform to the right, then spin attack to the left into the hole at the highest point below the ceiling. This maneuver is easier to perform while the platform is on its way down.

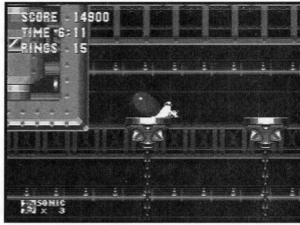

With Sonic you'll have to spin attack from this platform as it drops to reach the Special Stage in the left wall.

※ **BOSS:** The boss has two stages. The first time you'll be trapped between two force fields while Robotnik stands to the right. The beam at the top of the screen will move left and right to home in on you, then it charges up and shoots a beam straight down. You can't touch the yellow force fields on either side, which move in closer each time the beam shoots. Move next to either of the yellow force fields (you can touch the area at the bottom without getting hurt), then when the beam charges up and stops flashing off, quickly move to the opposite side. You can even charge up a spin attack while waiting for the beam to stop flashing, then spin to the other

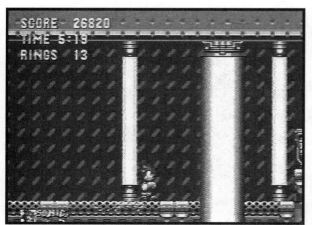

When the beam stop flashing off, quickly move to the opposite side of the screen.

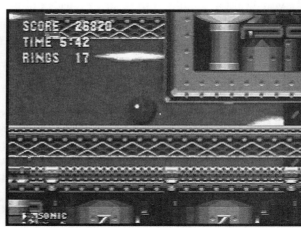

The floor will crush you if you don't run quickly to the roof of the airship.

side. Eventually the force fields will explode and Robotnik will make a run for it. Quickly run to the right as the floor rises. You must make it through an obstacle course to the top floor before the bottom floor crushes you. When you see the first rings (there are four), duck down and hit the buttons rapidly to charge up a spin attack, then push forward to run up the wall. Run into the spring on the right wall to shoot to the left quickly. If you're far enough ahead of the floor you can take time to collect lots of rings along the way. Use the spin attack to hit the Super Ring TV without hitting the spikes on the ceiling. When you reach the top floor go to the far right of the screen and wait for Robotnik to appear. He grabs onto the floor with two spiked hands while he hangs below in a protective globe. His pattern will vary, depending on if

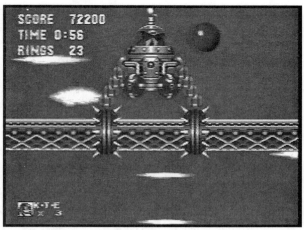

His pattern changes depending on if Sonic or Knuckles is attacking, but the basic strategy is to pounce as he rises, then jump over him between flames.

you're playing with Knuckles or Sonic. With Knuckles he'll shoot flames up four times, with a short burst between the second and third burst that's a great opportunity for you to float over him. Avoid getting cornered by the spiked hands. After four flames he'll rise up around the floor twice, shooting another burst of flames as he swings under the floor and at the top. Jump and pounce into him each time he rises, but stay clear as he swings at the top and bottom shooting flames. Repeat the pattern until he's defeated. With Sonic the pattern is much easier! You can hit him once right at the beginning as he rises. He'll shoot flames up once, then he'll wait a few seconds before shooting flames up again, then he'll swing around the floor four times without shooting any flames. Pounce away!

Sandopolis Zone, Act 1

SONIC/KNUCKLES STRATEGIES: The biggest fear we have of Sonic games is acts like this. The act is very large and complicated, making it diffi-cult to write a walkthrough. Read the section on enemies, and try going everywhere. The coolest part of the act is repelling off the sides of the buildings. The boss is to the far bottom-right, but you won't be able to go straight there without climbing and dropping a bunch of times. As long as you keep heading to the right, you'll find the boss. You can also sink down into the sand in several areas, but if the screen doesn't start scrolling immediately, quickly jump back up out of the sand or you'll sink to your death. There are a few walls that only Knuckles can bust through. If you can find the first wall near the beginning of the act while you're using Knuckles, bust through and climb to the upper-left ledge before the next wall to find an **extra life.**

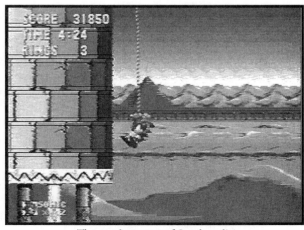

The coolest part of Sandopolis is repelling down the sides of the walls.

SONIC GOLD RING LOCATIONS (Special Stage): This ring is a bit tricky to find. After the first wall you repel down, go right. You'll have to push a block onto rollers. Ahead is an invincibility TV. Go up to the ledge above and go left to the thin sand waterfall. Go up the waterfall and jump over to the ledge on the left. Go past the wide sand waterfall (wider than the last one, at least), and ride the swinging platform to the left ledge. Keep going straight to the far left and you'll find the **first Special Stage Gold Ring.** From the Special Stage, go right and sink into the quicksand to reach a hidden area below. You'll end up on the path you were on before. When you reach that invincibility TV for the second time (it will be smashed if you grabbed it the last time around), go to the ledge above and climb up in the thin sand waterfall. Jump to the ledge on the left and go up in the wide sand waterfall to the very top, then go right into the cave. Go right, through the loop, and keep going right until you see a quicksand pit. Jump into the quicksand and sink to find a hidden area. Go left to find the **second Special Stage Gold Ring.**

KNUCKLES GOLD RING LOCATION (Special Stage): We searched *everywhere* and couldn't find one! Sorry.

ENEMIES: Plenty of new enemies to challenge you on this act. Anytime you see sand, beware of the Sandworms. They jump out of the sand in an arc, but they only stick to the top surface area, so if you're diving down deep into the sand you won't have to fear them. The Skorp is a robotic scorpion that slings its spiked tail at you. Your safest strategy is to wait until he turns around, then hit him from the back. Otherwise, try to time your hit for when his tail is extended.

BOSS: A large pyramid will rise from the sand when you reach the bottom-right area of the act, then the boss will appear from the door. The boss can't be pounced or hurt in any way. He'll try to stomp you when you approach, which is the only way to make him move. The trick is to lure him to the left side and make him jump into the quicksand. When he's on the edge of the ledge next to the quicksand, you must stay near him and keep jumping rapidly to avoid sinking, then quickly move out of the way and jump out of the sand as he leaps into it.

Climb up the thin sand waterfall and go left past the thicker one to find Sonic's first Special Stage.

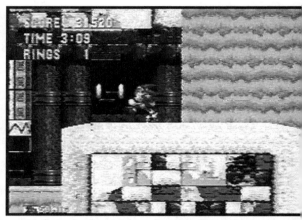

Go down in the quicksand pits to find hidden areas, including this one where the Special Stage is located.

Lure the stoney boss to the left ledge and make him jump into the sand, then leap for the land before you sink!

Sandopolis Zone, Act 2

✦ **SONIC STRATEGIES:** When you're on the sand slides, find the swinging platform above the inter-section of two slides and jump to it, then go to the left to find two Super Ring TVs. Go back to the swinging platform, then go down to the right on the slide to reach the first checkpoint. In the next room you must push the black switch on the ground, then get to the upper-left corner of the room and push the block onto the rollers (use the spin attack to push it easily). Jump on the block and make a jump for the door before the block stops moving or the door will close before you clear it. After the second checkpoint you'll be forced to release a cork and climb quickly ahead of the rising sand, twice! Further ahead are two walls to repel down. During the second repelling, Sonic will spin around 180° to grab rings and hit a wall on the opposite side, then go back and forth between the walls several times. The boss is a few steps past (and a long drop down) from the next checkpoint.

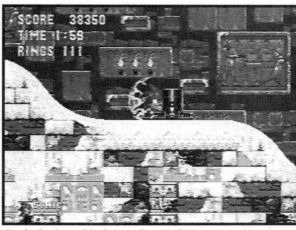

Push the large black switches in this area to open doors, then run quickly to get through them before they close.

✦ **KNUCKLES STRATEGIES:** At the beginning of this act you can choose to go to the right (the "Sonic path"), or grab onto the left wall and climb. Read the section below on the Special Stage Gold Ring to help you decide which path to follow. Pull every ceiling switch to turn the lights on and scare the ghosts away. Most of the ghosts can be pounced, but the timing is tricky. The lights will slowly fade back off, but you can keep pulling the same switch as many times as you like to brighten the room. Pushing the black switches will usually open a door nearby, which will slowly close as the switch slides back to its original position. You'll probably have to backtrack often once you find the door closing to re-activate the switch. There are corks on the ceiling in various areas that will release sand. As Sonic you have no choice — the only way to reach the top of the act is to release the sand and climb quick-ly as it rises. With Knuckles you can climb walls all the way to the top, which isn't necessarily less dan-

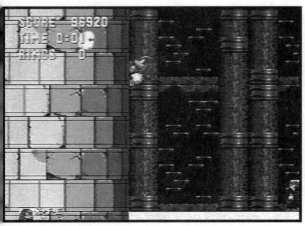

If you use Knuckles and climb up the left wall at the beginning of the act...

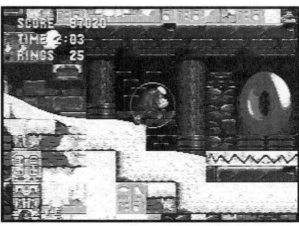

...you can reach the first Special Stage Gold Ring, and a few other cool items.

gerous since you'll have to worry about dropping into danger if you lose your grip on a wall. There is one particularly tricky black door switch near the end of the act that closes very fast. The only way to get through the door is to prop the block to the left of the switch against the switch, and the only way to get the block over to the switch is to raise the floor by releasing sand from above the door (climb up past the door and hit the cork on the ceiling). To the right of the next checkpoint is the boss.

✸ **SONIC GOLD RING LOCATION (Special Stage):** We searched *everywhere* and couldn't find one! Sorry.

✸ **KNUCKLES GOLD RING LOCATIONS (Special Stage):** From the beginning of the act, go to the left wall and climb to the top. When you find the light switch, grab it, then jump from below it to the wall on the left and climb up. A spring will take you to a bubble and Super Ring TV, then head to the

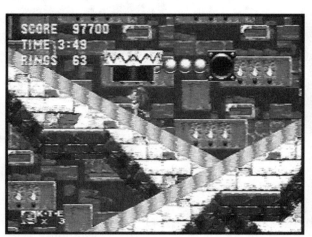

Watch for this swinging platform when using Knuckles, then follow the directions...

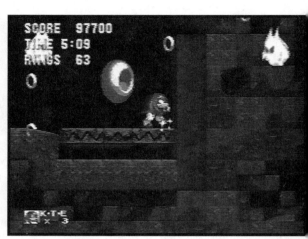

...to reach this second Special Stage Gold Ring in plain sight.

right, drop to the right of the spikes, and break through the wall on the right to find the **first Special Stage Gold Ring.** When you reach the large room with criss-crossing slides that go forever (actually you'll loop back to the top slide if you don't get off). Watch for a swinging platform between one of the slide junctions. When you're on the slide going from the top-right to the bottom-left, fall to the next

slide below going to the right. When you fall to the next slide below, jump and climb to reach the top-right of the slide. To the right is another slide going down to the right. Ride it down and go right to find the **second Special Stage Gold Ring** in plain sight.

✸ **BOSS:** The boss is a giant robot that marches across the sand while swinging its spiked arms. You must hit the boss in the head to knock his armor back, then hit the boss again to damage him before the armor returns. The arm on the front side of the boss is safe to climb onto when the arm is swinging forward, so jump on it and leap for the head, then land back on the arm and quickly jump back up into the head of the boss. If you see sparks forming at the head of the boss, beware of a beam that shoots to the ground. If

Knock the armor off the boss, then pounce into him once or twice.

you hit the boss while the beam is charging it will cancel the beam. If the boss makes too much progress across the room, and you're using Knuckles, you'll have to jump onto the left wall and float over into the head. If you're using Sonic, you'll have to defeat him before he gets too close to the wall.

Lava Reef Zone, Act 1

⚡ **SONIC STRATEGIES:** When you see the first checkpoint, hit it and grab the flame shield next to it for protection from the biggest threat in this act (fire!). Before reaching the next checkpoint you'll encounter a machine that drills into the floor below you and causes it to collapse. Stand to the left of the machine, clear of the shaking floor that is about to fall. After the floor falls, you can reach an extra life by using the flame shield to charge across the gap that now exists. Drop down through the gap and head right until you're riding on a rising platform with spikes across its bottom. Hold right to enter the wall. A lower hole in the wall has a Super Ring TV, while directly above you can find the **first Special Stage Gold Ring.** Ahead is another identical rising platform with spikes, then a third. When you reach the third spiked platform, ride it up to reach a lightning shield to the left, then jump to the ledge above and go into the wall on the right to find a room with 33 rings, and an **unreachable Special Stage Gold Ring** to the lower-right through the wall. Of course, that is it can't be reached with Sonic or Knuckles, but it could be reached if you had Tails (you *can* jump into a hole in the ceiling below it, but you can't jump high enough). Hmmm! I wonder what Sega has planned. Perhaps a *Sonic & Knuckles & Tails* with Lock-On Technology? Ahead you'll cross a bridge in front of a lava waterfall. There's a path straight to the right, but first climb up to grab a lightning shield and Super Ring TV. Jump on the rising spiked platform to the right and jump onto the spin attack-activated elevator to reach a ledge with an

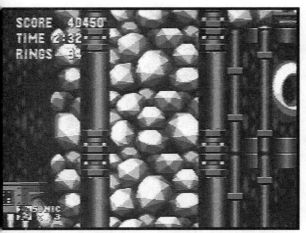

Jump into the wall to find a Special Stage Gold Ring, and a Super Ring TV directly below it.

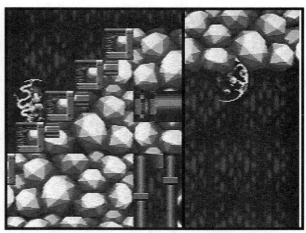

The unreachable Special Stage viewable through this wall has an access area below only Tails could enter. Hmmm.

extra life and 15 rings. Go back down to the bridge by the lava waterfall, then go to the right and take the lower path (you'll have to bust through the rocks with your charge attack). In the area below is a huge spiked ball that swings around a post. When you run past the spiked ball, it will begin to chase you. Keep running and skip the first hole in the floor to fall into the second, which has an extra life. The spiked ball will probably hit you, causing you to lose your shield. Go left and climb upward to find a spin attack-activated elevator, ride it up to the top, then go into the left wall to find a **second Special Stage Gold Ring.** After exiting the Special Stage, go up and right to find the same area where the first Special Stage gold ring is located (with the rising spiked platform). You've just looped around to where you started. Continue forward until you find the bridge with the lava waterfall, but this time climb up above the lower passage and continue to the right. Keep going until you reach a spin attack activated elevator with a hidden passage below it (you'll be able to see the rings in the hidden passage). You'll find a checkpoint, then you'll meet the boss.

✦ **KNUCKLES STRATEGIES:** There's a machine that drills into the rocks and causes part of the floor to drop in the Sonic version of this act, and in Knuckles version of this act it's right at the beginning. We hit it dozens of times and still didn't destroy it. Drop down and go right across the lava. When you reach the rising spiked platform, jump to the upper-right for a Super Ring TV, then climb the wall so your hands are on the bottom area of the largest stone. Jump and float to the left to reach an extra life (this takes practice, but it *is* possible. As you go forward use Knuckles floating abilities to clear the jumps across the lava. The first checkpoint is just ahead. The second checkpoint is far ahead, but there isn't much to point out between it and the first checkpoint. When you jump to a wall right before the second checkpoint you'll climb into it when you try to climb it. The checkpoint is inside this wall, along with 25 rings. When you find a spin attack-activated elevator trail ahead with no elevator, go down through the rocks to find the final checkpoint, and the boss for this stage.

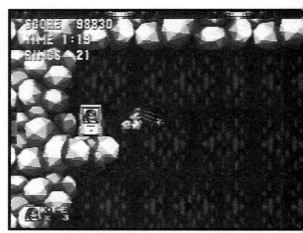

Jump and float across the room
to reach this extra life.

✦ **SONIC GOLD RING LOCATION (Special Stage):** Check the Sonic Strategies above for the location of *two* rings. Look for **Special Stage Gold Ring** in bold letters.

✦ **KNUCKLES GOLD RING LOCATION (Special Stage):** We searched *everywhere* and couldn't find one! Sorry.

✦ **ENEMIES:** Flames, lava, and other hot stuff. There are pipes that leak steam, and the steam will stick to you. The pipes are easy to pounce. There are also stones on the ground that have creatures under them, and the stone will explode when it sense you near it.

✦ **BOSS:** The boss is out of sight below the screen, but you will see two "tentacles" that rise on each side of the screen and shoot three fireballs each. If you have the flame shield the fireballs will not hurt you, so you can safely stand at the center of the screen and wait for the hand. You can hit the tentacles to destroy them (concentrate on destroying one before hitting the other, then it will be easier to attack or destroy the other). After the tentacles sink back down off the screen, a robotic hand rises and slaps the ground. Move left or right to avoid the hand (it will pause for a moment before slapping), then jump and hit the

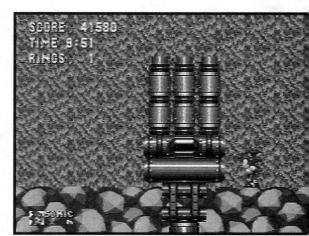

Keep moving to avoid the hand, then when it stops,
leap into the air and pounce it as it slams down.

hand before it disappears. If you move too far from the hand before it slaps the ground, you won't be able to hit the hand after it slaps the ground. Five hits and the hand is history.

Lava Reef Zone, Act 2

✦ **SONIC STRATEGIES:** Keep heading up and right as often as possible. The path is linear for almost the entire act. There's one area where you can choose two directions, but both paths will lead you to the same area. There are rolling logs with handles that you can grab onto. As Sonic is spinning around the metal log, you can launch upward by hitting any jump button. The best time to launch for maximum height is when Sonic is on the front side of the log, not the top.

✦ **KNUCKLES STRATEGIES:** After crossing the rolling log of spikes, climb up to find rings and a flame shield. Don't, I repeat, don't pounce on the Robotnik TVs or you'll lose rings or a life. Get rid of the exploding stone to the right of the Robotnik TVs, then jump into the wall to get sucked through a tube. Through this path you'll find lots of rings, another flame shield, and a checkpoint. From the checkpoint,

go to the right until you see spiked yellow platforms on a vertical conveyor belt. Jump to one of them, then jump back to the left under the moving block to get into the wall with a **Special Stage Gold Ring.** Continue through the stage to get sucked into another tube, and to hit a checkpoint. Grab the flame shield to the left of the checkpoint (don't let that spiked ball hit you and take your flame shield!). To the right is a button below a flame thrower that opens the door above it. Continue forward until you find the path to the Hidden Palace Zone. There's no way to avoid it, but there is a looping area that will keep you busy for hours searching for another path. The other stages in the game are for Sonic.

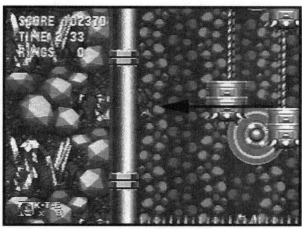

Jump to the spiked platforms, then jump to the left into the wall below the moving block to find the Special Stage.

✦ **SONIC GOLD RING LOCATION (Special Stage):** You'll come to a room near the beginning with two Robotnik TVs in the bottom-right corner. There are two paths leaving this room, but to find the ring you must go to the passage on the right above the Robotnik TVs. Keep following the path until you reach steel platforms with yellow stripes on a vertical conveyor belt. Jump on one of the platforms and leap into the top-left wall to find a hidden hole with the **first Special Stage Gold Ring**. After leaving the Special Stage, keep following the path to the right until you reach rolling steel logs with handles. When you reach the floor above the rolling logs, use the spring to enter the left wall for a flame shield and Super Ring TV. Use the same spring to reach the moving blocks above, then jump into the top-right wall to find a **second Special Stage Gold Ring**.

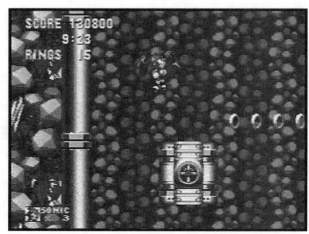

Use the springs to reach these moving blocks, then jump into the right wall to find the second Special Stage.

KNUCKLES GOLD RING LOCATION (Special Stage): See the Knuckles Strategies section above for the location of the **Special Stage Gold Ring** (it's in bold letters, too!).

BOSS: Knuckles finds a passage out of this act, with no boss to block him. Sonic will be knocked out by Knuckles, then he'll land above lava and face Robotnik. The moment you see the explosion, jump over to the right platforms and keep running to the right. The platforms that collapse have a bright white spot just below the gold — get off of them quickly. The targets on the platforms mark where Robotnik's missiles will land. After you hit the checkpoint, jump to the platforms sinking in the lava and keep jumping to the right until the screen scrolls down, then jump to the left across three platforms to find a flame

Watch out for the collapsing platforms while avoiding the targets that aim Robotnik's weapons

shield TV. The flame shield will make the next battle *much* easier. When you reach the bottom floor you'll be able to stand on the lava safely. As long as you don't hit the spikes on Robotnik's ship, or the spiked balls, you'll be able to stay alive easily. Even if you don't have the shield, this battle isn't impossible. The platforms you rode down to this bottom floor will help you stay off the lava and away from the spiked balls. The floor will tilt to the right (the left side will rise up), and the platforms will slide down toward Robotnik. Jump to the left and continue jumping onto each of the platforms to avoid hitting Robotnik. You don't have to hit his ship — the spiked balls he throws will ram into his ship as the floor tilts. The floor will flatten back out, then Robotnik will sink into the lava and appear on the left side. The floor will tilt the opposite direction. Use the same strategy as before. The pattern will repeat a few more times before Robotnik finally takes enough hits.

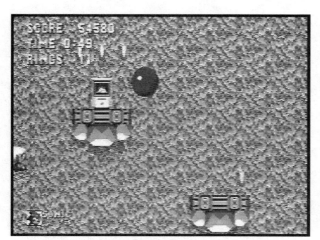

Grab this flame shield on your way down to fight Robotnik and you won't have to fear the lava.

Stay on the platforms while avoiding the spiked balls that crash into Robotnik's ship, eventually destroying it.

idden Palace Zone

* **SONIC STRATEGIES:** No enemies and only a few obstacles make this an easy climb. After hitting the checkpoint you'll face Knuckles in an extremely easy battle.

* **KNUCKLES STRATEGIES:** Run to the right and jump on the globe to enter the Sky Sanctuary Zone. No enemies, no Special Stage gold rings, no nothing!

* **BOSS:** Knuckles cruises right through this act, but when you're playing with Sonic you'll have to fight Knuckles here. It's an extremely easy battle. Stand at the center of the screen. During most of the battle Knuckles will jump and float across the screen. Simply jump up into him. Use spin attacks or pounces the rest of the time. Knuckles

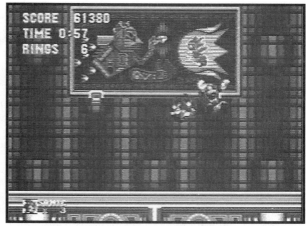

Sonic will have to fight Knuckles to get past the Hidden Palace Zone. Jump up into him while he's floating.

will make a run for the emerald to the right, but Robotnik will steal it and give Knuckles some shock therapy. What a traitor! Knuckles will help you through a blockade, then you'll both be warped up to the Sky Sanctuary Zone.

Sky Sanctuary Zone, Act 1

* **SONIC STRATEGIES:** Mini Robotnik soldiers are the tough enemy here. They float in the air and shoot laser beams. Jump the beam, then pounce them. There are transparent clouds and solid white clouds — the white clouds will bounce you up. Go to the right and up the tower, then to the far left to flashback to a classic Sonic boss.

* **KNUCKLES STRATEGIES:** Knuckles heads here directly from the Hidden Palace Zone. You must face off in a final battle against Mega-Sonic.

* **KNUCKLES' BOSS:** The boss is Mega-Sonic. His pattern is a bit unpredictable at times, but isn't impossible by any means. He jumps into the air, then the tricky part comes. He's going to shoot across the top of the screen and land on the opposite side, or he's going to bounce at the center of the floor and land on the opposite side of the screen. It's tough to figure out which is coming until the very last second. Just be ready to avoid the bounce, and try not to make a habit of jumping or you might mis-predict a bounce and jump up into him as he shoots across the top of the screen. The rest of the pattern is easy. When he lands, spin attack into him if he's facing you. If his back is to you, he's going to slide backwards so jump over him, then spin attack when he reaches the opposite side of the screen. Once he's defeated, he'll bow down for a moment, then he'll dig down deep within his soul and find enough ener-

When Mega-Sonic lands facing you, spin attack into him. If he lands with his back to you, jump over him.

gy to slide over to a large green gem. The gem will power him up for another battle.

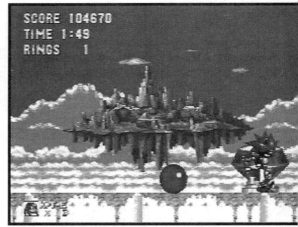

The only time you can hit Mega-Sonic during the second battle is right before he climbs back onto the green gem

- ⚡ **Mega-Sonic will be gold during most of the second battle,** and you won't be able to hit him while he's gold. When he stops in the top corner he'll swoop down at you (jump or spin away to avoid him), or he'll tilt his head back like a Pez dispenser and shoot fireballs. Stand far away and jump to avoid the three large fireballs he shoots. He'll drop to the ground, then he'll spin across the screen. Jump over him, then quickly spin attack him as he turns blue for a second before climbing back up onto the green gem. Stick near the green gem between attacks and Mega-Sonic will mostly stick to his three fireballs pattern. After a few hits Mega-Sonic will hover above you and shoot eight deadly rings outward. Stand below him and slightly to the left or right to avoid the rings that shoot straight down and diagonally. If you collect all seven emerald gaining the powers of Super Sonic, you'll get to enter a zone that you wouldn't get to play without th Super Sonic powers. However, if you collect the Super Knuckles powers you won't get to play an extr zone, but you will get a slightly different ending.

- ⚡ **SONIC'S BOSS:** The first boss you meet may look familiar. It's the first Sonic The Hedgehog bos ever, from the original Sonic game. This time, however, it's Mega-Sonic at the wheel instead of Robotni He's in a round ship that floats near the top-center of the screen. He drops a ball on a chain that swing from left to right. There's a platform on each side of the screen to jump onto, making it easier to pounc Mega-Sonic. The trick is to time your pounce on Robotnik as the ball is swinging toward you, then dro through the chain as the ball is to the far right and make a run for the left platform. Repeat the patter of pouncing, dropping through the chain, and running to the opposite platform.

- ⚡ Once you defeat Mega-Sonic the first time, you can teleport to the next floor up. Go to the far right t meet Mega-Sonic again, this time in another familiar vehicle from Robotnik's past. This one is from th Metropolis Zone of Sonic The Hedgehog 2. The round ship is surrounded by spheres that spin aroun

Deja Vu! It's the first boss from the first Sonic game! Pounce him, then jump through the chain and run to the other side.

Jump up and hit the second Mega-Sonic vehicle when the spheres are in a horizontal line.

it. The spheres are deadly, so you must time your pounces to avoid the spheres. The only safe time to hit the bottom of the ship is when the spheres are moving in a horizontal direction. The rest of the time you should avoid jumping anywhere near the ship. There are small clone bubbles that float out of the ship, which can easily be popped with a hit. Once you defeat him you'll have to climb up two floors to find a teleport ball to a higher area. Each time you approach a tower you will see several small animals, but beware of the Robotnik soldier that is chasing them out of the tower. An easy climb up another floor will earn you another teleport ball that takes you to a final battle with Mega-Sonic, this time standing on his own two feet.

The final Mega-Sonic vs. Knuckles battle is the same as it is with Sonic. Spin attack when he lands facing you.

Mega-Sonic on foot: His pattern is a bit unpredictable at times, but isn't impossible by any means. He jumps into the air, then the tricky part comes. He's going to shoot across the top of the screen and land on the opposite side, or he's going to bounce at the center of the floor and land on the opposite side of the screen. It's tough to figure out which is coming until the very last second. Just be ready to avoid the bounce, and try not to make a habit of jumping or you might mis-predict a bounce and jump up into him as he shoots across the top of the screen. The rest of the pattern is easy. When he lands, spin attack into him if he's facing you. If his back is to you, he's going to slide backwards so jump over him, then spin attack when he reaches the opposite side of the screen. Once he's defeated, he'll bow down before you and you'll be off to the Death Egg Zone.

Death Egg Zone, Act 1

SONIC STRATEGIES: This is one tough act! You'll have to face new and unfamiliar enemies, discover a few new obstacles, and survive much of the next act walking upside down on the ceiling! See the Enemies section below for some tips on how to deal with them. The wide blue platforms in this area will rotate and form steps. You must stand on the left side to make the right side rise, then quickly climb up the steps before they get too high. The elevators are covered with conveyor belts that sometimes change directions. They'll try to force you into the spikes on the walls while you're riding up. You'll see a countdown before being shot through the invisible tubes. While you're enjoying the ride be sure to watch for power-up items to head for once the ride is over. There is one elevator that has a conveyor belt on the bottom, so you can stand on it without sliding to the sides. This elevator will

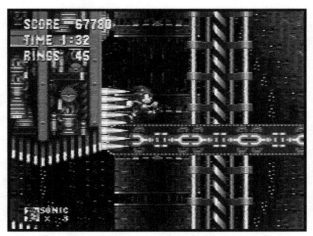

The elevators are covered with conveyor belts that try to force you into the spikes on the walls.

give you a long ride through a few different corridors, but when you see the next checkpoint jump for it before the elevator takes a plunge into a bottomless pit. After this checkpoint you'll find a room where you'll bounce around with the gravity pulling you to the right. The walls are covered with springs, and there appears to be no way out. The trick is to hit all of the buttons on the floating platform to make them red, then the door to the right will open. After you find the next checkpoint you'll meet the boss of this act.

$\bigstar$ **ENEMIES:** The spiked floating creatures will move above you, flash a light, then shoot a spike straight down into the floor. You'll be given plenty of time to move, but don't waste any of it. You can hit them from a diagonal direction as long as you avoid the sharp parts. The black balls that spin around a pole aren't very dangerous — they'll blow you up into the air as you jump over them. A wide-eyed robotic creature with a red hat spins a spiked ball around his chin, then shoots it out in a straight, horizontal line. Don't jump near them except immediately after the ball returns.

$\bigstar$ **BOSS:** The boss is a cylinder with a red eye and spheres spinning around it. The spheres will move up and down, then spread out when they're above the floor. When the spheres are not spread out, and are near the floor, make a leap for the red eye. As long as you hit it, you'll be bounced back to the sides, away from the cylinder. Each time you hit the eye one of the spheres will explode, and small spikes will shoot out in eight directions.

$\bigstar$ The eye will separate from the cylinder and float, surrounded by two platforms. The platforms

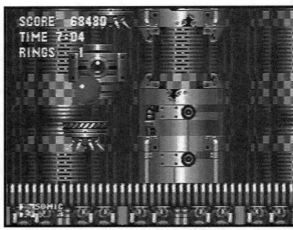

Pounce into the red eye of the boss when the spheres are near the floor, then bounce back to the left.

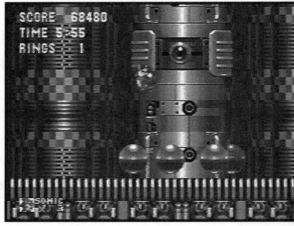

Stay on either platform and jump up into the eye as you swing below it. You're very safe on the platforms.

have spikes on the bottom, which are your only hazard as long as you stay on either of the platform (if you're on the floor you'll also have to avoid a huge laser beam shot straight down from the red eye) Stand on either platform and jump up into the eye. The platforms will both spin around the red eye a the same rate, increasing in speed, then decreasing back to a stop. Wait for the platforms to slow dow then hit the red eye again. Stay on the platforms the entire time and repeat this pattern until the bos is defeated.

Death Egg Zone, Act 2

$\bigstar$ **SONIC STRATEGIES:** This is more of the same from the last act, only now you have to master th controls while walking upside down (at least during most of the act). Before falling down into the firs tunnel you can grab a Lightning Shield and a Super Ring TV on the right side. If you fall into the hol before grabbing them, go down in the four-way junction and you'll be able to get enough momentum to get back up to the TVs. The path to the left in the four-way junction is tricky, so we suggest going to the right. Go to the right and ride the steps down, then go right to the next stairs that sink. Above these stairs is an extra life you can reach by jumping from the top step when the beam is on, then jumping again (you have to do this while you're upside down, which is the only part that makes it very tricky). You'll hit three more checkpoints before reaching the boss. It's a long and tricky trip, but as long as you stick to the basic strategies, and always keep at least one ring, you shouldn't have too much trouble (you've made it this far!).

BOSS: This is another boss that's confusing at first, because you can't pounce into the boss. It's a large floating sphere that drops small drones onto the floor with spikes on one side and wheels on the other. The trick to defeating the boss is to jump into one of the teleport tubes to reverse the gravity at a time when the spiked side of the drones will collide with the boss. Sounds easy? It is! Especially once you realize you don't have to pounce the boss!

Once you defeat the sphere boss you'll only have one more boss to beat — the massively huge Robotnik robot. If you have the Super Sonic powers (which is received after you collect all seven emeralds), you'll have to face the Robotnik robot once now (in two parts), then again in the Doomsday Zone. If you don't have the Super Sonic powers, you'll only have to fight him this first time, then you'll get a slightly less exciting ending sequence.

ROBOTNIK ROBOT: When the act begins, quickly run to the right and keep running until the screen stops scrolling. Robotnik will appear from the left side, with his metal hands being your first threat. Each hand has three fingers. Listen for the crashing rhythm of the sound. You'll hear the crash of his feet, then his fingers will come crashing down. There are even beats between the sound of his feet and the sound of his fingers. When you hear the first crash, of his feet, wait about half a second and jump high into the air in front of his fingers. You'll land on his

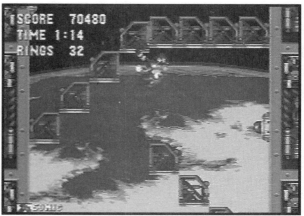
During much of this act you'll have to adjust to walking upside down.

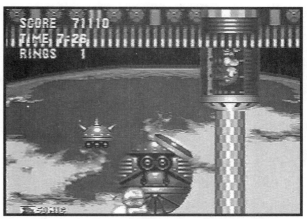
You can't pounce this boss. Reverse the gravity to make the spiked drones hit the boss.

Run to the right when the Robotnik Robot appears to avoid falling through the floor.

fingers as they crash down into the floor. The safest attack is to line up with one finger and keep pouncing that finger each time it comes down once, then wait for the next time. If you're feeling a little gutsy, you can line up with a finger and jump, then guide Sonic to land between two fingers to hit them each once. This is more risky, because every once in a while the game will glitch and you'll take a hit while waiting for the fingers to rise back up. You can also risk a spin attack between the hands, which will cause you to bounce between the fingers on the inner side of each hand. If you make the jump early enough, it's possible to pounce the fingers, bounce, and hit the fingers again a moment before they rise up. To do this you have to make the jump the moment you hear the feet crash into the ground, but if you jump too early you'll get hit by the fingers.

⚡ Once you destroy the hands run quickly to the right and keep running. The robot will chase you from the left side and the floor will collapse as the robot walks through it. The robot will shoot flames down to the floor and across to the right, which you can easily jump over. The flames will continue to come until you take action. If you jump into the nose of the boss. When the mouth opens on the boss you'll see a huge cannon that charges up and shoots a beam across the screen. It's possible to duck the beam sometimes, but it's very unsafe since there's no guarantee the beam will miss you (it depends on if the robot is moving up or down at the time). The only safe way to avoid the beam is to jump over it. The beam sucks in energy, which you can see, then it stops for a second before shooting the beam. When you see the energy stop getting sucked in, wait about half a second and make a high jump. The beam only lasts for a quick flash, and the timing isn't extremely critical. You can continue this pattern of hitting the nose, then jumping the beam, but you won't destroy the boss. The key to defeating the robot is to hit the nose, pounce the top area of the beam cannon, then run to the right and jump the beam. Be ready to jump the flames again, then hit the nose and repeat the pattern until the robot is defeated. Once the robot is defeated, keep running to the right to

Stand in front of one finger while they're pointing up, then jump when you hear the thump and land on it.

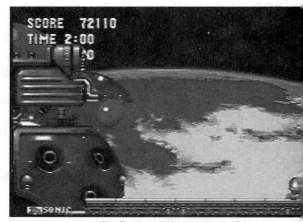
Jump over the flames, then leap into the nose to expose the laser beam cannon...

...pounce on the beam cannon, then run to the right and jump to clear the shooting beam.

avoid falling through the collapsing floor. Robotnik will appear once more carrying the main emerald. Hit him, run to the right, hit him, run to the right... you get the idea. If you collected all seven emeralds and have the Super Sonic power, you'll be off to Doomsday Zone, otherwise you'll get to see the normal ending sequence, which isn't much different than the "real" ending.

Doomsday Zone

⚡ **SONIC STRATEGIES:** You'll only get here if you've collected all of the emeralds to gain the power of Super Sonic. Once you complete the Robotnik robot you'll be flying through the sky chasing the robot.

⚡ **BOSS:** Thanks to the Super Sonic powers, this battle isn't too tough. Grab lots of rings while flying so you won't lose your powers. Hit the jump buttons to surge forward (you can hit it rapidly). As long as you have Super Sonic powers the asteroids and rockets will just make you spin a few times. When you reach Robotnik in his cool blue rocketship, he'll shoot guided missiles your way. You can't damage the rocketship, so use the missiles against him. Fly around the ship in a counter-clockwise direction to guide the missiles into the cockpit of the ship. Once the ship is destroyed, Robotnik will zip past you with the main emerald in his hands. This time you'll have to avoid asteroids and small bombs while ramming into Robotnik. The flames from his jetpack won't hurt you, but when you ram him you'll spin backwards for a moment. Eight hits will destroy the flying robot and you'll freefall with the main emerald until Tails rescues you.

Circle Robotnik's spaceship to guide
the guided missiles into the cockpit.

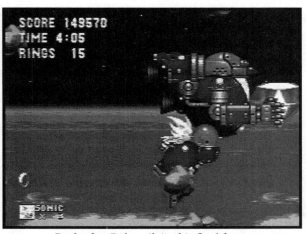

Rush after Robotnik in this final form,
using the jump buttons to charge into him.

Awesome Secrets!

⚡ **SAVE YOUR GAME!:** The best reason to go out and buy *Sonic The Hedgehog 3* (or buy it back from the guy you sold it to) is so you can save your progress in *Sonic & Knuckles*. There's no built-in battery in *S & K*, but the battery in *Sonic 3* will save your game, and when you finish *Sonic 3* you'll go straight into the first act of S & K. When you quit or lose all of your lives, your game will be saved, regardless of which game you're involved in. As a bonus, the emeralds you collect in Sonic 3 will carry over to S & K, so you can become Super Sonic or Super Knuckles that much easier.

SPARKSTER

CATEGORY: Platform
PLAYERS: 1

DEVELOPER: Konami
PUBLISHER: Konami

Introduction

Rocket Knight Adventures introduced the character of Sparkster to the Genesis, and now he's back in an all new adventure with tons of new enemies and obstacles. For those that missed out on the first adventure, Sparkster must travel through six stages of increasingly difficult challenges, mostly in a side-scrolling platform game, but also fighting it out in a "Rock-Em Sock-Em Robots" stage where you control a huge robot boxing another. Sparkster is jam-packed with challenging gameplay, so if you love platform games, check it out! The latest trend in video games is to release a Super Nintendo and Genesis game at the same time with the same name, but have both games feature totally different levels. That's the case with Sparkster, so if you love this game, be sure to check out the Super Nintendo version also.

The star of Rocket Knight Adventures returns with two different adventures: one for Genesis, one for SNES.

Basic Strategies

✸ Press A to attack with your sword, B to jump, and C to attack with a Rocket or Screw Attack. The **Rocket and Screw Attacks** are Sparkster's ultimate weapon. When Sparkster is charging at an enemy with either attack he will be "invincible", as long as he's not touching the enemy as he finishes the attack. As the gauge at the top of the screen turns all red, you'll be able to perform the Rocket Attack, and when it fills to white you can perform the more powerful Screw Attack. You can aim these attacks by pressing in the direction you want to attack, and you can use these attacks to reach higher platforms, or to rebound between walls to climb higher.

✸ There are **blue and red gems** to collect along the way. The red gems will spin the wheels in the slot machine at the top-right corner of the screen. Whatever item appears in all three spaces will be the item you receive. If the word "BOM"

Collecting the red gems (or 10 blue gems) will give you a spin of the jackpot wheels for cool power-ups.

appears, you must quickly move out of the way to avoid the bomb that falls. Collecting 10 blue gems is equal to one red gem. You can also collect Apples to restore some of your energy, or Meat to restore all of your life. You can also collect seven keys along the ways, called the **Keys to the Seals.** These keys look like a sword handle, and you'll see the first during the opening scene with Sparkrobo. There are Keys to the Seals during the Demo, then on Stage 1, Stage 2, Stage 3, Stage 5 (2 keys), and the final on Stage 6. We'll point out their location as we go (look for **Key to the Seals** in bold lettering).

Opening Demo: Sparkrobo

You can choose to play this part of the game, or hit Start to pass it by. If you defeat the other giant robot, you'll grab the first Key to the Seals. **WARNING:** If you hit Start to skip this "interactive demo", you won't collect the **first Key to the Seals.** It's very easy to beat the other robot. Use A to deliver a straight punch, B for an uppercut (strongest hit), and C to guard yourself. As long as you keep your guard up, you can't receive damage. At the beginning of the fight, put up your guard and wait for him to attack, then take three steps forward and swing your uppercut on the third step to hit him. Immediately put up your guard, then repeat the pattern after he shoots and until he's defeated.

The instructions are very easy to defeat this robot, and skipping this "demo" will skip the first key.

Stage 1

This first stage isn't too difficult, and it's a lot of fun. The only challenge to it is the length. It's long! If you can make it to the second stage, you'll be able to get a password when you lose all of your lives, then you can continue on Stage 2 later. From the beginning, practice your rocket skills by grabbing the blue and red gems above. Hold up on the control pad, then press C to shoot up to the gems. Also practice shooting up into the air, then changing directions and shooting into a different direction while still in the air. This will be an important skill to have later in the game. Go right and spin into all the enemies you see. As long as you use the Rocket and Screw attacks, you won't get hurt by the enemies. Be

Every item you see can be taken.
Try going through or around a wall.

sure to search high and low, using your rocket powers, to find items to grab. If you can see an item, there's a way to get to it. Try going through fake walls, or going around to the other side of a structure. Watch for a platform with a moving face. When you see a moving face, you can almost always pass through that wall or floor. Below the moving face is 11 blue gems. Grab them, then go left into the wall to find a secret passage with an **extra life.** Use your rebounding skills to rocket out of the room with the extra life.

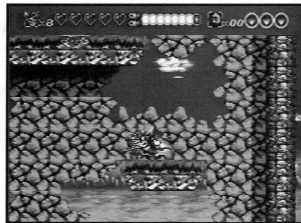

The first Key to the Seals is in the demo before Stage 1. The second is through the left wall in the second area.

In the **second area** you'll spin into a screw switch that opens the floor below you. As you fall down, hold left to enter a secret hole in the wall. You can also rocket back up to this hole in the wall. Inside is the **second Key to the Seals,** as well as several red gems. As you go to the right through this area, watch for another wall with moving faces, which you can walk through to collect many blue gems. If you continue to the right, through another wall with moving faces, and hit a screw switch, you'll land next to a spinning cylindrical machine next to a conveyor belt. The machine spins and spits out bombs that land on the conveyor belt. When you try to rocket through the machine, you'll be swallowed up, but you won't receive damage and the machine will spit you out on the left or right side unharmed. When it spits you out on the right side, continue to the right to find a tougher cylindrical machine. There's a second path along the top of this area that will still lead you to this machine, in case you didn't go through the walls with the moving faces.

The cylindrical machine boss will spin it's sections around, then when they stop you will be able to unscrew a screw if one is facing you. If a screw isn't facing you, the other holes will spit out bombs your direction. The pattern is easy: stand on the yellow block and wait for the machine to stop. If there's a screw on your side of the machine, the block will raise or lower to its level, then you can simply hold the direction pad toward the machine and press the Screw Attack button to shoot at the machine and pull out the screw. After the screw is removed, you'll shoot through the hole it leaves behind, then you can repeat the process from the other side of the machine.

After defeating the cylindrical machine, you'll enter the **third area of this stage**. The vines that reach down toward you can be destroyed with a spin attack to the tip. The droplets that fall will keep you

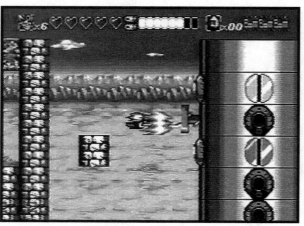

Stand on the yellow block next to the cylindrical boss, then spin attack if a screw appears on your side.

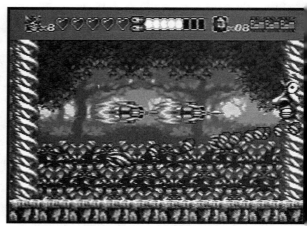

Hit this tree boss in the nose with a spin attack each time he reaches his arms out toward you.

from jumping — swing your sword to knock them off. The creatures in mine carts can be knocked out with a rocket or spin attack. To the lower-right of this area is the first boss. It's a tree with a big nose. Stand to the far left of the screen, then when he swings his arms or reaches them out toward you, jump straight up and spin attack to hit his nose. Quickly run back to the left and repeat the pattern until he's defeated.

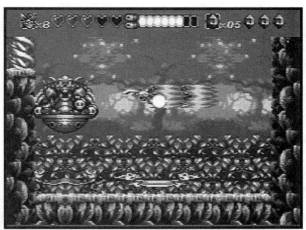

The creature in the sphere can't be hurt while he's spinning, so save up your attacks for when he stops.

✯ Go to the right until you reach another room where the walls close up on both sides. This time the **creatures in mine carts** will drop from the top of the screen. Stand at either end of the screen, then spin attack through them when they appear. When you defeat them all you'll be chased by a creature in a sphere. Run through the maze until you reach the room where you fight him.

✯ **The creature in the sphere** is protected when he spins, so spend this time concentrating on evasive maneuvers. If he corners you, use the spin attack to make yourself invincible while you quickly move away from him. When he stops spinning, spin attack into him as often as you can.

✯ The next part of this stage pits Sparkster on a **train.** Go to the right and keep off the tracks. Most of the boxes in this area contain enemies, so be ready to attack them after you break the box open. Using your sword is the key to avoiding any hits. Hit the box with your sword and save the spin attack for hitting the enemies when they appear. On about the sixth or seventh train car you'll find several blue gems to rocket up into. To the right are five boxes, then further right are several boxes surrounding metal drums.

Charge up into the air, then charge down diagonally into the nose of the train's head.

An **extra life** is hidden in the third box over on the bottom (it's on the right side of the metal drum). If you rocket into it you'll grab it, but if you hit it with your sword it will fall into the tracks and be lost.

✯ **The final boss** of this stage is the engine of the train, which is actually a robot laying on its back. He'll swing his arm up to hit you. Jump into the air, then rocket down into him and rebound back up into the air. Quickly rocket back down into him, repeating as fast as possible to avoid falling into his swinging arm. You must hit his head about a dozen times to destroy him and clear the stage.

Stage 2

✯ Fall into the first hole, then hit the **torch** on the wall to put out the lights, and make **hidden items** appear. There are several torches throughout this stage, so keep your eyes peeled. There's an **extra life** outside on the top floor, which is protected by a tornado. When you come out of the hole to the right of the extra life you must quickly rocket to the left and grab the life before the tornado catches you. To the far right is the entrance to the second area of this stage. A room below the entrance has a torch on the far left, and a hidden piece of meat on the far right that will give you full energy if you grab it quickly enough after hitting the torch.

⚡ **Second Area:** Go to the right, defeat the enemies, grab the blue gems and rebound up the passage to the entrance of the third area.

⚡ **Third Area:** Go left and up to the first passage on the right. The torch in this passage will make several enemies appear, so be ready to spin attack through them for blue gems. Go to the top passage and right, then take the first passage up (rebounding) to collect a couple of blue gems (don't hit the switch on the floor). Go back down and right to exit this area.

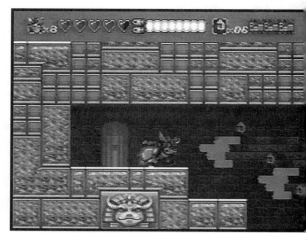

Hit the torches to dim the lights
and cause hidden items to become visible.

⚡ **Fourth Area:** Watch out for black spheres to come rolling down the halls in this area. Use your spin attack to pass through them safely. Go through the far right to find a passage down and left. The pits along this passage have blue gems, which you can choose to risk grabbing if you have the courage. When you reach the end of the passage to the far left, drop down and hold right to find the exit.

⚡ **Fifth Area:** You'll be back outside. Climb up to the first passage and go right. The top passage has the **third Key to the Seals,** but grabbing it is very risky because the ceiling collapses. If you want to go for it, go into the pyramid until you reach the first crystal, then rocket to the right, then go right, jump up, and rocket again to reach the second key. Back at the lower passage of the pyramid: the bottom floor has red lava, so do your best to avoid it. There's a floating platform to leap to if you land on the lava. Go to the far right, rocket attacking the enemies, then quickly drop down the passage (you'll only take one or two hits at the most if you go quickly, which will probably be better than if you take your time and still get hit a few times). Hit the switch when you reach the bottom floor to make a floating platform appear to the left. Use your sword to hit enemies (rocket attacking is dangerous over lava).

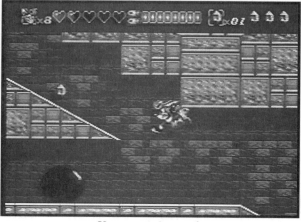

Use your spin attack
to pass safely through the black spheres.

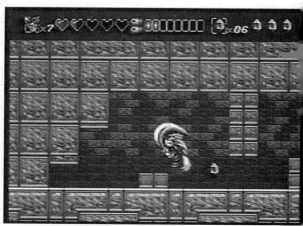

As you climb up the outside of the pyramid, enter the
top entrance if you want to risk grabbing the third key.

and duck as you enter the passage with spikes. Jump up on the next ledge and carefully move past the spiked plungers. Don't enter the mouth here or you'll end up at the entrance of this area again! Ride the moving platform below to the far left, then rocket up to the ceiling and enter the lower of the two mouths on the right.

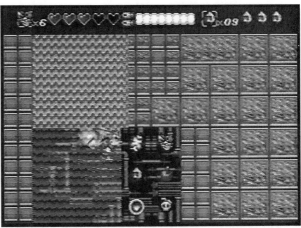

- **Sixth Area:** Spin attack through the enemies hanging from the pipe, then hit the torch to turn them into blue gems. Rocket up the passage, through the bats, then go up and left to find four red gems. Grab the pipe above the red gems (or where they were) and go to the far left. Sink down into the quicksand to find an extra life, meat, blue gem, apple, power-up capsule, red gem, rocket pack, and a bomb (I guess that's one of everything!). Go back up the quicksand and hang from the pole below the first face on the ceiling. Swing

Sink down into the quicksand to find one of every item available in the game, including a bomb to avoid.

your sword to make the mouth spit out bombs, then hit the torch at the top of the quicksand to turn the bombs into blue gems. Try to get out of the stream of gems before they turn back into bombs. Go down and to the left, then straight to the right across several lava pits until you meet a melting face.

- **Melting Face Boss:** Hang from the pole on the ceiling and stay to the far left. When the face rises up to your level, spin attack into it, then quickly rush back to the left. The face will spit steam at you. Wait until the very last moment before the steam hits you, then charge attack through it and into the face. Keep repeating the pattern, sticking to the top-left corner until the face rises to your level.
- Nearly every wall is covered with spikes in this area. When you hit the torches, you will be able to see **invisible blocks**, which you can stand on safely. Having good rocket skills in this area is vital, especially the skills required to perform several rocket attacks in a row without touching the floor. Use the floating platforms and the invisible blocks to reach the mouth in the upper-right corner of this area.
- **Snake Boss:** The next boss is a creature with a green head and a snake-like body. He jumps to the background and uses his tail to attack, then he jumps up to the foreground to attack. When he's in the background, move to the corner furthest from him and you won't get hit by his tail, then when he jumps

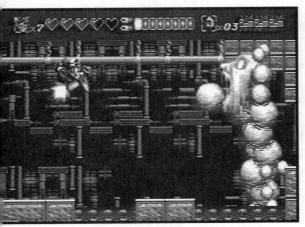

Hang from the pipe to the left of the melting face and use rocket attacks when he comes up to your level.

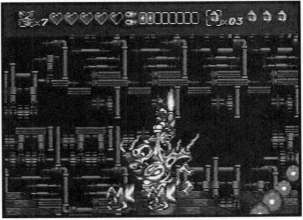

Wait for the snake boss to jump into the foreground, then use rapid rocket attacks to destroy him!

to the foreground rocket attack into the top-center of the room, then rocket attack straight down to hit him in the head. When you land on the ground, quickly rocket attack into his head again, then concentrate on avoiding his simple attacks. You'll only be able to get in one or two attacks before he retreats back to the background.

Stage 3

✦ This stage doesn't seem as long as the last, but makes up for it in difficulty. You'll board a ship at the beginning, then work your way through a maze of passages. Your objective is to **destroy the propellers** on the top deck of the ship. You can only hit the propellers from the metal side. Go up when you see the first arrow on a tube in the ceiling. Go left and use your sword to destroy the propeller, then go down the tube next to the propeller to reach the next. Destroy the next propeller, then go into the tube on the far right. When you drop out of the tube, jump back up into it, then when you reach the top of the ship, jump over the wall on the left to reach the **fourth Key to the Seals.** Go back down into the same tube to reach an area with an apple. Go back down the tube to come up next to a propeller, and destroy it. Jump back down into the tube, up into the one you come out of, then back down into the next one you come out of. Destroy the propeller in this area. Go back down into the tube, back up into the tube you come out of, back down into the tube you come out of, then jump over the wall on the left to destroy a propeller. Jump into the tube next to the propeller to reach another propeller. Jump into the tube again to reach the next propeller. Go back down into the tube to reach the final propeller, which you'll destroy from the left side. You'll be on the far left side of the ship. Jump down into the tube and you'll go inside the ship.

Use the tubes to reach and destroy every propeller on the top deck of the ship. Don't miss the key!

✦ **Inside the ship** you'll have to move quickly to the right to stay ahead of the screen as it scrolls. Many of the passages are blocked by a **green orb.** Attack it with two or three hits to destroy it. Near the halfway mark you'll have to travel along the bottom of the ship. You can walk on the top of the pole, or hang from it with your tail. There are robots hanging from the pole, which you must rocket attack if you're hanging, or run past if you're walking on the pole. When you get the chance, go back up into the ship, instead of trying to attempt jumping to the low hanging pole (much riskier). You'll be back hanging outside the ship for a bit longer, then it's back inside for the final distance. There are even more green orbs blocking your path in this area. Attack them

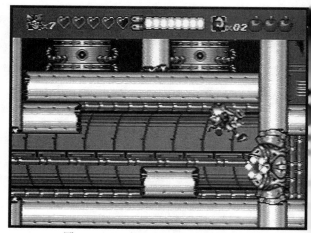
The green orbs are a pain to destroy, especially with the scrolling screen rushing you.

the moment you see them and you won't fall behind the scrolling of the screen.

The gremlin boss has a tricky pattern to learn, but once you know it he's mush easier to defeat. His pattern varies, but there are a few basic attacks that repeat. Always stand as far away as possible at the beginning of each attack. In one attack he changes into a **big genie** and sends out three streams of skulls. You must time a spin attack through the skulls a moment before they hit you. If you attack too soon, you'll end the attack halfway through the skulls and you'll be damaged. You'll shrink if the skulls hit you, then you'll have to hide out in the corner and hope you don't get hit until the shrinking wears off. **When the genie flexes his muscles,** he'll explode into several small gremlins. Move near the gremlins without letting them hit you, then attack the gremlin that has sparkles surrounding it (you can't damage the others). If the small gremlins are sucked up off the top of the screen, be ready to charge the sparkling one when they drop back down. When the first gremlin appears again, he'll shoot a stream of skulls, followed by another. Use the same strategy as before, charging through a moment before they hit you. The stream will curve around and follow you as you pass through them, so be ready to jump over them when you stop. Charging up at an angle might be an easier method to avoid them as they curve back, so give it a try if you're having problems with this part of the pattern. **When the gremlin shrinks to a medium size** (smaller than the first, but bigger than the tiny), he will run to one side and jump up the wall, then he'll

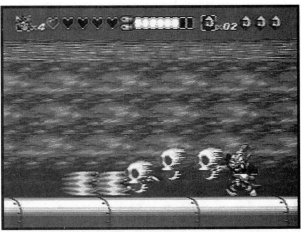
You must time the beginning of your spin attack through the skulls a split second before they hit you.

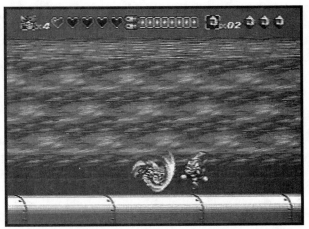
This little gremlin will run up the left wall, then the right. Keep chasing him, then attack as you cross paths.

drop back down, run to the other side, and jump up the other wall. Charge to each side of the screen and spin attack each time you cross paths. When the gremlin is defeated he'll transform into each of his previous forms before falling off the ship.

Stage 4: Sparkrobo Returns

It's time for some more fun in the **huge robot suit.** You'll be running to the right through a town. Use A to fire your fist while aiming up and down. When the view lowers to your feet, you must jump over the bombs dropped by the mutant while also jumping to kick the mutant when he's within reach. As your view raises back up to your head, an **oil can** will appear. The oil cans will give you energy, so make a huge effort not to punch them or you'll lose them. Near the end of this jog through town you'll have to face the robot that appeared before Stage 1 for a rematch. First he'll be in the background launching bombs at you. Hit the bombs that are in front of you, then when he moves to the left side you must move to the right side to avoid the bombs. After crashing into the wall, you'll have to fight the giant robot fist-to-fist. Use the same strategy explained at the beginning of this chapter.

Make every effort not to punch the oil cans (energy) while running in the Sparkrobo suit.

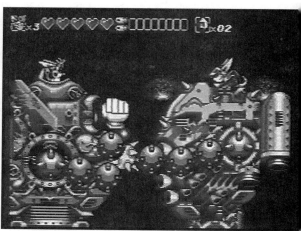

The fighting match between the giant robots is exactly like the battle before Stage 1.

Stage 5

✦ You must destroy the **four dragon heads that guard the yellow doors** in this area. Stand back and wait until your attack meter has reached full power, then walk toward the door and shoot up diagonally at the dragon heads before their fireballs hit you. You can't attack the legs of the gator heads, so wait until they drop down to the ground, or jump and attack to hit the head. The path to the next yellow door is linear, meaning you can only get there one way. Follow the path and take your time destroying each enemy as you meet them. Also be sure to search high and low for blue gems and other power-ups. Go straight to the far right to find meat (full energy), then come back to the left and climb to the top (the second passage has an apple). Destroy the spiked drones on the pole, then stand on the pole and charge to the right to break through the two yellow barrels. After passing through this doorway, rocket to the top-right to find a bunch of blue gems and a red gem. Another yellow door is below, and the exit to this first area is behind it.

✦ **Second Area:** Go to the right and drop to the bottom floor, then go left through the conveyor belt to grab an apple and hit a switch that open the door to the far right. Inside are several guards lined up along steps. Charge attack into the lowest one and rebound back to the left out of reach, then go for the next guard until all are destroyed. After defeating the final guard, go to the upper-left for nine blue gems. To the right of

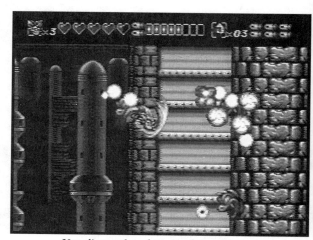

Use diagonal rocket attacks to destroy the dragon heads guarding the yellow doors.

the yellow steps are several pits with spiked poles. Jump over each pit to the next ledge between each two pits. When you get past the final pit, get ready to make a run for it! There's a beam that will chase you through a zig-zagging passage. Just hold right as you drop down to the floor in each passage, and quickly shoot up through the path of blue gems to reach the next passage. At the end of the passage are three guards and a green switch, but before hitting the switch go back to the last passage and climb to the top-right to find an **extra life** and the **fifth Key to the Seals** behind a wall with a shooting blue sphere (like those in Stage 3). Go back down and hit the green switch to open the gate, then attack the robot guard inside. There are two red gems directly up from the robot guard, and the exit for this area is behind the wall with the shooting green sphere to the right.

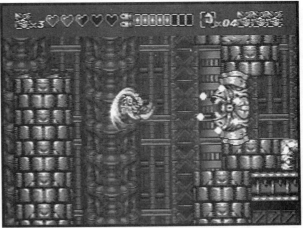

Blast through this blue sphere
to reach an extra life and the fifth key.

✸ **Third Area:** The background of this stage flashes. There are missiles that will appear on the left or right side of the screen. After a few seconds a crosshair will appear where you are standing, and if you don't move out of the path, the missile will hit you. Keep running to the right and breaking through the yellow blockades. Use the steps along the way to drop down or step up out of a missiles path. After the last blockade you'll drop to a switch. Hit it, then go left into the door that opens. Go to the upper passage to fight a mini-boss on a conveyor belt.

✸ **Yellow Boss on Conveyor Belt:** Stand close to the boss and use your sword to hit him. If you rocket attack, you'll rebound too far and will take several hits trying to get back over to him.

✸ Once the yellow boss is defeated, go to the lower floor and left. The enemies on beams in this area can be defeated easily, but you must hit the enemy and not the beam to destroy them. Further left is another mini-boss similar to the last. Use the same technique as before. Go left and drop down, then go into the path on the right to collect gems and meat (full energy). Go back to the left and chop

through the blockades. Climb up and right to the top floor. Under the first conveyor belts you can find two apples (enter on the right end of the belts). Continue to the right, checking the areas between ledges for gems and other power-ups. To the far right is the third boss, which is the same as the first two, only now he has friends.

✸ **Third Mini-Boss:** The yellow head returns, now riding up and down on a screw and accompanied by green guards. If you have plenty of energy, and you should if you collected all of the gems before this boss, you should get in close to the boss and attack him as you did the others, taking a break each time one of the guards appears, then continuing with the boss. You'll get hit once or twice each round by the boss, if you don't avoid the sparks, but it should only take

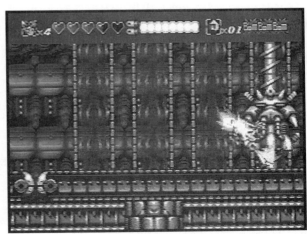

Move in close and use rapid attacks on the boss,
then attack each guard the moment they appear.

you three rounds to destroy it (with four to five hits per round). If you don't have full energy, stick to the far left and take on each guard that appears, then rocket to the head and hit it twice. Rocket back to the far left quickly before the beams appear with the next guard, and repeat the pattern. Go left and down to find the exit.

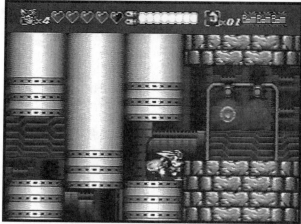

The first two sets of yellow tubes have the same pattern, but you'll need to move through the third more slowly.

✴ **Fourth Area:** There are two centipede skeletons with evil-looking heads at the beginning of this area. When you see the closing walls ahead, pass through each one at a time, then wait a moment to watch the pattern of the next closing wall. Hit the green switch, then immediately jump into the yellow pipes and stand on the center tube. Hold right on the control pad to walk into the next tube, then exit to the right out of the tube when you can. Use the same pattern for the second set of tubes. On the third set of tubes, stand in the first tube and ride it up to the roof, then quickly walk into the second tube before you get crushed by the ceiling. Ride the second tube down until you can enter the third tube, then continue on. Rocket into the guards ahead, then hit the dragon heads to pass through the yellow door.

✴ **Fifth Area — Tall Walking Robots:** Rocket into the bodies or heads of these robots. Each robot takes about six hits, depending on the strength of your rocket power at the time. When you reach the bottom floor you'll face two of these walking robots as the final boss for this stage.

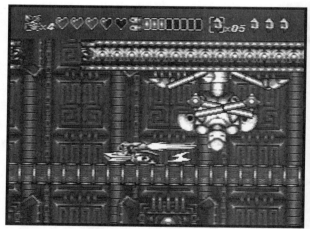

You won't have much luck avoiding this robot, so use rapid attacks to defeat it quickly.

✴ **Stage Boss — Two Walking Robots:** The yellow boss will attack first. When its arms are spread out, it will shoot a stream of bullets from its head. The bullets will aim where you're standing, so jump or move before they hit. When it's walking, the robot will spray bullets in a circle. Use your rocket attacks to fly through the bullets and to hit the robots body or head. It takes about a dozen hits to destroy each robot. The green robot will appear once the yellow is destroyed. He'll begin on the bottom floor, then he'll hop up to the top and hang from the ceiling. Stand on top of the barrier and use rocket attacks each time he comes your direction. After a few hits he'll drop to the bottom floor and spin on his head. Use the same strategy of rocket attacks to hit him safely. After this the robot will dance around in a few different patterns, mostly repeating. Keep hitting him until he hands you the **sixth Key to the Seals**.

Stage 6

✴ This is a short stage with only one boss. It's Axle, and he's fairly easy to beat. He appears to be your evil twin, giving him rocket powers similar to yours. The walls in this battle arena are electrified, so don't hit them unless you're in the middle of a rocket attack. Rebounding off the walls constantly is the safest way to fight this battle. Shooting across the screen at angles will increase your odds of hitting Axle. Once you defeat Axle, he'll give you the seventh Key to the Seals. If you collected all of the others, you'll have the Legendary Armor and the final battle will be much easier to complete. For the sake of those who didn't find all of the keys, we're going to cover the final stage without the Legendary Armor so you'll have a better chance of surviving. If you do have the armor, you won't have to be as cautious during this battle. You won't receive a "Stage Clear" signal here, but you'll go straight into the next stage after receiving the final key.

Use diagonal rocket attacks constantly during the battle against your evil twin, Axle.

Stage 7

✦ **The Evil King Gedol** is your final challenge. There are two parts to the challenge, beginning with King Gedol in his full body form, then ending with a battle against his head. Even without the Legendary Armor we were able to survive the first battle without losing any energy. Here's how: When King Gedol is in his transformation state, sucking in energy, you can attack him. The rest of the time you just want to avoid him as much as possible. Start attacking with sword swings when he appears, then watch his motions for a clue on how he'll attack. He always begins by spreading his arms straight out. If he then breaks into three clones that flash, he'll float around the room while shooting lightning beams from the ceiling. The beams will hurt you only if you are standing on the floor where they hit. Use your rocket attack to constantly shoot up and down at angles across the screen. As long as you keep moving and don't stay on the ground, you'll be safe from the beams. Attack the King when he returns to the center of the screen. If he spreads both arms straight out and begins flashing, asteroids will rain from the ceiling diagonally from the top-right to the bottom-left. Go to the left side of the screen and jump

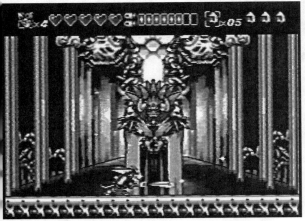

Attack King Gedol when he's sucking in enough energy to make his next transformation.

The lightning beams will strike into the floor, so as long as you're in the air you won't be hit by them.

straight up each time an asteroid is headed straight for you. You should be able to easily jump every asteroid that heads your way, but you can always spin attack into the wall to make yourself invincible for a moment if you feel an asteroid can't be jumped. In the final part of King Gedol's pattern, he'll spread his arms straight out and a cyclone will appear at the center of his body. Run to the left, then near the end of the cyclone use rocket attacks to move away from him more effectively. After performing each of these three attacks, King Gedol will swap bodies with you. You don't want to hurt Sparkster, because you're going back to his body in a few seconds, so hit the B button to teleport from side to side. The A button will start the cyclone, which can be hazardous to Sparkster so try to avoid it. After swapping bodies back, attack King

When the asteroids hit, stay on the far left side of the room and jump to avoid them.

Gedol and prepare to repeat the three patterns above until he's defeated, which shouldn't be long (he didn't make it past the first pattern when we beat him).

* **King Gedol's Head:** The final battle is against the King's swollen head. Look at it! It's huge!!! The only vulnerable part is the red gem between the eyes of the King. You must avoid the beams shot from his eyes while hitting the red gem whenever possible. Stay in either corner at the beginning of the battle. The beams will shoot at angles, but only hit the corners occasionally. Attack in between the beams, and be ready to jump out of the corner when the beams are headed there. The beams will always shoot straight out, and the aim rotates in a clockwise direction. Keeping this in mind, you can always stay ahead of the aim of the beams while attacking. When the head splits into two heads, the pattern is generally the same, and the red gem is still your target. Stand in front of the face with the gem and use jumping with spin attacks to hit the gem between beams, then slowly move to the left as the beams come around and work on the other head when the gem appears. After attacking the split head for a while, you'll be attacked by **King Gedol's hands**. You can't attack the hands. They shoot vertical beams

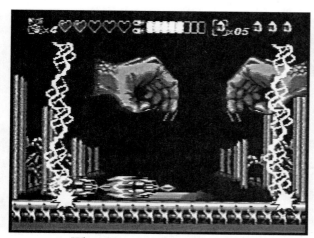

When King Gedol's head appears, hit the red gem at the center to damage him.

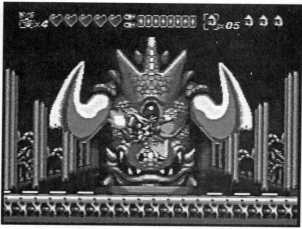

Avoid the vertical beams from Gedol's hands by rocket attacking through them at the last moment.

that begin between the hands and spread out across the screen. Quickly move to either corner when the hands appear, then use rocket attacks a moment before the closest beam hits you to avoid both of them. Move immediately to the opposite corner and repeat the pattern. After a few beams, the hands will attack by stomping down into the ground. Use the rocket attack to quickly move away from them. After a few hits, the head will reappear. The pattern is the same as before. Once you defeat him, you'll receive a final score and a decent ending sequence, which is even better if you have the Legendary Armor.

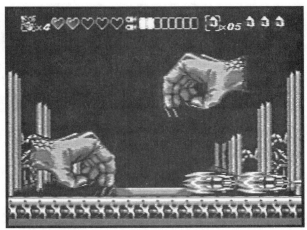

Run or use the rocket attack to move out of the way of the King's stomping hands.

"Sun For Hank" by Gavin Campbell and J. Douglas Arnold
There must have been a dozen variations of this sun produced before we finally gave in and accepted it.
See page 325 for more 3D information.

SUPER STREET FIGHTER II

CATEGORY: Fighting	DEVELOPER: Capcom
PLAYERS: 1-2 (Simultaneous)	PUBLISHER: Capcom

Introduction

Street Fighter II really doesn't need much of an intro-
duction. This one-on-one fighter is one of the most
popular games of all time. Not only has *Street Fighter
II* dominated the home and arcade markets, it has also
produced a flurry of sequels. *Super Street Fighter II* is
the newest addition to the *Street Fighter* series of
games. This version of *Street Fighter II* takes the original twelve world warriors and adds four new fighters: Fei Long, Cammy, Dee Jay and T. Hawk. The
Genesis version also adds features not found in its
SNES counterpart: additional sound effects, five speed
settings vs. three on the SNES, and an expert mode in
which you must battle all 16 characters instead of the
normal twelve to make it to the end.

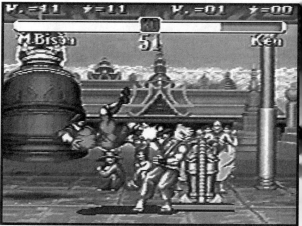

It's baaaack! Street Fighter has morphed ever-so-slightly
once again into this latest edition that's just soooo super!

Basic Strategies

✳ CONTROLS: Since the release of *Street Fighter II* for the Genesis, many companies have produced 6 button joypads/joysticks catering to the *Street Fighter II* player. We recommend the Sega 6-button controller
due to its price, lastability, and ease of use. A 6-button controller is a must for any true *Street Fighter II*
player. If you don't have a 6-button controller, you'll have to use the SELECT button to toggle between
punching and kicking, which makes some moves and combos nearly impossible to accomplish.

✳ For beginning players, we recommend the Tyco Power Plug. This extraordinary device connects to any
joypad or joystick and allows you to program in moves and combos which can be executed with the
touch of a button. Using the Power Plug may be considered as cheating by some players, but it's a great
way to learn how to time combos and improve your skills.

✳ The basic controls for each character in *Super Street Fighter II* are as follows: A = Short, B = Forward, C
= Roundhouse, X = Jab, Y = Strong, Z = Fierce. *Super Street Fighter II* allows you to reprogram these buttons for your own preference.

Learning Special Moves and Combos

✳ Each character has its own unique set of special moves. Mastering these moves for at least one character
is a key skill to learn when trying to master *Super Street Fighter II*.

✳ Throwing can be accomplished by walking up to an opponent and pressing Toward and a Punch button.
Throwing is one of the easiest things to learn in *Street Fighter II* and is also one of the most useful moves

in the game. Many players consider throwing to be cheap or "cheesy," but it's in the game and can be used effectively to win.

✥ By performing certain special moves together with regular hits, you can create a combination move, or *combos* as most players call them. Most combos require a lot of practice and timing. Combos are the most potent moves in *Super Street Fighter II* and must be mastered in order to become an expert *SSFII* player.

✥ Timing of joystick and button movements is the key to performing special moves and combos. A good way to practice special moves is to play two-player Vs. Mode games and use the second player as a punching bag. Do this until you feel comfortable performing a move.

✥ Neck Kick: The neck kick can be a devastating move, especially against rookie players. The object of the neck kick to jump over your opponent and time your hit so that it strikes before the opponent turns around to block it. If the opponent does not block this, it can be followed by one of the below combos.

✥ Charging means to hold the joystick in a certain direction for a given amount of time. Some combos require that you charge a move while performing others. Only certain characters have moves which require charging.

Balrog

SPECIAL MOVES AND TECHNIQUES

✥ Dashing Punch: Balrog's long-range Dashing Punch can be performed by charging back for two seconds then pushing Toward and any Punch button. The distance of the move depends on the Punch button used. This move can be used to catch your opponent off guard, but a well timed jab or projectile can easily stop it. Be careful when planning this move.

✥ Turning Punch: By holding down all three Punch buttons you can execute this sometimes deadly move. The longer you hold down the buttons before you release, the more energy the hit will take away. Due to the fact that Balrog leans back before he performs this move, it can easily be seen and blocked.

✥ The Turning Punch has a second of invulnerability. Throw a Turning Punch as a projectile is flying towards you to move through it untouched.

✥ Dashing Uppercut: Charge back for at least two seconds before pressing Toward and any Kick button to release this nasty uppercut. The uppercut works great against aerial targets.

MULTI-HIT ATTACKS AND COMBOS

✥ Fierce/Short/Dashing Punch: Here's a pretty easy combo for beginners. Jump toward your opponent with a late Fierce Punch and begin charging Back. Throw a standing Short Punch and follow it with a Dashing Uppercut.

If you're new to Balrog, try using this easy three-hit combo.

- Fierce/Jab/Roundhouse: Start this easy three-hit combo by jumping at your opponent with a late Fierce Punch. When you land, deliver a crouching Jab and follow it up with a crouching Roundhouse.
- Fierce/Jab/Jab/Fierce: Jump towards your opponent, immediately begin charging back, and throw a late Fierce. While still charging throw a crouching Jab. Throw a second Jab and begin the motion for a Dashing Punch. Finish this motion and press any Kick button to finish the devastating four-hit combo.
- Fierce/Short/Short/Dashing Uppercut/Fierce: This is one of Balrog's best combos. Start by jumping into your opponent with a late Fierce. Immediately begin charging back and deliver two crouching Fierce Punches (three if you're fighting a large character). Immediately after the series of jabs, follow it with a Dashing Uppercut. Wait a second for Balrog to regain his composure and then throw a standing Fierce Punch. This will result in a five-hit combo against a small opponent and a six-hit combo against larger opponents.
- Fierce/Short/Dashing Uppercut/Dashing Uppercut/Fierce: Here is the combo for all you expert players out there. Jump into your opponent with a late Fierce and begin charging back. Throw a crouching Short Punch and follow it with a short Dashing Uppercut. Immediately begin charging and throw yet another short Dashing Uppercut. (You must be *very* fast to do this!) Wait a second for Balrog to recover from his hits and throw a standing Fierce.

Blanka

Special Moves and Techniques
- Rolling Attack: Charge Back for two seconds, then press Toward and any Punch button.
- Electricity: Simply press any Punch button repeatedly to create an electric forcefield around Blanka's body.
- Vertical Rolling Attack: Charge Down for two seconds, then press Up and any Kick button.
- Beast Leap: Charge Back for two seconds, then press Toward and any Kick button.

Blanka Multi-Hit Attacks and Combos
- Fierce/Strong/Forward: Jump at your opponent with a late Fierce Punch and follow it with a standing Strong Punch as soon as you land. Finish it off with a crouching Forward.
- Fierce/Strong/Rolling Attack: Start out this expert-only combo by charging Back on the controller while jumping at your opponent and delivering a late Fierce. As soon as you land throw a double head butt (Back and Strong). After the first head butt connects, press Toward and Punch to execute the Rolling Attack. You must be charging throughout this entire combo until the end.

Cammy

Special Moves and Techniques
- Cannon Drill: Perform a Fireball with one of the three Kick buttons to perform Cammy's Cannon Drill. She has no projectiles to throw at you, so she hurls herself.
- Front Kick: Cammy's equivalent to the Dragon Punch is her Front Kick. Perform it by doing a Dragon Punch motion and pressing a Kick button.
- Spinning Knuckle: Perform a half-circle starting at the Back position and going counterclockwise to Toward, following it with any Punch button to execute Cammy's Spinning Knuckle attack. You can use this move to go through projectiles when timed properly.
- Air Throw: Catch an opponent in the air and press Away or Toward with one of the Punch buttons to throw him into the ground.

Cammy Multi-Hit Attacks and Combos

✤ Fierce/Forward/Forward: Jump at you opponent and deliver a late Fierce before you land. As soon as you touch the ground, deliver a standing Forward followed by a low Forward.

✤ Fierce/Fierce/Front Kick: Start this combo out by jumping at your opponent. Before you land, deliver a late Fierce. As soon as you land, throw a standing Fierce then immediately perform the motion for a Front Kick.

You can incorporate several different moves as the finishing hit in this combo.

✤ Strong/Cannon Drill: Start this combo by crouching near an opponent. As soon as they are off guard, throw a crouching Strong Punch followed by the motion for a Cannon Drill.

Make sure you charge up when beginning this two-hit combo.

✤ Forward/Forward/Forward/Cannon Drill: This one takes lots of practice and excellent timing to master. Start out by delivering a neck kick with a Forward. As soon as you land, deliver a standing Forward, then a crouching Forward, followed by the motion for a Cannon Drill. This will produce a devastating four-hit combo.

Chun Li

✤ Special Moves and Techniques
  Lightning Leg: If you can't do this move, you shouldn't be playing. Simply press any Kick button repeatedly.

- Fireball: Similar to Guile's Sonic Boom, simply charge Back for two seconds and follow by pressing Toward and a Punch button. Unlike Guile's Sonic Boom, Chun Li's fireball doesn't go all the way across the screen Learn the distance of Chun Li's fireballs to take maximum advantage of this attack.
- Whirlwind Kick: Similar to Guile's Flash Kick, charge Down for two seconds and follow by pressing Up and any Kick button at the same time. This kick can also be performed in mid-air during a jump.
- Head Bounce: Jump towards an opponent and press Down while throwing a Forward Kick.

Time Chun-Li's head bounce right and you can make an easy three-hit combo out of it.

- Wall Spring: Chun Li has the ability to spring off the side of the screen. Jump towards the wall, and when you touch it, press in the opposite direction to bounce off.

Chun Li Multi-Hit Attacks and Combos
- Fierce/Forward/Roundhouse: Jump at your opponent and land a deep Fierce attack at the last second. Follow this with a crouching Forward Kick and then a crouching Roundhouse. This basic combo is one of the easiest to perform in the game and most useful.
- Fierce/Fierce/Fireball: While jumping at your opponent throw a late Fierce Punch and immediately begin charging backwards. Throw a standing Fierce Punch and follow it with a Fireball.
- Fierce/Hurricane Kick: Start this combo by charging for a Hurricane Kick. Throw a standing Fierce and follow through with a Hurricane Kick. This combo is similar to Guile's Crouching Jab/Flash Kick combo.
- Roundhouse/Strong/Forward/Roundhouse: This is probably the hardest combo to execute for Chun Li. Start this combo by performing a neck kick with the Roundhouse button. Throw a standing Strong Kick followed by a crouching Forward and ending with a crouching Roundhouse. This combo takes perfect timing.

Dee Jay

Special Moves and Techniques
- Max Out: To throw Dee Jay's Max Out (Fireball equivalent), charge Back for two seconds then follow through by pressing Toward and a Punch button.
- Double Dread Kick: Perform this move the same as the Max Out; simply substitute a Kick for the Punch.
- Hyper Fist: Charge Down for two seconds and follow through by pressing Up and any Punch button. Continue rapidly tapping the Punch button as fast as you can to obtain as many as five hits.
- The Hyper Fist can be used to go through projectiles if timed properly. Just as the projectile gets near you, perform the Hyper Fist. If the opponent is close, keep tapping the Punch button to obtain a multiple-hit combo.

Dee Jay Multi-Hit Attacks and Combos

✿ **Fierce/Jab/Max Out:** Jump towards your opponent with a late Fierce Punch. Once you land, follow through with a Jab and immediately perform a Max Out.

Make sure you charge up in order to get your Max Out out as the finishing hit.

✿ **Roundhouse/Jab/Forward:** Jump toward your opponent with a late Roundhouse. As you land, throw a standing Jab followed by a low Forward Kick.

You can substitute a Dread Kick as the last move in this combo.

✿ **Forward/Jab/Strong/Hyper Fist:** Jump at your opponent delivering a late neck kick using the Forward Kick button. As you land throw a crouching Jab then a standing Strong Punch immediately following it up with a Hyper Fist. If done perfectly this combo can get up to eight hits!

Dhalsim

Special Moves and Techniques

✿ **Yoga Fire:** Perform this move just like Ken/Ryu's Fireball by pressing Down then doing a 90-degree circular motion to Toward following it with a Punch button.

✿ **Yoga Flame:** This move can be accomplished by performing a 180-degree half circle motion from Back to Down to Toward and following it with any punch button.

✿ **Yoga Teleport (Front):** Dhalsim has the magic ability to disappear and reappear in four different parts of the screen depending on which buttons you press. To Yoga Teleport in front of your enemy, press Back, then Down and Down/Back (imagine a backwards Dragon Punch). Follow this movement by hitting all three Kick buttons to appear far from your opponent or all three Punch buttons to appear right next to your opponent.

- Yoga Teleport (Behind): To Yoga Teleport behind your opponent press Toward, then Down, then Down/Toward (just like a Dragon Punch). Follow that movement by pressing all three Kick buttons to appear far from your opponent or all three Punch buttons to appear right next to your opponent.

- Dhalsim's Yoga Teleport can be a very effective weapon against opponents who use a lot of projectiles (Ken, Ryu, Chun Li, Guile, Sagat). As soon as you see the opponent start to throw a projectile, immediately teleport beside them and follow it with one of the below combos.

- A really cheap but often effective move is to throw a slow Yoga Fireball and time it so that when it hits your blocking opponent you can Yoga Teleport behind him and throw him while he is stunned from the block.

Dhalsim's Head Smash is one of the more powerful throw moves in the game.

Dhalsim Multi-Hit Attacks and Combos

- Forward/Flame: Start this hot combo out by pressing Down and Toward, and kick when the opponent is near. Right after that, start the Yoga Fire or Yoga Flame motion to send the opponent flying in a ball of smoke.

This is a simple yet effective two-hit combo.

- Jab/Fierce: This easy three-hit combo starts out by throwing a standing Jab when the opponent is close and immediately following it up with a Fierce Punch, which produces a head-butt.

- Jab/Jab/Roundhouse: This fairly easy combo can be accomplished when the opponent is near by delivering a deep Jab. Crouch and throw another close Jab, following with a Roundhouse slide (Down and Roundhouse). Since the initial Jab comes out quick, this combo is great against opponents that like to attack as soon as you get up.

E. Honda

Special Moves and Strategies

- Hundred Hand Slap: This move can be accomplished by rapidly pressing any Punch button. When the Hundred Hand Slap starts, you can slowly move Honda by pressing Back or Toward.

- The Hundred Hand Slap is a great move to catch opponents off guard. Even if they are blocking, this attack takes away a respectable amount of energy. Learn to use this move to finish off opponents, even when they are blocking.

- Butt-Drop: Possibly one of E. Honda's weakest special moves is his Butt-Drop. Charge Down on on the control pad for at least two seconds and follow by pressing Up and any Kick button at the same time. The stronger the Kick you use, the higher Honda will fly.

- Sumo Body Drop: When in the air, press Down and a Kick button to smash your opponent into the ground. This move is great to use against projectiles.

- Head Butt: In the case of Honda, these two words are not contradictory. To perform Honda's Head Butt, charge Back for about two seconds and follow it by pressing Toward and any Punch button. The stronger the Punch you use, the farther Honda files across the screen.

- E. Honda's Head Butt has a split-second of invincibility when it first begins. Learn to use this to your advantage when fighting opponents. It works especially well against aerial attacks and flying through fast-moving projectiles.

E. Honda Multi-Hit Attacks and Combos

- Strong/Head Butt: This combo takes a considerable amount of timing to execute. Start out by charging diagonally Down/Toward. Throw a Strong Punch and immediately follow it with a Head Butt.

- Roundhouse/Jab/Roundhouse: Jump toward your opponent delivering a late Roundhouse. Once you land, throw a quick standing Jab and end it with a crouching Roundhouse.

- Fierce/Strong/Fierce: Start this combo with a jumping Fierce attack. As soon as you land, follow it up with a Strong Punch and finish with a crouching Fierce.

- Fierce/Roundhouse: Jump into your opponent with a late Fierce Punch and follow it with a standing Roundhouse. This will result in a three-hit combo if you're close enough.

- Fierce/Hundred Hand Slap: This combo is considered cheap by many players, but it's in the game. Jump into your opponent delivering a late Fierce and continue tapping the Fierce button afterwards. This will result in a Hundred Hand Slap which, even when the enemy blocks, takes away a considerable amount of energy.

- Forward Neck Kick/Forward: Jump over your opponent delivering a forward Sumo Body Drop (Down and Toward). Once you land, turn around and follow it with a crouching Forward. This is a nice little three-hit combo.

You only have to execute two moves to get this three-hit combo.

Fei Long

Special Moves and Techniques

⚡ Rekka Ken: Fei Long's most powerful move is the Rekka Ken. Perform it by doing a Fireball motion.

⚡ Learn to throw up to three Rekka Kens together to create an easy combo. If your opponent is blocking series of Rekka Kens, be sure to use the Jab Punch for the third one in order to give you time to recove so that the opponent can't attack you. Use the Rekka Ken only when the opponent is open for a hit or to fake him out (only do one or two Rekka Kens instead of three).

⚡ Rising Dragon Kick: Start this motion by pressing Back and continue through by pressing Down the Down/Back followed by a Kick button. This move is similar to a Dragon Punch, only done backwards with a Kick button.

Fei Long Multi-Hit Attacks and Combos

⚡ Fierce/Strong/Fierce: Start this easy combo out with a late jumping Fierce Punch. Land and throw a stand ing Strong Punch followed by a crouching Fierce.

⚡ Fierce/Fierce/Double Rekka Ken: Start this combo out by landing a late jumping Fierce Punch. Land and throw a Jab following it with two Rekka Kens. This should produce a four-hit combo if done properly.

This is Fei Long's most popular combo.

⚡ Roundhouse/Fierce/Rekka Ken: Jump at your opponent with a late Roundhouse Kick. Land and throw a standing Fierce immediately following it with the Rekka Ken motion and a Fierce Punch.•

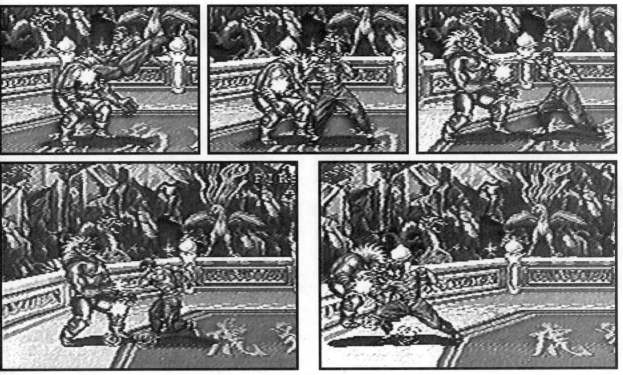

Master this combo and you'll be ready to take on the best.

⚡ Fierce/Fierce/Triple Rekka Ken: This five-hit combo can be accomplished by jumping at your opponent with a late Fierce Punch. Immediately after you land, throw a standing Fierce Punch follow by three Fierce Rekka Kens. Timing is critical with this combo.

Guile

Special Moves and Techniques

- Sonic Boom: Guile's well-known Sonic Boom attack is performed by charging Back for about 2 second then pressing Toward and any Punch button. Depending on the Punch button you use, the Sonic Boom will fly at different speeds (see Ken/Ryu Fireball).

Use a Sonic Boom to counter a Fireball, then throw a Fierce Punch to counterattack.

- Flash Kick: By charging Down for about two seconds, then pressing Up and a Punch button at the same time, you can perform Guile's Flash Kick. Depending on which Kick button you use, the Kick will go higher and take away more energy (see Ken/Ryu Fireball).
- Charging the above moves can be done in various ways. Guile can charge either of the moves by holding Down/Back at the same time. Guile can also charge moves when he's in the air, knocked down on the ground, or even before the start of each round. When using Guile, it is essential that you learn how to charge your moves at almost any given time.
- Leaping Knee: One of Guile's weaker moves is his Leaping Knee. To perform this simply press Toward and Forward Kick at the same time.
- Air Throws: Guile has two different kinds of throws which he can perform in the air. When both fighters touch each other in the air, press Down and a Kick button to throw your opponent into the ground or press Back or Toward and Punch to throw your opponent away from you. Guile's Air Throws are very effective weapons in his arsenal of attacks.
- Cornering: This strategy is just for Guile. Try getting your opponent trapped up against the wall. Once you've done this, don't let off the attacks. Learn which combos will repeatedly keep your opponent trapped against the wall.
- Vs. Ryu/Ken: When getting into a Fireball/Sonic Boom duel with Ken or Ryu you have a slight advantage. When close to your opponent, cancel out his Fireball with a Sonic Boom and immediately follow it up with a Fierce Punch.

Guile Multi-Hit Attacks and Combos

- Crouching Jab/Flash Kick: This is the first mini-combo you should try to master when playing with Guile. While crouching, hold Down and Back to block and charge at the same time. When the opponent is near, press Jab and follow it with a Flash Kick. Be sure to master this two-hit combo before you try any others.

Standing Jab/Flash Kick: Start this combo out by charging Down. When the opponent is near, stand up and throw a Jab immediately following it by pressing Up and a Kick button to execute a Flash Kick. This is one of the more complicated combos in the game, and perfect timing is critical to execution.

Jab/Sonic Boom: While holding Back to charge, throw a Jab and immediately follow it with a Sonic Boom. You can also substitute a Fierce instead of a Jab when starting this combo, though it's a little harder to do so.

Fierce/Fierce/Sonic Boom/Fierce: Start this massive four-hit combo by jumping at your opponent and landing a deep Fierce Punch immediately starting to charge afterwards. Follow this with a standing Fierce Punch and then a Sonic Boom, trailing it with another standing Fierce (due to the distance of the opponent, Guile should do a backhand Fierce attack for the fourth hit). You must start this combo with a very deep Fierce Punch for it to work effectively.

Fierce/Fierce/Flash Kick: Guile's hardest-to-perform and most devastating combo. Jump at your opponent and immediately start charging by pressing Down. Throw a deep Fierce Punch before you land and follow it with a standing Fierce Punch then a Flash Kick. If you can master this combo, then you're pretty damn good!

It takes practice to time the final Flash Kick in this combo.

Ken/Ryu

Special Moves and Techniques

Fireball: Perhaps the easiest and most used move in *Super Street Fighter II* is the Fireball. To perform a Fireball, simply push Down and continue to TOward in a 90-degree circular motion. Follow this by pressing a Punch button. A Jab Punch will deliver a slow-moving fireball, a Strong Punch will produce an average-speed fireball, and a Fierce Punch will result in a fast-moving fireball.

Ryu now has the ability to throw a Red Fireball. To do so, start by pressing Back, then follow through by pressing Down and Toward in a 180-degree circular motion. The Red Fireball will cause your opponent to catch on fire. If you do a Red Fireball close to your opponent it will knock them down (presuming they don't block it).

Hurricane Kick: To perform the Hurricane Kick press Down then Back in a circular motion followed by any Kick button. By using a Short Kick you will only fly a short distance, a Forward Kick will make you go a little farther, and a Roundhouse Kick will cause you to go twice as far as the Short Kick.

When you jump in the air you can also do a Hurricane Kick by performing the same motion. When performing a Hurricane Kick in the air, the Kick button you use does not effect the distance you fly; this is determined by how high you are in the air when you execute the Hurricane Kick.

The Hurricane Kick has a second of invincibility. Use the kick just before a Fireball hits you to spin right through it.

Dragon Punch: Ken and Ryu's most powerful move is the Dragon Punch. To perform one push Toward,

Down, then Toward followed by a Punch button. A light punch will perform a low Dragon Punch, whi[ch]
a hard punch will result in a high Dragon Punch.

✦ Ken's Fierce Dragon Punch is also known as a Flaming Dragon Punch. Ken's Dragon Punch also reach[es]
farther than Ryu's, but Ryu's takes away more energy per hit.

Ken/Ryu Multi-Hit Attacks and Combos

✦ Fierce/Fireball: When standing close to the opponent, press the Fierce Punch button. Immediately afterward[s]
follow it with a Fireball. This will cause a two-hit combo and is your first step towards learning more co[m-]
plex multi-hit combos. Once you get this one down, try doing a Fierce Punch followed by a Hurricane Kic[k]

✦ Roundhouse/Fierce/Fireball: Start this combo out by jumping in the air toward your opponent. Just befo[re]
you are about to land throw a Roundhouse Kick. Follow this immediately with a Fierce Punch and [a]
Fireball. This will send your opponent to the ground. A similar combo can also be done by substituting t[he]
first move in this combo with a Fierce Punch.

This is one of the most well-known combos in *Street Fighter II,* so make sure you know it.

✦ Fierce/Fierce/Hurricane Kick: Jump at your opponent and hit him with a late Fierce Punch. Throw anot[h-]
er Fierce Punch so that it hits him as soon as you land and follow it with a Hurricane Kick. This results [in]
a nasty five-hit combo with Ken and a three-hit combo with Ryu. You can also start this combo off with [a]
Roundhouse rather than a Fierce Punch.

M. Bison

Special Moves and Techniques

✦ Torpedo: Similar to Guile's Sonic Boom, you can perform M. Bison's Torpedo by charging Back for tw[o]
seconds and following through by pressing Toward and any Punch button.

✦ Scissors Kick: The Scissor Kick is the same as the Torpedo except that you finish it off with a Kick inste[ad]
of a Punch. Charge Back for two seconds then press Toward and any Kick button.

✦ Head Stomp: Yet another charge move. Press Down for at least two seconds and follow though by pres[s-]
ing Up and any Kick button at the same time.

✦ Flying Fist: Charge Down for two seconds and then press Up and any Punch button at the same time. Th[is]
move is great to confuse your enemy and get them crossed up (neck kick).

M. Bison Multi-Hit Attacks and Combos

✦ Jab/Torpedo: Charge Back on the control pad to get ready for a Torpedo. When the opponent is clos[e]
throw a crouching Jab and follow through with the Torpedo motion. This will result in an easy two-h[it]

combo. To turn this combo into three hits, jump into your opponent with a late Fierce before starting this combo.

• Fierce/Jab/Scissor Kick: Jump into your opponent with a deep Fierce Punch. Immediately throw a crouching Jab followed by a Scissor Kick. This creates a cool-looking three-hit combo.

This combo is easy to do and fun to show off.

Sagat

Special Moves and Techniques

Tiger Fireball: To throw Sagat's Tiger Fireball, start by pressing Down and follow through to Toward in a 90-degree circular motion. Follow this with any Kick button to throw a low Fireball or a Punch button to throw a high Fireball.

Learn to throw Sagat's Tiger Fireball at different speeds and varying heights to keep your opponent on their toes. A well-timed Tiger Fireball is sometimes Sagat's best weapon.

Tiger Uppercut: Sagat's Tiger Uppercut is executed the same way as Ken and Ryu's Dragon Punch. Press Toward, Down, Toward and a Punch button to finish the move. The height and strength of the Tiger Uppercut varies depending on the Punch button you use.

Unlike Ken & Ryu's Dragon Punch, Sagat's Tiger Uppercut is quite a bit more vulnerable going up. As a tradeoff, the Tiger Uppercut can take away more damage when timed right. Try to time Tiger Uppercuts so that they hit right before the opponent is about to land to take away large amounts of energy.

Tiger Knee: Perform a circular motion from Down to Toward to Up/Toward and press a Kick button to execute Sagat's Tiger Knee. This move is great as a combo finisher, but leaves Sagat open for attack when he misses.

Sagat Multi-Hit Attacks and Combos

Short/Tiger Uppercut: While standing close, throw a Short Kick and immediately follow it with the motion for a Tiger Uppercut.

Short/Tiger Knee: When standing close to the opponent, throw a Short Kick and immediately follow it with a Tiger Knee. This combo can hit three times if you are close enough to your opponent.

 Roundhouse/Short/Tiger Uppercut: Jump at your opponent and deliver a late Roundhouse Kick. On[e] you land, throw a crouching Short Kick and immediately perform a Tiger Uppercut.

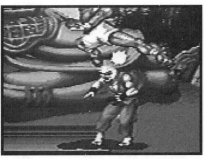 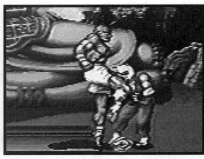 

You can finish the above combo with a Fireball as well as a Tiger Uppercut.

 Roundhouse/Short/Tiger Knee: Start this four-hit combo out by jumping at your opponent with a la[te] Roundhouse Kick. Once you land, start the motion for a Tiger Knee. When the control pad is in the down-rig[ht] position, throw a Short Kick. Finish the Tiger Knee and press Roundhouse to send your opponent flying.

 Tiger Fireball/Tiger Fireball: Get your keen timing skills out for this one. When far away from your opp[o]nent, throw a low Short Tiger Fireball. Wait for the Tiger Fireball to hit your opponent and immediate[ly] release a low Roundhouse Tiger Fireball. If timed perfectly, your opponent will get majorly flamed.

T. Hawk

Special Moves and Techniques

 The Hawk: Press all three Punch buttons simultaneously to perform The Hawk.

 Thunder Strike: Perform the motion for a Dragon Punch with any Punch button to execute this move. U[se] it to project yourself over fireballs and other projectiles.

 The Storm Hammer: Rotate the control pad 360 degrees and press any Punch button when close to pic[k] your opponent up and throw him into the ground.

 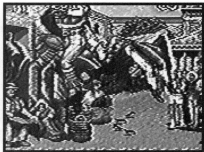 

T. Hawk's Storm Hammer is one of the most impressive throws in the game.

T. Hawk Multi-Hit Attacks and Combos

 Fierce/Jab/Roundhouse: This easy three-hit combo starts with a late jumping Fierce followed by a crouc[h]ing jab and finishing with a Roundhouse.

Body Splash/Jab/Thunderstrike: Start this combo out by jumping at your opponent with a late Body Splash (Down and Fierce). Follow through with a crouching Jab and then a Thunder Strike.

You can end this combo with a Thunder Strike or short attack.

Body Splash/Jab/Jab/Thunder Strike: Jump at your opponent with a late neck kick using the Body Splash. Immediately land and throw a crouching Jab followed by a standing Jab and finishing with a Thunder Strike.

Vega

Special Moves and Techniques

Claw Roll: To execute one of Vega's more popular moves, simply charge Back for two seconds and follow through by pressing Toward and any Punch button. The Punch button you use affects the distance of Vega's Claw Roll.

Backflip: Press all three Kick buttons simultaneously to perform Vega's normal backflip.

Double Backflip: Press all three Punch buttons to execute Vega's double backflip.

Wall Climb: To perform Vega's Wall Climb, charge Down for two seconds. Press Up and Right diagonally plus any Kick button to jump to the right, or press diagonally Up and Left to jump towards the left part of the wall.

Wall Bounce: Jump towards the edge of the screen. Just as you are about to touch it, press in the opposite direction to bounce off the wall.

Use Vega's backflip to go right through fireballs and other projectiles.

Vega Multi-Hit Attacks and Combos

※ Jab/Claw Roll: Start by charging Back for a Claw Roll. When the opponent is close, throw a standing Ja
and follow through with the Claw Roll motion. This will result in an easy two-hit combo.

Vega has a lot of quick two-hit combos like this one. If you're good, you should be able to add a third hit in somewhere

※ Roundhouse/Jab/Claw Roll: This combo can sometimes score an amazing six hits. Even if your opponen
blocks, it drains quite a bit of energy. Start out by jumping into your opponent with a late Roundhouse
Start charging Back for a Claw Roll and throw a crouching Jab, then immediately begin a fierce Claw Rol

※ Fierce/Jab/Roundhouse: Start this combo by jumping into your opponent with a late Fierce Punch. Onc
you land, throw a crouching Jab and finish it with a sliding Roundhouse (Down and Roundhouse).

Zangief

Special Moves and Techniques

※ Spinning Pile Driver: If you plan to be any good fighting with Zangief, you must learn this move. Rotat
the control pad in a 360-degree motion (starting at Toward is usually easiest) and follow by pressing an
Punch button.

※ Siberian Suplex: Rotate the control pad in a 360-degree motion and follow with any kick button.

※ Spinning Clothesline: Zangief's first of two deadly spinning attacks can be performed by pressing any tw
Punch buttons at the same time.

※ Double Spinning Lariat: This advanced version of the above moves requires you to press any two Kic
buttons at the same time to execute it.

※ Use the Spinning Clothesline to become invincible against projectiles. Just as the projectile is thrown a
you, execute one of the two spinning moves and you'll go right through it. The Double Spinning Laria
also makes Zangief invulnerable to low attacks.

※ Zangief is a thrower. Learn to throw when playing Zangief. Combos? Never heard of them. Zangief like
to throw...

TAZ: ESCAPE FROM MARS

CATEGORY: Platform   DEVELOPER: HeadGames, Inc.
PLAYERS: 1   PUBLISHER: Sega of America

Introduction

This is the second game from Sega featuring Taz as the main character, and while the first game was a decent platform adventure, this sequel is vastly improved with better graphics, better controls, and more creative stages. While it's no Sonic, Taz is a worthy choice of anyone who loves challenging platform games. There are six levels, each featuring two stages, with a familiar boss at the end of each second stage. The final battle takes place in Marvin the Martian's House against the little green guy himself. Other familiar faces include Yosemite Sam, Witch Hazel, and Gossamer (that cool orange monster) with his creator The Mad Scientist. Shrink and growth rays allow Taz to fit into small passages or stomp enemies.

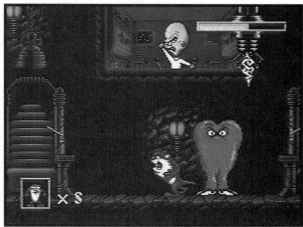

This second game from Sega featuring the Taz character
is a big improvement graphically and gameplay-wise.

Basic Strategies

There are lots of **collectable items** throughout each stage, but the majority of the items will hurt you when collected. If you see a bomb or other explosive-looking item, spin into it to knock it away. If the item is safe to eat, walk up to it and Taz will swallow it whole. First-aid kits are the most effective way to regain energy, but the food helps. Gasoline will give you flaming breath that will fry nearby enemies. The box of rocks will let you spit rocks for a while to knock out enemies. There are two bubbling beakers that will make you grow (blue) or shrink.

The **spin attack** (B button) is Taz's most effective weapon. Use the C button to jump, and the A button for actions like hitting switches, spitting flames after collecting gasoline, or spitting rocks after collecting a box of rocks. If you grab a mushroom you can use the spin attack to fly like a helicopter. Taz can also bounce between two close walls to climb up, and can spin along pipes (even upside-down).

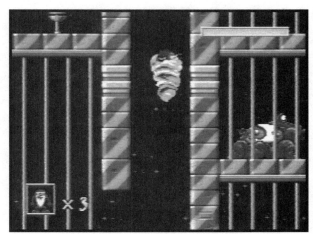

The climbing spin attack is the key to reaching
higher floors, and is usually the way out of a dead end.

- When using the **spin attack to knock out enemies** you will sometimes have to hit them more than once to defeat them. Be ready to hit the spin attack again the moment you bounce off an enemy.
- The blocks with Taz and a "1" on them are **1-Ups.** Even better are the blocks with Taz and a "C", which gives you an **extra continue.** If you can find either one of these on a stage be sure to remember their location. As long as you grab them before you lose a life you'll be able to keep playing. We'll point out the locations of every 1-Up and continue block we found — look for bold lettering in the next few pages for their locations.

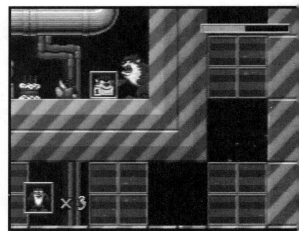

Keep an eye out for the 1-Up blocks and Continue blocks
If you lose a life, you can always go back for another.

Level 1: Mars

- **STAGE 1:** This first stage is a great place to practice the controls, since there aren't many enemies to get in your way. Clear out the enemies, then practice your spin attacks and spin climbing. After you hit the first transporter you'll find a **checkpoint** (Taz with a checkered flag). As you climb up the hill on the right look for a passage leading up that you can spin climb up into. When you reach the area with the square windows take the upper path, then when you reach the next shrink ray don't walk through it yet. Wait for Taz to regain his normal size, then go left and climb up the first passage you see. Take the passage all the way up, then left, and when you drop down go right and grab a **1-Up** with food items below. Go back to the shrink ray and continue on through this part of the stage. When you get into the maze of zoo cages it's important to know you can hold down and press jump to go down through the purple and yellow floors. You can also jump up through these same floors. Hit another transporter and you'll find the first Exit.
- **STAGE 2:** This stage begins with several tricky leaps from elevator to elevator. Get to the far left, then use your spin attacks on the pipes. When you reach the far side you'll find a **checkpoint** and several spike pits. Fall down the first pit past the checkpoint to hit a shrink ray, then rush to the far right to find a **continue block (C).** Wait until Taz goes back to his full size, then jump up to grab the continue. You'll have to use spin climbing to get out of this area and to the next transporter. Jump over the pits, spin along the pipe, climb up the steps, then spin climb to the next transporter. In the final area there are a few good food items to pick up, so be careful not to spin into them. Spin climb to the **checkpoint**, climb to the top-right, then drop down to the

Wait until the shrink ray wears off,
then make a leap for this continue block.

next transporter, which leads to the Exit.

BOSS: This first boss is an alien elephant. His trunk pops out at the bottom-center of the screen and spins around in a clockwise direction, then a counter-clockwise direction. During this time you must use the spin attack to circle the entire room, staying ahead of his trunk. The first time it spins only one revolution each direction, but then increases by one revolution each time this part of the pattern comes back around. The rest of his attack involves three spiked balls that bounce a few times before exploding. Pick a spot on either side and move as necessary to avoid them. The moment the third spiked ball explodes, the eyes of the boss appear. This is the only time you can hit him, so walk up the left or right corner, jump toward the center of the screen and spin attack. Spin into him four times and you're off to Mole World!

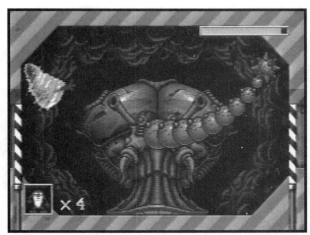

The corners of the room allow you to spin completely around the walls to avoid the alien elephant's trunk.

evel 2: Mole World

STAGE 1: Go into the first dirt area to find a box of rocks, then skip the other dirt areas and go all the way to the right. Spin into the wall to climb upward along the ceiling. Jump over the torches as you go to the far left, then climb up and head to the far right again. After you hit the **checkpoint,** go down into the next dirt area and spin into the left passage, then go straight down as much as possible to find an empty area with food. Go to the right and follow the passage until you hit air again, then go to the upper right until you see two torches (one shorter than the other). Jump over them, then go down in the dirt and spin climb up the next area. A mole guards the top of this passage you spin up, so try to keep spinning in the passage until he shoots, then finish climbing up and knock him out. The exit is to the right.

STAGE 2: An underground drilling machine is to the left, but it's moving to the right so keep moving as quickly as possible (without getting too careless). There are tons of drills, spikes and conveyor belts to avoid. Stick to the higher paths as much as possible. From the very beginning of this stage go into the dirt and climb out onto the ledge on the right, then leap over the torch on the left to reach a **1-Up** block. As long as you grab this block, you'll be able to keep trying to get through this stage without ever running out of lives, and it's still possible to finish the stage before the drilling machine catches up. There's a large block of dirt near the end of this stage — stay in the lower paths within the dirt to find the path to the Exit ahead.

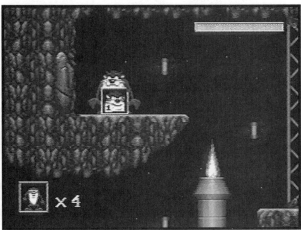

As long as you grab the 1-Up on Stage 2 you can keep trying without running out of lives.

BOSS: You'll be falling down a cavern while avoiding an odd machine controlled by a mole. You'll begin on two falling rocks, but if you fall off you can choose to fight the battle on a group of three falling rocks or one wide rock at the center. You can't plummet to your death, so keep falling until you find the rocks you're comfortable on. We preferred the three rocks, because they had the widest separation. Stand on the far right rock and wait for the missiles to drop, jumping to avoid the one that will hit the rock you're on. As it explodes, jump across to the middle, then the left and be ready to jump up between the left wall and the machine with a climbing spin. When the mole is finished playing with his beam weapon, fall down on the right side and land on the right rock, then spin attack the mole that appears on the bottom of the ship. Repeat the pattern until he's defeated.

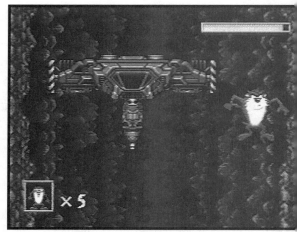

You can't fall too far, so fall until you land on a set of rocks you like. Hit the mole when he shows his head.

Level 3: Planet X

STAGE 1: Go to the right and climb up to ride on the back of a floating alien. Go left and up, then the far right to find a box of rocks. Be careful to avoid the red claws that drop from the ceiling — the second one is very difficult to avoid, so take your time. After the second claw, go to the far right to fin a medical kit (energy). When you hit the waterfall, grab the medical kit at the top. Use your spin attac to climb up the waterfalls. After grabbing the medical kit, fall to the next floor below and go to the pla form on the right to find a checkpoint marker and a hamburger. Climb the passage to the upper-rig to find a **1-Up,** which you can reach if you use the nearby mushroom as a propeller and go throug the wall. Be sure to land to the left or right of the 1-Up so you don't spin into it and knock it awa

Use the mushroom to go to the top-right, then go into the dirt and left to find another medical kit. Climb down and left to land in more water, then leap over the red tentacles as you ride the water to the right. Use your climbing spin technique to climb up the next narrow passage, then go right and drop down into more waterfalls. Watch for a checkpoint marker on the right. From the checkpoint go to the right across the floating aliens, then through the dirt to find a mushroom. Take it to the top-left and go through the dirt, then cross more floating aliens. Go up and right to find the exit. If you see a pit of spikes, wait for a moment to see if a floating alien is nearby.

STAGE 2: There is a **1-Up** at the beginning of the stage. Drop into the waterfall, then immediately jump right to reach a ledge. Go right over the

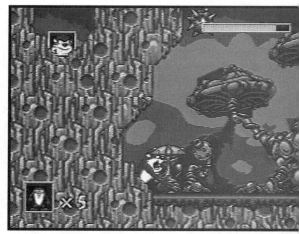

When landing near the 1-Up using the mushroom, be careful not to knock the 1-Up away.

spikes and through the wall to find the 1-Up. As you continue down the waterfall, be ready to leap over the arms and head of an octopus. Below the octopus is a box of rocks. Go left from the rocks and pass through the dirt, then take the water down to another octopus. Jump to the right after the octopus and go under the three claws, then hit the water and take it down to the left, then down to the right. Leap to the right on the first ledge to knock out a bomb, then go under the two claws to reach a cake. Go back into the water and jump to the next ledge on the right to find food. Jump back into the water and keep going down until you see an octopus with one arm. Leap to the ledge on the right after the octopus and climb up until you find dirt. Go up inside the dirt, then go right to reach another waterfall. Jump in and leap to the first ledge on

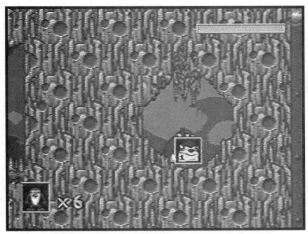

On Stage 2 you can find a 1-Up in the wall near the very beginning of the stage.

the right, then go right to find a **checkpoint**. Drop down to the right of the checkpoint, then go to the first ledge on the right and continue leaping to the right until you reach the exit sign.

STAGE 3: Go to the left under the four claws and grab the mushroom, then carry it back to the right and propel up in the area after the fourth claw. Keep going up and left until you hit a dead end, then go straight to the right and down at the next wall. When you get below the wall go around it and up on the right side of it. Keep going up and left again until you reach a secret area in the ceiling with a **turkey** to eat. Go back out of the ceiling and to the far right, then go up all the way, left over the wall, down under the wall, then up the left side of the same wall. Continue to the upper-left corner again, then go right to the wall and down. To the right, under the claw, is a medical kit (and a bad cake). The **checkpoint** is directly below. Hit the checkpoint, then go up along the right wall. Continue going up until you hit **another checkpoint,** then go through the dirt to meet the boss.

BOSS: The boss is a **snake.** The corners of the room will allow you to spin in a complete circle from floor to wall to ceiling to wall and back to the floor. If the snake is going to hit you, use the spin to go around him on the walls. You can only hit the last piece of the snake, which is marked with red dots.

Use the corners of the room to spin completely around while waiting for an opportunity...

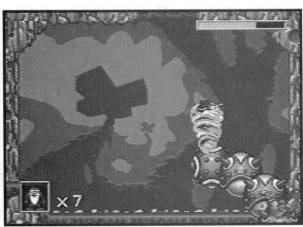

...to spin attack into the snake's tail. You can only hit him once each time he appears.

Use your spin attack to hit the last piece off. After you hit the snake once when he appears, you'll ha[ve] to wait until he disappears and reappears before you can hit him again. Stay near a corner and be read[y] to spin, then if the snake is in a safe area wait for your opportunity, jump, then spin into his tail. Aft[er] removing all of his body parts you'll have to hit his head.

Level 4: Mexico

⚡ **STAGE 1:** I knew my geography was weak, but I hadn't realized that Mexico was anywhere *near* Mars! On the first stage you have to jump across the backs of bulls and mules and stagecoaches until you reach the front of the line. It's one of the easier stages, so make a run for it and stop for any food you see along the way, which is plenty. When jumping between two animals that are far apart from each other, use your spin attack to soar through the air.

⚡ **STAGE 2:** This stage is also fairly easy (that last level was just too difficult!). You can go inside the buildings through the double doors. There's a **1-Up** in sight through a window of one of the first buildings, and you can grab it if you enter the doors to the left. Eat the gas so you can breathe fire at the enemies. Try to climb up narrow passages with your spin attack whenever possible. When you reach a dead end, not far from the beginning of the stage, you must enter a door and spin to climb up inside the building. There's a **continue block** straight to the right about four screens, but you have to jump down through the floor to find it. Keep going until you reach the exit sign at the far bottom-right corner.

⚡ **BOSS:** It's time for a bullfight. The trick to winning the bullfight is to spin run from the bull as he charges, then jump at the very last second so he'll crash into the wall. When the bull is dizzy from a hit, walk about one screen length away from him and wait for him to charge, then *run!* It takes seven hits to knock him out.

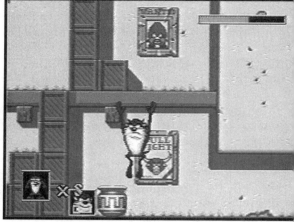

Jump down through the floors
to find this valuable continue block.

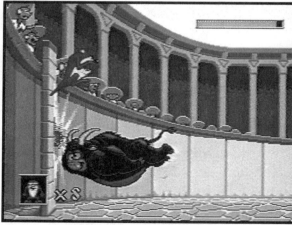

Timing is everything when trying
to make the bull ram into the wall.

Level 5: Haunted Castle

⚡ Go to the far right to collect a gas, then fry the flies as you climb. You'll have to hit a switch to raise [a] gate at the top. When the flames along the passage to the right hit the ground they can still burn yo[u] until they completely disappear, so time your jumps accordingly. When you get to the far right, clim[b] the steps to hit a switch, then go back down the steps and jump down through the floor. As you wal[k] through the next door, be prepared to jump over and run from **Yosemite Sam.** As you exit out the other side and go down the steps, be careful not to spin into the box of rocks and hamburger at the bottom of the steps. Go to the right across the steps that pop in and out of the wall, then take the steps up at the junction to meet **Witch Hazel.** Jump over her cleavers and climb up the steps that pop in and out above to reach gas, then hit the switch to the left. Go back down to the junction and take the steps down to find a medical kit and a **checkpoint**. Directly above the checkpoint is a box of rocks you can climb to on the steps to the right, then go right to grab fruit and hit a switch. Straight across to the right is the next area you want to go to, but you'll have to use the steps that pop in and out of the wall below to reach it. Go all the way to the top-

You must find your way around the Haunted Castle to hit switches and avoid Yosemite Sam.

right, then jump down through the floor and go left past **Yosemite Sam and his dragon** to reach a switch. Go to the right and fall off the ledge to reach the floor below, then leap left over the spikes to reach a door with an exit sign hidden inside.

STAGE 2: Go down the steps and right to find a trick wall next to a fire pit. Press up in front of the trick wall to go inside, then go right and come out of the other door. On the opposite side of the next fire pit is a turkey, but you'll have to take a hit from the fire to reach it. Continue going to the right and down the steps, then when you reach the bottom floor go left for a medical kit. Go to the far right to find a **spiral staircase** to spin up to the top floor. Hit the **checkpoint**, then go left to find gas and a **1-Up** block. Go right and down the first steps to the bottom, then right to spin up the next spiral staircase. Grab the food at the top, then spin climb upward. There isn't enough room to jump over the flies, but if you spin climb in the small arch above the fly you can stay above it until you can safely drop back down. Keep going left until you see a hamburger and gas in windows above, then enter the door to the left to reach both items. While still inside the wall, go up and right to the next door. Go through

the door and jump to the upper left, then continue left to find the next **checkpoint**. Further left is gas and a spiral staircase to spin down. Be ready to avoid a Witch Hazel at the bottom, then quickly go left and climb upward. Go left and down the next spiral staircase, then right and up another climb to the exit sign.

STAGE 3: The background of this area is green. Go right and use the conveyor belts to reach a ledge in front of a solid door in the upper-right area. Go down through the next set of conveyor belts to the bottom, then left to find more conveyor belts. Use the conveyor belts to reach the upper-left, then go left and down to the bottom floor. Go right until you find a **checkpoint**. To the upper-left is a hamburger. Grab it, then go back to the marker and go to the far right across

Stage 3 is a maze of conveyor belts. Use the Checkpoints as a checkpoint when trying to follow our guide.

the conveyor belts. From the far right conveyor belt, go up and left to find another checkpoint marker, then spin climb up the passage on the left and go right to find a very tricky set of conveyor belts placed a bit too close to steam vents. This area is very frustrating, and taking your time won't help. Try to climb as quickly as possible. When you reach the top conveyor platform the steam vent can't reach you, so time your jump to the ledge on the left carefully, and spin when jumping to clear the distance. Go left to find the exit sign.

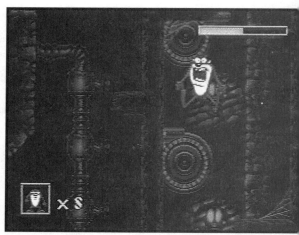

These three small conveyor belts are placed near steam vents that will knock you to the floor. Ugh!

✦ **BOSS:** The boss for the Haunted Castle is the mad scientist and his orange creation, Gossamer. Get ready for a cool little battle. The toughest part is dodging Gossamer while waiting for a chance to pounce him. You need to jump to pounce him, but when you jump he'll also jump. The trick is to jump as he's walking towards you, then as you land run under him before he lands from his jump. He'll stop every once in a while, giving you a chance to pounce him easily, but be ready to dodge him again immediately after. After the second or third pounce in front of either chair he'll sit in the chair, giving you a chance to run to the other chair and hit the switch. The switch causes a machine to come down and swap your brain with Gossamer's. Now you'll be able to control Gossamer, so jump up on the chair and punch or pounce the zapper that the mad scientist is controlling.

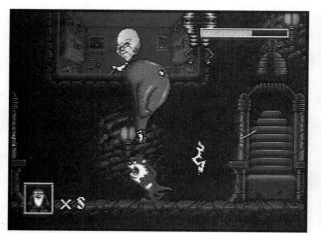

Fake Gossamer out with a jump, then run under him before he lands. Knock him into a chair...

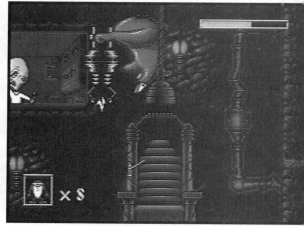

...then switch brains for a while so you can destroy the mad doctor's electric bolt generator.

Level 6: Marvin's House

✦ **STAGE 1:** Ugh! The final level! Go to the right, avoiding the spiked creature, and ride the box up, then leap to the next block and take it to the room on the left with a box of rocks. The path ahead is linear (only one way to go), but when you reach the next door (just like the first door), go up to find a blue potion that will make Taz big and invincible, then rush to the right before the potion wears off. Stick to the higher ledges, then about the time the potion wears off you'll find a bone on the floor above you. Grab it and give it to the dog below, then climb back up and go to the far right for a room with a **medical kit** (and a bomb). Go back to the dog, then go right and drop down the first tube you see. You'll land in a pit with walls that close in. When they get near enough, spin climb up them and go left. Keep going to the far left, then drop down and go right. There's a passage in this area where you must spin climb in a hole in the ceiling to get over a slow-moving spiked creature. Go right and drop to find a **checkpoint marker,** then go left to find a hamburger (and two bombs). You'll enter a **cloning room,** and as you walk out

After you enter the cloning room you can have your twin help you reach higher platforms.

you'll be followed by a familiar looking creature. He follows your lead, only a second behind. Jump on his head, then leap to the platforms above for food. The rest of the path to the left is linear until you reach another tube leading down. As you fall down the tube use your spin attack and hold left to enter a passage with a **continue block** (don't spin into it!). As long as you make it this far into the level you can always grab this continue block (even if you lose a life and come back). You might want to build up a few continues in case you have trouble with the incredibly tough next stage and the final boss (of course, you could always continue playing for practice to see what's ahead). As you continue down the tube hold right to land on the next ledge. Go right and drop off the ledge, then keep going right to find a secret tunnel in the wall — a very long tunnel — with a hamburger, a **1-Up,** and a bone (no use for the bone that we could find, since you'll drop it if you carry it too long). There are a lot of bombs in the next area, so be ready to spin attack. When you reach the second cloning room you'll have a trickier set of jumps to make in order to reach the ledge above. You must get your clone to jump to the platform above with you, then stand on his head and jump, then leap from his head to the right as he jumps. Be ready to rush past Marvin's dog to the exit sign.

STAGE 2: This confusing stage has arrows that spin you upside down and sideways, along with **four colored laser beams** that must be deactivated. Each laser has a button-shaped power source that is destroyed by three spin attacks. If you reach the boss you'll be able to battle him with any remaining lives, but once you lose all your lives you must continue back at the beginning of Marvin's House. From the start of the stage, go right and use the box above to go up. Jump into the up arrow to flip and walk on the ceiling, then leap to the right and hit the right-pointing arrow to flip sideways and land on a wall to the right (blue beam is above to the left). Go down and drop to the right to battle a suc-

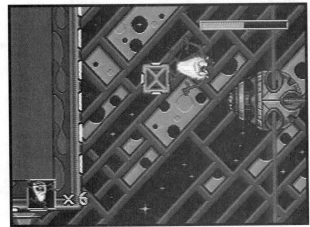

You must find the power button for each colored laser beam and smash into it with a spin attack.

tion-cupped green wheel. Spin along the walls until you reach a right-pointing arrow to hit. Go dow
along the floor and continue spinning to the left wall and up to the ceiling. Drop upward to the ne
ceiling (upside down). You should see some furniture and three boxes. From the top box, go right ar
hit the arrow pointing down, then go right and jump over the next arrow. Spin attack the green whee
then go right and walk through the yellow laser beam (you have to take this hit). In the room to th
right is the power button for the blue laser beams. Spin attack it three times, then go right and dro
down in the floor to three arrows pointing left and hit them to drop into the room with the yellow las
beam power button. Attack the power button with three spin attacks. Go into the passage on the uppe
left and keep going left to find that furniture we pointed out earlier. Go to the passage above and le
then drop down a few floors to find the red laser beam power button. Destroy it, then go out the pa
sage on the bottom-right to find your way to the exit.

BOSS: It's **Marvin the Martian** in a giant robot with long skinny ledge and Marvin's helmet. At fir
this boss seemed impossible, but the trick is to use the small orange platforms on the robot's knee
You can make the jump to these platforms from the ground, then spin attack the brush on the robot
helmet. You can also use the green part of the robot's shoe and the orange platform on the secon
joints of the legs to stand on, but jumping from the knee gives the best angle for effective hit
Sometimes you can bounce from the brush onto the second joint in the leg, then attack again immed
ately. If you beat Marvin, you'll get to witness one of the coolest ending sequences we've seen in
while. Luckily Sega and HeadGames (the developers) realize the importance of rewarding us game
for our hard work (and hard-earned cash spent buying the game in the first place!). Thanks, guys!

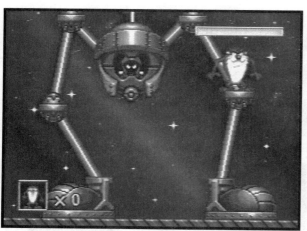

You can jump to the platform on the knee
of Marvin's robot from the ground...

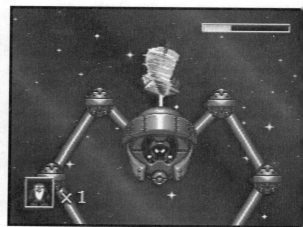

...then leap up and spin attack
into the head of the robot.

URBAN STRIKE

CATEGORY: Flight Sim/Shooter   DEVELOPER: Granite Bay Software
PLAYERS: 1   PUBLISHER: Electronic Arts

Introduction

Urban Strike is the third in the popular series of heli-copter sim games from Electronic Arts that began with 1992's *Desert Strike* and continued with 1993's *Jungle Strike*. *Urban Strike* has more missions than the previous games—a whopping ten in all—and sev-eral of the missions let you control the pilot as he scampers around inside buildings and blowing stuff up. *Urban Strike* isn't quite as tough as the previous games, but there are still some tricky parts, hence this detailed chapter.

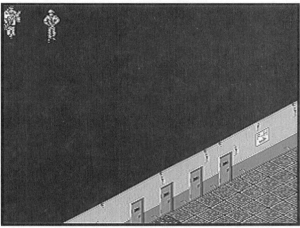

The programmers of *Urban Strike* scattered Elvis Presley all over the game. Must've seemed funny on paper.

Campaign 1: Hawaii

💥 Select Cossack or Freeperson as your co-pilot.

MISSION 1: VISITORS CENTER

💥 Your first mission is to destroy the two radar build-ings near the coast. They aren't very well guarded, so you won't have much trouble. Use two Hellfires on each building to destroy them quickly.

💥 There's a downed chopper on the beach with the missing co-pilot Legal. Fly south of the western radar building to find Legal surrounded by a cou-ple of foot soldiers. Take out the soldiers and scoop up Legal. Blow up the chopper after you pick her up to keep it out of Malone's grubby hands.

💥 You can also get the Super Winch while complet-ing this mission. Fly to the far west side of the campaign zone and destroy the buildings there until you find the Winch.

Fly along the beach to find the MIA co-pilot Legal next to her downed helicopter (and a few enemy soldiers).

MISSION 2: TELESCOPE MIRRORS

✹ You're going to skip this mission for the moment, because there are still too many enemies roaming the zone, and if even one of the mirrors get damaged, the entire campaign is a failure. Better to skip ahead for now and come back for the mirrors later.

MISSION 3: STEALTH SHIPS

✹ There's an extra life in the building (well, it's a hut, really) between two of the lower stealth ships.

✹ Each stealth ship's gun is active until the ship sinks completely below the water, so whack the ship with missiles and then fly out of range instead of gloating at your handiwork.

MISSION 4: PLASTIC SURGEON

✹ This is *very* easy. Fly to the surgeon's house in the northwest corner of the map, kill the wimpy guards, destroy the house, and pick up the surgeon.

MISSION 5: ENEMY BRIDGE

✹ Start at the northwest corner of the bridge, then fly southeast while unleashing a stream of Hydra missiles to break it into several sections. Don't slow down or deviate from your path—just keep going straight ahead and shooting missiles like a crazy person. If you don't destroy the entire bridge on one pass, you'll just have to make another.

MISSION 2: TELESCOPE MIRRORS

✹ *Now* you're ready for the mirrors. You can get up to four, but you only *need* to get two of them. Make sure the path to the barge on the north side of the zone is clear of gunboats and other enemies. You don't want to encounter anything as you tow the mirrors.

✹ Hit the well-reinforced trucks with missiles to blow them up, then carry the mirrors to the barge and set them down carefully on the circles. Once you pick up a mirror, you can't grab any items until you set the mirror down again, so make sure you have adequate fuel and ammo before grabbing a mirror.

MISSION 6: GREEN BERETS

✹ Fly south to the island, then fly east of the island and rescue the civilians from the shark. (You can kill the shark with a quick burst of chain gun fire.)

When you destroy a stealth ship, move out of range until it's completely sunk to avoid getting shot.

Zoom straight down the bridge and unleash a stream of missiles to blow it to pieces.

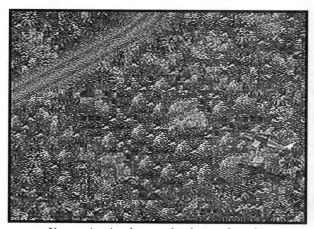

You can't miss the purple plume of smoke being released by the Green Berets.

Return to the island and pick up the smart bomb. With the smart bomb attached to the winch, fly west to the Green Berets. Look for a purple plume of smoke and drop the bomb on the patch of dirt near the plume to create a landing zone. Shoot the first two enemy soldiers that appear and start picking up the Berets.

At this point, you should switch from the Mohican to the Blackhawk, the fat yellow chopper at the north landing zone. It can hold many more passengers than the Mohican, and has double the armor, although its weapons suck. Use the Blackhawk to scoop up Berets until the mission is complete. Return to the Mohican and fly back to base.

Campaign 2: Baja Oil Rigs

Make sure to choose Legal as your co-pilot.

MISSION 1: RADAR STATION

Along with the lightly defended radar station, destroy all the structures along the coast to uncover items for you to pick up later on. There's a Super Winch under the building on the far left side of the coast.

MISSION 2: SMALL OILRIGS

Each of the two oilrigs has two Phalanx rocket launchers on the corners that need to be disabled. Once they're gone, you can safely strafe the oilrigs to kill the guards and reveal items. The rocket launchers take three Hellfires each to destroy, but less than that if you get lucky and destroy the part of the oilrig supporting the launcher. Take care not to damage the Blackhawk chopper on the southern oilrig; you need it for the next mission.

MISSION 3: PASSENGERS

As soon as you destroy the fourth Phalanx, the passenger ship on the west side of the zone starts to sink. You have a whopping three minutes to save at least fifteen passengers. Make sure you got the Super Winch before starting this mission—you vitally need the extra pick-up speed.

Land on the south oilrig and switch to the Blackhawk, then head for the sinking ship. Pick up the passengers in the water first—they need more immediate help than the ones if lifeboats. Use a quick chain gun burst to take out the shark circling around the ship. Some of the passengers are far away from the ship, so use the map to

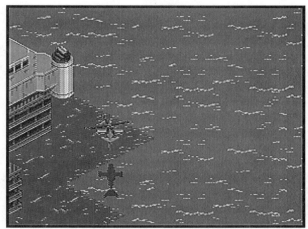

The oilrigs can't be safely attacked until the Phalanx rocket launchers are taken out.

You only have three minutes to save at least fifteen passengers from the sinking ship.

locate the ones who've drifted away. Drop off your passengers at the north oilrig, *not* the Main Base. Return to the south oilrig and switch back to the Mohican.

MISSION 4: DESTROYER

Shoot the chopper to the north of the destroyer, then shoot and destroy the cannon on top of the ship. There's an armor repair under the cannon on the stern of the ship. Grab it before sending the destroyer to the bottom of the sea with a few well-placed missiles.

MISSION 5: RUSSIAN SUB

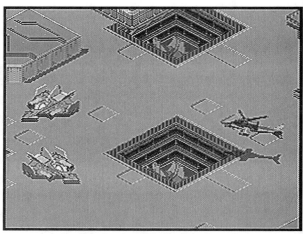

Although this is a rescue mission, you should use the Mohican instead of the Blackhawk because of the Mohican's better weaponry, which you need to deal with the enemy presence around the sinking sub, especially the enemy choppers. You'll need to make at least two trips because of the Mohican's wimpy storage capacity, but the sub soldiers aren't in danger of drowning, so there's no hurry. After you've rescued all the soldiers, go to the ship west of the sub and pick up the crate. Return to the sub and drop the crate on the marked circle to complete the mission.

MISSION 6: JET FIGHTERS
AND MISSION 7: MAIN OILRIG

Don't miss the F29s in the elevators
as you blow the main oilrig to hell.

Now it's time to strike the main oilrig, which is bloody huge. Shoot the rocket launchers on the corners first to give yourself a much easier time with the enemies on the rig itself. The co-pilot Stinger is inside the building on the northwest side of the rig; there's an armor repair on the west side; and there are F29s scattered all over the place. Don't miss the F29s placed inside the elevators. A landing pad appears when you uncover the entrance into the rig. Land on the pad to dash inside. This is the first time in the *Strike* series you get to experience life outside the helicopter!

Campaign 3:
Inside Oil Rig

MISSION 1: GUN CAMS

As you run through the oil rig, you need to shoot the barrels and missile piles to uncover ammo and armor repair items. When you destroy a barrel or missile pile, you usually draw the attention of an enemy soldier or two; shoot them from long range with your machine gun. The ammo and armor crates will be picked up when you even get close to them, so stay at a distance until you really need them. You don't want to pick up, and possibly waste, an item. One last note to remember: enemy

One well-placed grenade is all you
need to destroy a gun cam.

soldiers are killed by nearby explosions of barrels, missiles, or whatever.

✺ Use a well-placed grenade to destroy each gun cam. You can usually hit them while standing just out of their range so that you don't get hit yourself.

MISSION 2: ENEMY F29

✺ You need to finish this mission before finishing Mission 1, since the F29s are all placed near the entrance. Use your machine gun to destroy the surprisingly fragile aircraft.

MISSION 3: AGENT

✺ There's an armor repair under the missile pile near the agent. Squeeze through the gap in the wall south of the agent and use a few grenades to destroy the pill box guarding him. Talk to the agent and remember the button he tells you to push on the beacon.

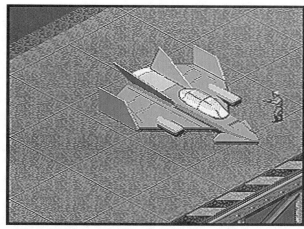

These F29s don't last for long under a constant stream of machine gun fire. (Then again, neither do you.)

MISSION 4: BEACON

✺ There are several pill boxes and soldiers along the path to the beacon. Grab the armor repair on the north side of the zone along the way, because you'll need it. The last pill box before the beacon also has an armor repair underneath it. Touch the beacon and press the correct button to activate it. Now you need to run back to the ladder before the rig is blown to kingdom come.

✺ To make your escape just a little bit harder, more soldiers and pill boxes have been placed on the path: three soldiers and eight pill boxes in all. (All the pill boxes are encountered closer to the exit.) Use your grenades to quickly wipe out the pill boxes and advance onward. If you didn't save any ammo packs earlier on, you're going to be in big trouble here.

Campaign 4: Mexico

✺ Make sure to choose Stinger as your co-pilot.
✺ There's a Super Winch in the northwest corner of the zone, in a group of five closely spaced buildings.
✺ Look for an extra life in a building directly west of the GAV field (Mission 5).

MISSION 1: SCOUT TEAM

✺ Hit the watch towers and foot soldiers around the camp one at a time. Use a single Hydra to take out each watch tower instead of chain gun fire; it's quicker and easier. When the defenses around the camp are down, hit the enemy soldiers inside the camp. The square bunker on the southwest side of the camp can't be destroyed, so don't waste ammo on it. Pick up the scouts; one of them tells you that there's a guy inside the bunker being tortured.

Destroy the defenses around the perimeter of the camp before flying in and rescuing the scouts.

Touch down on the landing pad and your co-pilot runs inside. Meanwhile, a tank attacks you from the north. Hit it with missiles to destroy it quickly. Drop off the scouts and come back to pick up your co-pilot and more scouts. When you scoop up the final scout, the building blows up.

MISSION 2: ENEMY CAMP

Approach the enemy camp from the north; you need to fly through a deadly Danger Zone if you attack from the west. This is quite a tough mission, so take it slowly and destroy one enemy at a time. Do not fly deep into the camp or you'll be quickly destroyed by enemy crossfire. There are flak cannons inside some of the buildings to make your job even tougher.

MISSION 3: CONTRACTORS

Fly to the building with the contractors inside and use your chain gun to blow up the paratroopers dropping out of the sky. It's important to take out as many paratroopers in the air as possible; once they land, they can return fire and are obviously more dangerous. Keep shooting the paratroopers until the contractors all scurry out of the building at the same time. Two tanks roll onto the scene at the same time, so destroy them before scooping up the contractors to complete the mission.

MISSION 4: GAV PLANS

An easy mission. Blow up the hexagonal buildings and pick up the blue plans inside each one. When you get both plans, you learn which button to use to hot-wire the GAV in the next mission.

MISSION 5: GAVS

Shoot the soldier on top of the control box on the west side of the GAV field. Hot-wire the box by pressing the button indicated in the plans (which was C every time we played the game). A landing pad appears; set down the Mohican and you run into the GAV for a little spin.

Drive to the southwest side of the GAV field and start shooting each GAV one at a time. Attack them

Shoot as many of the falling paratroopers as you can while they're still in the air.

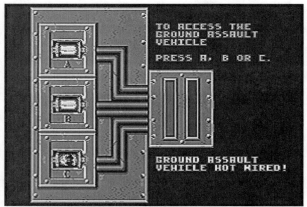

Press the correct button and you get to take control of the extremely well-armored GAV.

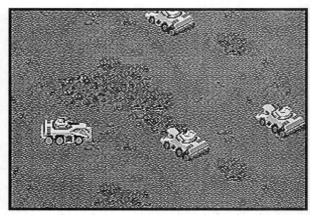

Shoot the enemy GAVs from behind and remember that you're absolutely loaded with missiles.

from behind, which forces them to turn around to return fire. Some of the GAVs don't move when you shoot them, while others get aggressive and attack you. Stop firing when a GAV explodes so you don't destroy any item inside. You can also position yourself so that the attacking GAVs shoot and destroy other GAVs. Take out all the GAVs to complete the mission.

MISSION 6: FACTORY

✴ Hit the building on the west first to uncover the smart bomb inside. Don't pick up the smart bomb right away, because several tanks attack when the building is destroyed. There's also a GAV guarding the factory. The best thing to do is to return to the GAV, get inside, and blow up the GAV guard. Then return to the Mohican, pick up the smart bomb, and drop it in front of the factory to blow it up. If you screw up with the first smart bomb, fly back to the west to pick up another one.

Campaign 5: San Francisco

MISSION 1: GOLDEN GATE AND BAY BRIDGE

✴ Three of the four bomb attachments on the bridges are being guarded by hover planes, which are the nastiest enemies yet. Do not use missiles to knock the bombs off the bridges; this might cause them to explode. Just use a burst of chain gun fire to knock off the bombs, then missiles to destroy the hover planes.

✴ After you disable the bombs on the first bridge, fly northwest along the fog line to the second bridge. Shoot the hover plane along the way to reveal an extra life.

MISSION 2: RADIO TOWER

✴ Fly due south to the tower. There are several soldiers hiding in the fog around the tower. Use chain gun bursts to take them out, then use a long burst of fire to destroy the tower. You can also destroy the Victorian buildings nearby to uncover items (although you lose points for destroying civilian targets). One of the houses has Elvis inside.

MISSION 3: CORP HQ WEST

✴ Most of the corporate buildings are defended by only two soldiers on each rooftop, armed with bazookas. Hit one building at a time, killing the soldiers and then destroying the building. The hardest part of the entire mission is dealing with the hover planes around the buildings.

MISSION 4: ARMY BASE

✴ Attack the army base from the north, clearing the area of troops and vehicles. Leave the buildings

Knock off the round bombs on the bridges with the chain gun, not with missiles.

Most of the corporate buildings are guarded by two soldiers, one on each side of the rooftop.

alone for the moment. Look for a single soldier placed in between three smart bombs. Shoot him (carefully!) and pick up a bomb. Fly south to the field of tanks and drop it in between them to cause a massive chain reaction. When the mission is completed, destroy the buildings to reveal items. There's an extra life in this area. When you take it, a tank shows up; shoot the tank to reveal an armor repair.

MISSION 5: MICRON LABS

The labs seem lightly defended, but as soon as you start attacking, bad guys show up and start shooting. Trick the vehicles into shooting the lab buildings to save ammo and make your job easier.

MISSION 6: HOMEBASE

A simple and difficult mission. Just blow the crap out of the attacking hover planes with your missiles. The faster, the better!

MISSION 7: HENCHMAN

Destroy the red car driving along the road. Don't waste time or ammo on the enemies along the road, just blow up the car quickly.

MISSION 8: ALCATRAZ

There are ammo, fuel, and armor repair items under the buildings on the island. (The armor repair is on the far right if you need it quickly.) Don't be afraid to fly back to the mainland if you need supplies—the enemy's not exactly going anywhere. Keep blowing structures up until a landing pad appears. Touch down and you run into the prison.

A not-so-smart enemy soldier stands in the middle of a threesome of smart bombs.

Shoot this car to annihilate the henchman inside. He didn't deserve to live anyway!

Campaign 6: Alcatraz

Elvis is hiding out in this campaign. To find him, play through the campaign until you reach the northernmost sensor. Now walk around the north wall to the northwest corner of the zone. There's Elvis in his trusty jumpsuit. Thank ya verra much!

MISSION 1: SENSORS

You can't complete this mission all at once; you simply need to take out sensors as you move through Alcatraz and complete the other missions. The sensors are linked to gates placed throughout the prison. Once you destroy a sensor, you can destroy the gate it's linked to with a single machine gun bullet. Lastly, the sensors are unarmed, so you can destroy them with machine gun fire instead of grenades.

MISSION 2: BLUEPRINTS

✦ The blueprints are guarded by two armored guards, and very easy to destroy, so the best thing to do is grab them before using your grenades on the guards. You can also shoot the guards when they are between you and the blueprints, but this is dangerous. There's an armor repair underneath the computer on the desk, ammo underneath the drawing board, and a sensor nearby.

MISSION 3: WEAPONS

✦ Blow up the first two weapon crates. The first one has a sensor, and the second has a guard and an ammo pack. The sensor is linked to the gate blocking the path to the remaining five crates. Blow those crates open to find ammo, armor, and a few more guards.

MISSION 4: LONG HAUL

✦ With all the sensors destroyed, you can see Long Haul's prison cell. There are two cannons and a few soldiers between you and the cell. Use grenades to destroy them quickly. When you release him, he runs like hell for an exit—but *not* the same exit you used to enter the prison, so keep that in mind. Shoot anything that gets in your way. When Long Haul stops next to the pillar, walk behind it to replenish your armor. This is crucial!

Pick up the fragile blueprints before you start shooting at the enemy guards.

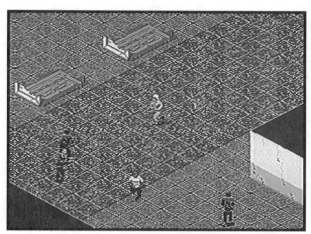

Follow Long Haul as he runs like hell through the prison to make his escape.

Campaign 7: New York

✦ Make sure to choose Long Haul as your copilot.

MISSION 1: FINANCIAL HQ

✦ You start the mission under attack by a flak cannon and bazooka-armed soldier. Time your lift-off between the soldier's bazooka blasts and take him out before he can reload. Nail the second soldier and the flak cannon to clear the zone.

✦ There are four buildings that need to be destroyed to complete the mission. The southern two buildings are slightly taller than the surrounding buildings, and a slightly different color. Shoot them with the chain gun to blow them up and destroy the radars inside. The northern two buildings are more obvious, since they're both labeled with big "MALONE" signs.

- Shoot all the structures on top of the buildings to uncover items, including the rooftop swimming pools. It's vital to find as many items as possible.
- To get the Super Winch, simply fly to the south edge of the zone, then fly west until you see the Winch on top of a building. It's impossible to miss.

MISSION 2: CIVILIANS

- Rescue the civilians from the burning buildings around the city. Soldiers will pop out to attack while you're picking up the civs, so you should have the Super Winch. Once you're filled with civvies, head for one of the three UNLOAD CIVILIANS zones. You get 100 armor points for each civ rescued. There will be additional civilians even after you complete the mission, so save them for when you need armor.
- You can skip Mission 2 and save it for later, but you won't be able to locate the other missions, so you need to know where the mission areas are found.

MISSION 3: CHOPPERS

- Look closely at the map and you'll see four red dots, with one of the dots separated from the rest. This separate dot is a radar building that needs to be destroyed before you tackle the choppers.
- Use your missiles to hit most choppers on the buildings before they take off. You only need one Hellfire to destroy each chopper. Once a chopper takes off, it takes more ammo to destroy it. If you're running low on armor, grab and rescue a few more civilians. Don't bother destroying all of the choppers—just take out enough to complete the mission.

MISSION 4: NAFTA MEMBERS

- Destroy the east target on the map first; it's a radar building. Once it's gone, fly west to the burning building to pick up the NAFTA members. (They run out of the building onto the nearby rooftop.) One of the members has important information about the bomb inside the Trade Center.
- You need to make several trips to the landing zones in order to rescue 16 members and complete the mission. When you rescue the 16th member, a landing pad appears. Set yourself down and your co-pilot runs into the building to defuse the bomb.

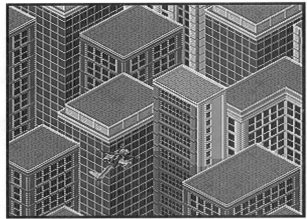

Look for these buildings that are slightly taller than the surrounding structures.

Each helpless civilian is worth a very helpful 100 armor points, so grab as many as you can stuff into the chopper.

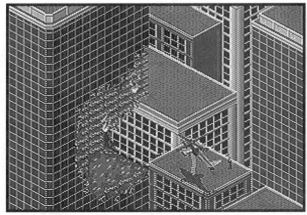

Grab the NAFTA members as they run out of the big hole in the side of the Trade Center.

MISSION 5: TRADE CENTER

✴ Cut the correct wire to defuse the bomb. (Don't cut the green wire!) Your co-pilot returns to the Mohican and an enemy chopper attacks you. Blow it up and return to the base to complete the campaign.

Campaign 8: Las Vegas

✴ Make sure to select Long Haul as your copilot.

✴ Look for a Chapel of Love at the north end of the campaign zone; it's a lighted building with a colorful heart on the roof. Blow up the building to reveal a bride, groom, and two Elvis impersonators. You can pick up the Elvises or shoot them; pick up the happy couple for extra points at campaign's end.

✴ There are two extra lives in the campaign, but both of them are in dangerous areas and can't be grabbed immediately. The first life is in the center of the zone, inside a bandstand (it looks almost like a hot-air balloon!). The second life is next to the southwest roadblock, out in the open and ready to be picked up.

MISSION 1: COMMANDER

✴ The Super Winch can be obtained right at the start of the campaign. Just fly directly south from the base to find it out in the open.

✴ There are oodles of Danger Zones in Vegas, and you should avoid them at all costs. One mistake is usually fatal. To fly to the Commander, go south to pick up the Super Winch, then southwest to the edge of the campaign zone, taking a big detour around the roadblock. Then fly west until you reach the Commander's red armored truck.

✴ One Hellfire will destroy the Commander's truck. He isn't driving past enemies, which makes you job easier. The Commander runs a short distance and then stops, allowing you to shoot his driver. He blows up when you shoot him, because he was carrying a bomb that would've destroyed your chopper had you picked it up. The Commander reveals the location of the numerous radar sites.

MISSION 2: RADAR

✴ Avoid attacking enemy forces unless they are directly between you and a radar site. Destroy the civilian buildings to uncover items, especially the Quickie Marts and gas stations, which almost always have something inside. When you reach a radar site—look for a small rotating dish—shoot until it blows up, then wait for the smoke to clear and shoot the structure that the radar was operating on. If you stray into a Danger Zone while flying

Look for small radar dishes on the targets before you start firing.

MISSION 3: ROADBLOCKS

✴ The roadblocks are placed at the four corners of the campaign zone, and all heavily defended. Make sure your armor is filled up before you make your first roadblock attack run. Stay around the edges of the campaign zone as you fly from roadblock to roadblock to avoid most of the enemies. Don't smash into the powergrid on the north side of the zone, though! Use a barrage of missiles to destroy the vehicles around each block, then turn around when safely out of weapon range and make another run.

MISSION 4: STRIP

This mission has you blowing up enemy vehicles along the Strip, a long road with cool hotels placed generously along its length. Start at the northeast end of the Strip and shoot your way southwest, taking one enemy at a time and flying away when you need ammo, fuel, or armor. Do not be tempted to stray too far into the Strip or you'll be caught in a fatal crossfire. Destroy buildings along the Strip to reveal more goodies.

MISSION 5: POWERGRID

Destroy the four cannons around the powergrid building with a barrage of Hydra missiles. You should be able to destroy all the cannons without taking much damage at all. Blow up the powergrid to reveal ammo, fuel, and an armor repair to max out your Mohican before tackling the final missions.

MISSION 6: CASINO

The casino itself is indestructible, so concentrate on the cannons surrounding the building. (These cannons are also indestructible until you take out the powergrid.) It's dark, so refer to the map to see the cannons' exact locations. When all of the cannons are taken out, a landing pad appears near the casino.

MISSION 7: CASINO

Set yourself down on the landing pad near the casino and you run inside.

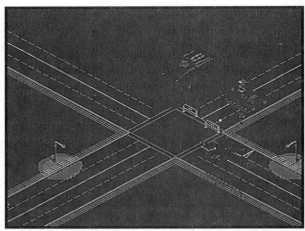
When you blow up the vehicles near a roadblock, the roadblock is often caught in the explosions.

The fabulous Caesars–er, Neros hotel and casino on the Strip in Las Vegas.

Campaign 9: Casinos

MISSION 1: PIT BOSSES

All six of the slot machine groups near the start of the level have ammo inside, and a few of the soldiers also have ammo. You can only find armor repairs at two locations, however.

Shoot through the glass wall at the start of the casino and nail the first pit boss (dressed in black) with a grenade. Now head toward the northeast corner of the casino, where most of the bosses are waiting. Use the machine gun when a pit boss has his back turned to you or when you're attacked by a purple-uniformed guard, and make extra-sure to avoid the slot machines with the machine guns mounted on them. These suckers take away your armor extremely quick.

✦ On your journey northward, look for a group of three slot machines between two pillars. Shoot the left machine to reveal Elvis and an armor repair. An armor repair appears here after you complete each mission, so be sure to return here when you need to.

MISSION 2: CASHIER BOOTH

✦ Make sure you have at least four grenades before attacking the booth—three to blow it up and a fourth to kill the guard inside. Once you nail the boss, it's a very simple task of picking up the three hostages and the ammo crate.

MISSION 3: V.I.P.

✦ There are five guards between you and the room where the V.I.P. is being held. They're all of the wimpy purple variety, so your machine gun will do just fine. Use the gun to blow up the V.I.P. room and then a grenade to dispatch the guard—just make sure you don't kill the V.I.P. in the blast! The V.I.P. tells you the location of Malone.

MISSION 4: MACHINE GUNS

✦ Four of the five change booths are defended by machine guns inside. (The southernmost change booth is hiding the shuttle, but you can't destroy it until you hit the other four.) The best technique here is to lob two grenades at a booth to destroy it, back out of range, and then move into range and destroy the gun with a third grenade.

MISSION 5: SHUTTLE

✦ Destroy the south change booth and walk onto the shuttle to be whisked into Malone's underground chamber for the final campaign!

Visit the King after each completed mission to pick up another armor repair.

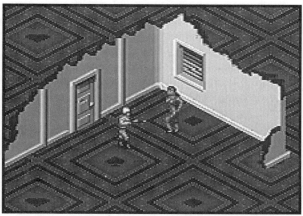

This V.I.P. has the information you need to complete the mission.

Walk into the shuttle to speed off to the final mission and the confrontation with Malone.

Campaign 10: Underground

※ Make sure to select Long Haul as your copilot.

MISSION 1: ENEMY WEAPONRY

※ This is the hardest mission of the campaign; get through this with two or three lives and you should be able to finish the entire campaign easily. Destroy the enemy weapons and soldiers and frequently refer to the map to find new ones. Use missiles-a-plenty on the tougher vehicles, and don't stray too far east into the Danger Zone.

※ There's ammo, fuel, and *two* armor repairs in the southeast corner of the map beneath the weapons there. Try to hold off on reloading or rearmoring as long as possible.

MISSION 2: ENEMY BARRACKS

※ The barracks are huge, square buildings at the north side of the map being guarded by flak cannons and foot soldiers. Take out the defenses of each barrack and then the barrack itself. There's nothing inside the barracks, unfortunately.

MISSION 3: CENTRAL CONTROL

※ The control panels are lightly guarded by foot soldiers and harmless scientists. As you destroy the control panels, the screens they're connected to go dim, so you might as well blow them up too.

MISSION 4: LASER CONTROL

※ Even easier than Mission 3. Destroy the control panels around the yellow steel shell until you get the mission complete message.

MISSION 5: EXPOSE LASER

※ Blow open the steel shell protecting the laser. That's it!

MISSION 6: MALONE'S QUARTERS

※ With nearly all the underground forces already destroyed, this mission ain't too much of a problem. Blow up the building and grab Malone as he scampers away from the rubble.

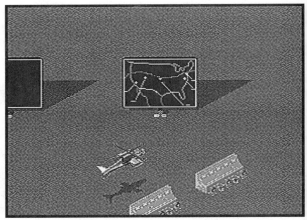
The central control panels are lightly guarded at best. Take 'em out along with the video screens.

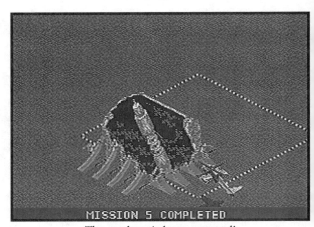
MISSION 5 COMPLETED
The madman's laser exposed!

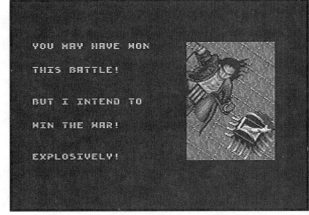
Pick up the psychotic Malone and drop him on top of his own laser to win the game.

MISSION 7: CAPTURE MALONE

✹ As you pick up Malone, you realize that you've got a big problem: his body is loaded with dynamite! You can't bring him into the chopper, and you can't put him down—or can you?

MISSION 8: DESTROY LASER

✹ Fly southwest to the exposed laser and drop Malone squarely on top of it. He blows himself and the laser to hell. Heh heh. Fly northwest to the base and land to witness the sucky ending.

Top-Secret Tips

✹ PASSWORDS: Use these passwords to access any campaign in the game.

      Campaign #1 (Hawaii): YZ9NHLWVNBF
      Campaign #2 (Baja Oil Rigs): CNHLGBR4NBF
      Campaign #3 (Inside Oil Rig): ZLGBWD3PFZD
      Campaign #4 (Mexico): 9BWDR6MJYNM
      Campaign #5 (San Francisco): NDR63P7VZLT
      Campaign #6 (Alcatraz): H63PMJT4SYL
      Campaign #7 (New York): LPMJ7VSXFZR
      Campaign #8 (Las Vegas): GJ7VT4FKYNM
      Campaign #9 (Casino): BVT4SKYCZLT
      Campaign #10 (Underground): WR63PMT4SYL
      Ending Credits: D3PMJ7SXFZD

✹ ELVIS SIGHTINGS: Here are the missions where you can find the King of Rock and Roll.

      Campaign #1: Shoot the guarded hut on the far left side of the zone.
      Campaign #2: Complete all the missions and fly to the wrecked submarine. You'll see Elvis in a nearby tugboat.
      Campaign #5: Elvis is inside one of the houses in the southwest corner.
      Campaign #6: Play through the campaign until you reach the northernmost sensor. Now walk around the north wall to the northwest corner of the zone.
      Campaign #7: After completing Mission 5, look for Elvis on a rooftop in front of the Empire State Building.
      Campaign #8: Elvis is here twice. The first time, he's guarding the Radar Commander; the second time, he's inside the Chapel of Love.
      Campaign #9: Elvis is hiding inside one of the slot machines.

VIRTUAL BART

CATEGORY: Platform+   DEVELOPER: Sculptured Software
PLAYERS: 1   PUBLISHER: Acclaim

Introduction

Somewhere buried deep in the contract between Matt Groening, the creator of The Simpsons, and Acclaim, the publishers of this game, must have read a paragraph containing the words, "every game featuring the character of Bart Simpson must be difficult to control, frustrating to play, and nearly impossible to finish." Acclaim has outdone themselves once again to abide by that contract. The six "events" in Virtual Bart are tougher alone to complete than the average entire game. The majority of the enemies are impossible to avoid, the jumps are often into an area you haven't been before, and those jumps are usually into a deathtrap waiting to spring. Of course everyone knows that, by law, every platform game must contain an ice level where you slip and slide out of control, but the programmers of Virtual Bart

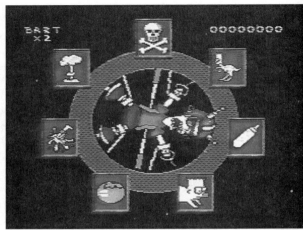

For the video game challenge of a lifetime dive into the Hellish world of Virtual Bart!

made the extra effort to throw in two ice levels. If your in the mood for an enormous challenge, this is your game. If you have high blood pressure, you might want to consider playing something else.

Basic Strategies

✦ Check each events section for specific basic strategies and controls on that event. Overall, the only general strategy is to use the Practice option to master each of the individual events, then attempt to play each one on the wheel. The biggest threat on the wheel is the top position, which flashes between a banana (extra spin) and a skull (lose a spin). Class Picture was our personal favorite event, since it doesn't feel as impossible as the rest of the events, and it was fun to play the first few times around. Doomsday Bart is one of the easiest, featuring Bart on a post-apocalyptic motorcycle ride. Mt. Splashmore would place third in difficulty, with the three platform stages being the most difficult.

Use the practice option to master each of the events separately, then attempt the wheel of torture.

Class Picture

We're going to start with our favorite of the six events. In this stage you must toss tomatoes or eggs at your classmates without hitting any of the adults. Use the B button to throw the tomatoes. By pressing left, right, or up and left or right diagonally, you can aim the tomatoes or eggs to the sides. The easiest aim is directly straight ahead. The only way to master this event is lots of practice. After a few runs you'll get a feel for the timing of when to throw and how far. It's very easy to throw a bit too close or too far, but practice will also pay off for aiming. When you hit a kid on any of the rows the first time, another kid will appear. After that kid is taken out, an adult will appear. Since having adults in the foreground rows will make hitting the kids in the background tougher, you should concentrate your efforts on hitting the kids that are the furthest back first. Once you complete the first group of kids, you'll be faced with the group again, only this time they're walking on the playground and they can move up and down the screen while walking from side to side. They also tend to change direction (up or down) all the time, making them very tough to nail. If you make it to the second round, then fail to hit all of the students or do hit an adult, you'll be sent back to the wheel. However, when you land on the Class Picture position on the wheel the next time, you'll begin on the second round.

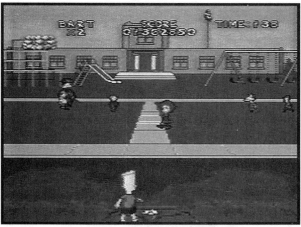

Take aim and fire away.
Practice is the only way to master this event.

Doomsday Bart

The second easiest event to master is the motorcycle ride, but that will mostly depend on your driving skills. There's not a lot of advice to give. Avoid the enemies as much as possible. Some will give you popsicles when you beat them up. Avoid the rocks and squirrels to keep your speed up. Hit the nitros cans to increase your speed for a few seconds. You have an unlimited supply of water balloons, so fire them continuously to hit any enemies that swerve in front of you. Make a major effort to grab any popsicles you see. Energy and time are your two biggest enemies during this event. As you get closer and closer to the finish line there are more rocks, more turns, and more aggressive enemies. As long as you avoid the rocks and skulls in the road, you'll be able to easily outrun the enemies and you'll have a better chance of reaching the finish line in time.

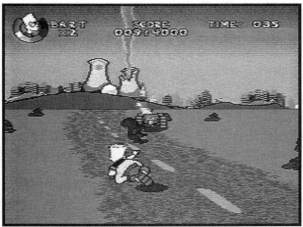

Avoid the rocks, skulls and squirrels
to keep your speed up during the final miles.

Mt. Splashmore

✦ This waterslide is the third easiest event. It can be very difficult to figure out which tube to go into at each of the junctions, but the trick is to check the back of the shirt on the man directly before the junction. There are lines on the shirt that point in the direction of the tunnel you should enter. Since it's far too difficult to spot the shirt and react immediately, hit the Start button to pause the game the moment you see the junction, then make your decision and hold the controller as you take the game off of pause. Try to grab the clocks along the way. We were totally unable to grab any of the popsicles for energy, or the bodyboard for speed, but we still managed to survive.

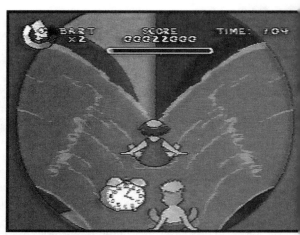

Pause the game when you see a junction coming up, then study the back of the man's shirt for direction.

Baby Bart

✦ This probably qualifies as the easiest of the platform events, in the same way that you vote for a guy that you don't trust just because you don't trust the other guys more. Use A to jump, Down + A to jump down, B to **shoot your pacifier** (control the aim with the control pad), and C to open your **diaper chute** (safe only from higher limbs). You'll begin with a climb across several trees. Your goal is to reach the clotheslines to the far right, but to get there you'll need to climb to the top-right side of the trees. Always try to stay on the higher limbs of the trees to increase your odds of grabbing a branch if you fall. There's an **extra life** worth grabbing about halfway through the trees on a low limb. When you reach the last tree and you can see the clothesline to the right, climb to the top of the tree and jump to the right, then open your diaperchute when you reach the highest point in your jump to get the maximum float over to the clothesline.

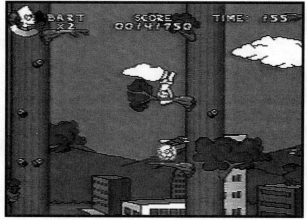

Grab this extra life on a low limb halfway through the trees.

Use your diaperchute to launch from the top of the last tree, then aim for the clothesline or trampoline.

CLOTHESLINE: Always stay on the higher lines so you'll have a chance to catch yourself if you fall. As you walk to the right, constantly spit out your pacifier in hopes of hitting oncoming enemies or obstacles. You can't walk across the clothes hanging from the clothesline, so hop down to a lower line to walk past the clothes, then hop back up to the top line. When you reach the end of the clothesline, stand on the bottom line on the far right and leap for the strings hanging from the **floating balloons.** You can still shoot your pacifier, as well as move up or down the strings to avoid enemies and obstacles. Jumping will also help in your defense, but grabbing the string on your way down is mostly based on luck. There's an **extra life** worth going for (if you lose a life after grabbing it, at least you'll be even).

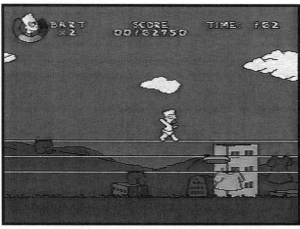

Stick to the higher clothesline to increase your chances of grabbing on as you fall.

BABY CARRIAGE: You must guide the carriage up or down one of the four lanes (two lanes on the streets, plus sidewalks on each side). Avoid the holes, oil, obstacles, enemies, and anything else that doesn't look like solid pavement. You can easily stick to the top two lanes (sidewalk and top road lane) for the majority of this scene. There's an **extra life** and a popsicle along the bottom, but grabbing them is very risky and nearly impossible. If you want to go for them, then extra life comes up right after the third fire hydrant on the bottom sidewalk.

SEALS: As is apparent, you must act like a circus freak and leap across the balls balanced on the noses of the seals. If you leap across the tree trunks to the left there are **two extra lives** to grab. Timing the jumps across the seals is extremely challenging (much more frustrating than fun). Jump to a seal as their rising so you'll have the maximum time to make the jump to the next seal. Take as mush time as you have to judge the next seal and make the jump. If the next jump is looking too risky, you can always risk jumping back to the last seal. It's possible to make the jumps all the way across without going back or using your diaperchute. There are eight seals to clear, then from the eighth seal you must leap and

Stick to the top two lanes during the majority of this event. Tap up and down to change lanes quickly.

Leap from the ball on the nose of the seal before it goes below the fence, or you'll fall to your death.

use your diaperchute to land on the **trampoline,** leap high into the air, then use your diaperchute again to float into the circus tent.

* **CIRCUS TENT:** There's an extra life above the first trampoline to the left. Grab it, then use the diaperchute to get back to the trampoline. Climb up to the top of the post. You can take your time shooting the clowns with your pacifier, or make a quick run to the top enduring the few hits you'll receive. From the top of the post, jump for the **trapeze.** You must grab the exact spot at the center of the trapeze handle to keep from falling (most games are a little more forgiving). Using your diaperchute can make grabbing the trapeze a little easier. From the first trapeze, jump off to the right and float down using your diaperchute. Go through the rings if you really want to (you won't gain points unless you collect the popsicles

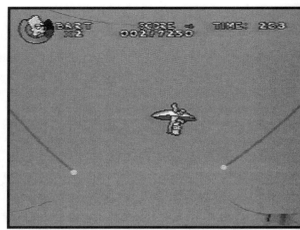
Use your diaperchute between trampolines and trapezes to increase your time to react.

located in a few of them), then keep an eye out for a trampoline to land on. Bounce to the right across the trampolines, using the diaperchute to safely guide yourself to the next trampoline. Climb up the next post, then go across the next six trapezes carefully. From the sixth trapeze leap to the right and float down with your diaperchute in search of another trampoline to land on. There are jumping clowns in between each of the next trampolines. Time your jump as they're going down so you can make it over their head, then float to the next trampoline. You can shoot the clowns with your pacifier, but it takes about 20 hits to knock them out. Jump into the cannon to launch out of this frustrating event!

Pork Factory Pig Bart

* There are three basic parts to this complicated event. The first part is the easiest, and the last part is the second easiest. The ice box in between is way too hard. Begin by running to the right as you enter the meat packing plant. Jump and bounce on your tail to hit the switches that let the pigs escape (A to jump, Up + A to bounce). Go to the far right and ride the elevator up one floor, then go left and climb up to hit a switch. Go back to the elevator and go up another floor. Go left, behind the green wall, then jump up to the conveyor belt and hit the switch. Whenever you see an arrow with a cross through it, don't go in that direction or you'll be Spam. Go left and enter the door opened by the switch you just hit. Jump up to the conveyor belt above, then go right and leap over the funnel to avoid being processed. Enter the door to begin the search for the three keys.

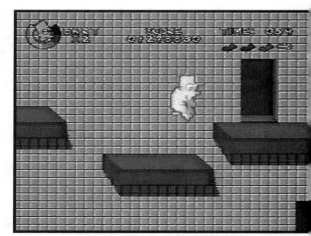
Press Up + A to bounce on your tail to higher ledges.

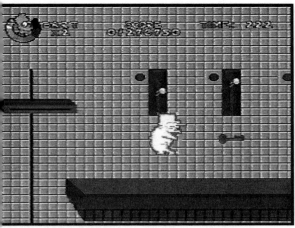

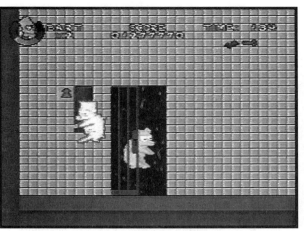

Hit the switch to activate a key color,
then search for the key while it's activated.

Use the keys to free the pigs,
then grab the gold key to enter Krusty's freezer.

THE SEARCH FOR THREE KEYS: You must find three keys, one red, one blue, and one green. Go up the elevator to reach the three switches on the right. When you hit a switch, a colored light will appear next to it, indicating that key is now in sight. Hit the left switch to make the green key appear immediately, then grab the green key. You can go free the pig below immediately, or hold on to the key until it's more convenient to go down there (like on your way back up after falling). Hit the second switch to get the blue light, then go left from the switches and drop down to the floor at the bottom of the elevator. Go left and enter the door at the end of this floor, then enter the next door to the left. Go right to grab the blue key, then go back to the switches. The blue key will release the pig to the left of the pig released by the green key. Hit the third switch to activate the red light, then go to the floor at the bottom of the elevator and go to the right edge. Drop to the platform below, then grab the red key. The red key will release the pig in the bottom-right corner below the switches. When the final pig is released, go back to the switches and collect the gold key. Go back to the floor below the elevator, then enter the door on the left side of this floor. Go to the right to enter Krusty's freezer.

THE FREEZER: This is the toughest part of the entire Virtual Bart game. You'll have very loose controls on the ice, making the already-complicated leaps even more impossible. From the first area you must climb up to the top of the room. Before doing that, go to the left along the bottom ledges to find an **extra life.** Continue bouncing across ledges to the far left for **another extra life.** If you can make it back to where you started this room, you'll be in good shape. Go to the left along the conveyor belts until you see a blue block. When the block is out from the wall, leap to it, then jump onto the metal screen and ride it up. As you ride up, do your best to avoid falling off as the blocks of ice fall from above. When you reach the top of the path for the metal screen, leap to the left onto the ice block and continue leaping left down the ice blocks (we know it's impossible, but that's what you gotta

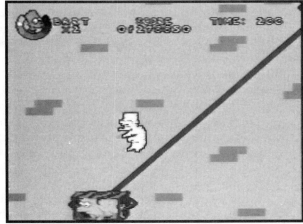

Climbing to the top of the freezer is the toughest part of this game. Especially jumping across these ice blocks.

do!). As you leap to the first ice block, you have to leap from it before the claw drops it. While leaping from the first block to the left, the next ice block will be almost as far as you can jump, but not quite. After about four or five blocks you'll reach a solid conveyor belt. This is a checkpoint, so if you lose a life you'll restart here. Jump to the next belt on the left, then go to the far left side and bounce on your tail until you can jump to the metal screen. When the metal screen reaches the top of it's path, jump to the right and climb up the conveyor belts to reach the next metal screen. At the end of it's path, jump from the metal screen to the convey-or belt, then jump to the next belt and wait for the blue block to pop out of the wall. Jump onto the blue block, then quickly jump to the next platform and enter the door. Ugh! If you've made

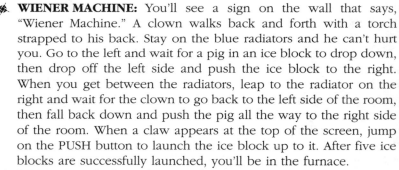

Push these pigs in ice to the far right of the room, then launch them up as the claw passes overhead.

it this far you shouldn't have much trouble with the rest (especially with the hot tip we have coming up).

- **WIENER MACHINE:** You'll see a sign on the wall that says, "Wiener Machine." A clown walks back and forth with a torch strapped to his back. Stay on the blue radiators and he can't hurt you. Go to the left and wait for a pig in an ice block to drop down, then drop off the left side and push the ice block to the right. When you get between the radiators, leap to the radiator on the right and wait for the clown to go back to the left side of the room, then fall back down and push the pig all the way to the right side of the room. When a claw appears at the top of the screen, jump on the PUSH button to launch the ice block up to it. After five ice blocks are successfully launched, you'll be in the furnace.

- **FURNACE:** Climb to the top of this room, helping a pig escape along the way (on the left side of the room near the top). When you reach the top you'll have to walk under metal plungers that crush you while avoiding steam and crossing a conveyor belt. No problem! Ugh!!! When you reach the right side (it's a checkpoint), fall off the ledge and hold left for a second to land on a ledge directly below (on the left side of the large pot of blood — well, what would molten metal be doing in a slaughterhouse?!). From this platform you can take a major shortcut by falling off the left side at the correct moment. The block to your right is in sync with a block below you. If you fall when the block to your right is out, you can safely land on the block below you. Even if you miss that block, there's a chance of landing on the floor safely below the pot of blood. As you fall, hold right so you'll fall against the side of the pot of blood, then stop holding right so when you clear the bottom of the pot of blood you won't go too far to the right (and get crushed). It's a tricky jump (see the picture), but it's a lot eas-

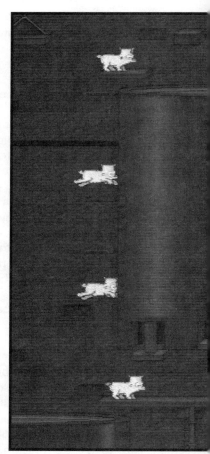

Take a major shortcut from the top of the furnace to the bottom by dropping at the right moment.

ier and less risky then going to the far left, then down, then back to the right where you'll land on this shortcut. Go right and you'll enter the office.

OFFICE: The boss is three executives. Go to the far left of the office and pounce on your tail, then when one of the executives runs over to you pounce him a few times. After about 6-8 hits the two executives will be conquered and you'll only have one guy left. The plump guy will chase you until you

Stand to the right of the desk and face right, then when the plump executive approaches...

...run to the right as he stomps and the books from the bookcase will hit him in the head.

stop, then he'll leap towards you (and stomp you if you don't move). When he lands, books will fall from the bookcases on the wall in the background. Stand on the right side of the main desk and face right, then as the plump guy approaches and begins his leap, quickly move to the right. He'll stomp, the books will hit him, then he'll run back to the left. Hooray for Bart!

Dino Bart

Climb the first steps you see to grab a growl, then climb the second set to get a popsicle. The growl works like a smart bomb, defeating all enemies on the screen. To the far right is the main mountain to climb. Along the way are tons of enemies (including your family members), and very few power-ups. You're better off avoiding most of the enemies. Climb up the platforms to the second floor, then go all the way to the right to collect two popsicles, an extra life, and a growl. Try to save one of your growls for the

Use the growls as a smart bomb to defeat any and all nearby enemies.

family members. Most family members will give you a popsicle or an extra life when you defeat them. You can easily pounce on most enemies (in the Super Nintendo version of Virtual Bart you'll bounce to the sides, making the pouncing of enemies extremely difficult!). You can also use your tail to hit enemies. Continue climbing up to the first cave entrance, pouncing humans along the way to keep your energy up. Barney's burps are impossible to avoid, so move in close and knock him out before his burps knock you out.

- ✻ **INSIDE THE FIRST CAVE:** Go to the right and climb up the steps quickly. Large boulders will fall from above, but their speed makes them impossible to totally avoid, so make a run for it. There's a growl at the exit of the cave.

Pounce the family members
to collect popsicles for energy.

- ✻ **BACK OUTSIDE:** Go to the far left for a popsicle, then climb up and use a growl to knock out Mr. Burns and Smithers. Continue climbing up and right, past Krusty, until you reach Lisa and Maggie. From the floor below them, leap to the platform on the right, then continue to the right until you reach the next cave.

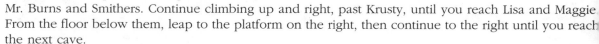

- ✻ **INSIDE SECOND CAVE:** Avoid the green goo while leaping over the holes. When you reach the red lava pit, jump from platform to platform to the other side. You don't have to press up or down to reach the higher or lower platforms. On the opposite side of the lava pit, quickly run up the hill (again, avoiding the boulders is nearly impossible even with the reflexes of a hummingbird). At the top of the hill, fall down the first hole for an extra life, then climb back up. To the right is Mr. Burns and Smithers, and this time they have boulders and, I'm guessing, a donut in amber. You must avoid the grey boulders dropped by Smithers while hitting the donuts in amber with your tail back up at Mr. Burns. We searched and search but couldn't find a "safe spot" or pattern that would avoid hits. It takes nine hits to knock them out. The best spot for hitting the donuts back up at Mr. Burns is from standing with your head directly below Smithers. Continue to the right to exit.

Avoiding the boulders is nearly impossible,
so race through them quickly.

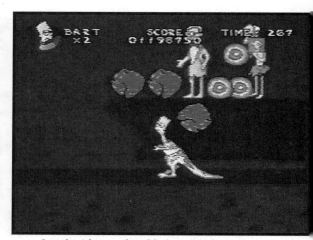

Stand with your head below Smithers, then use
your tail to hit the donuts back up at Mr. Burns.

✸ **BACK OUTSIDE, ON ICE:** Run to the right and grab the popsicle. Climb up as high as you can. When you can't see the next step, try looking down for another step, or wait a few seconds to see if a pterodactyl flies by. You can safely ride on the back of the pterodactyls. If you fall from them, you'll land in or on a partially frozen lake. You're best off staying on the pterodactyls as long as possible. To the right is a large lake with ice blocks moving horizontally and vertically. Jump to each ice block that appears until you end up between Moe and Homer. As you float to the left, stand on the left edge of the block and swing your tail rapidly to knock out the blocks below Moe, then as you go to the right, stand on the right edge and knock out the blocks below Homer. Continue until both are defeated.

You can safely ride on the backs of the pterodactyls, and the path across their backs is safer then below.

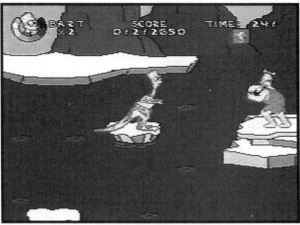

Stand on the edge of the block and use your tail to knock down Moe and Homer.

"Just in Time for Dinner" by Adam Dotson
These 3D stereo pictures are tougher to view, but worth the trouble. Train your left eye to view the right image, and your right eye to view the left image. See page 325 for more 3D information.

TOP-SECRET TIPS

Cheaters never prosper, but at least they have more time to watch *Beavis and Butt-head,* so if you wan't to destroy a perfectly good $60 game, simply punch in one of the cheats included here and see the 20-second or less ending sequence with little or none of that annoying challenging gameplay. All codes are assumed to be entered on Controller 1 unless otherwise stated. Whenever a plus (+) appears between two buttons, you must press both buttons at the same time.

ALADDIN

Stage Select: Pause the game and press A, B, B, A, A, B, B, A to skip to the next stage.
Debug Menu: At the options menu, press A, C, A, C, A, C, A, C, B, B, B, B to get the debug menu. Cheat Mode makes Aladdin invincible, Start on Level allows you to choose the level you start on, Freezability allows you to view each frame of animation (by pressing START to advance), and Map View Mode allows you to scroll around on the screen without Aladdin.

ASTERIX

Passwords: Level 2: INSULA; Level 3: CONDOR; Level 4: VIENNA; Level 5: AVALON; Level 6: DULCIS.

AWESOME POSSUM

Secret Options Menu: At the title screen, after the song has played, press C, B, C. Press and hold Left on the control pad and press B, C. You should hear a tone. Press A to access the Secret Options Menu with infinite lives, invincibility, and a level select.

BATMAN RETURNS (CD)

Level Skip: Go to the Batman Options screen and highlight Game Type. Now highlight Driving, hold the control pad Left and press B. Highlight Driving Controls, hold the control pad Left and press B. Repeat this all the way down to Option 7. Once you reach Option 7, repeat the trick back up to Option 1. You'll hear a ringing noise to indicate that the cheat worked. During the game, pause and press C to skip ahead one level.

BATTLECORPS

Level Select: Pause the game and press B, A, B, A, Right, A, C, A, START.

BATTLETOADS/DOUBLE DRAGON

Super Warp and Mega Warp: At the Character Select screen, press B, A, Down, C, A, Down. Pick a character and you're sent to the Super Warp screen to choose a starting level through Stage 5-2. You also begin with five lives instead of three. For the Mega Warp, press Down, Up, Up, Down, C, A, B. Pick a character and you're sent to the Mega Warp screen to choose a starting level through Stage 7. You also begin with ten lives instead of three. These cheats don't allow you to view the ending sequence; when you finish the game, the Dark Queen says to try playing through the game without cheating.

BRAM STOKER'S DRACULA

Stage Select: Wait for the battlefield to begin scrolling across the screen. Press Down, Right, A, C, Up, Left, Up. You should hear a laugh. Start a new game and press START to pause. Press Up and look at the score box. You should see numbers appear for each stage of the game. Select a stage and press START to skip there.

BRUTAL (CD)

Play As the Bosses: At the title screen, press C, A, B, A, Left, A to control the Dalai Llama, or Up, Down, A, B, C, C, B, A, Down, Up for Karate Croc.

Password: Enter this to play as Kung Fu Bunny with all of his special attributes: KU5YVDUW5!3DAMQF ABCL8ME.

BUBSY THE BOBCAT

Passwords: Chapter 1: JSSCTS; 2: CKBGMM; 3: SCTWMN; 4: MKBRLN; 5: LBLNRD; 6: JMDKRK; 7: STGRTN; 8: SBBSHC; 9: DBKRRB; 10: MSFCTS; 11: KMGRBS; 12: SLJMBG; 13: TGRTVN; 14: CCLDSL; 15: BTCLMB; 16: STCJDH.

CASTLEVANIA BLOODLINES

Nine Lives: At the option screen, set the BGM to 05 and the SE to 073, then press START. Once you're at the title screen, enter Up, Up, Down, Down, Left, Right, Left, Right, B, A (the classic Konami code). Return to the option screen and you can set the Game Level to Expert and the number of lives to nine.

Unlimited Lives: Enter the code for Nine Lives above, then begin the game (lives and difficulty don't matter). The moment you die, tap reset and begin the game again, but choose a different character than before. When the game begins, you'll be on the same level you died on with the same number of lives.

Level Select: At the title screen, press Up, Up, Down, Down, Left, Right, Left, Right, B, A. The number that appears at the top of the screen is the stage select.

CHAKAN THE FOREVER MAN

All Weapons: Select practice mode and start the game. Position yourself onto the small platform above the sky portal and press Start. Select and use the Passage spell. You've now passed twelve levels and have all of the weapons at your disposal.

CHUCK ROCK II

Level Skip: Pause the game and press B, A, Right, A, C, Up, Down, A. The game should unpause. Pause again, hold A, and press Right to skip ahead one level.

CLIFFHANGER (CD)

Level Skip: You need two controllers for this trick. At the title screen, press START, C, B, A, Right, Left on Controller 2. During the game, pause and press C to skip ahead one level.

COMBAT CARS

Race Any Track: At the Options screen, highlight EXIT and press A, B, and C at the same time. Press START and you can start on any of the 24 tracks.

CYBERCOP

Password: Go to level five and enter FXAKBXAMGNAVGSGUIKOTBKDP for plenty of items and access level 7 on your security card.

Slow Energy Restoration: Pause the game and wait for a long period of time. Unpause the game and your energy will be restored.

DOOM (32X)

Invincibility: You need a 6-button controller to use this trick. Pause the game and press START, X, Z, MODE and Up at the same time.

Infinite Ammo: You need a 6-button controller to use this trick, Pause the game and press A, C, MODE, and Up at the same time.

DOUBLE DRAGON V

Reserve Points +2: Up, C, B, A, Down, A, B, C, Left, C, B, A, Right, A, B, C.
Reserve Points +3: Down, Right, A, C, Up, Left, A.
Reserve Points +4: Right, A, Down, A, C, A, Left, B, Up, Down.
Boss Code: C, Right, A, B, A, B, B, Left.
Nine Continues: A, Left, Left, Down, A, A, Left, Left, Down, A.
Disable Dizzy: Left, A, Down, Down, A, Right.
Disable Throws: B, A, Down, Left, Up, C.

DOUBLE DRIBBLE: PLAYOFF EDITION

Password: Enter B01K2 Q2N to play as Phoenix vs. San Antonio.

DOUBLE SWITCH (CD)

Hidden Video Scene: Play through the game until you reach Act III–much easier written than done. Once you've made it, intentionally lose the game by letting the Power Box get turned off or by letting Eddie capture the girls. When you lose, the screen goes dim and the Game Over video clip starts to play. Quickly press Left, A, Up, Right, A before the clip ends. (This code spells the name Laura, which is also the name of one of the characters in the game.)

DRACULA

99 Lives: Here's the next best thing to unlimited lives. When the words "Beware" are scrolling across your screen, press A, Left, Up, C, A, Right, Down. A border will appear on the screen. Start the game, then during the game press A+Start simultaneously. Unpause the game and you'll have 99 lives. You can do this trick again at any time to reset your life counter to 99.

DUNE

Level Passwords:

LEVEL	ATREIDES	HARKONNEN	ORDOS
2	DIPLOMATIC	DEMOLITION	DOMINATION
3	SPICEDANCE	SPICESATYR	SPICESABRE
4	ETERNALSUN	BURNINGSUN	ARRAKISSUN
5	DEFTHUNTER	DARKHUNTER	COLDHUNTER
6	FAIRMEAT	EVILMENTAT	WILYMENTAT
7	ASKLIKENNY	ITSJOEBWAN	SLYMELANIE
8	SONICBLAST	DEVASTATOR	STEALTHWAR
9	DUNERUNNER	DEATHRULER	POWERCRUSH

ECCO THE DOLPHIN

Debug Mode: Press Left or Right and pause the game when Ecco is facing toward you, then press Right, B, C, B, C, Down, C, Up. The debug mode appears with the header "The Dolphin." This works for the Genesis and Sega CD versions.

ETERNAL CHAMPIONS

Overkills: Here's how to do the Overkill moves for each of the game's characters. Trident: Position yourself in front of the rock on the left or the mermaid statue on the right. Attack from the outside (hitting the opponent into the center of the screen) with C or Z. Tentacles appear from the water and pull your opponent beneath the waves. Midknight: Place your opponent's knee on the right side of the doorway frame on the left-of-center shed. Your victim should be to your right. Hit C or Z and watch a helicopter fly past and blow your opponent into meaty chunks. Jetta: Position your opponent's head in front of either of the red columns closest to the center. Hit C or Z and the ground opens up to swallow your opponent. Shadow: Standing to the opponent's right, align your opponent with the center neon letter. Hit C or Z to knock your opponent into the second neon letter. Zap! Blade: Position your opponent in front of the fan with their knee all the way over the black bar that's right next to the first set of windows on either side of the fan. Hit C or Z to send your opponent backwards into the fan. Slash: On the left side of the screen is a small rock with a flat surface on one side of the top. Align your opponent with the rock and hit them from the right with C or Z. A dinosaur appears and eats your foe. Larcen: Line up your opponent with the CH or ER in "Chicago Theater." Hit them with C or Z and watch the drive-by shooting. Xavier: Line up your opponent with the corner building in the background (the lightest-colored building on either side). Your opponent should be close to the fire. Hit C or Z to knock them into the flames. RAX: Line up your opponent in the middle of the large left spotlight shining on the floor. Stand to the opponent's left and press C or Z.

FATAL FURY 2

Dip Switch Mode: Press Down, Down/Left, Left, Down/Left, Forward, Y (Terry's "Power Geyser" move) during the Takara screen. Select the Options screen and choose Dip Switch. Use trial and error to figure out what each of the switches do (moving the fifth to 1 will allow you to perform a Super Ultra Attack by pressing the Mode button with Y).

Boss Code: At the Takara screen, *quickly* press Right, Down, Right, Down, Down, Left, B. Select the Arcade Game mode and you'll be able to choose any of the last bosses.

Nine Continues: During the continue screen, press Down, A, B, C, C, C, C, C, C. You can repeat this trick each time you reach the continue screen.

FIFA INTERNATIONAL SOCCER (CD)

Power-Up Passwords: On the Options Screen, enter the following codes. Invisible Walls: C, C, C, B, A, A, A, B; Curve Ball: B, A, C, B, C, C; Crazy Ball: C, A, B, C, C, B, A, C; Dream Team: A, A, B, B, C, C, A, A; Super Power: B, A, B, B, B, B, B, B, B, B, B; Super Goalie: A, A, A, A, A, B, B, B, B, B; Super Offense: A, A, A, A, A, B, C; Super Defense: B, B, B, B, B, C, B.

Hidden Video Scene: Enter the Coaching/Stats screen and move the soccer ball next to Formations, Coverage, or Strategy. You can see a hidden video for each of these selections by highlighting it and pressing A.

FLASHBACK

Walk Through Walls: Walk up to a wall in any stage of the game. Turn away from the wall, then hold the A button and point the control pad away from the wall. The instant you see Conrad start to run, quickly release the A button and point him back at the wall. He should walk right through it. This trick might kill you or crash the game, but it's fun to play with.

GENERAL CHAOS

Secret Mode: You need two controllers for this trick. First, press START to pause the game. Press and hold A and B on Controller 1 and C on Controller 2 at the same time. A faint bubbling sound tells you that you're in the Secret Mode. You can now use of the the following three cheats. MAXIMUM MEDICS: Press A and C on Controller 1 and B and Down on Controller 2. BATTLE ADVANCE: Press A, C, and Up on Controller 1 and B on Controller 2. FULL-SCALE WAR ADVANCE: Press A, C, and Down on Controller 1 and B on Controller 2. Note that these tricks benefit the Chaos Army; to benefit Havoc's guys, simply perform the Controller 1 actions on Controller 2 and vice versa.

THE INCREDIBLE HULK

Special Moves: These are the kind of moves you'd normally find in a fighting game. Super Stomp (defeats enemies when standing on them): Down, Up, Down, A. Pile Driver: Grab the enemy and press A+B. Bear Hug: Grab the enemy and press A. Shoulder Tackle: Toward, Toward, C, Toward.

INDIANA JONES AND THE LAST CRUSADE

Level Select: When the Lucasfilm logo appears, press A, B, C, B, C, A, C, A, B. The screen will turn blue and the word "SHHHHHHH" will appear. Now you can select your starting level and starting point within the level.

JAGUAR XJ220

Easy Finish: Enter your name as MAR, then choose the World Tour option. Pick a country and start a race. When the lights turn green, pause the game and press A, B, and C at the same time to win the race!

JAMMIT

Chill Passwords: Game 1: TZMYNYN; Game 2: THMSLNS; Game 3: DNWYGLL; Game 4: DLMRVNN; Game 5: MRNLYNG; Game 6: MKGLSCK; Game 7: THMSCSY; Game 8: JRBRGHT.
Roxy Passwords: Game 1: DKRBNSN; Game 2: STPKRNR; Game 3: SSNHYDN; Game 4: JNFRBCN; Game 5: LRNCHLS; Game 6: PLWRHDS; Game 7: STWSPKN; Game 8: BBSKNNR.
Slade Passwords: Game 1: MRKYMCY; Game 2: HNSFJLD; Game 3: DWGTSTN; Game 4: DMDWYDZ; Game 5: TRYBRNM; Game 6: BRNMCMN; Game 7: JSPHKSC; Game 8: PHLSRGR.

JUNGLE BOOK

Lots of Codes: Pause the game and press the buttons as indicated to perform the trick. L, R, U, and D are Left, Right, Up, and Down on the control pad. ABBAABBA: Takes away all but a few seconds of time. (This was a code in Virgin/Disney's previous game, *Aladdin*.) UUDDLRLRBA: Resets the timer and fills up all weapons. (This is the classic "Konami code.") BAABBAABABBAABBA: Skip to the next level. CAABCAA: Go directly to the snake boss with one life. BALUU: Move to Baloo's stage with one life. RADBAD: Go to the monkey boss with one life. LUALUA: Go to the orangutan boss with one life. ACACACACBBBB: Go to the last boss (Khan) with one life. BADCARLARD: View the ending sequence. ABBACABB: Modify the palette (and restart the current level). LARDBALLCRUD: All the sprites are upside down.

JUNGLE STRIKE

Passwords: Use these passwords to start with ten lives and all the co-pilots. Campaign 2: RXVWT74S6KB; Campaign 3: 9WT7NL6MHBV; Campaign 4: X7NL4SHPG94; Campaign 5: VL4S6MGCZVH; Campaign 6: WS6MHPZJFTZ; Campaign 7: TMHPGCFDYN3; Campaign 8: 7PGCZJYK34X; Campaign 9: NCZJFD3BR67.

JURASSIC PARK

Debug Mode: Enter the password NYUKNYUK and the words "Second Controller Enabled" will appear. Plug in Controller Two and use it to go to any point in the game. Pressing Start on Controller Two will disable the second controller.

KRIS KROSS (CD)

Totally Hidden Video: At the "Choose A Caller" screen, press and hold A, then B, then C, then Right. You'll see footage of an audio taping session. Press START while the footage is running to see additional footage of the designers selling the "Make My Video" game concept.

LOTUS TURBO CHALLENGE

Automatic Qualification: Enter MANSELL as your password and start the game. You'll automatically qualify in every race, even if you run out of time.
Infinite Turbos: Enter SLUGPACE as your password and start the game. You now have an infinite number of turbos at your disposal.
Level 3 Tip: Hit the logs to launch over the streams and puddles that slow down the car.
Level 7 Tip: Drive under the trucks to collect bonus points for being such an insane driver.
Passwords: Night: SLEEPERS; Fog: HERBERT; Snow: BUSINESS; Desert: APPLEPIE; Interstate: STANDISH; Marsh: MALLOW; Storm: TEA CUP.

LOTUS II

Hidden Game: Go to the player name screen and change player 1's name to POD PLEASE and press B. You get to play a secret game that's kind of a cross between *Galaxian* and *Centipede*.

MADDEN NFL '94

Skip the Playoffs: Select a playoff game, then press Start. All games will be finished. Go right and press Start again. Continue this trick until you reach the finals.

MARKO'S MAGIC FOOTBALL

Passwords: Level 2: HAUNTING; Level 3: BSTOKE; Level 4: GUNGETNK; Level 5: ECTOPLSM; Level 6: JAWS; Level 7: GARAGE; Level 8: TRAFFIC; Level 9: ELF; Level 10: KRUSTY; Level 11: BARREL; Level 12: CRABTREE.

MEGA TURRICAN

Level Skip: During the game press Start to Pause, then press Right, Left, Down, Right, B. When you unpause, the "Stage Clear" will appear.
Invincibility: Pause the game and press A, A, A, B, B, B, A, A, A, then unpause.
Level Back Skip: Pause the game and press Right, Left, Down, Right, A. Unpause the game and you skip back one level.
Controller Flip: Pause the game and press Up, Up, Down, Down, Left, Right, Left, Right, A, B. Unpause the game and you now move in the opposite direction that you push on the the control pad.

MICRO MACHINES

Infinite Lives: Press Start to pause the game, then press B, Down, C, Down, Up, Down, Left, Down.

Faster Car: Press Start to pause the game, then press Up, Down, A, B, Left, Right, C.

Higher Difficulty Level: Press Start to pause the game, then press Left, Right, Left, Right, Up, Down, Start, Down.

Much Higher Difficulty Level: Press Start to pause the game, then press Left, Down, Up, Down, Right, Down, A, Down.

Better Handling Car: Press Start to pause the game, then press A, Up, B, Down, C, Left, Start, Right.

Extra Crash Power: Press Start to pause the game, then press C, Up, Left, Right, A, B, A, C.

MORTAL KOMBAT

Super Cheat Code: At the Game Start/Options screen, press Down, Up, Left, Left, A, Right, Down. (This spells DULLARD, in case you were wondering.) A top-secret menu item called Cheat Enabled appears. Highlight this option and press START for a hidden configuration menu with the following options. FIGHTER 1/FIGHTER 2: This controls which players are seen in the Demo mode. PLAN BASE: This allows you to change the order of the characters you fight by choosing from four different paths to the top. CHOP-CHOP: Allows you to choose which material you'll be shattering in the block-breaking bonus round. 1PLAY CHOP/2PLAY CHOP: Determines the frequency with which the Bonus Stage appears during the game. Choose 1 to make the Bonus appear after evry battle or 6 to appear after every six battles. 0 turns off the Bonus completely. DEMO: Shows you different sequences from the game; pick a scene and press A to view it. Cameo shows the biography of the character selected under FIGHTER 1; Biography 1/2 shows you the ending sequence for the character; Battle Plan shows the order in which you'll fight the other characters; Medal shows the pre-fight screen with the characters selected in FIGHTER 1/2; Chop-Chop sends you directly to the Bonus Stage. FLAG0: Turn this flag On to start each battle with Player 2 in Danger mode. This doesn't work against the second character in an Endurance match, or in the first round of a fight against Goro. FLAG1: Same as FLAG0, except for Player 1. FLAG2: You always have a silhouette flying in front of the moon on The Pit stage, needed for raching Reptile. FLAG3: Strange silhouettes fly in front of the moon. FLAG4: Causes Reptile to appear at the beginning of every battle. FLAG5: You havee infinite credits. FLAG6: Compuer opponents perform fatalities when they defeat you. FLAG7: Locks in the background at the Palace Gates stage all the way up to the third Endurance Match. BLOOD ON: Turns on the blood and fatality moves. CHEAT ON: Turn this Off to deactivate all the flahs simultaneously. 1ST MAP: Selects the starting scenario or background.

MORTAL KOMBAT (CD)

Super Cheat Code: This code is the same as the Super Cheat Code described above for the cartridge version, except that several of the options are renamed to make it clearer what they do. For example, FLAG2 is renamed MOON.

MUTANT LEAGUE FOOTBALL

Passwords: Monster Cup Trolz vs. Bots: GVSLBN3J884XG; Monster Cup Things vs. Slammers: BCV6CMW7DNX8F.

NIGHT TRAP (CD)

Annals of Digital Pictures: Watch the credits at the end of the game. When the words "In Memory of Stephen D. Hassenfeld" appear on the screen, press Up, A, A, A, A, A. You'll be shown video footage that was shot in Pawtucket, Rhode Island, in December 1986 when Tom Zito (the president of Digital Pictures) demonstrated a prototype of the NEMO game system for a group of executives from the Hasbro toy company. The game being demonstrated is *Scene of the Crime,* an early prototype of *Night Trap.*

OUTRUNNERS

Virtua Racing F-1 Car: On the titles screen, press Left, Right, Left, Right, B, C, A. When you enter the car selection screen, you'll be able to choose the Virtua Racing car.

PHANTASY STAR IV

Sound Test: Finish the game and watch the ending. Press START at the title screen, highlight CONTINUE, and press B.

PINK GOES TO HOLLYWOOD

Cheats: Plug in both control pads. Hold A and C on Controller 1 and B on Controller 2 while turning your Genesis on. If the trick works, you'll hear a crash sound after the TekMagik logo fades out. Start the game, then press Start to pause the game. Use Controller One to activate the cheats. Press C to make the cheat menu appear. Press Left or Right to choose the number of the stage you want to play. Press B to become invincible. Press A to restore your health meter.

POWERMONGER

Password: Use this massive code to play the final territory: TJ3DP2TJW7TI5PJ3DJ4PJLIKPHAKJEKOGQ.

PRIZE FIGHTER (CD)

Hidden Video Scene: Press and hold A, then B, then C, then Right at the Options menu while holding down each button until the sequence begins.

PUGGSY

Extra Level: Go to the Options Menu and select the Password Option. Enter the password 123,765,444 177,075,537   457,337,735. This password will open a new island with a new area.

REBEL ASSAULT (CD)

Easy Level Passwords: Asteroid Field Training: BOSSK; Planet Kolaador: ENGRET; Star Destroyer Attack: RALRRA; Tatooine Attack: FRIJA; Asteroid Chase: LAFRA; Walker Assault: DERLIN; Stormtroopers: MOLTOK; Rebel Transport: MORAG; Yavin Training: TANTISS; TIE Attack: OSWAFL; Death Star Surface: KLAATU; Surface Cannons: IRENEZ; Power Relays: LIANNA; Death Star Trench: PAKKA; Ending: NORVAL.
Normal Level Passwords: Asteroid Field Training: BOTHAM; Planet Kolaador: HERGLIC; Star Destroyer Attack: LEENI; Tatooine Attack: THRAWN; Asteroid Chase: LWYLL; Walker Assault: MAZZIC; Stormtroopers: JULPA; Rebel Transport: MORRT; Yavin Training: MUFTAK; TIE Attack: RASKAR; Death Star Surface: JHOFF; Surface Cannons: ITHOR; Power Relays: UMWAK; Death Star Trench: ORLOK; Ending: NKLLON.
Hard Level Passwords: Asteroid Field Training: BORDOK; Planet Kolaador: SKYNX; Star Destroyer Attack: DEFEL; Tatooine Attack: JEDGAR; Asteroid Chase: MADINE; Walker Assault: TARKIN; Stormtroopers: MOTHMA; Rebel Transport: GLAYYD; Yavin Training: OTTEGA; TIE Attack: RIFHII; Death Star Surface: IZRINA; Surface Cannons: KARRDE; Power Relays: VONZEL; Death Star Trench: OSSUS; Ending: MALANI.

REVENGE OF THE NINJA (CD)

View All Scenes: At the Game Start/Options screen, press Right, Left, Up, Down, Right, Left, Up. A new option called Test Mode appears. This lets you view all of the normal, death, and ending scenes.

RINGS OF POWER

Naughty Intro: You need two controller for this trick. While the Genesis is off, hold down A, B, C, START, and Down/Right on Controller 2. Turn on the Genesis and keep holding down the buttons until the Naughty Dog that usually scrolls across the screen is replaced by a topless woman!

ROBO ALESTE (CD)

Level Select: At the Option menu, set the Sound to 3A, the Level to Hard, and the CD-DA number to the stage you want to play. Hold B and press START. A new option called Continue appears; select it to start on your chosen stage.

ROBOCOP VS. TERMINATOR

MA-17 Code: Pause the game and press C, B, A, B, B, A, B, B, C, B, B, C, C, B, B, C, B, C, A, C, C, A, A, A, B, B, B, A, C, A. This fills the game with screaming female enemies, flaming skeletons, and blood.
TurboCop Mode: Pause the game and press A, B, C, C, B, A, C, B, A, C, B, A, A, A, C, A, C, B, C, A, C, A, C, A, B, C, B. RoboCop jumps and walks faster.
54 Lives: Pause the game and press C, C, A, A, B, B, C, C, A, A, B, B. You see a secret screen with programmer John Botti.
Invincibility: Enter the TurboCop code, then go all the way to the left side of the screen on Level 1. Press Up and C and the screen displays a photo of the M.I.T. Network. You're now immune to enemy bullets.
Maximum Weapons: Pause the game and press B, A, C, C, C, A, B, B, A, C, C, C, A, B. Unpause and press Down, A, B, and C at the same time. Let go of the buttons when your favorite weapons appear at the top of the screen.
Drop Through the Floor: Pause the game and press A, B, C, C, C, B, A. Push Down and C to drop through the floor. Re-enter the code every time you want to drop.
Secret Level: Halfway through Level 2, you'll drop from a suspended wire behind a building. Move around to hear Robo picking up power-ups. Go all the way to the left of the building to enter the secret OCP offices.

THE SECRET OF MONKEY ISLAND (CD)

Passwords: Part One (The Three Trials): 3076, 3176, 3177, 3377, 3777; Part Two (The Sea Voyage): 6200, 6297, 6377, 2323; Part Three (Underneath Monkey Island): 9430, 9433, 1436, 8742, 7310, 7377; Last Part (Guybrush Kicks Butt): 9898, 8989.

SHADOWRUN

Debug Menu: At the title screen, wait for PRESS START to flash and press A, B, A, C, A, B. Start the game and press START to access the statistic screen. Press A to access the pocket secretary and move down past the Save/Load Game option to the Invisible option. Choose a cheat from the menu.

SHAQ-FU

Blood Code: At the Option screen, press A, B, C, C, B, A.
Play as Any Character in Story Mode: At the option screen, set the music to the character you want to play in the Story Mode. Now press Up, Down, B, Left, Right, B. On the overhead map, you'll see Shaq, but you'll fight as ther character you've chosen.

SHINING FORCE II

Config Mode: At the SEGA logo, press Up, Down, Up, Down, Left, Right, Left, Right, Up, Right, Down, Left, B, START.
Hidden Battle: After finishing the game and watching the credits, wait for about three minutes at the jewel screen. A box saying "And more..." will appear on the screen. Press C to enter a secret battle with twelve bosses.

SHINOBI III

Infinite Shuriken: Go to the Options menu and change the S.E. setting to Shurikin. Move up to the Shurikins setting and change it to read 00. Wait a few seconds, and the double-zero turns into an infinity symbol.

Invincibility: Go to th Options menu and go to the Music setting. Choose the tune HE RUNS and press B to heear it, then listen to JAPONESQUE, SHINOBI WALK, SAKURA, and GETUFU. You should hear a brief tone when you hit B to hear the last tune. Start the game and you're invincible.

SILPHEED (CD)

Stage Select: During the intro sequence, press Down, Down, Up, Up, Right, Left, Right, Left, A, B, START. Press START at the title screen and a stage select appears.

SKITCHIN'

Passwords: Denver: 01J4 HXWG HZ0M; San Diego: RTZZ GPXC RIRC; Seattle: 0DJZ MRXV 0KPZ; San Francisco: JURL EJEX X2BG; Los Angeles: FDKL MCXX FD3L; Washington: KC42 OPJ2 XTVB; Toronto: F2KR HNEN G1N4; Detroit: FTL4 MOGU F1DI; Chicago: RAQZ O3VI XVHB; Miami: 0TAM MGTW 0K2K; New York: R2ZK E3XO GKMO.

SNATCHER (CD)

Secret Jordan Names: Enter these names into the Jordan computer at Junker HQ. ADACHI, INAMURA, JEREMY, KIMBERLEY, KIRITA, KOJIMA, KUSHIBUCHI, MICHAEL, NOSE, SAITOU, SASAKI, TOGO.

Secret Videophone Numbers: 44-3723 (Inamura), 39-6004 ("Isabella"), 41-6766 (Jeremy), 33-3333 (Kushibuchi), 79-6641 (Sasaki), 44-6454 (Togo). Dial each number several times for maximum effect.

SONIC THE HEDGEHOG

Slow Motion: At the title screen, press C, C, Up, Down, Down, Down, Left, Right, Start. During the game, press Start to pause and press A to return to the demo, B to activate smooth slow motion, and C to activate frame-by-frame slow motion.

SONIC THE HEDGEHOG 2

14 Continues: At the title screen, select the OPTIONS mode, then move down to the SOUND TEST box. Play the following sounds: 01, 01, 02, 04. Move up to the PLAYER SELECT box and press START to begin a new game. When you run out of lives, the continue screen appears with 14 continue symbols. There are two side effects to this cheat: Song #04 plays through the entire game, and there are no sound effects.

SONIC THE HEDGEHOG 3

Debug Mode: When Sonic appears on the title screen, press Up, Up, Down, Down, Up, Up, Up, Up. You must enter this quickly the moment you see Sonic begin to appear. This is very, *very* hard to do, but it works.

Eighth Special Stage: Rumored to have been removed from the U.S. version, but here it is! Enter the Debug Mode above, then go to the Options and change the music tune to 1F. Press C, then highlight Stage 2, hold the A button, and press START to begin. You can also play this stage in a normal game by selecting 1F, exiting the debug screen, and resuming a saved game. When you're about to enter a large gold ring for the Special Stage, hold A until the Special Stage begins. If you get the emerald in this stage, the game will show the usual scene of Sonic and the emerald, but it won't show up on the save screen.

Extra Animation: Enter the Debug Mode above, then hold down C and preess B to make Sonic go through all his frames of animation, including some that aren't normally seen in the game.

SONIC CD (CD)

High Scores of Game Designers: Press Right, Right, Up, Up, Down, C on the title screen.

Secret Demo Mode: Play the Time Attack mode until your total time is less than 37'27"57. Go back to the title screen and there's a new selection on the menu called D.A. GARDEN. It's a visual sound test–you can move the globe around the screen with the control pad as the game's characters fly around in the foreground. Press A to choose a tune, B to change the direction of the globe (hold B to make it spin faster) or hold C to zoom in. Release C and hold again to zoom out.

Bonus Round Time Attack: Play the Time Attack mode until your total time is less than 30'21"05. You can access a new series of challenges by pressing Left on the control pad while the Time Attack menu is on the screen.

Visual Mode: Play the Time Attack mode until your total time is less than 25'46"12. There's a new menu selection called VISUAL MODE. It lets you watch the game's opening sequences, both endings, and a pencil test.

Sound/Music Test: Press Down, Down, Down, Left, Right, A while the title screen is flashing PRESS START. You move to a hidden Sound Test menu with options for listening to sound effects, digitized samples, or digital audio tracks straight from the CD.

Secret Bonus Round: Using the Sound Test, set all three menu items to 07 and press START. You get to play a secret special stage with Dr. Robotnik lurking in the background. Defeat the stage and you get a condensed credit screen that's different from the ones you see when you beat the game.

Hidden Screens: Enter the following numbers on the Sound Test screen to see hidden screens. 46, 12, 25; 42, 04, 21; 44, 11, 09; 42, 03, 01.

Debug Mode: Using the Sound Test, set the numbers to 40, 12, 11 and press START. You'll see a cool screen with Tails next to a race car. Return to the title screen and start a new game. Press B to change Sonic into different objects; while he's changed, press A to pick a different object or C to place the object on the screen.

Stage Select: At the title screen, press Up, Down, Down, Left, Right, B. A Stage Select menu appears with access to all of the game's levels, including the past, present, and both future versions. You can't start a game from any stage with this trick–you're sent back to the title screen as soon as you clear a stage.

Title Screen Tricks: You need two controllers for this trick. At the title screen, hold the A button and press Up, Down, Down, Down, Down, Up. You hear a chime. Use Controller 2 to manipulate the clouds; Left to zoom out, Right to zoom in, Up to tilt the horizon at you, Down to tilt the horizon away from you, A or C to rotate the clouds, and B to speed up the movement.

SOLDIERS OF FORTUNE

Passwords: Use these to play as any combination of characters. Brigand and CPU Thug–World 2: M8HT3WJ8KQ44; World 3: 8HBBTX2MCHTJ; World 4: RCT7C4MYR854. Navvie and CPU Scientist–World 2: LQ1LX2#81Q59; World 3: C48YLCVLM0GM; World 4: CRR56F82GN5K. Mercenary and CPU Navvie–World 2: ZBVBHSQPT73Q; World 3: GQZHHMW1#70H; World 4: 40R52P7FZP1C. Gentleman and CPU Navvie–World 2: Q3BK7PYNS794; World 3: LV6W7QK0NYB5; World 4: RW#75#FJ40TH. Thug and CPU Navvie–World 2: ZB2S4HKXWBFG; World 3: GJGJK#PBBDH_; World 4: 4H76263NP0R4. Scientist and CPU Navvie–World 2: 7LJLHPHMWBN1; World 3: 3B5YXP5D#8H9; World 4: H485R9CQT93B.

Mega Password: Enter the password BZ2C60QRL35 to start on Level 2 with 30,000 coins (which allows you to buy 30 lives, full health, skill, and weapons).

SONIC SPINBALL

Level Skip: Go to the Options menu, then press A, Down, B, Down, C, Down, A, B, Up, A, C, Up, B, C, Up. You should hear a sound effect. Go to the title screen and hold A+Start to go to Level 2, B+Start to go to Level 3, or C+Start to go to Level 4.

STELLAR FIRE (CD)

Stage Select: Enter the Start Game/Difficulty menu and highlight Normal. Press A to cycle through the difficulty settings and hold the A button down when you get back to the Normal setting. While holding A, press and hold C and START, then while holding all threee buttons, press Up on the control pad. You hear a chime to indicate you've skipped a stage. Keep pressing Up to skip as many stages as you want. Choose Start Game to play on your chosen stage. Press Up seven times to view the ending sequence.

STIMPY'S INVENTION

Ren Passwords: City 1: 8900003; City 2: L9NH2WZ; Pound 1: 8710003; Pound 2: L9N22W6; Outdoors 1: 8520007; Outdoors 2: RC452WZ.
Stimpy Passwords: City 1: 8700004; City 2: D2NG4WY; Pound 1: 871000B; Pound 2: 2LN24WZ; Outdoors 1: 872000G; Outdoors 2: F3444WN.

STREET FIGHTER II: SPECIAL CHAMPION EDITION

Key Configuration: If you want to configure your buttons without using the Options screen, select the character you want to use, then hold the Start button. You'll fly to the next stage, then a Key Configuration screen will appear.

STREETS OF RAGE 3

9 Lives: You need two controllers for this trick. At the Options screen, highlight the number of players. Press Up, A, B, and C at the same time on Controller 2. Press Right on Controller 1 and you can select up to nine lives.
Same Character Code: At the selection menu, move the cursor to 2 Players. Press Down and C at the same time and you should hear a tone. At the Select Player screen, both players should be able to choose the same character.
Play as Roo: At the title screen, press B and Up at the same time, then press START. You can now choose Roo on the Select Player screen..
Play as Shiva: Play the game to the end of Stage 1, where you must beat Shiva. Once you beat him, quickly press and hold B. Continue to hold down B until the next stage begins. When your character dies, the game asks if you want to continue. Select Yes and you can choose Shiva as your character.

SUNSET RIDERS

99 Continues: Go to the Options screen and play sound 0E. Press START to exit the Option screen and select your character by pressing A. When the player smiles at you, press and hold A, B, and C until the game starts. You'll have 99 continues.
Sonic-Style Edit Mode: Play sound test 1.3, then exit and press START. Press A and B to select your player and keep holding them until the game begins. You can now press B to change your player into different pieces of scenery.

SUPER STREET FIGHTER II

Battle Trick: Select Group from the Title Screen to get to the "Battle Mode Select" screen. On Controller 2, press A, B, A, B, A, B, B, A. You'll hear Vega laugh. Select 8 as the number of characters, then go to the Selection Screen. Each player can select up to eight of their favorite fighters.

SYLVESTER & TWEETY

Loads of Codes: Enter any of the following codes at the Stage Prop screen which appears when you press START during the game. Extra Time: Up, A, B, C, C, A, Up, C, C, C, Up. The clock is reset to zero. Extra Energy: A, A, A, B, B, A, B, C. Sylvester's health is restored. Extra Points: C, C, C, C, B, C, A, A, C, B, A. Increases your score by 10,000. Extra Continues: Right, Left, A, A, B, Up, C, A, B, B, C. Adds one continue. This can be used repeatedly. Invincibility: B, B, Up, A, Left, Right, Down, Right, B, B, C. Skip Train Level: C, C, B, C, A, B, C, A, B, C, Down. Use this on the Mayhem Express level to skip ahead. See End Credits: Down, Right, A, B, B, B, C, C, B, A, A.

TEENAGE MUTANT NINJA TURTLES TOURNAMENT FIGHTERS

Special Moves: You can only use these moves when your energy gar is 25% or less, but they kill your opponent with a single hit. Leonardo: Press Back, Toward, Down/Toward, Down, Down/Back, C. Donatello: Press Toward, Back, Down/Back, Back, C. Raphael: Press Back, Toward, Down/Toward, Down, Down/Back, C. Michelangelo: Press Toward, Back, Down/Back, Down, C. Casey: Press Toward, Back, Toward, C. Ray: Back, Toward, Down/Toward, Down, Down/Back, C. April: Back, Down/Back, Down, Down/Toward, Toward, C. Sisyphus: Back, Toward, Down/Toward, Down, Down/Back, C.

THE TERMINATOR

Secret Options Menu: Hold the control pad Right at the Start Game/Options screen, then press B, C, B, B. Release the pad and the cursor changes from an arrow into a square. Press START to find the secret menu.

TERMINATOR 2: THE ARCADE GAME (GENESIS VERSION)

Level 3 Tip: Here's a simple and brilliant tip for the seemingly impossible Level 3. (We printed a complete walkthrough in Awesome Sega Genesis Secrets 3.) The gunner on the back of the truck moves his gun to the left or right just before the Hunter-Killer appears om the screen. Aim at the correct side of the screen before the HK attacks.

Level Skip: At the title screen, press the following sequence twice: Up, Down, Left, Right. You'll hear Arnold say "Excellent!" During the game, pause and press B and C simultaneously to skip ahead one level.

Stage Clear: At the metallic title screen, press Up, Down, Left, Right, Up, Down, Left, Right. A voice will say "excellent!". During the game, press Start to pause, then press B+C simultaneously to clear the stage.

TOEJAM AND EARL

Fixed World: When you play the Fixed World, the ship pieces are on Levels 2, 6, 10, 12, 15, 17, 20, 21, 23 and 25.

TYRANTS

Hidden Game: Select the LOAD option and enter the password JOOLS. You'll activate a cool hidden game that looks a bit and plays a lot like the ancient coin-op Sinistar! Press A for thrust, B to fire, and C to use a smart bomb. Pick up the objects that the enemies you destroy leave behind for more bombs.

VIEWPOINT

Stage 1 Warp Zone: Midway through the stage, the enemy forms a circle with four red enemies inside. Destroy all the red enemies and the center of the wheel to make the warp to Stage 2 appear. The easiest way to destroy enerything is with a bomb.

Stage 2 Warp Zone: Midway through the stage, there are two catlike animal statues. Behind one of the cats is the warp to Stage 3.

Stage 4 Warp Zone: Midway through the stage are several hills and mountains. Behind one of the mountains is the warp to Stage 5.

VIRTUA RACING

Mirror Image: The feedback in the steering of the coin-op game made this very entertaining, but without the steering wheel it basically sucks (especially at a retail price of nearly $100!). If you want to add some challenge to the game, hold A, B, and Up as you turn your Genesis on, then keep holding the buttons while pressing Start. You should see the Mode Select screen with an extra blue box on the bottom-right with the words "Virtua Racing" written backwards. Select this mode and the tracks will be completely reversed.

WIZ 'N LIZ

Super Difficulty Level: When the SEGA logo appears, press and hold A, B, and C, then press START twice. You'll hear a voice say "Yeah!" Go to the Options menu and highlight the Difficulty Level option. Select the Super Wizard setting.

X-MEN

Stage Select and Other Cheats: Disconnect Controller 2 from your Genesis before you turn the power on. At the title screen, press and hold A, C, and Down on the control pad and hit START. Next, when Magneto's face is on the screen, disconnect Controller 1, plug it into into the Controller 2 socket and hit START. Disconnect the controller again and plug it into the Controller 1 socket. Hit START to choose a difficulty level and complete the code. Choose a character and walk to the right. You'll see eight panels on the wall; each panel represents a different stage. Crouch down in fromt of a panel and press C to warp to the stage. You can refill your Health and Mutant Ability meters at any time simply by pressing START to pause the game. You can also summon Rogue, Archangel, Iceman, or Storm as many times as you want.

Mojo's Crunch: Play through the level, find Mojo, and defeat him. Then keep going to the right until you find the Danger Room exit floating in the air. (It looks kind of like a computer.) It's not a real exit, so jump and hit the exit to blow it up. Now here comes the stupid part: to reset the computer and finsh the level, you have to press the RESET button on your Genesis. No, really. When you hit RESET, the screen fills up with binary code, the computer resets (but not your Genesis), and you get to play the final level. *Don't* hit RESET at any other time or you'll reset the Genesis for real.

ZERO TOLERANCE

Final Level Password: Enter !zoPHYYJ1 as your password to play on the final level.

"Corey's Favorite Book" by J. Douglas Arnold
This 3D stereo picture can be viewed if you cross your eyes correctly. This picture was captured using a special camera designed to take 3D pictures. See page 325 for more 3D information.

"Parrot in Paradise" by Joan D. Arnold
This 3D stereo picture can be viewed if you cross your eyes correctly. This picture was captured using a special camera designed to take 3D pictures. See page 325 for more 3D information.

STEREOGRAM TIPS

It's those weird little images filled with random dots or twisted patterns that have taken the country by storm. We've been including them in our books for several years (long before they were trendy!), and we've got a few new ones for ya right here in this book. There are totally original images you won't see anywhere but in our books.

In case you haven't seen these before (boy, you must lead a very sheltered life!), here are a few tips for viewing them. The image appears to be a random jumble of dots, but by refocusing your vision, you'll see three-dimensional images literally jump out of the page. You don't need 3D glasses to view SIRDS. All you have to do is learn how to view them. Some people can see SIRDS right away, but it takes others several days, so keep trying until you get it. We guarantee you'll be blown away.

Technique #1: Hold the book one to two feet away from your face. Relax your eyes and focus about a foot or two beyond the book. Don't cross your eyes! Focus into the distance. Once your focus is right, it will take a few seconds or a few minutes for your brain to pick out the 3D image on the page. If you focus too far into the distance, try moving the book farther away from your face.

Technique #2: Look directly at the two fusion dots at the top of the SIRDS. Relax your eyes and look through the page so that the two dots separate into four dots. Now adjust your focus so that the center two dots overlap and create a dark third dot. You're now focused on the SIRDS.

Technique #3: Hold the book extremely close to your face and look into the distance. Hold your look long enough for your eyes to focus. Now slowly move the book away from your face, holding the book steady. Look at the fusion dots with your peripheral vision. They will fuse and form a third dot when the book is a foot or two from your face. You're now focused on the SIRDS. If you lose your focus, keep practicing until you can hold it.

Technique #4: We learned of this technique recently, and it seems to work great for several people that had problems with the other techniques. When you view a SIRDS, you must focus your eyes exactly twice the distance that the paper is from your eyes. An easy way to do this is to stand in front of a mirror, hold the SIRDS against the mirror, then look at your eyes. Try to hold the focus of your eyes looking at your eyes in the mirror as you slide the book up slowly into view.

The SIRDS throughout this book are simple drawings, and are not actual clues to a game. If you can't view them, for whatever reason, don't feel like you're missing a crucial clue. They are just totally awesome 3-D drawings.

Index to Stereograms

AWESOME SEGA GENESIS SECRETS 4

THE BEST GAMES! THE MOST SECRETS!

by ZACH MESTON & J. DOUGLAS ARNOLD

MORTAL KOMBAT • STREET FIGHTER 2 • ALADDIN
JURASSIC PARK • ROCKET KNIGHT • SHINOBI 3
SHINING FORCE • JUNGLE STRIKE • CD GAMES
ZOMBIES • AERO THE ACROBAT • MANY MORE!

ISBN# 0-9624676-26
320 Pages • Retail Price: $11.95

Includes complete chapters for 22 games:

Aero The Acro-Bat
AH-3 Thunderstrike (CD)
Aladdin
Bart's Nightmare
B.O.B.
Ecco The Dolphin (CD)
General Chaos
Gunstar Heroes
The Haunting
John Madden Football '94
Jungle Strike

Jurassic Park
Mortal Kombat
Mutant League Football
NHLPA Hockey '94
Ranger X
Rocket Knight Adventures
Shining Force
Shinobi 3
Street Fighter II: Special Champ. Edition
Time Gal (CD)
Zombies Ate My Neighbors

Plus secrets, codes and tricks for 48 other games!

AWESOME SEGA GENESIS SECRETS 3

ISBN# 0-9624676-34
320 Pages • Retail Price: $11.95

Includes complete chapters for 33 games:

Batman Returns
Batman: Return of Joker
Battletoads
Black Hole Assault (CD)
Cobra Command (CD)
Cool Spot
Ecco the Dolphin
Fatal Fury

Flashback
Galahad
Joe Montana '93
John Madden '93
NHLPA Hockey '93
Night Trap (CD)
Out Of This World
Outlander

Prince of Persia (CD)
Road Avenger (CD)
Road Rash 2
Secret Monkey Island (CD)
Sewer Shark (CD)
Shadow of the Beast 2
Side Pocket
Sonic 2

Streets of Rage 2
Sunset Riders
T2: The Arcade Game
Team USA Basketball
Teenage Mutant Turtles
Tiny Toon Adventures
Wonder Dog (CD)
World of Illusion

Plus secrets, codes and tricks for 40 other games!

AWESOME SEGA GENESIS SECRETS 2

ISBN# 0-9624676-50
288 Pages • Retail Price: $11.95

Includes complete chapters for 31 games:

Alisia Dragoon
Cadash
Chuck Rock
Desert Strike
Devilish
Dragon's Fury
Earnest Evans
Exile

Golden Axe II
Joe Montana II
John Madden '92
Kid Chameleon
Krusty's Super Fun House
Mick & Mack's Global
Gladiators
Mystical Fighter

Rolling Thunder II
The Simpsons
Sol-Deace
Splatterhouse 2
Steel Empire
Super Off Road
Syd of Valis
Taz-Mania

The Terminator
Thunder Fox
Toki: Going Ape Spit
Trouble Shooter
Two Crude Dudes
Valis
Wonder Boy/Monster Land

Plus secrets, codes and tricks for 50 other games!

AWESOME SEGA GENESIS SECRETS 1

ISBN# 0-9624676-42
256 Pages • Retail Price: $11.95

Sonic the Hedgehog
Shining In The Darkness
Air Buster
Alien Storm
Arcus Odyssey

Batman
Castle of Illusion
Decap Attack
El Viento
Midnight Resistance

MUSHA
Quackshot
Saint Sword
Shadow Dancer
Spider-Man vs. The Kingpin

Streets of Rage
Strider
ToeJam and Earl
Vapor Trail
Wardner

DUNGEON MASTER 2 — SKULLKEEP: THE OFFICIAL STRATEGY GUIDE

ISBN# 1-884364-039 • 144 Pages • Retail Price: $12.95 • Available: NOW
Includes huge fold-out map of main floor!

Dungeon Master 2--Skullkeep is the sequel to the best-selling adventure game of the 1980s. This official book, written with the full cooperation of FTL--the developers of *Dungeon Master* and *DM 2*--is filled with detailed maps, hundreds of screen shots, and information straight from the programmers. Covers all versions of *DM 2*, including the Sega CD, IBM PC, and Macintosh.

VAY: THE OFFICIAL STRATEGY GUIDE

ISBN# 0-884364-101 • 144 Pages • Retail Price: $12.95 • Available: NOW

Working Designs follows up the massive success of Lunar with a brand-new role-playing adventure. VAY features an all-new cast of characters in a lengthy adventure pitting good against evil. Includes detailed maps of every dungeon, tons of screen shots, a complete walkthrough, and charts of all weapons, items and monsters.

HEIMDALL: THE OFFICIAL STRATEGY GUIDE

ISBN# 0-884364-020 • 120 Pages • Retail Price: $12.95 • Available: NOW

Heimdall: The Official Strategy Guide is filled to the margins with in-depth information on every aspect of JVC's role-playing adventure game: maps of every location, background information on the history of *Heimdall,* and even a complete walkthrough of the quest. Written with the full cooperation of JVC, this is the only strategy book on the market for this spectacular title.

LUNAR: THE OFFICIAL STRATEGY GUIDE

ISBN# 0-884364-004 • 132 Pages • Retail Price: $11.95 • Available: NOW

Written by the creators of the Gaming Mastery Series with the cooperation of Working Designs, *Lunar: The Official Strategy Guide* is the ultimate guide to the ultimate Sega CD role-playing game. Includes detailed maps of every dungeon, tons of screen shots, a complete walkthrough, and charts of all weapons, items and monsters.

POPFUL MAIL:
THE OFFICIAL STRATEGY GUIDE

ISBN# 1-884364-187 • Over 120 Pages • FULL COLOR! • Retail Price: $16.95
FOR THE SEGA CD: The most anticipated role-playing game is from the master Japanese translators at Working Designs. In the tradition of Lunar and Vay comes Popful Mail. This time the action is side-scrolling, with tons of areas to explore, people to talk to, and beasts to fight.

AWESOME SEGA GENESIS SECRETS 5

ISBN# 1-884364-055 • 320 Pages • Retail Price: $12.95 • Available Now

Animaniacs
Ballz
Battletech
Beavis & Butt-head
Contra: Hardcorps
Dynamite Headdy
Earthworm Jim
Ecco 2

Heart of the Alien CD
Madden NFL '95
Mickey Mania (Cart + CD)
Mortal Kombat II
NBA Jam
NBA Live '95
NHL Hockey '95
Panic! CD

Sonic & Knuckles
Sparkster
Super Street Fighter 2
Taz: Escape From Mars
Urban Strike
Virtual Bart

AWESOME SUPER NINTENDO SECRETS 4

ISBN# 1-884364-063 • 384 Pages • Retail Price: $13.95 • Available Now

Ballz
Beavis & Butt-head
Demon's Quest
Earthworm Jim
Final Fantasy III
Illusion of Gaia
Indiana Jones Adventures
Jungle Book

Madden NFL '95
Mickey Mania
Mortal Kombat II
NBA Jam
NBA Live '95
Pac-Man 2
Sparkster
Street Racer

Stunt Race FX
Super Adventure Islands 2
Super Bomberman 2
Super Punch Out
Super Street Fighter II
Virtual Bart
Vortex

3DO GAMES SECRETS

ISBN# 1-884364-179 • 288 Pages • Retail Price: $12.95 • Available Now

Alone in the Dark
Crash N Burn
Dragon's Lair
Escape From Monster Manor
FIFA Soccer
Gridders
Guardian War
The Horde
The Incredible Machine

John Madden Football
Jurassic Park Interactive
Lost Files of S. Holmes
Mega Race
Night Trap
Off World Interceptor
Out Of This World
Road Rash
Samurai Shodown

Sewer Shark
Shadow
Shock Wave
Soccer Kid
Star Control II
Super Street Fighter II Turbo
Total Eclipse
Twisted
Way of the Warrior

ORDER FORM
THE HOTTEST SECRETS AND STRATEGIES!

The best walkthroughs, secret passwords, maps and strategies.
Become an expert! Satisfaction guaranteed! If not, return for a full refund!

TITLE	PRICE	TOTAL
Awesome Sega Genesis Secrets 1 (ISBN 0-9624676-42)	$11.95	$ _____
Awesome Sega Genesis Secrets 2 (ISBN 0-9624676-50)	$11.95	$ _____
Awesome Sega Genesis Secrets 3 (ISBN 0-9624676-34)	$11.95	$ _____
Awesome Sega Genesis Secrets 4 (ISBN 0-9624676-26)	$11.95	$ _____
Awesome Sega Genesis Secrets 5 (ISBN 1-884364-05-5)	$12.95	$ _____
Awesome Super Nintendo Secrets 1 (ISBN 0-9624676-69)	$11.95	$ _____
Awesome Super Nintendo Secrets 2 (ISBN 0-9624676-77)	$11.95	$ _____
Awesome Super Nintendo Secrets 3 (ISBN 0-9624676-85)	$11.95	$ _____
Awesome Super Nintendo Secrets 4 (ISBN 1-884364-06-3)	$13.95	$ _____
3DO Games Secrets (ISBN 1-884364-17-9)	$12.95	$ _____
Popful Mail: The Official Strategy Guide (1-884364-18-7)	$16.95	$ _____
Dungeon Master 2: Official Strategy Guide (ISBN 1-884364-039)	$12.95	$ _____
Heimdall: The Official Strategy Guide (ISBN 1-884364-020)	$12.95	$ _____
VAY: The Official Strategy Guide (ISBN 1-884364-101)	$12.95	$ _____
Lunar: The Official Strategy Guide (ISBN 1-884364-004)	$11.95	$ _____
Subtotal		$ _____
Air Shipping ($4.00 in U.S. and Canada; $5.00 Foreign)		$ _____
Total (Check/Money Order/Credit Card in U.S. funds)		$ _____

Name _____

Company _____

Address _____

City _____ State _____ Zip _____

Visa/Mastercard # _____ Expiration Date: _____

Signature: _____ Phone: ( ) _____

SEND TO: SANDWICH ISLANDS PUBLISHING
P.O. Box 10669, Lahaina, Maui, Hawaii 96761
Fax orders: (808) 661-2715

FREE INFORMATION!

Get on the
Gaming Mastery Series
Mailing List and:

- Learn about new book releases months in advance.
- Receive special newsletters with exclusive tips.
- Get special offers and news of upcoming games.

Name _____ Age _____

Address _____

City _____ State _____ Zip _____

Where did you buy this book? _____

Game Systems Owned:
- ☐ 3DO
- ☐ Super Nintendo
- ☐ Game Gear
- ☐ Turbografx-16
- ☐ Atari Jaguar
- ☐ Genesis
- ☐ GameBoy
- ☐ NES
- ☐ Saturn
- ☐ 32X
- ☐ Lynx
- ☐ Other: _____
- ☐ Sony Playstation
- ☐ Sega CD
- ☐ PC-Compatible

Three Favorite Games (any system): _____

Fill out this form or write the info on a piece of paper
and mail it to us: **SIP, P.O. Box 10669, Lahaina, HI 96761**